Hong Kong Architecture 1945–2015

Charlie Q.L. Xue

Hong Kong Architecture 1945–2015

From Colonial to Global

 Springer

Charlie Q.L. Xue
Department of Architecture and Civil
    Engineering
City University of Hong Kong
Kowloon Tong
Hong Kong

ISBN 978-981-10-1003-3   ISBN 978-981-10-1004-0   (eBook)
DOI 10.1007/978-981-10-1004-0

Library of Congress Control Number: 2016939925

Printed on acid-free paper

This Springer imprint is published by Springer Nature
The registered company is Springer Science+Business Media Singapore Pte Ltd.

Preface

The Impetus for This Book

Hong Kong, a Chinese territory located at the tip of the South China Sea, was the last British overseas colony. During its 150 years of colonial rule from 1841 to 1997, the colonial leadership combined with a Chinese effort from the administrative to grass-roots levels made Hong Kong unique. In addition to its values and lifestyle, this city-state has its own social, political, and economic systems. Hong Kong laid down the framework for the city proper during its first hundred years of development from 1841 to 1945. The 50 years following World War II saw Hong Kong transition from a defensive outpost into an international financial hub. The urban architecture seen in the city today was formulated mainly during the 1980s and fermented to maturity. Since 1978, when China opened its doors, Hong Kong has served as an example of economic success, and its experiences have directly contributed to the success of mainland China. In the 1990s, the per capita GDP of Hong Kong once surpassed that of UK, its suzerain.[1] After the handover of sovereignty in 1997, Hong Kong became one of China's many cities. Since then, it has contributed its wealth of experience to other parts of China.

In the 1950s and 1960s, Hong Kong was busy relocating refugees and developing local industry. From the 1970s to 1990s, the rise of the "four Asian dragons"—Hong Kong, Taiwan, South Korea, and Singapore—was manifested in their remarkable construction boom. Hong Kong architecture during the half century from 1946 to 1997 was shaped by government's policies, local social and technical forces and products created by local and expatriate planners, architects, and builders. The tiny island took its own path apart from UK and China. Hong Kong's architecture is the result of a pragmatic economy and property speculation, and is

---

[1]During 1993 to 1998, the per capita GDP of Hong Kong was higher than that of the UK.

The data of per capita GDP is available from (International Bank for Reconstruction and Development 2014).

free from political ideology. The independence and uniqueness of its built environment are worth exploring.

Although the port city was shaped in the nineteenth century, the buildings constructed before the war were mostly demolished when the economy took off in the 1970s. The buildings constructed after the war mostly followed modernist principles and resonated with the modern architectural movement in the Western world during the 1950s. These buildings of the 1950s and 1960s have become endangered as a result of the tide of redevelopment encouraged by high commercial profits. More than half of the post-war buildings have been or are being replaced by new skyscrapers. Some buildings in the central business district stood for less than 30 years before they were replaced by a new generation of skyscrapers. This modern heritage deserves further exploration. My study of Hong Kong architecture is further motivated by the following questions.

- As one of the major economic pillars, how did urban architecture help Hong Kong's transformation and economic miracles in its last 50 years before the sovereignty handover?
- How did the building projects represent and symbolize the various stages during this period of transformation?
- What are the driving forces for building development in different stages?
- What contributions has Hong Kong architecture made to China, Asia, and the world?

Although many books and articles have considered Hong Kong's urban architecture and construction, a comprehensive and resourceful English volume related to post-war architecture has not yet appeared. I have written and published several books, chapters, and papers about contemporary Chinese mainland architecture (including a few about Hong Kong architecture) for decades, and hope to extend my study to this corner of the South China Sea to compare developments in mainland China and Hong Kong. By answering these questions, I hope to establish a framework of Hong Kong architecture from 1945 to now, contribute to the architectural history of this vibrant city and enrich the discourse of city-state development. On the practical side, a study of Hong Kong architecture would reveal its design and development and provide a reference for architects, developers, government, scholars and members of the public. Hong Kong architecture involves the development, design and management of a high-density environment, and its study should be useful and meaningful for other cities facing similar problems.

Other Studies of Hong Kong Architecture

Scholarly works inspire the study of Hong Kong architecture in the following ways. Due to space limitations, only the most representative works are discussed.

British Colony and Hong Kong History

British overseas colonies reached their heyday in the nineteenth century. Home's *Of Planting and Planning: The Making of British Colonial Cities* (1997) covers the entire sweep of British colonial urbanism from Africa to Asia. Building design was partly mentioned. Ngo's *Hong Kong's History: State and Society under Colonial Rule* (1999) offers a colonial history perspective of Hong Kong. Several books have described the history of Hong Kong in different ways. For example, Akers-Jones (2004) focuses more on the human rather than administrative aspects, but provides many insights into the recent history of Hong Kong. Welsh (1997) evokes the history of Hong Kong and the characters of those who shaped it, from its buccaneering origins to its post-war growth. Wang's (1997) book includes two parts, one involving archaeology, society, policy, urban development, and economy and the other involving education, culture, religion, and social customs. Ching and Faure (2003) analyze the social formation of Hong Kong, the interaction between its government and society, the internal and external factors underlying its social evolution, and the emergence of its culture and identity. Li (2012) reveals the government decision process in the last colonial administration period through reading the released archives in London. Blyth and Wotherspoon (1996) examine the oral histories of more than 30 people. Lui (2012) analyzes the social factors experienced during the 1970s. The last two books provide a voice from grass-root citizens, which are rarely heard in formal historic accounts. As a piece of cultural critique, Abbas' book (1997) relentlessly expounds the essence of "disappearance" culture in the last colonial years.

Some books mention Hong Kong's regional history. Girard et al. (2011) explore the notorious Kowloon Walled City before its final clearance in 1992. Lee and DiStefano (2002) examine the threats of recent development to two of the oldest villages in Hong Kong's New Territories. No matter how strict the law was enacted, people have their own innovative ways of resistance, resilience, and survival. They created "architecture without architects." Many similar books, mainly published by non-government organizations, take a nostalgic approach to post-war life in Shek Kip Mei, Shau Kei Wan, Lamma Island, and other areas. The government has also recorded population, housing, and other changing statistics in its annual reports and other documents.

Urban Studies of Hong Kong and the Statutory System

Urban studies of Hong Kong usually refer to items such as the city's geography, estates, reclamation, land use, municipal construction, administration, policies and town planning. Victor F.S. Sit established a framework for Hong Kong's urban development in *Hong Kong: 150 years, Development in Maps* (2001, 2010) which consists of the city's geography, history, economy, city, society, community, and environment statistics. Sit compiled a factual panorama of the city.

Alexander Holmes and Joan Waller's *Hong Kong: Growth of the City* (2008) takes a series of important cities as references and analyses their growth and evolution in tables to show Hong Kong's developmental history. Feng Bangyan's Chinese book entitled *One Hundred Year History of Hong Kong Real Estate*

Property (2001) attempts to reveal and dissect the historical progression of the city's real estate against its economic and population development backgrounds in the twentieth century. Living in and speculation of real estate have been the driving force of urban construction and building design in Hong Kong.

Ho's several English and Chinese books (2004, 2008, 2011) focus on Hong Kong's harbor, land, infrastructure and construction development history over a 150-year period. These books consider data from the government and professional bodies and present them in statistic tables and figures. Bristow (1984) records the history and progression of land policy implementation from the viewpoint of land-use planning. In another book, Bristow (1989) covers the historical and conceptual origins of new towns and satellite towns worldwide and the Hong Kong cases, in addition to development procedures and controls, design aspects and problems, and the role of government and the private sector in catering to the public need. As the difficulties of accessing the materials of half a century ago, Bristow's books give a reliable source. More critical review of public housing comes from Castells et al. (1991), who studied the public housing in Hong Kong and Singapore and linked "collective consumption" with the cities' economic growth.

Cheng (2000) has written several books introducing the development clues of Hong Kong's roads and streets with abundant historical pictures. Nissim explains both the historical development and current practice of land administration. The Hong Kong government has also published urban study materials that consider the city and its statutory system. For example, the government manual entitled *Hong Kong Planning Standards and Guidelines* provides criteria for determining the scale, location and site requirements of various land uses and facilities. Lu and Chan's (1998) Chinese book about Hong Kong's urban planning is a systemic monograph that introduces the formation and development of the urban planning framework after World War II in Hong Kong. Other books consider recent case studies to extensively explore Hong Kong's economy, town planning, building control, urban renewal, and housing price problems (Lai 1997; Lai and Fong 2000; Leung and Yiu 2004). Yiu's e-museum of building control and land administration focuses on the changing policy of building control and its consequences for building development and design.

Hong Kong architecture

Most of the books and articles about Hong Kong architecture have been published in the Chinese language. Lung Ping-yee's pioneering *Ancient and Current Hong Kong Architecture* (1991) outlines Hong Kong architecture from the early nineteenth century to the end of the 1980s. Peng's (1990) edited collection of architects' and scholars' articles written about Hong Kong's history, housing, commercial, and new town development covers the period to 1990, with all authors knowing Hong Kong well at the time. Zhang and Lau (1998) analyze the formation of Hong Kong's port in the late nineteenth and early twentieth centuries by comparing Shanghai and Yokohama. The Hong Kong Institute of Architects (HKIA) published a Chinese book entitled *Hundred Years of Hong Kong Architecture* (2005), which consists of chapters on tenement housing, public and private housing, and vernacular buildings. The book is intended for consumption by the general public at the expense of academic depth. Two by-product books from the HKIA investigation, including *Loving Architecture* (comprising dialogues with 15 veteran architects) and *Jianwen zhuji* (a biography of old architects) were published in 2007, and serve as vital records of famous architects between the 1950s and 1980s. Gu (2011) records the endeavor of Chinese architects and clients to construct the Chung Chi College buildings at the Chinese University of Hong Kong in the 1950s and 1960s. These books delineate a line of development from the post-World War II period to 1970. Other Chinese books have been written by cultural commentators and published by non-government organizations (Woo 2005; Fang 2006), and express personal ideas and observations. Except for Gu's bilingual book, none of the aforementioned books are accessible to the English-speaking world.

Some English books have focused on Hong Kong architecture. Walker and Rowlinson (1990) describe the Hong Kong Construction Association's 70 years of building construction. Their book provides information about milestone building projects from the 1920s to 1980s. Denison and Guang (2014) tell a story of architect Luke Him Sau from Hong Kong, London, Shanghai, and then Hong Kong. In their book about Hong Kong's high density, Shelton et al. (2011) describe the city's land constraints, planning innovations and peculiar situation. Three books including Christ and Gantenbein's *An Architectural Research on Hong Kong Building Types* (2010), Frampton, Solomon and Wong's *Cities Without Ground - A Hong Kong Guidebook* (2012) and Zhang's *Invisible Logic* (2009) demonstrate a lasting research interest in the high density and design strategies of Hong Kong. *Cities Without Ground* focuses on this interest in the academic and professional worlds. It uses digital axonometric drawings of various traffic interexchange areas and attempts to exaggeratedly demonstrate Hong Hong's intricate high-density environment and pragmatic solutions. *Cities Without Ground* most typically represents the fresh psychology when a (foreign) visitor first arrives in the city.

Books by Chung (1990) and Lampugnani et al. (1993) include large-format design case pictorial introductions and cover articles. Both books focus on prominent building cases completed before 1991. The property market has always been a major driving force behind Hong Kong's economy. The books *Professional Practice for Architects* (1998) and *Building Design and Development in Hong Kong* (2003) cover a wide range of topics related to building design and property development practices in Hong Kong. The government departments publish materials about their work, such as books about public housing (Yeung and Wong 2003; Leung 1999), and reports related to subways (Tang et al. 2004) and public buildings (ASD 2006).

Journals in China and abroad occasionally publish design works or articles about Hong Kong. Hong Kong trade magazines such as *China Architecture & Urbanism, Building Journal, Vision, Pace, Space, Hinge, Perspective, Hong Kong Institute of Architects Journal* and *Asian Architects and Contractors* frequently print stories about built projects in Hong Kong using little text and analysis. They record ample factual material and timely information.

Conclusively, there is a plethora of publications related to Hong Kong's history, society, geography, urban planning, environment, and construction especially in the Chinese language. However, quality writing about post-war Hong Kong architecture is rarely published. Although professionals know about many buildings and events, they have not yet captured them in writing. In view of this gap, I published a Chinese book entitled *Contextualizing Modernity: Hong Kong Architecture 1946–2011* in the summer of 2014. It was warmly welcomed by readers in Hong Kong, Taiwan, and mainland China. This English edition lends its findings a broader scope and consolidates the other chapters.

From Colonial to Global

My observations of Hong Kong architecture in this book are set against the background of Greater China and world architecture. I have read most of the aforementioned materials and immersed myself in the life of Hong Kong over the past 20 years, following the construction of key buildings and participating in design projects and social events. My view of Hong Kong architecture was gradually formed during a process of close examination, experience, and contemplation.

Most books on architecture highlight built works with attractive and tasteful pictures. Initially, I intended to focus on building design and formal evolution in this book. The deeper I looked into historical materials from half a century ago, the more I felt the pulse of Hong Kong's development and found it to be closely associated with the building form. Behind the form and evolution of the building hide governmental policy and control, a societal vision, various forces and architects' creativity. Some buildings deserve description and broadcasting. Some buildings are generic, and only serve the operation of the busy capitalist urban machine and provide usable space to owners, end users and speculators. These buildings lack prominent qualities and glamor. During Hong Kong's transition from last British colony to international Asian metropolis, buildings were produced, consumed, and quickly demolished or replaced. That is the meaning of Hong Kong architecture and also the departure point of this book. The text and illustrations provided in this book explain this process.

A "colony" is a type of territory expansion in which people migrate from a central region to an outlying region. The ancient Romans conquered the vast territories from Minor Asia to North Africa and Northern Europe. Overseas colonization started from ocean navigation and venturing expansion. Vast land of Latin America, India and Far East fell to the hands of European colonists. British colonists built Hong Kong Island into a trade outpost and military base during the first hundred years after its occupation in 1841. In the turbulent years of modern Chinese history, Hong Kong acted as a refuge, a buffer zone, and an enclave between political powers and cruel wars. The cultural seeds of East meets West were planted from its inception as a port city.

Looking at the 50 years of Hong Kong history from 1946 to 1997, an obvious demarcation line can be drawn in 1971. Post-war reconstruction turned a new page for Hong Kong after the dark days of Japanese rule. After the war, the British Colonial Office took close care of its outlying colonies. London directed the governance of Hong Kong, which stepped into the free capitalist world. Meanwhile, the Chinese mainland suffered from endless turmoil as a result of internal war and political movements. The Territories received an influx of migrants from the Chinese mainland in the 1950s and 1960s, providing a direct supply of labor for the newly sprouting industry.

From 1946 to 1970, Hong Kong society was busy coping with various emerging disasters such as an inundation of refugees, squatter area fires, resettlement of the urban poor, economic embargos, and street riots. As observed by Ackbar Abbas, "other cities like Los Angeles or Tokyo were built on seismic fault lines or volcanic soil; Hong Kong seems to have been built on contingency, on geographic and historical accidents, shaped by times and circumstances beyond its control and by pragmatic accommodation to events" (Abbas 1997). Hong Kong experienced gains and losses. The transitioning immigrants improved its culture and technology, and money escaped from Shanghai after the communists came to power in 1949. Therefore, Shanghai had the dominant influence over the culture.[2]

Although boasted as a sample of "laissez faire" economic policy and "active non-intervention," the urban architecture of the period was characterized by strong government leadership and specific investment, in the types of public housing and buildings constructed. Settling the refugees, providing shelters for low-income people, regulating the developmental potential and dense conditions, building schools and hospitals—all of these active governmental measurements thoroughly modernized an otherwise dilapidated port city full of squatter areas. As Castells et al. concluded, millions of people lived in a "realm of collective consumption" due to the government's housing and social welfare endeavors.[3] Partly because of the rigorous economic situation, government buildings were designed with authoritative modernist language, mainly designed by expatriate architects in the public sector. The architectural magazine at the time reflected an enthusiastic pursuance of modernist method (Tan and Xue 2013).

Early in 1967, decolonization began silently in Hong Kong "because Britain was set on a course of withdrawal" (Fauer 2003). Hong Kong gradually decided its own developmental path. More Chinese elites began participating in political and administrative affairs. The installation of new governor Sir Crawford Murray MacLehose in 1971 marked a new economic era and social life in the territory. To be considered one of the greatest governors, Sir Crawford introduced more social

---

[2]Harvard University Professor Leo Lee called Hong Kong's culture in the 1950s "Shanghainesed." See (Lee 1998). The architects from Shanghai were active in this period, a fact that partly supports Lee's judgement.

[3]"Collective consumption" is used to describe people in the "developmental nations," where housing and other welfare are mainly supplied by the government. See (Castells et al. 1991).

welfare and public services to thoroughly cure the society.[4] The governor and his cabinet established a new way of governance: "As for Hong Kong, its very lack of resources or means of being independent was always curiously enough a factor for its favor: it meant that more could be gained all around by making the city work as a port city—by developing infrastructure, education, international networks. This was a position that both the colonizer and the colonized could agree on, a position of cute correspondence or collusion" (Abbas 1997).

Under this "collusion" and consensus, private investments started to surge, especially those from full-fledged Chinese (family) consortiums. In many ways, their financial forces surpassed those of the government and the old-brand British companies and merchants. The government was keen to introduce these (Chinese) elites to the Legislative, Executive and Urban Councils. The private sector, private and public cooperation and semi-public sector (e.g., mass-transit railway [MTR]) dominated urban construction. This situation was quite different from that seen in the 1950s and 1960s. A watershed moment occurred in 1971, when the government and private forces led Hong Kong through its colonial years in the last half-century in two stages, respectively. The government channeled economic activities into a more thriving direction.

After 1970, Hong Kong's economy gradually boomed and its society found stability. From 1971 to 1997, Hong Kong saw its economy take off and witnessed the prosperity and internationalization of the city. A significantly important factor supporting Hong Kong's economy was the open-door policy adopted on the Chinese mainland in 1978. After 28 years behind the iron curtain, China opened its windows and let its people see the affluent lifestyles, advanced technologies, and management practices of Western countries. However, the West was located far away, with the nearest example being economically successful Hong Kong. China's patriarch Deng Xiaoping (1904–1997) circled the four special economic zones on a map—Shenzhen, Zhuhai, Shantou and Xiamen—all of which were located in southern China and close to the capitalist world of Hong Kong, Macau and Taiwan.[5] The intention of China to learn about capitalist (economic) success was obvious.

People and companies on the Chinese mainland were eager to learn from the West, and multinational corporations showed an intention to enter the China market. Hong Kong acted as a transition point that collected money from both sides.[6] Meanwhile, the opened Pearl River Delta provided ample land and labor for Hong Kong's manufacturing industry. Factories in Hong Kong were moved

---

[4]In most of the history books about Hong Kong, Sir Crawford Murray MacLehose was warmly lauded as a leader who brought Hong Kong into a new era. The main measurements are social welfare, public services and eliminating bribery. See (Cheng 2007).

[5]For more about modern and contemporary Chinese history and Deng Xiaoping's achievements, see (Spence 1990) and (Goodman 1994).

[6]Hong Kong gained from both the Western and Chinese sides in the early years of the open-door policy. See (Zweig 2002). Such gains also took place in architectural design. See (Xue 2006)[1] and (Xue 2006)[2].

northward to Shenzhen, Dongguan, Shunde and other towns in Guangdong Province. These factories made products in China and traded from Hong Kong. The land in Hong Kong was freed for office buildings. In 1997, the tertiary and service industries in Hong Kong contributed 85 % of the city's GDP.[7] The city transformed from a light-industrial base into a service center. Supplied with all of the preceding advantages in a "borrowed place and borrowed time," the people in Hong Kong created an economic miracle, growing its GDP steadily at 7–9 % annually over a sustained period (Hughes 1976) and (Castells et al. 1991).

To support these changes, skyscrapers designed by international architects were erected to soar over the central business district (CBD). Landmark buildings served as headquarters for multinational companies and were glorified as physical landmarks. To disperse the population pressure in the city center, new towns were planned and accommodated the increasingly expanding middle class. Consequently, MTR was developed and transit-oriented development (TOD) was enacted for the convenience of residents and the working class.

The diverse and vital economic development since the 1970s was led by private forces. The society and people tended to earn more money instead of political disputes. The austere modernist design language was gradually replaced by more decorations and somewhat "post-modern" manner. The architectural magazines with academic inquiry folded and gave way to more commercial trade magazine (Xue et al. 2016).

The early 1990s saw the end of the Cold War and the "end of history" around the world.[8] During this period, Hong Kong was proceeding toward the sovereignty transition. After Hong Kong is returned to China, it was no longer a British colony and outpost, instead it would merge to the network of Pearl River Delta and will lead China towards the world with its unique system. After 1997, Hong Kong society became more open, civic-oriented and democratic as the world entered a globalized, informational, and consumerist era. People enjoyed more individual and materialistic lifestyles, convenient communication and freedom of speech and civic life. Furthermore, Hong Kong's town planning, urban design, heritage conservation and sustainable development attracted societal attention and engaged the active participation of the public.[9] The professional cooperation between the Chinese mainland and Hong Kong also became more interactive.

Based on the preceding understanding of Hong Kong's contemporary history, this book is divided into three parts, with Part I covering the post-war period to 1971, Part II covering the period of 1972–1997 and Part III covering the post-1997 period. Each chapter discusses a particular topic.

---

[7]For more about the growth of the tertiary industry in Hong Kong, see (Zheng 2016).

[8]I borrow the concept of Harvard University Professor Francis Fukuyama. See his influential book (Fukuyama 1992).

[9]In the twenty-first century, all public buildings require design competition or tendering within a "two-envelope system"—one economic, and one design professional. Many public projects have undergone numerous public hearings and consultations. See (Cheng 2007).

Chapter 1 describes the post-war reconstruction in Hong Kong and how the government used resettlement housing to soothe the society and support new industries when thousands of workers required shelter. Chapter 2 analyzes the planning and design of public housing and buildings in tandem with their Western counterparts. The pioneers of the modernist architectural movement drew blueprints for ideal urban living in the 1920s and 1950s. Their dreams were realized in the crowded Far East. Expatriate British architects in the Hong Kong government brought in fresh ideas of modernist design and provided examples for their peers.

Chapter 3 categorizes the different types of architects and examines the strategies they adopted during the post-war reconstruction period. Educated in the US and UK, the first generation of Chinese architects, who had escaped from mainland China in 1949, filled the gap before the local talents were trained and matured. This chapter is devoted to "immigrant architects" and supplements studies of the first generation of Chinese architects and their achievements on the Chinese mainland. Chapter 4 reviews the evolution of government control and building regulations. To scientifically manage the urban architecture on the narrow land available, the government continuously updated the building regulations, which forcefully shaped the appearance of the buildings on the Hong Kong streets. The constraints both challenged and inspired developers and architects.

Chapters 1–4 mainly refer to the timeframe of 1946–1971. Their discussions of certain building types such as public housing and buildings focus on cases seen in later years so that readers may comprehend the fully evolving picture of these types of buildings and their development tracks.

With the enhancement of quality of life and an increase in the middle-class population, private housing started to thrive in the 1970s, driven by the growth of powerful (local Chinese) commercial developers. To begin Part II, Chap. 5 describes several representative private residential estates from the period. Most commercial developments are gated communities decorated with classical architectural clichés. On the contrary, the examples provided in Chap. 5 exhibited a forward-looking spirit and contributed to an active street life. Chapter 5 also depicts the evolution of the shopping mall in Hong Kong in terms of its design characteristics and why such buildings have flourished. Given the increasing popularity of consumerism, which has led the world economy, the shopping mall has arguably become a quasi and alternative "public space" for people living in narrow environments. Chapter 6 considers the "rail town" and mega-structures that attempt to solve the problems encountered in high-density cities. Such crowding problems challenge most East Asian cities. First proposed in the Western world, TOD also made its way to Hong Kong. New towns, TOD and public-private partnerships are mutually indispensable in achieving a compact city.

A colony is formed to connect with the outside world and outside forces. As Robert Home pointed out, "while the concept of the colonial city is still useful for the development theory, all cities are in a way colonial. They are created through the exercise of dominance by some groups over others, to extract agricultural surplus, provide services, and exercise political control" (Home 1997, p. 2). King also argued that the colonial city was the forerunner of the current global metropolis

(King 1990). As Hong Kong began to take its own path, the wave of globalization arrived at its shores. Globalization is a process of interaction and integration between the people, companies and governments of different nations, a process driven by international trade and investment and aided by information technology. Globalization affects and is affected by business and work organization, economics, social-cultural resources and the natural environment (Globalization101 2016). The International Monetary Fund identified four aspects of globalization: trade and transactions, capital and investment movements, the migration and movement of people and the dissemination of knowledge (International Monetary Fund 2016).

Chapter 7 depicts the work of international architects in Hong Kong in the 1980s, when the current CBD waterfront townscape was crystalized. Hong Kong has been a stepping-stone for foreign architects' expeditions in China. The construction of a convention center in Wanchai and a new airport in Chek Lap Kok represented the apex of this trend and injected confidence in the sovereignty handover. Meanwhile, both local and expatriate Hong Kong architects alike started to export their designs to China and Asian countries. The 1980s saw the heyday of Hong Kong's economy and architectural design.

Hong Kong's awareness of the importance of finding roots increased when its society accumulated a certain amount of wealth in the global era. The awareness consciously resisted and subtly balanced the capitalist greed and cultural supermarket to some degree.[10] Hong Kong architects discovered the potential and challenges involved in their own land. Chapter 8 considers representative designers and their works to this end. The explorative journey did not cease after 1997; rather, the baton was passed to the new generation.

If the 50 years from 1946 to 1997 represented a rising trajectory of Hong Kong, the 18 years after 1997 made its architecture more comprehensive, and as such deserve a separate piece of the territory's history. Part III highlights two salient trends that have been witnessed in the last 20 years. The first is the conservation of heritage buildings. The second is design competition and public consultation, both of which have reflected Hong Kong's buoying democracy and civic society. During the economic boom in the 1980s, people were unaware of the importance of conservation, and the government was able to decide and implement large-scale infrastructural or building projects with little public engagement. This top-down method was subverted when the political and social situation was transformed. In the twenty-first century, any matter of historic value is highly sensitive and politicized. Design competitions bring some new ideas that affect local conventions, and public consultation engages more stakeholders and citizens. Those who make decisions about public buildings hear different voices and solicit many schemes. However, the process is costly, noisy and time consuming.

From public housing and buildings to private housing and shopping malls, from shantytowns to rail villages, from refugee architects to locally trained designers,

---

[10]Gordon Mathews uses the term "cultural supermarket" to describe the abundant choices in life. See (Mathews 2005).

from one-way government decisions to public engagement, the last 70 years have seen a wide range of building types and progress. The aforementioned chapter topics chart the leap forward of Hong Kong from colony to global city from an architectural perspective.

The three periods of Hong Kong modern architecture are listed in the following table based on their driving forces and architectural outcomes. Although the table contains preliminary ideas and contents that can be further adjusted, it shows the rubric of the relationship between the causes and effects of architecture during the 70 years under examination.

Table 1 Summary of social conditions, driving forces and outcome of urban architecture in Hong Kong

Period	Social and economic conditions	Driving forces	Outcomes in urban architecture
1946–1971	Unstable domestic and international situations, crises typical of the Third World; wave of industrialization.	Settling refugees; clearance of squatter areas; housing for low-income citizens; **government-led modernity**.	Public housing; public buildings for urgent societal needs.
Demarcation event	Installation of Governor Sir Crawford Murray MacLehose in 1971.		
1972–1997	Economy taking off; shift from manufacturing to tertiary industry; bridging China and the Western world.	Driven by the **property market** and private investment, especially from **Chinese capitalists.**	Large-scale private middle-class residential estates; shopping malls; CBD designed by international architects; new towns and TOD; heritage buildings giving way to commercial interests.
Demarcation event	Sovereignty returned to China in 1997.		
1998–Now	Bumps in economy; economy slowing down; economy gradually surpassed by neighboring competitive cities like Shenzhen, Shanghai and Singapore; divided opinions in society.	Civic society; **public engagement**; awareness of the importance of **sustainability** and **finding roots.**	Public and institutional buildings through international design competitions; green architecture; renovation of heritage buildings.

In Search of Identities

The change in Hong Kong's imprint from a colony to a global city inevitably influenced several characteristics of the city's architecture. First, after World War II, colonies in Asia and Africa gradually achieved independence, strange flowers grown from the local and Western cultures. When the wave of globalization pushed forward, these former colonies soon became nodes of global cities such as Singapore, Kuala Lumpur, Taipei, Hong Kong and Shanghai (semi-colony) and played roles in the world economy. Although the imprint might not have been obvious in the individual buildings, it was embodied in the continuous development of the period. Chapters 2, 6 and 9 extend this observation.

Second, architectural design strategies were motivated by Hong Kong's high-density environment, hilly topography and compact infrastructure. Land resources were always in short supply. When Sir Abercrombie enacted the Hong Kong Plan in 1948, he was amazed that the city had "the highest density in the world." This density is now almost four to eight times its size during Abercrombie's era. On several university campuses, the height difference reaches hundreds of meters. The mega-structure MTR stations and their vicinities form many "rail villages" that accommodate almost half of the population. The territories' high density, hilly topography and "infrastructure urbanism" led to many special design treatments and construction effects. Chapters 4–6 look at the designs implemented to suit Hong Kong's unique topographical and environmental situations.

Third, the pragmatism of the architecture developed over time. Hong Kong is generally defined as a "city of materialism" when compared with other cities of religion, political power and romance.[11] A building's function must be rational, and the building should deliver its maximum usable or saleable floor space. A building is a machine for living and working that yields commercial value. The traditional relationship of "architect: building work" sometimes disappears in the city. The commercial determination of the developers decides the building plan, while architect only acts as an "Authorized Person" for drawing submission, and occasionally "beautifies" the elevation. Although Hong Kong tourism materials portray a red-sail junk positioned against a background of skyscrapers, ideas such as "integrating the East and West" and "custody of Chinese culture," which have haunted architects in mainland China and Taiwan, never burden Hong Kong architects. This pragmatic attitude is also partly shaped by the city's narrow lands, thrift-conscious conditions and fast pace of life. Pursuing efficiency and mass production, elaborating functions and exploiting technology advancements coincided with the design principles of modern architecture. This modern architecture opposed the classical (eclecticist) architecture that dominated the influential buildings of Hong Kong before the war. Gaining global popularity after World War II, many architects and

---

[11]See (Bell and De-Shalit 2011). The authors discussed nine cities, including Jerusalem, Montreal, Singapore, Hong Kong, Beijing, Oxford, Berlin, Paris and New York, using their own "strolling" anecdotes and extensive storytelling. Hong Kong's ethos is defined as "materialism."

architectural educators adopted architectural modernism (Frampton 1992). The expatriate British and some local architects designed a series of (public) works in the 1960s and 1980s that demonstrated the features of modernist architecture, including simplicity and clarity of form, the elimination of unnecessary decoration, visual expression of structures, clear edges, the use of industrially-produced materials and machine aesthetics. Chapters 2, 5, 6 and 8 provide examples of the buildings that fit these categories.

From drawing board to concrete entity, a building is the result of the joint force of a hundred hands, a thousand drawings, many machines and huge amounts of material. However, the architect's design is the soul of a building. After the war, public housing and buildings were mostly designed and supervised by architects from the Public Works Department who had come from Britain or other Commonwealth countries. Through public buildings, the government achieved its social plan and architects realized their ambitions. The second force of architects came from the Chinese mainland (mainly Shanghai) after accumulating practical experience for 20–30 years and serving clients from China. Local (trained) architects debuted in the 1970s. The third force comprised large (British expatriate) firms such as Palmer & Turner, Leigh & Orange and Spence & Robinson, which had been set up in the late nineteenth century and survived over several generations. Since 1980, international architects have participated in the design of corporate headquarters. Chapters 2, 3, 7, 8 and 10 provide details about how these architects make their brainchildren. The conclusion foresees the "made in Hong Kong" design and its future potential.

Architecture is the container of life. Every era has its own architecture. In the years when women wore *qipao*[12] and boat ferries were the only means of crossing the harbor, tenement housing and the first generation of public housing sheltered the Chinese people. The information and digital age requires more sophisticated, comprehensive and flexible architectural spaces. The text and illustrations included in this book demonstrate buildings from decades ago and in part represent the living scenarios and paces of former generations. Regardless of their lengths, the following chapters serve to delineate Hong Kong's transition from colony to global city from an architectural perspective. To avoid exhaustive descriptions, the chronology in the appendix supplements the major events in the construction of modern Hong Kong.

The 1990s saw the emergence of globalization and building products in Hong Kong. The last 70 years of architectural development in Hong Kong present interesting contrasts and rich colors. Most of the following chapters were developed from independent research papers that were either working papers or published in journals.[13] These papers represented the outcomes of the research team over the

---

[12]*Qipao*, an old-style Chinese woman's cloth popular in the 1920s–1960s. It is sometimes seen as a symbol of traditional beauty in the Republic of China. See (Lee 1999).

[13]See the chapter notes and reference bibliography.

past five years. Although the chapters are grouped by period in Parts I–III, each chapter can be read as a topical paper.

An author requires a platform to launch his inquiry. My 25 years of observation, experience and contemplation in Hong Kong are reflected throughout this book. Inspired by Bell and de-Shalit's book, which captured the authors "strolling" through nine Eastern and Western cities in addition to providing strict academic accounts (Lee 1999), I add a personal account of a specific Hong Kong environment at the end of every chapter in *italics*. According to Walter Benjamin (1898–1940), this attitude of *flâneur* or "civicism"[14] combines personal experience and emotion with the macro narrative of urban architecture for the benefit of readers. My life experiences in other Chinese cities, the U.K., the U.S. and other countries allow me to consider the "ethos" and building types in Hong Kong with a degree of sensitivity. The selection and prioritizing of chapter topics, buildings, events and people are driven by my understanding of Hong Kong's values. The insertion of personal experiences and stories may be challenged as superficial and impressionistic. The profound masters' works mentioned previously should address these concerns. Urban scholar Anthony King also described his findings in relation to traveling and moving to new places (King 2004).[15] As we are convinced that the ultimate purpose of architecture is to better the lives of people, a description of life within the architectural context better illustrates the subtle quality of the built environment. In past decades, some "academic" architectural journals have served only to boost individual ideas such as Descartes, Husserl, Heidegger, Merleau-Ponty and Derrida rather than physical buildings themselves. It is time to counterbalance this trend.

Looking at the Far East, Shanghai was once a splendid metropolis in the 1920s and 1930s. When the European cities were limiting their building height to 80 feet, Shanghai was building skyscrapers from 18 to 24 stories high in the 1930s. Its building height was just the second after that of New York City (Denison and Guang 2006, 2008). After 1938, Shanghai was dragged to Sino-Japan war, internal war and behind the iron curtain during Mao's leadership. Shanghai and other Chinese cities picked up from 1978 when the open-door policy was adopted. During Shanghai's absence in the urban and skyscraper construction, Hong Kong timely took Shanghai's talent/fund and relayed to build capitalism and skyscrapers.

Since 1950, various parts of Greater China have taken their own paths. Mainland China implemented a socialist planned economy and in 1978 embraced the open-door policy. Design institutes have designed buildings in mainland China as part of the national plan. "National form and socialist" content has been highlighted in the official buildings of Beijing. In Taiwan, official building design has been influenced

---

[14]Walter Benjamin (1898–1940) was a French social scientist. He invoked the image of the *flâneur* —the man who walks aimlessly through the street—as a way of examining the rise of capitalism, consumerism and urbanism in nineteenth century Paris. See (Benjamin and Tiedemann 1999). "Civicism" was a term advanced by Bell and de-Shalit, who argued that loving a city was easier than loving an abstract state. See (Bell and De-Shalit 2011).

[15]In this intimate and comprehensive book, the author introduced his life experiences in Britain and the United States.

more by the Beaux-Arts method, and architectural design has inherited Japanese and American conventions.[16] During the period of marshal law, architecture reflected an official ideology, similar to the situation in mainland China. When marshal law was lifted, modernist flowers blossomed (Shyu and Wang 2008; Fu 2014). In Macau, the main construction took place after large-scale reclamation and the construction of ocean bridges, with talented Portuguese architects playing a major role.[17]

Compared with architects in other areas of Greater China, Hong Kong architects were less affected by ideology. At first, they embraced the modernist principles without hesitation when forced to face the problems of mass construction and limited budgets. This was apparent in a series of public buildings constructed in the 1950s and 1960s. In tandem with the worldwide trend, design standards and tastes were much better than they were in other areas of Greater China. Since the 1970s, backed by the solid design and management abilities they accumulated in past decades, Hong Kong architects have sustained this momentum and taken their designs to mainland China, Taiwan and Macau. This book intends to determine how they built this momentum. I sincerely hope that it provides fresh material for analyzing the architectural streams in Greater China and the rest of Asia.

References

Abbas, A. (1997). *Hong Kong: culture and the politics of disappearance.* Minneapolis: University of Minnesota Press.
Akers-Jones, D. (2004). *Feeling the Stones: reminiscences by David Akers-Jones.* Hong Kong: Hong Kong University Press.
Architectural Services Department (ASD). (2006). *Post 97 public architecture in Hong Kong.* Hong Kong: Architectural Services Department, HKSARG.
Bell, D., & De-Shalit, A. (2011). *The spirit of cities - why the identity of a city matters in a global age.* Princeton: Princeton University Press.
Benjamin, W., & Tiedemann, R. (1999). *The arcades project.* Cambridge, Mass.: Belknap Press.
Blyth, S., & Wotherspoon, I. (1996). *Hong Kong remembers.* Hong Kong: Oxford University Press.
Bristow, M. (1984). *Land Use Planning in Hong Kong: history, policies and procedures.* Hong Kong: Oxford University Press.
Bristow, R. (1989). *Hong Kong's new towns: a selective review.* Hong Kong: Oxford University Press.
Castells, M., Goh, L., & Kwok, R. (1991). *The Shek Kip Mei syndrome - economic development and public housing in Hong Kong and Singapore.* London: Pion.
Chen, Y. (2014). *Hong Kong: a city state - how to restore its local culture.* Hong Kong: Tian chuang press. 陳雲. (2014). 香港城邦論II—光復本土. 香港: 天窗出版社有限公司.

---

[16]For more about the general development of modern Chinese architecture, see (Xue 2006)[1], (Zhu 2009) and (Xue 2010).

[17]The scholarship related to Macau architecture was based mainly on its colonial history and heritage buildings from the 16th to early 20th centuries. For example (Liu and Chen 2005). Modern architectural development since 1960 is rarely covered in both the Chinese and English literature.

Cheng, J. (2007). *The Hong Kong Special Administrative Region in its first decade.* Hong Kong: City University of Hong Kong Press.

Cheng, P. (2000). *Hundred Years of Kowloon Street.* Hong Kong: Joint Publication Ltd. 郑宝鸿. (2000). 九龙街道百年. 香港: 三联书店.

Ching, M., & Faure, D. (2003). *A History of Hong Kong 1842–1997* (2nd ed.). Hong Kong: Open University of Hong Kong.

Denison, E., & Guang, Y. (2006). *Building Shanghai: the story of China's gateway.* Hoboken, New Jersey: Wiley-Academy.

Denison, E., & Guang Y. (2008). *Modernism in China - architectural visions and revolution.* New York: John Wiley & Sons Ltd.

Denison, E., & Guang, Y. (2014). *Luke Him Sau, architect.* Chichester: John Wiley & Sons Inc.

Fang, Y. (2006). *One building two system – the opportunity and challenge of Hong Kong architecture.* Hong Kong: Wan Li Book Co. 方元 (2005). 一樓兩制 - 香港建築的機遇和挑戰. 香港:萬里機構,萬里書店.

Fauer, D. (2003). *Colonialism and the Hong Kong Mentality.* Hong Kong: Centre of Asian Studies, The University of Hong Kong.

Frampton, K. (1992). *Modern architecture.* London: Thames and Hudson.

Fu, C. (2014). *A history of modern architecture in Taiwan.* Taipei: Architectural Institute of Taiwan.

Fukuyama, F. (1992). *The end of history and the last man.* New York: Free Press.

Girard, G., Lambot, I., & Goddard, C. (2011). *City of darkness.* Chiddingfold: Watermark.

Globalization101. (2016). What Is Globalization?. *Globalization101.org.* Retrieved August 28, 2015 from http://www.globalization101.org/what-is-globalization/

Goodman, D. (1994). *Deng Xiaoping and the Chinese revolution.* London: Routledge. Retrieved August 28, 2015.

Gu, D. (2011). *Chung Chi original campus architecture.* Hong Kong: Chung Chi College, Chinese University of Hong Kong.

Home, R. (1997). *Of Planting and Planning: the making of British colonial cities.* London: E & FN Spon

Hughes, R. (1976). *Borrowed place, borrowed time: Hong Kong and its many faces.* London: Deutsch.

International Bank for Reconstruction and Development,. (2014). *World Development Report, 1990-2014*(1st ed.). New York: Oxford University Press. http://siteresources.worldbank.org/INTPOVERTY/Resources/WDR/English-Full-Text-Report/toc.pdf

International Monetary Fund,. (2016). *Globalization: threats or opportunity.* Washington, D.C.: IMF Publications.

King, A. (1990). *Global cities: post-imperialism and the internationalization of London.* London: Routledge.

King, A. (2004). *Spaces of global cultures: architecture urbanism identity.* London: Routledge.

Lai, L. (1997). *Town Planning in Hong Kong, a critical review.* Hong Kong: City University of Hong Kong Press.

Lai, L., & Fong, K. (2000). *Town Planning Practice: context, procedures and statistics for Hong Kong.* Hong Kong: Hong Kong University Press.

Lampugnani, V., Pryor, E., Pau, S., & Spengler, T. (1993). *Hong Kong architecture—the aesthetics of density.* New York: Prestel Verlag.

Lee, L. (1999). *Shanghai Modern: the flowering of a new urban culture in China, 1930–1945.* Cambridge, Mass.: Harvard University Press.

Lee, L. (1998). Hong Kong: as Shanghai's otherness. *Dushu,* (12), 18–23. 李欧梵. (1998). 香港, 作为上海的"她者". 读书, (12), 18–23.

Leung, M. (1999). *From Shelter to Home: 45 Years of Public Housing Development in Hong Kong.* Hong Kong: Hong Kong Housing Authority. 梁美仪 (1999). 家 – 香港公屋四十五年. 香港: 香港房屋委员会

Leung, A., & Yiu, C. (2004). *Building dilapidation and rejuvenation in Hong Kong*. Hong Kong: Hong Kong Institute of Surveyors and City University Press.

Li, P. (2012). *Governing Hong Kong: insights from the British declassified files*. Hong Kong: Oxford University Press. 李彭广 (2012). 管治香港- 英国解密档案的启示. 香港: 牛津大学出版社

Liu, X., & Chen, Z. (2005). *Heritage architecture of Macau*. Nanjing: Southeast University Press. 刘先觉,陈泽成 2005 澳门建筑文化遗产 南京:东南大学出版社

Lu, H., & Chan, L. (1998). *The Introduction of Urban Planning in Hong Kong*. Hong Kong: Joint Publishing Ltd. 卢惠明、陈立天 (1998). 香港城市规划导论. 香港: 三联书店.

Lui, T. (2012). *The 1970s we might know*. Hong Kong: Chung Hwa Book Co. 吕大乐. (2012). 那似曾相识的七十年代. 香港: 中华书局.

Mathews, G. (2005). *Global culture/individual identity: searching for home in the cultural supermarket*. London: Routledge.

Peng, H. (1990). *Hong Kong architecture*. Beijing: China Architecture and Building Press. 彭华亮主编. (1990). 香港建筑. 北京:中国建筑工业出版社.

Shyu, M. S., & Wang, C.-H., (2008). *Rustic & poetic - an emerging generation of architecture in postwar Taiwan*. Taipei: Mu Ma Press. 徐明松、王俊雄 (2008).粗旷与诗意:台湾战后第一代建筑. 台北 木马文化.

Shelton, B., Karakiewicz, J., & Kvan, T. (2011). *The making of Hong Kong-from vertical to volumetric*. New York: Routledge.

Spence, J. (1990). *The search for modern China*. New York: Norton.

Tan, Z., & Xue, C. Q. L. (2013). Trade magazines and the reflections on cities—about the contemporary urbanism of Hong Kong (1965-1984). *Architectural Journal*, (11), 14–19. 谭峥、薛求理(2013). 专业杂志与城市自觉—创建关于香港的当代都市主义(1965-1984). 建筑学报, (11), 14–19.

Tang, B., Chiang, Y., Baldwin, A., & Yeung, C. (2004). *Study of the integrated rail-property development model in Hong Kong*. Hong Kong: Research Centre for Construction & Real Estate Economics, Dept. of Building & Real Estate, Faculty of Construction & Land Use, the Hong Kong Polytechnic University.

Walker, A., & Rowlinson, S. (1990). *The building of Hong Kong*. Hong Kong: Hong Kong University Press.

Wang, G. (1997). *Hong Kong History: new perspective*. Hong Kong: Joint Publication.

Welsh, F. (1997). *A history of Hong Kong*. London: HarperCollins.

Woo, M. (2005). *Hong Kong Style*. Hong Kong: TOM (Cup Magazine) Publishing Ltd. 胡恩威 (2005). 香港风格.

Xue, C. Q. L. (2006).[1]*Building a revolution: Chinese architecture since 1980*. Hong Kong: Hong Kong University Press.

Xue, C. Q. L. (2006).[2]*The global impact: overseas architectural design in China*. Shanghai: Tongji University Press.

Xue, C. Q. L. (2010). *World architecture in China*. Hong Kong: Joint Publishing Ltd.

Xue, C. Q. L., Tan, Z., & Xiao, Y. (2016). Architecural magazine in Hong Kong for a century. *World Architecture*, 36(1), 40–44.

Yeung, Y., & Wong, K. (2003). *Fifty years of public housing in Hong Kong: a golden jubilee review and appraisal*. Hong Kong: Chinese University Press.

Zhang, Z., & Lau, S. (1998). *City Image of Central, Hong Kong*. Beijing: Pace Publication Ltd. 张在元, 刘少瑜. (1997). 香港中环城市形象. 香港:贝思出版公司.

Zheng, K. (2016). Industry upgrading and shifting in Hong Kong. *Doc.mbalib.com*. Accessed 23 May 2015. http://doc.mbalib.com/view/496cb46082e8ebea3cd71d69f1df267c.html Accessed 23 May 2015.

Zhu, J. (2009). *Architecture of modern China*. London: Routledge.

Zweig, D. (2002). *Internationalizing China: domestic interests and global linkages*. Ithaca: Cornell University Press.

Acknowledgement

Thanks to the open-door policy adopted in China in 1978, an apprentice from a steel casting and tempering plant entered college. One thing that has left a deep impression during my formative years in the 1980s was the design of Jinling Hotel in Nanjing. I remember standing in the city center during my visit to Nanjing, looking up at 37-story high Jinling Hotel—which was designed by a firm based in Hong Kong, P&T Architects & Engineers Ltd. At the time, it was a much-talked about design in the Chinese architectural circle. I began to appreciate Hong Kong as one of the architectural design powerhouses.

In the Science Hall of Shanghai, Dr. Tao Ho and other Hong Kong architects delivered a different "Chinese voice" to the students and professionals in Shanghai. In 1989, I was staying for nine months in Hong Kong, a distant outpost in relation to the Chinese capital that was overwhelmed by a dramatic political storm at the time. That short stint ushered in a longer (or perhaps permanent) stay that started in 1995—an academic nomadic found his oasis at the tip of the South China Sea. Without the encouragement, guidance and help from Professors Dai Fudong, Yuan Sitao, Xiang Bingren, David Lung, Stephen Lau, Sivaguru Ganesan and Julie Mo, I would never have imagined settling down in Hong Kong.

While I was busy compiling books and writing papers on contemporary Chinese architecture and overseas architectural design in China, friends reminded me that no proper study had been done on Hong Kong architecture. That triggered my interest and I began to pay attention to the surrounding architectural details, which we normally take for granted. Preliminary exploration brought in several grants from CityU's internal funding and later the National Natural Science Foundation of China (NSFC, Project No. 51278438), which made the investigation and this book possible. I sincerely thank the reviewers and the committee at NSFC.

I owe a great debt to my mentor, Mr. Chung Wah-nan, a widely respected predecessor in Hong Kong modern architecture, who filled me with the knowledge of the Hong Kong society, its people and building designs. Mr. Chung continuously instills Chinese factors into architectural design and urban construction in his architectural design practice, writing and lectures. His instructions and noble intellectual spirit have nourished me in many ways. Hong Kong architects like Mr Chung Wah-nan are the heroes of this book. I have followed their works and instructions and tried to weave their creations into this volume. I would also like to thank Tao Ho, Andrew Lee King-fun, James Kinoshita, Remo Riva, Rocco Yim, Simon Kwan, Patrick Lau, Ronald Philips, Raymond Fund, Dominic Lam, John Cheng, Nicholas Lai and Corrin Chan.

Conversations with my colleagues and friends have enriched my understanding of Hong Kong and its transition from 20th to 21st centuries. I would like to express my gratitude to Raymond Wai Man Wong, Kevin Yap, Brian Mitchenere, Gu Daqing, Jia Beisi, Stan Fung, Pu Miao, Wang Jun and Chen Longgen.

My study of the urban architecture of Hong Kong was in parallel with my observation of new architectural developments in mainland China, Taiwan and Macau. The research project is supported by my colleagues, assistants and students. They are Lu Yi, Li Lin, Carmen Tsui, Tan Zheng, Zou Han, Xiao Jing, Ding Guanghui, Yin Ziyuan, Zang Peng, Liu Xin, XiaoYingbo, Chan Ka Chun, Zhai Hailing, Li Yingchun, Hui Ka Chuen, Ma Luming, Chan Chiu Kwan, Vivian Lo and Kwan Young Yee.

The content of the book was first presented in a Chinese book: *Contextualizing Modernity: Hong Kong Architecture 1946–2011*, published by Commercial Press of Hong Kong in 2014. The book was warmly accepted when it was published and entered the bestseller list in Hong Kong. My special thanks to Dr. Han Jia for her insight and meticulous work, as well as to her supervisor Mao Yongbo and the editorial team.

After listening to the feedback on the Chinese book, I have re-written the materials in the English edition. Thanks to the decision of Leana Li and comments from anonymous reviewers, I feel honored that this book is ranked among the Springer social science list. Leana Li and her team deliver the book in an academic manner.

Drawings and pictures are an indispensable part of an architectural book. In addition to the above design masters, many other people and organizations have kindly provided well-appreciated images used in the book. Here, I would like to thank: Edward Stokes, Bryan Lu, Bernard Lim, Weijin Wang, Chris Law, Shirley Surya, James Law, Winston Shu, Chan Lai Kiu, Wong Suen Kwok, CityU, PolyU, HKU and government departments. In the past 70 years, many buildings have been built and demolished, but the hand-made drawings from these design masters are largely kept in the government departments or archives. When I read those faded ink lines or documents from decades ago, my heart was filled with awe and respect for the architectural accomplishments of the past era. These documents allow us to have a close look of the Hong Kong past. We can't help but to thank the people who have kept our past. This book also aims at keeping and reconstructing the architectural history of the island, especially the history of the buildings that once sparkled brilliantly and later ended up in dry rot.

Summer 2016   Charlie Q.L. Xue

Contents

Notes

- Since 1976, Hong Kong government has adopted the international measuring system. All submission drawings to the government must use the metric unit. The international system is used in discussing engineering and construction issues. However, the trade of housing transaction, sales agent, interior and furniture design still use the empire system of foot and inch. This book uses the British system when discussing buildings in the 1950s and 60s, or when citing popular informal sayings especially in housing unit size. The other descriptions use the international system.
- Since 1983, Hong Kong dollar has been pegged with US dollar. 1 US dollar stands for HK$ 7.72–7.78. When dollar is referred to in this book, it means Hong Kong dollar.
- When the building's year is referred, it usually means completion year. For example, PolyU campus (1980) means that the campus was completed in 1980.
- Illustrations are credited unless the author's own pictures.

Part I
Government Led Modernity

The Japanese invasion and civil war changed Hong Kong and also brought opportunity. The inundated refugees and wealth demanded shelter and also provided manpower and investment for manufacturing industry. Hong Kong launched unprecedented battle of building resettlement and public housing, which marked the territory's civilization and progress. Public building not only provided place for people's basic life but also taught modern aesthetics. The expatriate, local, and immigrant architects found their way of contributing to the post-war reconstruction. One of the design armies was escaping from the Chinese mainland regime, and their works in Hong Kong, Shanghai, Nanjing, and Tianjin formed a perfect picture of modern Chinese architectural history. Behind the various performances of real estate and architectural design was the government building control, which shapes the identity of different periods.

Chapter 1
Reconstruction and Resettlement After the War

1.1 Dilapidated City After the War

Japan surrendered the Second World War on August 15, 1945. After a hard and bitter struggle lasting three years and eight months, Hong Kong was liberated with the help of Allied Forces. The British fleet re-entered the waters of Hong Kong and a military government temporarily administered the colony. During the Japanese invasion, Governor Sir Mark A. Young (1886–1974) was imprisoned in Hong Kong, Taiwan and Shenyang. He resumed his duty on May 1, 1946. At the time, Hong Kong was severely wounded and waiting to resurge.

During its occupation, Japanese deliberately demolished buildings and snatched ironmongery to make weapons. The Allied Forces bombed Hong Kong heavily before the liberation in 1945. About 20 % of Chinese tenements were either destroyed or seriously damaged. An estimated 20,636 buildings serving as tenement-type housing for 160,000 people and European-type housing for 7,000 people (70 % of all European-style housing) were lost. Except for the busy Des Voeux Road and Queen's Road, the Mid-Level and Causeway Bay fell into dilapidation due to bombings and fires. Most of the streets, such as Lockhart Road in Wan Chai, Seymour Road and Robinson Road in Mid-Level and Woosung Street and Shanghai Street in Kowloon, were left empty and in disrepair. Factory and trading stopped, the market went quiet and public transportation was only "symbolically" maintained in limited areas. Trash piled up in the streets and food and fuel supplies became inadequate. Compared with the city, the rural areas in the New Territories were partly exempt from war disasters (Chen and Guo 1997).

Only new construction and major repairs could cure most of the housing deficiency. The pace of reconstruction was slow because property owners were discouraged by the high cost of building materials and labor at the time. For example, a looted European-type house might have cost twice as much to repair than it was

10 years earlier. In 1952, the cost of repairing a building was six times higher than it had been pre-war and the high prices prevented many clients from repairing.[1] The University of Hong Kong was badly damaged, mainly due to looting, same as many of the colony's schools. The industrial buildings were only lightly affected in comparison. The return of life to the port resulted in a flow of labor from China. The revival of Hong Kong, based as always on its entrepot trade, was slowly under way. As Hong Kong was struggling to restore itself to normal life, the Communists and Nationalists were engaged in a fierce civil war on the Chinese mainland. The money of the National Government in Nanjing depreciated drastically. Hong Kong had to lend a hand to the Chinese National government.[2]

Despite damages, houses had to be managed in service. Migrants entered into Hong Kong at a rate of 100,000 people a month. By the end of 1946, the population had grown from 600,000 to an estimated 1.6 million people, the level it had reached before the war. The annual report that year described "serious overcrowding" and recorded that "many of the newcomers … had no knowledge of urban life and were ignorant of the rudiments of sanitation. Thousands sought shelter in damaged premises with no sanitary fittings and drew their water from polluted wells." The tremendous pressure created by too many people trying to squeeze into far too few houses posed tough problems for the government. Many expatriates and their families returned to Hong Kong and packed the only hotels in Hong Kong Island and Kowloon.[3]

In addition to physical building, the complex housing economies and especially the landlord-tenant relationship had to be restored. The great influx of people during the Sino-Japanese War led to the passing in 1938 of the Prevention of Eviction Ordinance, which conferred upon tenants a certain measure of protection against excessive rent and eviction. Upon the restoration of the Civil Administration in May 1946, a committee under the chairmanship of Mr. Leo D'Almada, Q.C. was appointed to report on the practical workings of the Landlord and Tenant Proclamation. The committee report noted the following: "The acute housing shortage prevailing in the Colony can only be remedied by large-scale new building. In view of the high cost of materials and wages, we are of the opinion that to place any restriction upon the rents of new premises would be to discourage such enterprises and inevitably to prolong the serious situation." In 1955, the ordinance was amended. When clients prepared to repair buildings, they did not need to excessively compensate the tenants. This restored confidence in rebuilding and new investment. At the time, Hong Kong businessman Fok Ying-tung created a method of pre-selling housing units and mortgage repayment that stimulated more middle-class individuals to buy property (Chen and Guo 1997) (Figs. 1.1 and 1.2).

---

[1]The figures and quotes of this chapter are mainly taken from the *Hong Kong Annual Report 1957*, Hong Kong Government Publication Bureau (1958). The post-war situation partly references Graye (1951).

[2]According to the *Hong Kong Annual Report 1948*, Hong Kong loaned 10,000 t of rice to the Shanghai government in 1948. See (Hong Kong Government 1949).

[3]*Hong Kong Annual Report 1946*, Hong Kong Government Publication Bureau (1947).

Fig. 1.1 Pottinger Street, Central, 1946. Courtesy of Harvard-Yenching Library and The Photographic Heritage Foundation (HK)

Fig. 1.2 Townscapes of Hong Kong in the eyes of Hedda Morrison, 1946. Courtesy of Harvard-Yenching Library and The Photographic Heritage Foundation (HK). **a** Trade and shipping. **b** Chinese residencies in the Hong Kong Island

1.2 Planning for the Fifty Years

After the Second World War, the British government of Labor Party enacted the
Colonial Development and Welfare Act of 1945. This is a sign that the British
government concerned deeply on and controlled tightly its outlying colonies.
According to the Act, the British government allocated one million pounds, of
which Hong Kong gained 500,000 lb to support its 10-year comprehensive welfare
plan. The plan included the construction of a fishery wholesale market in Kennedy
Town and a pier in Aberdeen, in addition to the purchase of diesel engines for
fishing boats. One item referred to a 10-year town plan,[4] which the Hong Kong
government invited Sir Leslie Patrick Abercrombie (1879–1957) to oversee.
Abercrombie was the most famous town planner in Britain and had worked in the
planning field for more than 30 years. Before the end of the war, he had led the
planning of London County (1943), the Greater London Plan (1944) and the
planning of more than 20 shires and cities such as Plymouth, Bath, Edinburg, Hull
and Bournemouth. He was the founding editor of the *Town Planning Review* and a
professor at Liverpool University and University College London (UCL).[5] After his
retirement from UCL, he served as a consultant for the planning of Malta, Cyprus,
Karachi and Australia. In 1947, he was one of the founding members of the
International Union of Architects and acted as its first chair. Abercrombie continues
to be recognized as the most influential town planner of the 20th century.[6]

Abercrombie visited Hong Kong from November 2 to December 6, 1947.
During these 37 days, he visited various places and had discussions with government officials and locals. In September 1948, he sent three copies of The Hong
Kong Preliminary Planning Report to the Hong Kong government.[7] The report
categorized 108 articles into three parts. Part I detailed the scope of the report and
defined its timeline, economy and limitations. Early reports of the Hong Kong
government before the war, such as those related to David J. Owen's port city and
W.H. Owen's housing supply, were referenced in this part. Part II focused on
general development proposals for the harbor; population size and groupings;
housing density and redistribution; shops and workshops; industrial locations and
zoning; roads; the tunnel; railways; the removal of military services; the central
area, open spaces and New Territories; and tourism and ancillaries (infrastructure).

---

[4]*Annual Report on Hong Kong For the Year 1946*, Hong Kong Government Publication Bureau
(1947).

[5]The *Town Planning Review* was founded by Sir Patrick Abercrombie in 1910 and has been run
since then. It is the most recognized journals in the field of urban and regional planning.

[6]For details of the life and career of Sir Patrick Abercrombie, see Amati and Freestone (2009),
Dehaene (2004), Lai (1999). The award of urban planning in the World Congress of Architects
was named after Abercrombie. This honor is awarded to an excellent urban planning project in
every congress. Moreover, *Town Planning Review*, which was founded by him in 1910, is still
running today and is one of the leading planning journals in the world.

[7]For details of the pre-war town planning of Hong Kong, see Xue et al. (2012).

Part III detailed how to realize the proposals, such as by setting up a planning arm of the government and enacting statutory measurements.

Abercrombie had good ideas that included the establishment of a garden city, satellite towns and organic dispersion. These ideas had proved effective in his Greater London Plan and in the post-war urban construction in other European cities, and he looked forward to applying them to the Far East.

Abercrombie hoped that the Hong Kong report would cover both short- and long-term policies, and direct private enterprises in a way such that their operations would fall into a general and agreed-upon form of planned development. The report did not "assume a final and finite plan passed in all its details as a 'Town Planning Scheme', but a plan of 'Development' using the word in its strict sense and allowing for revision from time to time in the light of changing requirements and technical accomplishment" (Abercrombie 1948). It observed that Hong Kong faced two constraints, a shortage of land and an unlimited reservoir of possible immigration. Abercrombie suggested that new towns be built on the outskirts of Kowloon and in the New Territories, that the colony be divided into industrial and residential zones and that the military bases be removed from the city centers. Kwun Tong and Chang Sha Wan were designated industrial areas. Abercrombie pointed out that "Hong Kong is perhaps more deficient in public buildings than any other town of comparable size in the world: there is no town hall, civic hall, art gallery, museum, public library, theatre or opera house" (Article 81). Although Hong Kong Island and Kowloon were home to one million inhabitants, the two sides were separated by a stretch of water less than a mile wide. Abercrombie used seven articles to explain the necessity and technical possibilities of constructing a tunnel or bridge between Victoria and Kowloon (Fig. 1.3).

Sir Patrick observed, "The population has become used to densities which over large areas must be some of the highest in the world." When Abercrombie handed the report to the Hong Kong government at the end of 1948, the People's Liberation Army was pushing its front forward from north to south. Many refugees were pouring into Hong Kong. The population exploded from 600,000 people in 1945 to three million people in 1949. Already stressing the limits of its tattered fabric, Hong Kong achieved a new urban density of over 50,000 people to the square mile, one of, if not the, highest in the world.

The Hong Kong Preliminary Planning Report was carefully reviewed inside the government and consensus was reached in the early 1950s.[8] However, the Korean War broke out and the report had to be shelved. According to The Hong Kong Annual Report 1957, "These were drastic and expensive measures, which still might have been feasible if Hong Kong had been able to snatch two or three years of tranquility in the hazardous post-war world ... As events and people crowded upon the Colony, the planners found themselves more and more absorbed in

[8]About the comment and attitude of Hong Kong government towards Abercrombie's report, see Bristow (1984), Home (1997).

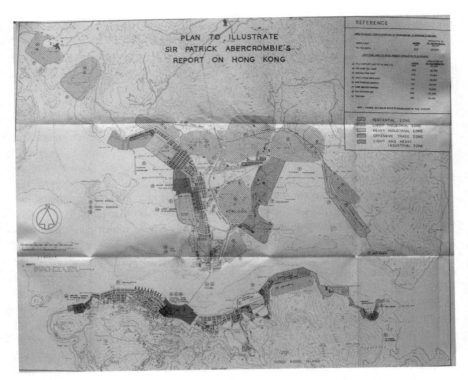

Fig. 1.3 Zoning in Abercrombie's planning report, 1948. From HK government archive

immediate problems. Yet the signposts erected by the Abercrombie Report have not been forgotten nor their broad directions obscured." In January 1953, a town-planning arm was established under the Land and Measurement Office of the Public Works Department (PWD). The Department of Planning was formally established in 1990.

Although Abercrombie's proposals were not immediately realized, they influenced later urban planning policies and directions. Many administrative and legislative actions followed his suggestions (Lai 1999). Abercrombie wrote that "extensive reclamations are also possible at Gin Drinkers Bay and Tsun Wan … Much less reclamation is possible on Hong Kong Island itself … Kennedy Town, the bay from Yaumati Ferry to Murray Road … east of North Point … Naval Dock, Causeway Bay … Shaukiwan Bay" (Abercrombie 1948). The reclamation of Kwun Tong was completed as early as 1952; Kennedy Town, Naval Dock and Causeway Bay by 1953; North Point by 1957; Yau Tong (in East Kowloon), Ma Tong Wai, Kowloon Bay and Hung Hum Bay by 1967; and Cheung Sha Wan (in West Kowloon), Gin Drinkers Bay and Tsuen Wan by 1983, continuing up to 2002. Debate over the reclamation of Victoria Harbor in 1997 has proved the predictions of Abercrombie 50 years ago.[9] In 1972, 24 years after Abercrombie's suggestion, the first cross-harbor tunnel opened from Hung Hom to Causeway Bay, allowing vehicles to run from the peninsula to the island. The new towns received millions of residents from city area and alleviated the pressure of city.

1.3 Sheltering Refugees

In the early 20th century, continental Europe and the U.K. made great strides to develop early industrial cities into civilized and garden cities. Improvements in hygiene, residential health and social housing made dirty and backward ghettos into livable cities. Inhabitable environments were transformed into modern civilizations. In the 1920s, a lot of veteran soldiers and workers moved into decent housing in countries like Germany, Scotland and Austria. After WWII, the sector of social housing grew strongly in Europe but variedly among countries.

In the early 20th century, the core concern of city management in Hong Kong was to control the density of Chinese tenement areas and prevent the spread of diseases when large amount of migrants flew in. Early building ordinances were promulgated for that purpose. In the 1930s, the colonial government set up a housing committee and appointed Wilfred Herbert Owen as its commissioner. In a report released in 1940, Owen suggested that government should improve residents' living conditions instead of merely relying on the private market. However, the report had to be shelved due to the outbreak of the Pacific War in 1941.[10] Nothing was achieved in mass housing before the war.

Just after the Japanese invaders were expelled, Communists and Nationalists entered into civil war on the Chinese mainland. Many refugees poured into Hong Kong and the population exploded from 600,000 people in 1945 to three million people in 1950. To cope with the wave of refugees, the government designated some hilly areas for residents to squat. The city underwent a rapid and ugly physical change. By 1951, shantytowns spread like an unsightly rash around the permanent buildings of Victoria and Kowloon, filling the valley floors and mounting the steep hillsides. The most extensive of these flimsy settlements were on the north-west outskirts of Kowloon. However, large communities disfigured almost every hillside

---

[9]On June 27, 1997, a motion entitled *Protection of the Harbour Ordinance* proposed by civil activists and Legislative Council member Christine Loh was passed in the Legislative Council three days before the sovereignty handover and later became Chapter 531 of the Hong Kong Law. The motion stated that the harbor, as a special public asset and a natural heritage of the Hong Kong people, was subject to the "presumption against reclamation" principle. It primarily called upon the government to withdraw plans for reclamation of the harbor and to take urgent measures to ensure its protection and preservation. Protection of the Harbour (Amendment) Bill 1997 (Minutes) 10 Feb 98, Legislative Council document. http://www.legco.gov.hk/yr97-98/english/bc/bc04/minutes/bc041002.htm, Accessed 20 May 2015.

[10]About housing and planning before WWII, see Xue et al. (2012).

and vacant lot on both sides of the harbor. Before the physical housing by the public fund, the government had to encourage the charity groups to take care the housing for refugees.

In 1948, using a donation of £14,000 from the Air Raid Distress Fund of the Lord Mayor of London, a group of enthusiastic British people founded a non-profit organization to help those in need of housing. Over the course of 60 years, this organization has grown into its current incarnation as the Hong Kong Housing Society. Other such organizations include the Hong Kong Model Housing Society, Hong Kong Economic Society, Hong Kong Settlers' Housing Corporation and Hong Kong Citizens Housing Company. While other volunteer organizations were building huts, these four organizations began building multi-storey housing for the poor in the dense urban landscape of Hong Kong as early as 1950. In a cramped city, building multi-storey housing is indeed insightful.

In 1951, the Model Housing Society built the five-storey Model Housing Estate in the remote countryside of North Point. After more than 60 years, the estate is still in use. Although the Housing Society is actively running on billions of dollars in investment, other organizations have disappeared over time (Fig. 1.4). In the beginning, these organizations mainly provided affordable rental housing for low-income families. They were later involved in various homeownership plans (such as the "sandwich class housing scheme"), rural public housing and aging rental house and urban renewal. The efforts of the Housing Society complement the government's work. Its housing standards have always been a bit higher than the government's resettlement standards.

However, these charitable organizations were unable to solve all the housing problems. When refugees built squatter areas along the foot of mountains, government allowed independent contractors to build small huts to sell on

Fig. 1.4 Model Housing Estate, 1951

hire-purchase terms. Hong Kong Settlers' Housing Corporation built more than 1,500 small and large cottages with HK$20–25 monthly repayment terms. In some remote areas, government only controlled roads, firebreaks, communal water supply and latrines. Building construction was "tolerated" (Will 1978). Within two years, the squatter areas were scattered around Kowloon and part of Hong Kong Island. Fire disasters have frequently taken place in squatter areas like Kowloon City, Diamond Hill and Tsuen Wan since 1950. On Christmas Day of 1953, an enormous fire broke out in the squatter area of Shek Kip Mei and 50,000 people lost their homes. Throughout history, fires have prompted the rebuilding of cities and sometimes served as catalyst of urban planning and regulations. Before the fire, the government began preparations to build public housing. The fire pushed the government to speed up the pace of resettlement.[11]

The government committee recommended a pilot scheme at Shek Kip Mei and also set up a new section called Resettlement Department. Architectural Office in the Public Work Department undertook the task of design and construction supervision. The government felt that the resettlement of the squatters was not possible until specific areas within the urban boundaries were freed for intensive development to accommodate the original inhabitants at a higher net density, while providing roads, services and open space in the same areas. "The overall effect was that the stage was set for a compact city form with extremely high density residential and commercial form which has given Hong Kong the characteristics that make it unique when compared with other large cities of the world" (Smart 2006, p. 5).

Mark I, the first generation of public housing, typically took the form of resettlement houses. Rooms were arranged back-to-back around long corridors. The standard government allocation for a family of five people was a flat of 120 ft^2.[12] The monthly rent was HK$14. When the squatter residents were earning HK$2 a day, smaller units sized at 86 ft^2 were made available at a monthly rent of HK$10. As a comparison, private flats sized at 300 square feet in the city area asked for HK$100 a month.[13] According to the author's measurements, the net area of a room in the Mei Ho Building (1954) was 2.2 × 2.8 m. These rooms were arranged back-to-back and a hole was opened in the partition wall in each room for ventilation. The Mei Ho Building contained 62 such standard rooms. The plan had an H-shape, with the central part between the two wings offering public toilets and baths. Storerooms were positioned at the ends of the wings. The two wings were spaced 10 m apart. According to Robert Home's study, such type house was

---

[11]Alan Smart's book provides another insight into the fire and public housing in Hong Kong, see Smart (2006).

[12]Since 1976, Hong Kong government has adopted the international measuring system. All submission drawings to the government must use the metric unit. The international system is used in discussing engineering and construction issues. However, the trade of interior and furniture design still use the empire system of foot and inch. This book uses the British system when discussing buildings in the 1950s and 60s, or when citing popular informal sayings. The other descriptions use the international system.

[13]For details on the rental of public and private housing in the 1950s, see Tu (2003).

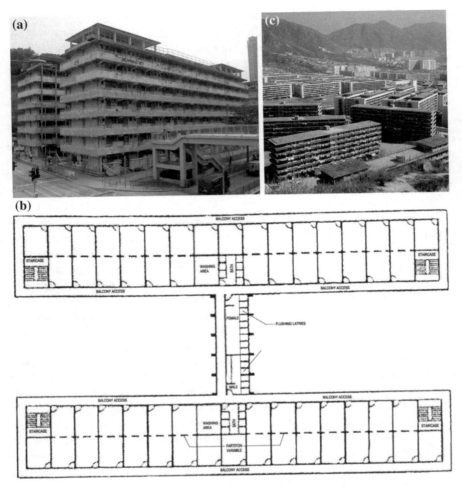

Fig. 1.5 Mark I—the first generation of public rental housing. **a** Over 40 such blocks existed in Shek Kip Mei till 2006. **b** Plan of Mark I public housing. Two wings are residential units, the center is toilet. **c** Mark I public housing in Chai Wan, a remote area in the HK Island. From HK Government archive

influenced by the earlier Improvement Board chawls in India (Home 1997, p. 204) (Fig. 1.5).

Eight blocks of H-shaped buildings six storeys high were constructed in 1954. Another nine blocks of seven-storey buildings were built in Shek Kip Mei. These included 8,500 living units and served as homes for 50,000 people.[14] From 1954 to

---

[14]For details on the dimensions of Mark I settlement houses, the author read the drawings of the Mei Ho Building and verified them on site. The unit number of 8,500 comes from Ho (2010).

1961, 115 blocks of H-shaped buildings and 31 blocks of I-shaped buildings were built in Shek Kip Mei, Tai Hang Tung, Lei Cheng Uk, Hung Hom, Lok Fu, Wong Tai Sin, Jordan Valley, Kwun Tong and Chai Wan. Kwun Tong and Chai Wan were remote areas in the 1950s and located far away from the workplaces. People were reluctant to move to these faraway areas.

A standard unit sized at 120 ft^2 accommodated five or more people. Using beds as a basic module, it was difficult to put four beds into a room, let alone other "home" functions. Although simple, these rooms offered happy homes for many residents who had originally lived in squatter areas. As "machine for living", low-cost shelter housing presented a repetitive, monotonous and sometimes monochrome face. Notwithstanding this, the roofs sheltered people from bad weather and the estates provided helpful neighborhoods. The modernist method of designing mass housing with little decoration was efficient and effective to solve the housing problem of urban poor. Many Housing Authority publications and Hong Kong memoirs recorded the pleasure of residents when they moved into the resettlement housing and started new lives.[15] Building settlement housing allowed people to move away from the squatter areas. The demolished squatter areas gave way to new higher-density construction both in public and private sectors, which formed the main construction work the government performed in the 1950s and 1960s.

1.4   Supporting the Industry

While Hong Kong was facing a dilapidated townscape, the Chinese mainland was changing drastically. Many capitalists, mainly from Shanghai, moved to Hong Kong with their families, employees and money. They invested in various types of manufacturing such as textile, enamel, aluminum, rubber and plastic. Hong Kong placed no limitations on immigrants and implemented a policy of a free economy that encouraged an influx of money. The arrival of these merchants soon raised the demand for buildings.

In 1951, Hong Kong presented a pleasing picture of thriving growth. Miniature skyscrapers were already rising steeply from the mass of three- and four-storey tenements in the two cities of Victoria Harbor. The slim concrete towers pointed to the end of the age of flat colonial architecture. The old porticoed, heavily pillared building with its high ceilings, fans and broad verandahs would soon be as out of date as the pith helmet. The new trend in both commercial and domestic architecture was the functional block of air-conditioned buildings six to ten storeys high,

---

[15]For details on the life and feeling of public housing residents, see Leung (1999), Blyth and Wotherspoon (1996), Liu (2010).

(a)   (b)

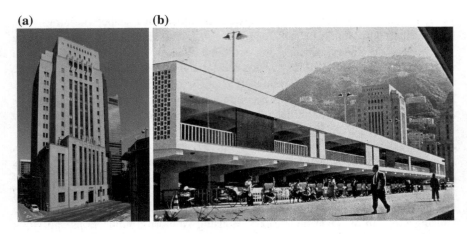

Fig. 1.6 Trendy buildings in the 1950s. **a** Bank of China headquarters, designed by Palmer & Turner, 1952. Picture shot in 2016. **b** Carpark in front of Star Ferry pier, concrete structure displayed its role. The background is HSBC building, 1957. Courtesy of Mr. Chung W.N.

making the maximum use of the site available. In 1957, the average building height was seven storeys. In the city, the older office blocks were being systematically demolished to make room for loftier buildings that would accommodate many more people on the same amount of ground space. In the suburbs and on the peak, apartment blocks were rising where villas had once stood, and former lawns and gardens were being turned into sites for garages and car parks (Fig. 1.6).

Manufacturing led to additional land demand. The new capital and labor influenced an industrial revolution in the colony. However, as a major factor of productivity, land was in short supply. The first wave of industrial revolution took place in Kowloon, with many factories and especially textile plants emerging in Mongkok and Ma Tau Wai. These areas developed in the direction of Tsuen Wan, which soon became an industrial town creating textile, enamel, rubber shoe and plastic products. In view of this trend, the government established the Kwun Tong industrial district in 1955.

The industrial development increased the employment rate. More workers and white-collar employees demanded low-cost housing. The non-profit Hong Kong Housing Society obtained land at one-third the market price and government welfare funding covered the site formation costs. Moreover, the government provided low-interest loans for building.

To help its employees, the government launched a project that encouraged local civil servants from the pensionable establishment to form co-operative housing societies to which land would be offered at one third the upset price and loans could be made on easy terms. 238 such societies were organized, which built over 5,000

Fig. 1.7 Civil Servants'
co-op housing built in the
1950s

living units for civil servants.[16] The scheme evoked a brisk response and construction on the first block of civil servants' flats began at Belcher Gardens in 1954.
One of these buildings is located on Po On Road in Cheung Sha Wan. The building
is five storeys high and has no lift. Each of its unit floor areas is 1,200 ft^2 in size.
With no extra decoration, the building is pragmatic and comfortable for living.
After more than 50 years, it still serves as housing for retired civil servants. In the
1950s and 1960s, 15 % of public housing was left for low-grade government
workers. In addition to housing its employees, the government encouraged enterprises to solve living problems for their staff. Private companies and factories, such
as Hong Kong Bank, the Jockey Club, universities, tram and bus companies and
power plants, built staff quarters on their premises. Textile companies constructed
dormitories for their employees next to their factories. In 1957, public and private
sector investment in housing reached $100 million to keep up with the population
increase (Fig. 1.7).

After the war, many government departments suffered from a shortage or lack of
office space. The 1950s saw the large-scale construction of government buildings.
The Colonial Secretariat building was built in 1847 and expanded through three
phases to house many government departments. All of the buildings adopted a
modernist aesthetic and were completed in 1956–1959. This area came to be known
as "Government Hill" on Lower Albert Road. Staff quarters consisting of concrete
buildings six to seven storeys high were built in Leighton Hill, Queen's Garden and
King's Park. The plans of these buildings followed the same basic pattern,
achieving the economy of mass-production. In 1951, married police quarters (for
junior staff) were built on Hollywood Road. The building was seven storeys high,

---

[16]The housing blocks built in the 1950s are usually four to five stories. Voice of rebuilding taller
blocks was high in the 21st century. For the co-op houses of civil servants, the owners should pay
back the full land premium and the new developers should pay additional land premium. This will
involve billions of dollars, which impedes the redevelopment. See *Tai Kung Pao*, January 3, 2014.

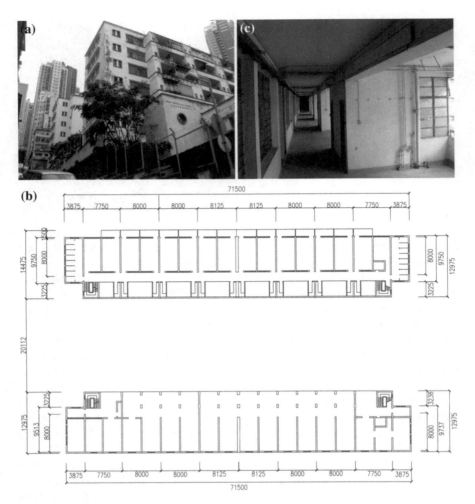

Fig. 1.8 Married police quarters, 1955. **a** Seen from street. **b** Plan. **c** The *left hand side* is living units, the *right hand side* is open kitchen

with one side comprising the living units and the other side comprising the kitchen. The design made use of a long corridor as a social function.[17] A similar experiment was undertaken in the U.K. and soon brought to Hong Kong. The government architects were mostly from the U.K. and had absorbed the prevailing modernist trends in Europe (Fig. 1.8).

---

[17]Private toilets were installed in units in the 1970s. In 2000, the building was vacant. In 2014, it was remodeled into a community creative place.

1.5   Conclusion: Resettling for Normal Life

Defeating the Japanese invaders, the Hong Kong government faced tremendous challenges in tackling and housing the pouring refugees. Abercrombie's report gave the territory a rational blueprint for the years ahead, while the Hong Kong government had to settle refugees and clear squatter shanty towns as its first priority. The helping hands from government, charitable organizations and some employers tirelessly alleviate the plight of laboring people. Technically, these resettlement houses might be rough, simple and did not reach the civilized threshold, they were practical, efficient, effective and machine-like. The resettlement housing alleviated the plight of refugees in time. When laboring people had little worry about their housing, they could devote whole-heatedly to the work and industry. The large scale sheltering gave the emerging industry a timely and powerful support. Both government departments and non-profit making organizations contributed to this positive process. "Hong Kong began as a harbor city and has continued to be built that way. After the war, it was intended to become a safe refuge for ships and people alike."[18]

When I was in Hong Kong in 1989, I lived in the University Hall of Pokfulam, overlooking the ocean to the west. A listed heritage building, the U-Hall was known as Douglas Castle in 1861. Entering the lane to approach 144 Pokfulam Road, you feel that the noisy world is shielded out. The heavy forest on both sides whispers as a delicately decorated white castle appears through the leaves. Opposite the road is Bethanie, built in 1870, a former church and sanitarium for French missionaries. In the late 1980s, Bethanie was the property of Hong Kong University, serving as the U-Hall boys dormitory and office for Hong Kong University Press. This mid-level area was typically devoted to European residences in the forms of early colonial plantations. European and local Chinese residents were separated into two worlds. Walking south along Pokfulam Road, one must pass the shabby squatter community known as Pokfulam Village before reaching the elegant, newly built living area known as Chi Fu Garden, and their substantial differences and proximity create a strong visual contrast. Shanty homes were erected at random in this area, where the road zigzags like intestines. You could purchase vegetables for two dollars in the narrow and dark streets. Pokfulam Village was one of many postwar squatter areas. The government vowed to eradicate all such slums before 1995, but as of 2015, Pokfulam Village remains.

Down from the main Hong Kong University campus, the end of Pokfulam Road leads to Sai Wan and Kennedy Town, where large amounts of Chinese people have settled on the two sides of the hilly streets since the end of the 19th century. Shophouses have been replaced by crowded pencil towers, and the roots of banyan trees firmly hold onto the meager amounts of soil in the gaps between stones in retaining walls. In 1989, Kowloon Walled City was full of residents and gangsters. I dared not enter and instead only looked at the dark buildings mushrooming across the street.

---

[18]*Hong Kong Annual Report 1957*, p. 14.

The Walled City represents "architecture without an architect"; it grew up according to local needs without government control. Strolling through Sai Wan, Tai Kok Tsui and other old derelict districts, it becomes apparent that Kowloon Walled City is everywhere. Family-based workshops can be seen in these streets, where they work on mechanical parts, car garages or ironmongery, industries that were prosperous in the 1950s and fed many families. In front of the workshops, ongoing welding and sawing projects invade the sidewalks, leaving pedestrians to find their way in the vehicular lanes. Although Hong Kong is a global city, the shabby traces of its identity before and immediately after the war are still embarrassingly apparent in certain areas, in contrast to its fabulous rival Singapore.

References

Abercrombie, P. (1948). *Hong Kong preliminary planning report.* Hong Kong Government.

Amati, M., & Freestone, R. (2009). "Saint Patrick"—Sir Patrick Abercrombie's Australian tour 1948. *Town Planning Review, 80*(6), 597–626.

Blyth, S., & Wotherspoon, I. (1996). *Hong Kong remembers.* Hong Kong, New York: Oxford University Press.

Bristow, R. (1984). *Land use planning in Hong Kong: History, policies and procedures.* Hong Kong: Oxford University Press.

Chen, X., & Guo, Z. K. (Ed.). (1997). *Hong Kong record, Ancient to 1959* (Vol. 1). Hong Kong: Chung Hwa Book Co. 陈昕、郭志坤主编 (1997). 香港全纪录 卷一 远古-1959. 香港: 中华书局.

Dehaene, M. (2004). Urban lessons for the modern planner—Patrick Abercrombie and the study of urban development. *Town Planning Review, 75*(1), 1–30.

Graye, H. (1951). Looking back December 1941-1951. *The Hong Kong and Far East Builder,* June Issue, 12–13.

Ho, P. Y. (2010). *The history of the construction industry 1840–2010.* Hong Kong: Commercial Press. 何佩盈 (2010). 筑景思城 – 香港建造业发展史 1840–2010. 香港:商务印书馆.

Home, R. K. (1997). *Of planting and planning: The making of British colonial cities.* London: Routledge.

Hong Kong Government. (1947). *Hong Kong annual report 1946.* Hong Kong Government Printer.

Hong Kong Government. (1949). *Hong Kong annual report 1948.* Hong Kong Government Printer.

Hong Kong Government. (1958). *Hong Kong annual report 1957.* Hong Kong Government Publication Bureau.

Lai, L. W. C. (1999). Reflections on the Abercrombie report 1948: A strategic plan for colonial Hong Kong. *Town Planning Review, 70*(1), 61–87.

Leung, M. Y. (1999). *From shelter to home—45 years of public housing development in Hong Kong.* Hong Kong: Housing Authority.

Liu, Z. P. (2010). *We all grow up in So Uk—A collective memory of public housing life in Hong Kong.* Hong Kong: Chung Hwa Book Co. 刘智鹏 (2010). 我们都在苏屋邨长大 – 香港人公屋生活的集体回忆. 香港:中华书局.

Smart, A. (2006). *The Shek Kip Mei Myth: Squatters, fires and colonial rule in Hong Kong* (p. 2006). Hong Kong: Hong Kong University Press.

Tu, E. H. E. (2003). *Colonial Hong Kong in the eyes of Elsie Tu.* Hong Kong: Hong Kong University Press.

Will, B. F. (1978). Housing design and construction methods. In L. S. K. Wong (Ed.), *Housing in Hong Kong—A multi-disciplinary study* (pp. 91–127). Hong Kong: Heinemann Education Books (Asia) Ltd.

Xue, C. Q. L., Zou, H., Li, B., & Hui, K. C. (2012). The shaping of early Hong Kong: Transplantation and adaptation by the British professions, 1841–1941. *Planning Perspective, 27*(4), 549–568.

Chapter 2
Modernism Coming to Town—Government Low-Cost Housing and Public Buildings

The word "modern", according to the Oxford Dictionary of English, means primarily "relating to the present or recent times as opposed to the remote past, characterized by or using the most up-to-date techniques, ideas, or equipment… denoting a current or recent style or trend in art, architecture, or other cultural activity marked by a significant departure from traditional styles and values."[1] In *Architecture and Modernity*, Hilde Heynen pointed out that "modernity is what gives the present the specific quality that makes it different from the past and points the way towards the future. Modernity is also described as being a break with tradition, and as typifying everything that rejects the inheritance of the past (Heynen 1999, p. 9)." She further discerned the modernity and modernism. "Modernity, then, constitutes the element that mediates between a process of socioeconomic development known as modernization and subjective responses to it in the form of modernist discourses and movements. In other words, modernity is a phenomenon with at least two different aspects: an objective aspect that is linked to socioeconomic processes, and a subjective one that is connected with personal experiences, artistic activities, or theoretical reflections… Architecture operates in both realms: it is unquestionably a cultural activity, but it is one that can be realized only within the world of power and money (Heynen 1999, pp. 10–11)."

Reflected in architecture, "modernity" transits to "modern architecture." There are many description and definitions of "modern architecture". Duanfang Lu concisely summarized this social and architectural phenomenon, "Originating in interwar Europe, modernist architecture—as a way of building, a knowledge product, a style of life consumer item, and above all—a symbol of modernity, has traversed national boundaries throughout the world (Lu 2011, p. 1)." Lu further observed that although modernist architecture was extensively adopted in the third world, history books only focus on its development in the West (Lu 2011). During Hong Kong's course of post-war reconstruction, economic condition was weak and

---

[1]Oxford Dictionaries Language Matters, http://www.oxforddictionaries.com/definition/english/modern. Accessed 26 May 2015.

© Springer Science+Business Media Singapore 2016
C.Q.L. Xue, *Hong Kong Architecture 1945–2015*,
DOI 10.1007/978-981-10-1004-0_2

construction workload was massive. Therefore, principles of modernist architecture were consciously or unconsciously adopted in a natural way. This chapter examines government subsidized low-cost housing and public building, and see how the modernist design method was applied to these building types.

2.1 Welfare Housing and Modernist Architectural Ideal

Hong Kong returned to the British rule after the war in 1945, while the two opposite forces in China, Chiang and Mao, did not claim the territories.[2] The reconstruction of Hong Kong was parallel with that of the UK and other colonies. According to the analysis of historian David Faure, "there were many indications that even in the 1950s, the watchful eye of London over Hong Kong was being relaxed". After the Suez Crisis of 1956 the taste of native British people for colonies was over. The number of people the Colonial Secretary was responsible decreased sharply in the 1960s, and the Colonial Office itself was merged into the Foreign Office. The British troops were being withdrawn from the Middle and Far East. "The devaluation of the pound sterling in 1967, left no illusion about Britain being able to serve the colonies as their governments' banker. Hong Kong continued to draw selected inspiration from Britain, but the late 1960s was the time when Hong Kong came into its own (Fauer 2003, pp. 73–74)."

After the initial stage of post-war construction, the light- and manufacturing industry, mainly family-based and "cottage type" workshop, led the economy in Hong Kong. The products of shoes, watch, toys and textile were sold to American and European countries. The industrial towns Kwun Tong and Tsuen Wan emerged with preliminary shape to accommodate factories and warehouses. Because of the endless "class struggles" and socialist movements in the Chinese mainland, people escaped the country and penetrated the Hong Kong borders intermittently. In 1962, a new wave of illegal immigrants poured to the territories, partly because of the natural and artificial disasters in the Chinese mainland.[3] In 1961, the median age of three million Hong Kong population was 19 years old.[4] A young and energetic society provided ample labor for industry and its assembly line.

To catch up the opportunity of industrial wave, help the industrialists and settle the citizens, the Hong Kong government opted to build large scale public housing

---

[2]After WWII, both political and military forces Chiang and Mao wanted to collaborate with the US, and hence its alliance UK. When the two sides of Taiwan Strait were in hostile state, Hong Kong acted a neutral place. See Spence (1990).

[3]About the natural and artificial disasters in China mainly caused by Communist Party's wrong policy from 1958 onward, see Dikotter (2010).

[4]The median age of 1961 was from Fauer (2003). Compared with 2012, 50 years later, the median age was 43, people over 65 years old accounted for 13 % of all population. From Hong Kong Government, *Economic Report* (2013).

for the low-income workers. Resettlement housing mentioned in Chap. 1 was the first step. Large scale public housing was being planned since 1956. As analyzed by Castells et al. "the mechanism concerning the relationship between the state, economic development, and public policy (exemplified by public housing) may indicate a positive interaction between economic development and public housing, and more broadly, between the role of the state in housing, urban amenities and social services (what we called collective consumption) (Castells et al. 1991, p. 2)."

Further, Castell et al. found that "although there are very important elements of intervention in the production and accumulation processes, particularly in the 1980s, the main form of intervention takes place in the realm of collective consumption, with the center of such intervention being located in the public housing program. Government supported housing, health, education, transportation, and subsidies of foodstuffs and basic daily consumption items, have been crucial elements in ensuring a proper production and reproduction of labor, in making labor cheaper without lowering its quality, in providing a safety net that has enabled an entrepreneurial population to take risks by investing and creating businesses, and in providing the basis for social stability since the early 1970s, that has made possible steady growth and economic improvement in an otherwise highly volatile situation (Castells et al. 1991, p. 4)." This comment echoed Le Corbusier's warning suggestion in the 1920s, "housing or revolution?"[5]

From 1964 to 1970, the public sector on housing completed and delivered more than 25,000 housing units each year, which was 60 % more than the private sector during the same period.[6] In the 1964–65 fiscal year only, the total number of completed housing units from both public and private sectors reached 61,600 when population in the territories was 3,507,900. For every 1,000 people, there were 17 units newly completed.[7] This number is much higher than the annual housing production of Hong Kong in the 21st century.[8]

To build housing in such large scale on small island and peninsula lands, modernist architectural ideas and method found their application. The modernist architecture took place in European countries mainly between WWI and WWII, that is the 1920s and 30s. The pioneers advocated social responsibility, form following function, rationality, technology expression, building economy, no extra-decoration and machine aesthetics. After WWII, the modernist ideals were partly revised and

---

[5]"Housing or revolution" was a proposal for the government in the 1920s, see Corbusier (1925).

[6]The housing units number of the 1960s is from Hong Kong Government, *Report of Housing Board* (1972).

[7]Source same as above. The figures in the 1960s are about two times higher than the housing units completed in the years of 21st century. Also see Hong Kong Government, *Hong Kong Annual Report*, 2001–2014.

[8]In the 21st century, both private and public housing production are lower than 20,000 units a year, because of the economic downturn and difficulties of finding suitable land. See *Hong Kong Annual Report*, 2001–2014.

adopted all over the world, and for good and bad, developed to "internationalism" in somewhere.[9]

From Gropius' workers' houses in Dessau in 1925, Weissenhof settlement in Stuttgart in 1927 to Unité d'Habitation Marseille designed by Le Corbusier in 1947, mass housing was always an experimental field for modernist architects, including in European and American towns. The Netherlands, Austria, Britain, France, Denmark, Sweden, East Germany and the Soviet Union each experienced large-scale social housing construction. Although these countries have different policies, percentage of rental (or ownership) and outcomes in social housing, their huge dimensions, immense scales and societal atmosphere contrasted sharply with those of traditional towns.[10] Le Corbusier's ideas of "city of tomorrow", "modular" and "L' Unité" had an opportunity to experiment in such large scale construction of workers' housing. In the 1950s, the Chinese government also built workers' residential areas in Beijing, Shanghai and other provincial cities to achieve its lofty communist ideals. The low-standard apartment buildings were largely funded by socialist companies and supplied to their employees.[11]

Public housing in Hong Kong was firstly designed as temporary resettlement shelter, but soon elaborated in a more appropriate and beautiful form, as evidenced by the first group of low-middle class housing estates. The building examples in this chapter are unfolded in this background.

2.2 Mass Production of Public Housing

In 1954, the government established Resettlement Department and building section in Urban Council, whose aim was to resettle the squatters, release the land for more intensive construction and to provide housing at a minimum standard of 35 ft^2 (3.2 m^2) per person and with rentals that could be afforded by families of the monthly income at HK\$ 300–900 (US\$60–180).[12] Finance was provided from the Colony's Development Loan Fund with low interest rates and sites were allocated at one third the assessed market value of the land.

The first low-cost estate project was North Point Estate completed in 1957, designed by Eric Cumine, FRIBA (1905–2002). Cumine had designed luxury apartment buildings in Shanghai in the 1920s and in Hong Kong in the 1950s and

---

[9]For the definition of architectural modernism, I follow the books of Frampton, Curtis and other classical books. For example Frampton (1992), Curtis (1987).

[10]For the social housing in European countries, see Scanlon et al. (2014). The book mainly discusses the policies enacted by the various countries. For the design of European housing, see Dijk (1999) and Scoffham (1984).

[11]Housing in China is mainly a social and policy problem instead of design. For the design part, see Lu et al. (2001) and Xue (2006, Chap. 6).

[12]In the 1950s, a university graduate of engineering could earn around HK\$400 a month, see Wang (2010).

made his name known in designing for upper class (see Chap. 3). His design for the low-income residents demonstrated same high quality. The North Point Estate is located on a site of 2.6 ha, three street blocks facing the harbor, with a waterfront length of around 400 m. The designer divided the building to three blocks, with three big courtyards facing the harbor. In the two side courtyards, point buildings are inserted to increase the land efficiency. The central court serves as bus terminals and front plaza for cross-harbor ferry pier. The buildings occupy 26 % of the site area, with a plot ratio of 3.5. The gross density is around 4,800 people per ha. The indent of building mass not only creates ample public space for families and children, but break through the feeling of monotony caused by too long elevation (Fig. 2.1).

Housing buildings are 11-storey high. Every two families form a group, such groups are connected in a central corridor like a long spine. The units on two sides of corridor are staggered. Light and cross-ventilation are attracted through the side windows of corridor, so that people would not feel boring in the long corridor. Every unit has self-contained kitchen, toilet, hall, two bedrooms and balcony. The headroom is 8 ft 1 in. (2.4 m), lower than the private housing. The building was constructed with simple reinforced concrete frame, brick infill walls, concrete floor, steel windows, hardboard doors and brick partitions. The yellow-painted balcony slabs cantilever out and lively decorated the white external wall. North Point Estate contained 1,955 living units and housed over 10,000 residents. The construction of North Point Estate cost $33 million, its standard is two to three times more expensive than the later construction.[13] The high cost was reviewed and criticized within the Housing Authority. However, Cumine's design let people see in the 1950s, that low-income housing buildings could be designed in such a decent, comfortable and beautiful way—which could parallel with the private apartment. However, this very first work of Housing Authority was completely demolished 45 years later in 2003. The land was sold to private developer, and a group of luxury high-rise apartments with harbor view are soaring up.

North Point Estate was in the Hong Kong Island, the area was considered as "satellite town" of Victoria City in the 1950s. After the success of North Point Estate, Eric Cumine was further commissioned by the Housing Authority to design So Uk Estate in the "New" Kowloon area in the late 1950s. So Uk, a triangle site is located on the foot of mountain, the edge of Kowloon. Cumine planned the site into two parts: lower and mountain. In the lower part, long slab buildings line the periphery and form courtyards, while in the mountain part pointed trident towers stand on the hilltop. The plot, which is around 7.8 ha in size, comprises 5,152 living units and 33,345 people, about the population of Salisbury, England at the time (Will 1978, p. 115). It also includes open and covered public spaces, a community hall, two primary schools of 24 classes, post-office, clinic, kerosene service store and more than 30 shops. The standard of units was by and large the same, however the housing blocks of 8-12-16 stories high present different shape and form. They were designed by various famous architects at the time, Wai Szeto, Luke Him Sau,

---

[13]Construction data from *Hong Kong Annual Report 1957*, Hong Kong Government.

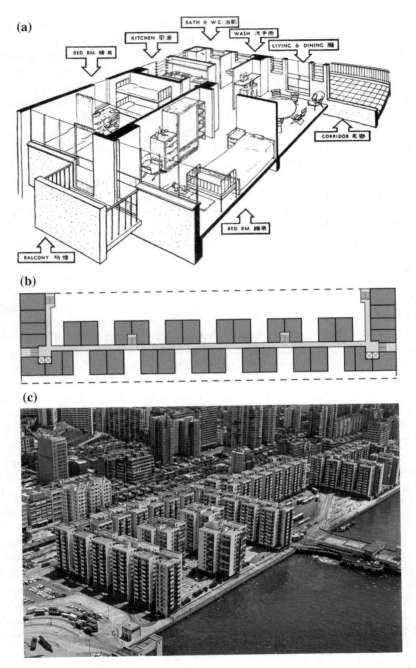

Fig. 2.1 North Point Estate—the first project of Housing Authority, 1957. **a** Interior of unit.
b Plan. **c** The building blocks are arranged around three courts facing the harbor. (**a**) and (**c**) from
HK Government archive. (**b**) Drawn by Xiao Yingbo

Fig. 2.2 So Uk Estate in Kowloon, 1962 **a** Master plan. **b** Housing blocks in the lower part. **c** Housing blocks in the mountain part

Chau & Lee and Leigh & Orange (also see Chap. 3). The participation of private architects made the design diversified (Fig. 2.2).

So Uk was once the largest housing projects in the Far East. Residents moved into So Uk in 1962. After years struggling in the squatter areas and cramp environment, the low-income residents felt being peacefully and happily sheltered. Many children grew up in So Uk and became lawyer, teacher, politician and medical doctor later (Lau 2010). Such an estate, which embodied blood and sweat of so many designers, workers and collective memory, no longer exists today. In the 21st century, Housing Authority reviewed estates of over 40 years and gradually demolished them to yield land for higher and denser construction.

Apart from Cumine, the other firms in frontier participated in the public housing design, for example, Palmer & Turner (P & T). Before the war, P & T was active both in Shanghai and Hong Kong and designed the most notable building—Hong Kong and Shanghai Banking Corporation headquarters in Central in 1936. P & T's design Choi Hung Estate, four hectares in size, was completed in 1964. Eight blocks of slab building of 21 storeys high extend horizontally and perpendicularly. Additional seven-storey blocks thread through the tall buildings. The ground floors of the low-rise buildings offer daily shops for residents. Two primary and secondary schools are located in the center. These residential blocks consist of 7,448 units. The floor areas range from 21.4 to 69.2 m and house 19,700 people. This kind of clear—edge slab building had never appeared in the portfolio of P & T. Bank of China designed by the company was completed in 1951, it is basically a recycled version of

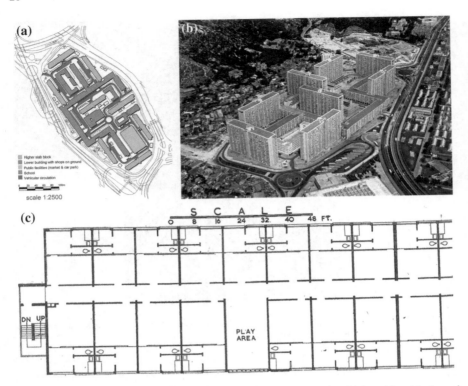

Fig. 2.3 Choi Hung Estate, 1964 **a** Master plan. **b** The estate comprises high and low blocks and schools. **c** Drawing adapted by Chan Chiu Kwan. (**b**) from HK Government archive

its Shanghai predecessor. Prince Building in Central was completed in 1965. Both buildings followed the line of commercial eclecticism. Serving the low-income residents, P & T resolutely explored new method of design. The layout of Choi Hung with many long slab building reminds people of the similar large scale housing developments in Europe, especially in Amsterdam and Rotterdam in the 1950s. In Europe, such scale housing complex is usually four to five stories; however in Hong Kong, it is 20 stories. Providing housing for mass residents, the Hong Kong government adopted a more resolute way (Fig. 2.3).[14]

Choi Hung Estate was a milestone of the first decade of Housing Authority. After 10 years, the in-house architects started to design by themselves. One of the first batch projects designed by Housing Authority is Wah Fu Estate located in the southwest corner of Hong Kong Island. Completed between 1967 and 1969, Wah Fu Estate is a slab building with a broken line and L-shaped residential blocks arranged along its contour lines. High-rise buildings are located in the back. This

---

[14]For the housing design in the Netherlands, see Dijk (1999), especially cases from pp. 125 to 128 and the chapter on post war reconstruction.

Fig. 2.4 Wah Fu Estate, 1969–1972. **a** Master plan. **b** Pedestrians and daily activities are in the podium level. **c** Shops are close to the bus stations. **d** The estate is in the corner of Hong Kong Island. From HK Government archive. Drawing by Zang Peng

design allows more units to face the sea. The plot of 10 ha accommodates 4,800 units, which are home to 16,000 people. A library and a market are located in the center. The southwest side of the estate is a waterfront park with a promenade more than 600 m in length. Residents often stroll and exercise in the park. As it was far away from the city area, it was planned like a new town, with more public facilities. People were reluctant to move in because of its remote location (Fig. 2.4).

In 1973, the government restructured and established Housing Authority to direct the public housing construction. The prominent project of the new Housing Authority was Oi Man Estate, which was built on the highland of Ho Man Tin, Kowloon in 1973–1975. Slab buildings are located in the center and double-wing twin towers are located at the periphery. The center is also home to a shopping arcade, "mushroom" hawk stalls and a kindergarten. The 10-ha hilly plot accommodates 6,300 units and houses 19,600 people.[15] "Oi Man", in Chinese, means "loving the people". The estate was conceived and erected under the new policy of Governor MacLehose in the early 1970s, which was regarded as a thriving and healthy period in Hong Kong's modern history. Her Majesty Queen Elizabeth II visited the estate when it was completed in 1975. Chinese President-designate Xi Jinping visited in 2009, as it was considered a representative grass-roots residential estate (Fig. 2.5).

---

[15]The public housing figures come from the website of the Hong Kong Housing Authority, http://www.housingauthority.gov.hk/tc/index.html, Accessed on 21 April 2014. The plot size of the public housing estate is read from Google maps.

Fig. 2.5 Oi Man Estate, Ho Man Tin, 1975 **a** Main road linking the estate to the city. **b** Shops in the center. **c** Master plan. **d** Scene in home. From HK Government archive

Table 2.1 Summary of early prominent public housing projects

	North point Estate	So Uk Estate	Choi Hung	Wah Fu Estate	Oi Man Chuen
Completion year	1957	1962	1963	1972	1975
Designer	Eric Cumine & Partners	Planned by Cumine and designed by various architects	Palmer & Turner	Housing authority	Housing authority
Site area (ha)	6	7.8	11	10	10
Living units	1,955	5,152	7,488	4,800	6,300
Habitants	Over 10,000	33,345	19,700	12,800	19,600
Density (units/ha)	325	660	680	480	630

Living units range from 19 to 55 m^2

A summary of the five early Housing Authority projects is listed in Table 2.1 for an easy comparison. From the 1960s, the density was controlled between 480 and 680 units per ha, triple the density Abercrombie planned in 1948. Developing upward and rational planning made this possible.

2.3 Living Machine with Human Touch

According to a statistics in the early 1970s, 33 % people living in the resettlement housing, government low-cost housing and Housing Authority/Housing Society housing were full-time employed, which was higher than the Hong Kong average of 30.8 %, although the household income was lower than the groups in the private housing.[16] It is obvious that government low-cost housing positively encouraged residents' active life and supported the burgeoning industry.

The provision of public housing saved money for the lower class. After more than 10 years, some public housing residents accumulated considerable wealth. In 1978, the government put forward its "home ownership" plan. Lower-middle-class residents were able to buy residential units, which were of a higher standard and bigger size than those of public housing and at an affordable price. These "ownership" buildings were located near the public housing, allowing residents to enhance their living standards and remain in the communities they considered familiar. When these "rich" residents moved up, the vacant public housing units were allocated to needy people in the pipeline. Home ownership buildings presented a new form of design (Fig. 2.6).[17]

In the 1980s, home ownership building plans were designed in trident or cruciform shapes and had six to eight units per floor. In the 1990s, the government put forward "harmony" type public housing, a cross plan involving four wings with four units in each wing. Sixteen units shared the central core, which had six lifts. The typical floors were stacked up higher than 30 storeys. A "concord" type was designed for the home ownership buildings. It was also a cross plan, with eight units per floor. The floor areas of the units ranged from 500 to 900 ft^2 in size. The central core could support more than eight units. The wings and gaps in the cross plan allowed for more ventilation and daylight for the kitchens and toilets. Therefore, they provided better conditions than the earlier public housing.

---

[16]The statistic data is from *Hong Kong population and housing census, 1971 main report*, Hong Kong Government, 1971; Luke S.K. Wong's article analyzed the phenomenon, see chap. 6. Socio-economic characteristics of public housing provision, in Wong (1978).

[17]The allocation of public housing was made by the Housing Authority according to the accumulated points of applicants. The basic requirements are the applicants' income and asset. The threshold standard is adjusted according to the income and inflation index every year. In 2015, the median level monthly income of Hong Kong is $18,000 (US$2322). The ceiling of income and asset for applying public housing is as follows: for 1 person family, income below $10,100 a month, asset below $236,000; 2 people family, $16,140, asset $320,000; 3 people family, $21,050, asset $417,000; 4 people family, $21,050, asset $487,000; 5 people family, $29,050, asset $541,000; 6 people family, $32,540, asset $585,000; 7 people family, $36,130, asset $ 626,000; 8 people family, $ 38,580, asset $ 656,000; 9 people family, $43,330, asset $ 724,000; 10 people and above family, $45,450, asset $780,000. To apply for government subsidized homeownership house, the family's monthly income should be below $46,000. In 2013, more than 170,000 people were in the pipeline to wait for unit of public housing. For the income, see *Statistic Report 2014*, Hong Kong Government. For the qualification of public housing, see *Tai Kung Pao*, 27 February 2015.

(a)   (b)

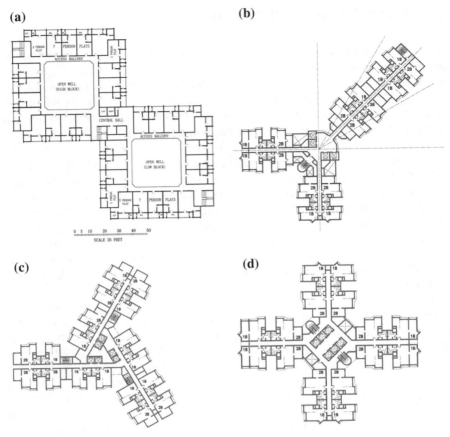

(c)   (d)

Fig. 2.6 Block plans used during the 1970s through 1990s. Drawn by Zang Peng. **a** In the double court plan, the lift is in the connection part. It is efficient, but the court and open corridors bring annoyance for residents. **b** One of the plans in Harmony Type. **c** Harmony type: trident plan. **d** Harmony type: cruciform

The standard of home ownership house was enacted by government, but mainly developed by Housing Society, a not-profit making organization run from 1948 (see Chap. 1). Because the standard of home ownership housing is higher than the public rental housing, the design has more room to display and this produces many excellent works.

In 1980, Palmer & Turner designed Sui Wo Court in Shatin, a Housing Society project. Three groups of towers in high and low land surround a shopping arcade. The roof of shopping arcade is car parking. Under the roof is wet market. Each group consists of three residential towers. Inside the tower, the designer set the lift stopping in every three floors. In this way, more common space is created. The method of three floors sharing a lift was seen in I.M. Pei's design of student dormitory at University of Hawaii at Manoa in 1960. This design creates compact plan and efficiency of using the lift. Similar design was adopted again in the Clague Garden Estate in Tsuen Wan in 1988. Lift stops on floors 3, 6, 9 and so on to make the plan more compact. "Sky gardens" were designed for placement on floors 3, 12, 21, 30 and 39. All of the housing units in Clague Garden Estate were sold to residents at affordable prices. Both projects were designed by James Kinoshita the director of Palmer & Turner, who was keen to learn from the other Modernist masters at the time. Public and subsidized housing design gave an opportunity for architects to realize their modernist dream. Although sharing lift by several floors represents an innovation in design, the building is not necessarily convenient for the disabled. Such a method was never used when the building regulations were amended for barrier-free purpose (Fig. 2.7).

The low-cost Prosperous Garden Estate is a typical Housing Society project. Its four buildings comprise 896 units that range from 500 to 800 ft^2 in size. The units were sold to "sandwich class" (lower-middle class) buyers, who typically dwelled in units that size. Another building comprising 668 units ranging from 100 to 500 ft^2 in size was rented according to standards similar to the government's public housing regulations. Prosperous Garden is located on the old streets of Yau Ma Tei, where the land was collected from the owners piece by piece. Ng Chun Man Architect and Associates conducted the planning and design. The buildings were completed in 1995. The garden pavement extends from inside to outside. The garden faces a shopping arcade that houses the elderly habitation center of the Housing Society. The historic Yau Ma Tei police station is also located nearby. Residents also have access to the Broadway Film Center, a theater that screens experimental films and cooperates well with the estate. When people walk from the old district to this area, they experience a nice pedestrian environment and a lively atmosphere. Prosperous Garden sets an example for the urban renewal of Yau Ma Tei (Fig. 2.8).[18]

In the 21st century, the government has defined buildings more than 30 years old as "old buildings." Much of the old public housing of the 1950s–1970s has been demolished to make way for taller buildings and denser planning that offers better amenities and environments. The Lower and Upper Ngau Tau Kok Estates are examples of this wave. The Ngau Tau Kok estate was built in 1969 to accommodate workers in the Kwun Tong industrial area. The plan to rebuild was initiated in the 1990s and began in 1998. It was conceived as "rebuilding and resettling locally." Phase I of three buildings was completed in 2002 and affected residents were invited to move in. All nine of the 40-storey towers in the Upper Ngau Tau Kok Estate were completed in 2009. The residents of the Lower Estate moved in and the vacant Lower Ngau Tau Kok Estate was demolished. The construction of the Lower Estate was completed in 2016 to house more residents (Fig. 2.9).

The designers and consultants studied the wind direction and microclimate of the estates during the planning stage. The building blocks are arranged so that

---

[18]The description of the Housing Society was found on the website of the Hong Kong Housing Society, http://www.hkhs.com/chi/about/index.asp. Accessed on 10 January 2015.

Fig. 2.7 Housing Society's projects designed by Palmer & Turner. **a, b** Sui Wo Court, 1980. Under the car park is the wet market and shopping arcade. **c** Clague Garden Estate, 1988. Courtesy of Hong Kong Housing Society

ventilation can go through the site and permeate the gardens and homes. From the mass transit railway (MTR) station in Kowloon Bay, residents walk over a pedestrian bridge to the estate. Pedestrians and vehicles are kept completely

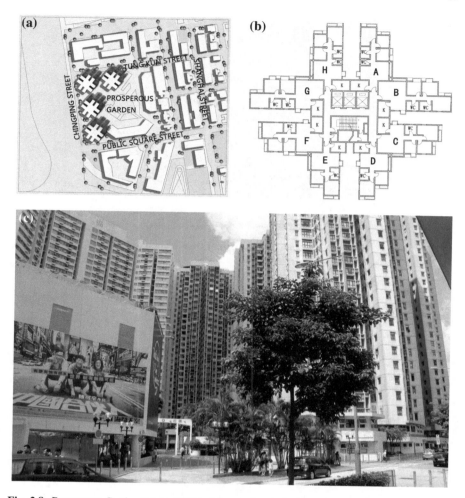

Fig. 2.8 Prosperous Garden Estate, 1995. **a** Master plan. **b** Typical floor plan. **c** The estate mixes rental and home-ownership blocks. Drawn by Zang Peng

separate. People move around on the lawn and through the flowers and shrubs on the upper deck and vehicles run in the streets. The covered pedestrian path is 1,000 m long and crosses over several streets in addition to central and peripheral gardens. The path is enriched by various treatments such as a semi-circular entrance, *pai-lou* (Chinese styled gate), wide steps, escalators, ramps and tensile structures. Old furniture, iron decoration and shop brands occasionally appear as reminders of the estate's history. The space close to the residential buildings is rendered with a more delicate landscape and hard pavement. The degree of privacy increases from the street toward the homes. The Upper and Lower Ngau Tau Kok Estates are no doubt representative examples of public housing in the 21st century (Fig. 2.10).

Fig. 2.9 Ngau Tau Kok Estate, 1969—the first public housing project using prefabrication. The buildings were demolished in 2009 for higher density new development

Fig. 2.10 Upper Ngau Tau Kok Estate, 2012. **a** Housing blocks of 50 stories. **b** More delicate landscape design closing to the housing entrance. **c** Market in the estate

The preceding examples are all high-rise and high-density buildings. Although the living units are small (no bigger than 50 m^2 in floor area), the public spaces, whether open or covered, are amply suited for residents' activities and play. Wet markets, supermarkets and daily shops are located within a radius of 200 m. The public housing offers a picture of peaceful, busy and warm life. The government controls the building density through plot ratio and coverage. From the 1960s until now, public housing has created very high, if not the highest, record of living density in the world.

In the social housing built in the U.S. and U.K. during the 1950s, long corridors link many housing units. Over the years, these corridors have become hotspots for crime. In Hong Kong, the early public housing adopted long and L-shaped plans that partly blocked ventilation. When a cross-plan is used, more gaps, ventilation and daylight are generated between blocks. A cross-plan also shortens corridor length and better protects the safety of residents.

Public housing is built by the taxpayers' money and the investment has to be accountable. From the outset of public housing, the planning tended to be high density. The sample estates described in this chapter usually have a density of 400–600 living units a hectare. This scale of mass housing was never seen in the private sector in the 1950s and 60s. Building components are reduced to the simplest form and repeat in large amount so that the limited resources can serve more people. Extra decoration is almost none, except for some brick laid hollow wall in staircase, which is economical, ventilated and delightful. The public housing estates, with rows of slab blocks dotted with pointed blocks, present the machine aesthetics—repeat, rhythm, clustered buildings surrounded by garden. They are surprisingly similar with Le Corbusier's precedent designs.

Along this direction, public housing first adopted prefabricated components early in 1969 to save on construction costs and time. These prefabricated components have included external wall slabs, staircases and parts of floor slabs. The modular system and standard units encourage mass housing production and decrease the wet work in construction sites. In the late 1990s, prefabricated components accounted for 60 % of public housing production. Prefabrication factories can be found in Shenzhen, Dongguan and other Pearl River Delta towns. Prefabricated external walls cladded with tiles and installed with window panes (no glass) are shipped to the sites, ready for installation (Fig. 2.11).

The machine is a bit austere for human life. The planning of public housing in Hong Kong focuses on community infrastructure such as public transportation, hospitals and parks. Most public housing estates provide convenient access to buses, mini-buses, MTR and shuttle bus transport to MTR stations. Private companies run the buses and mini-buses in Hong Kong. The Housing Authority and Department of Transportation, MTRC and private bus operators coordinate the public transportation. Moreover, public housing estates surround many parks such as Chai Wan Park, Lok Fu Park, Kowloon Walled City Park, Ngau Chi Wan Park, Po Kong Village Road Park, Shek Kip Mei Park, Tin Shui Wai Park, Tsing Yi Northeast Park, North District Park and Central Kwai Chung Park. These parks provide nice leisure and amenity spaces for grassroots residents.

Public housing estates are usually close to traffic interchange hubs used by tens of thousands of residents. In the 21st century, the Housing Authority began setting up large-scale shopping malls in the estates. For example, there are decades-old public residential towers located near Yau Tong MTR station. The station podium connects to a five-storey shopping mall known as "Domain," the floors of which are

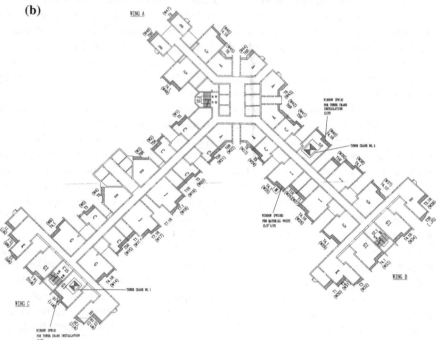

Fig. 2.11 Pre-fabrication of public housing. **a** Components are shipped to the site. **b** Prefabricated components are mainly used in the external wall. Courtesy of Housing Authority

connected to roof gardens of various levels, opposite streets and neighboring estates. In Choi Tak Estate of Kowloon Bay, a shopping mall was built on the mountain and served residents located on the mountain and plain. Some residents enter the shopping mall from the ground floor and others living on the higher levels enter from the fifth floor. The high and low levels cooperate seamlessly. From the

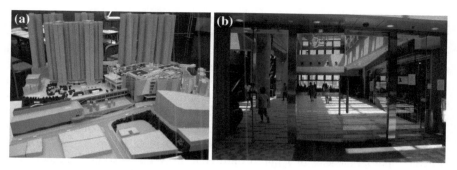

Fig. 2.12 Shopping mall in the public housing area, developed by Housing Authority. **a** Domain shopping mall is between the Yau Tong MTR station and public housing, 2012; **b** the atrium of shopping mall on the top of hill, Choi Tak, Kowloon, 2010

high level, shoppers can overlook Kowloon Bay and the harbor (Fig. 2.12). The public housing estates built in the 21st century enjoy the similar or even better natural and man-made environment than the private housing. In districts like Kowloon Bay and Tseng Kwan O, private and public housing estates share public space, shopping mall, community service and public transportation. This practice no doubt enhances the convenience and status of public housing, hence residents' sense of belonging.

Social housing practices demonstrated the determination of the government to improve the living conditions of grassroots residents. Since the early 20th century, the planning and building of social housing for the urban poor have been significant concerns for radical intellectuals and social activists. The construction of social housing after the war partly realized the dream of a social utopia. In terms of living conditions and standards, public housing in Hong Kong is far behind its Western counterparts. However, its modernist ideas and pragmatism echo practices in the U.K. and Europe and explore its own suitable path.

2.4   Public Building—Social Consciences

Public housing gives people home. Our homes embody our individual tastes and the public buildings in a city express our collective values. In a capitalist society, public buildings are essential social assets that balance private and civic interests while providing convenience and comfort to the entire community. Good or bad, the performance of public buildings affects most people rather than a handful of users/owners in the private sector. During the post-war construction in the UK and Europe, public buildings like performance and cultural centers greatly boosted citizens' morale and sense of belongings.

Dattner offers several suggestions for the goals of civil architecture. First, it must present a modest monumentality and not be excessive or insufficient in scale.

Second, it must have the noble aspiration to preserve and enhance public life. Third, it must be sustainable, exhibit an economy of means, do more with less and conserve material, human and natural resources. Public architecture must set a special example by being efficient, long lasting and energy conserving. Fourth, it must have contextuality, in that it should respect and express the natural topography. Fifth, it must offer inclusiveness and accessibility. A public building should include necessary functional parts to serve the people well, be convenient to access and offer a space in which all are included, valued and welcomed. Sixth, it must accept the contradictions raised by a multicultural society's multiple interpretations of civic structure appropriateness. Seventh, it must educate. Winston Churchill recognized the didactic dimension of architecture in his statement that "we shape our buildings, and then they shape us (Dattner 1995)." Although postulated in an American context, these criteria cover the basic tasks of a public building, including its social service functions and its roles as a collective symbol and a reflection of citizens' desires, expectations and dignities.

Bainiassad states that Hong Kong architecture is inherently public and that its "publicness" is an integral part of local culture. Public institution architecture has always occupied a central, subtle and decisive role in the quality and state of civility in a city. Ng attempts to explain the social reasons for the unique features of Hong Kong's public architecture. He explains that people living within this compact city need and aspire to a more acute use of public space. In a local context, common spaces and buildings naturally form an extension to city living.[19] This also significantly improves spatial efficiency in city planning and building design. Consequently, public buildings are becoming multi-use, multi-value and multi-level. Mixed-use environments offer enhanced spatial efficiency and flexibility, which optimizes their usability at different times of the day and year.

Until the pre-war period, Hong Kong was mainly developed to satisfy the interests of British merchants and the ruling class. In the 100 years spanning 1841–1941, the colony was busy coping with the problems of early settlement, an influx of refugees, hygiene in the dense city areas, exports and productivity, and internal and external pressures. The government had little attention, energy and budget to spend on public facilities.

It was also very difficult for early colonial officials to finance and report to London about large-scale public investments on the barren Hong Kong Island, as the initial colonial policies of Hong Kong were principally biased to encourage short-term profit garnered from Chinese trade. Construction of public architecture was thus scarce. Some notable typologies of public architecture were Catholic and Christian churches, Buddhist and Taoist temples and tycoons' clubhouses, which served a small group of people. The government did not invest in any of these buildings. Other government buildings such as government houses and magistrate

---

[19]Both Bainiassad and Ng's words are from Architectural Services Department, HKSARG, *Post 97 public architecture in Hong Kong'*, Hong Kong: Architectural Services Department, HKSARG (2006).

buildings predominantly followed colonial standards along with slight Victorian or Edwardian decoration. It was not until the 1970s when the economy was booming and society became stabilized after a period of social unrest and international warfare that the Hong Kong government had the financial ability to begin building the colony into a citizen-friendly city with an enormous investment in community building.

In 1967, a severe riot took place in Hong Kong and homemade bombs were thrown in the streets.[20] The newly arrived governor and his cabinet thought that a good supply of public housing and facilities would be the best way to soothe the social unrest. The administration adopted a people-oriented policy and started numerous massive civil infrastructure projects. Public architecture, including resettlement estates, city halls, libraries, sport complexes, hospitals and schools, eventually came to form the urban landscape of the Hong Kong territory. The local youths adopted healthy lifestyles in the midst of extremist anti-social behavior.

In 2014, the average gross domestic product per capita in Hong Kong is close to US$40,000 (World Bank 2015). Half of the population is still living in flats less than 50 m^2 in size.[21] Public facilities and space have become indispensable parts of people's lives. People go to city halls to see performances and participate in amateur arts activities. Children and the elderly go to the library to do homework and enjoy the air conditioning. The public spaces are frequently very busy.

The majority of public buildings in Hong Kong were designed and had their construction supervised by government architects from the former Public Works Department (PWD). Most of Hong Kong's architects and planners came from Britain and the Commonwealth nations during the early colonial years. During the 1950s, the staff members at the PWD were mainly young professionals and eager to display their talents in the territory. Modernism was widespread in Europe and America, and the designers of public buildings in Hong Kong generally adopted modernist principles. From an economic standpoint, the modernist attitude and method solved the functional problems and requirements of mass production. From an aesthetic standpoint, it conformed to the prevailing world trends in the 1950s–1970s.[22]

The works of these designers formed part of Hong Kong architectural history after the war, when big projects were seldom launched by private sector and eclectic method was mainly used in commercial buildings. In the late 1950s, government architects designed Elizabeth Hospital in Kowloon, which housed 1,300 beds.

---

[20]The riot in Hong Kong in May 1967 was triggered by a confrontation between the factory owners and workers. It was soon developed to a movement of "anti-British colonial rule" by the leftists in Hong Kong, influenced by the Cultural Revolution in the Chinese mainland (1966–1976). The riot lasted for seven months and included workers and schools' strikes, paralysis of public transportation and a toll of 52 lives. See Cheung (2009).

[21]These figures are from the *World Development Report*, Oxford University Press, New York, 2015 and *Hong Kong Yearbook*, HKSAR Government, 2014.

[22]In talking about modernist architecture, the authors follow the discussion and definition of classical writings like William Curtis and Kenneth Frampton. See Curtis (1987), Frampton (1992).

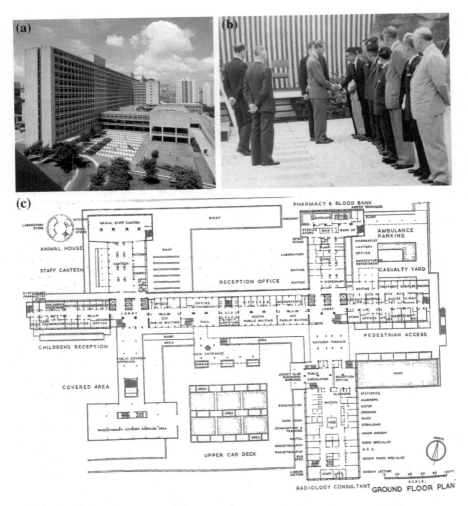

Fig. 2.13 Elizabeth Hospital in Kowloon, 1963. **a** The hospital was the largest of its kind in the Commonwealth when it was completed. From HK Government archive. **b** The Prince Philip, Duke of Edinburgh meeting the design team of PWD, 1962. **c** Ground floor plan. Courtesy of Dr. H.K. Cheng, J.P

The sheer wall concrete structure had a clear edge and was tidily expressed in the elevation. When it was completed in 1963, Elizabeth was the largest hospital in the Commonwealth. That same year, it was awarded the Bronze Medal by the Royal Institute of British Architects (Fig. 2.13).[23]

---

[23]For details of the design of Elizabeth Hospital, see *The Hong Kong Society of Architects Year Book 1965.*

The PWD was dissolved in 1982. A new department known as the Architectural Services Department (ASD) was established in 1986 as the architectural services provider to government institutions and departments. Other functions of the PWD included checking private-sector drawings and enforcing building control. These functions were transferred to the Buildings Department. Since the 1980s, local architects have dominated the agency and the British influence has faded. Local government architects are currently shaping public buildings based on their understanding of indigenous culture and Western ideas.

173 public building projects built from 1955 to 2011 are considered in this chapter to gain an overview of contemporary Hong Kong public architecture. The building projects are classified according to their typologies and completion periods. Essential facilities such as hospitals, government offices and municipal services buildings constitute 70 % of the typologies. Cultural centers, museums, libraries and sport facilities account for 22 %. In terms of construction periods, the 1950–1960s comprises 10 %, the 1970s comprises 8 %, the 1980s comprises 30 %, the 1990s comprises 28 % and the 21st century comprises 24 %. The rate of public building construction by quantity stabilized after the surge of mass production from the early post-war period to the 1980s.

Among the public buildings built in the post-war construction, **City Hall** is a most prominent case. A city hall is a type of public building commonly found in continental European and British cities since the end of the 19th century. It usually embodies the pride, and serves the needs, of citizens. However, during the first 100 years of colonial rule, Hong Kong did not have a decent city hall. The proposal to build one arose during the post-war reconstruction of the early 1950s. A city hall council was formed in 1950 to represent voices from 55 civic organizations. In 1954, the government completed reclamation of the sea in front of Statue Square. The land was designated for the construction of a ferry pier and a city hall, and architects were recruited from Britain (Fig. 2.14).

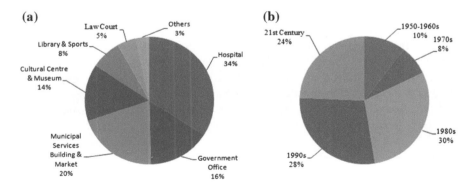

Fig. 2.14 Statistics of the public building. Drawn by Hui Ka Chun. **a** The distribution of typologies for 173 selected public building projects built from 1955 to 2011. **b** The distribution of construction periods for 173 selected public building projects

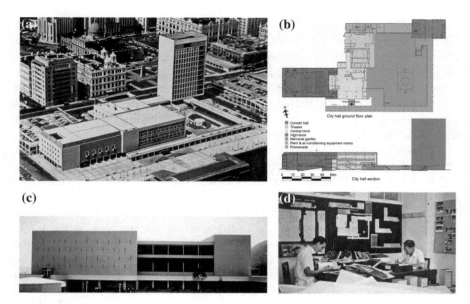

Fig. 2.15 City Hall, 1962. **a** A model of modernist architecture in Hong Kong. **b** Plan. **c** Elevation facing the courtyard. **d** Designers Alan Fitch (*right*) and Ronald Philips. Couresy of Mr. Ronald Philips

Designed by government architects at the PWD and completed in 1962, Hong Kong City Hall is located in Central on Hong Kong Island.[24] Its style embodies the minimal elegance of modernism. It was the territory's first-ever entirely local-oriented center for culture, comprising facilities such as a concert hall, a library, a theatre and a marriage registry.

The low block of Hong Kong City Hall houses a 1,434-capacity concert hall, a 463-capacity theatre and 3 restaurants. The high block houses the marriage registry and a public library. The memorial garden and shrine located in the center were built to honor those who died in World War II. The low block of the concert hall is located on one side and the high block of the library is located on the other. The two are skillfully linked by the small theatre and courtyard colonnade around the memorial garden. A crisp and simple design language was used in the construction of the building, which exhibits a well-balanced horizontal and vertical composition. Hong Kong City Hall is an example of a Bauhaus building (Fig. 2.15).

Hong Kong City Hall was built to communicate a modest monumentality for important ceremonial occasions such as governor inaugurations and the welcoming

---

[24]The City Hall was designed by the Public Works Department, mainly through the pens of Alan Fitch (1921–1986) and R.J. Phillips (1926–), who graduated from the Universities of Durham and Essex. *Far East Architect & Builder*, Hong Kong, April 1959; Nov., 1965. For details on the initiation and site selection of City Hall, see *Hong Kong Annual Report, 1951; 1953. Far East Architect & Builder*, Hong Kong, April 1959; Nov. 1965.

of British Royal family members. Its performance venue, library, marriage registry and garden have enhanced and enriched public life. The building was also constructed according to a minimalist philosophy. Its functional provisions did not consume more materials than needed. "Less is more" was a sustainable notion in the 1960s, when the economic situation was stringent. City Hall is located in the heart of Central. Originally aligned with the Queen's Pier and Edinburgh Place Ferry Pier, it was easily accessible to visitors from across Victoria Harbor. It is multifunctional and welcomes all age groups for any purpose. It educates the public in music, culture and literature, creating a diversified civic life for citizens inside and outside the building.

When City Hall was conceived in the mid-1950s, the surrounding buildings in Central were mainly classical (including the Supreme Court, completed in 1905; and the Hong Kong Club, completed in 1897) and Art Deco (including the Hong Kong Bank headquarters, completed in 1936, and the Bank of China, completed in 1951). The other commercial offices were designed according to an obscured and cliché language. City Hall served as a venue for royal rituals, such as inaugural ceremonies of new governors sent by Her Majesty and to welcome the Queen, princes and princesses. The design did not adopt the current model of royal family buildings, but embraced an asymmetrical, open and light-hearted aesthetic. The young designers from the U.K. bravely followed new examples from their home country, such as the Team X, Brutalism and "tropical modernism" movements of the 1950s. They sought to make the building plain and intimate for its citizens.[25] City Hall provoked a modernist movement in Hong Kong.

During its preparation, the same group of architects designed a government office building known as "Government Hill" that exhibited a plain box form, long central corridors and rooms on two sides. After 50 years, City Hall was listed as a Class I heritage building and part of "Government Hill" faced the threat of the bulldozer.[26] The north of City Hall is currently undergoing a reclamation and the Queen's Pier has been relocated. The convenient connection to water and the collective memory of the last colony have thus been lost forever (Fig. 2.16).[27]

The design of City Hall led to a modernist trend in Hong Kong. The government architects who conceived grand public buildings in the 1950s worked out of a

---

[25]The design intention of City Hall was reported in *Ming Pao Daily News*, 10 May 2007. For an explanation of "tropical modernism," see Uduku (2006).

[26]In 2011, the departments in the "Government Hill" moved to the new government headquarters in Admiralty. The west wing of "Government Hill" was proposed to be demolished to give way to high-rise office buildings. The proposal met severe protest in society. The protesters thought that no matter how dull it was, the "Government Hill" had witnessed a piece of Hong Kong history after the war and should be preserved totally. See *South China Morning Post*, 20 June 2012.

[27]In the 21st century, the reclamation project was carried out in Central to build a traffic bypass to alleviate the traffic pressure and pave a new waterfront park. The Star Ferry wharf and Queen's Pier had to be removed or demolished. The demolition of the two piers triggered several protests from Hong Kong society, especially young people. The occupation of Queen's Pier and confrontation with the police and construction workers lasted for several days and attracted media attention. See *South China Morning Post*, 1 Aug 2007.

Fig. 2.16 Statue Square. **a** Stature Square after renovation in the 1979. **b** Design sketch by Alan Fitch. **c** Pavilion and pond in the Square. Couresy of Mr. Chung W.N

two-storey shelter in Central.[28] The design of City Hall was first committed to Professor Brown Gordon in the early 1950s. It was later handed over to the Architectural Office in the PWD and was mainly designed by Alan Fitch (1921–1986) and Ronald Phillips (1926–). Alan Fitch went on to design Statue Square (1963). The lawn and pond were organized in rectangular shapes and flanked by long concrete pavilions. They symphonized with City Hall in front. Ronald Phillips went on to design Murray Building on Garden Road for the office of government

---

[28]In 2011, the government headquarters were moved to the Admiralty new building. There was a plan to demolish the west wing of "Government Hill" built in the 1950s and provide land for office towers. This was protested in society as the building witnessed the post-war history of Hong Kong. See *South China Morning Post*, 20 June, 5 December 2012.

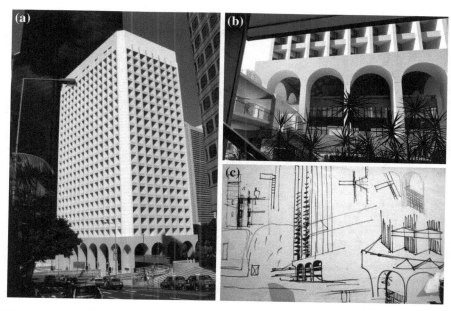

Fig. 2.17 Murray Building, Central, 1970. **a, b** The building serves for governmental department. **c** Design sketch by Ronald Philips in the 1960s. Courtesy of Mr. Ronald Philips

departments, mainly Public Work Department. The old two-storey high colonial building was dismantled and re-erected in Stanley. The new Murray Building of 27 floors was completed in 1970 and another excellent example of modern architecture in Hong Kong. In 2014, plans were made to convert the Murray Building into a hotel designed by Foster & Partners, who basically respected the original design (Fig. 2.17).

In the relatively backward early 1960s, the completion of City Hall brought fresh air to the city center of Hong Kong. After its opening in 1963, some other cultural facilities were built in new towns like Shatin, Tsuen Wan and Tun Men in the 1980s. Before 1997, all public buildings were designed by government architects and the qualities varied. The Cultural Center of 1989 and Central Library of 1997 were severely criticized in Hong Kong society for their mediocre design.[29] The dreary situation of public building design was broken through in 2000 when the **Museum of Coastal Defense** was standing on the hilltop of east Hong Kong Island.

The shortest distance between Hong Kong Island and Kowloon Peninsula is located at the 400-m channel in Lei Yue Mun. As early as 1844, the British built barracks at Saiwan to the south of the channel. By 1885, facing possible attacks from France and Russia, the British decided to construct batteries on the headland

---

[29]See Xue et al. (2013). The paper discusses the importance of public space in the East Asian environment.

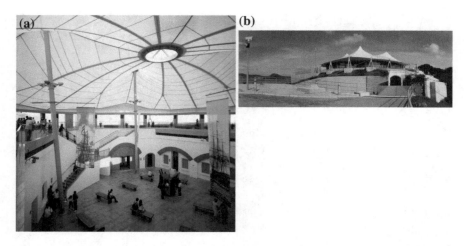

Fig. 2.18 Coastal Defense Museum, 2000. **a** The tensile structure covers the main sunken space. **b** New buildings crouching on the hill. Courtesy of Architectural Services Department (ASD), Hong Kong Goverment

to the south of the Lei Yue Mun Channel. Designed and built by the Royal Engineers, the redoubt was the core of the Lei Yue Mun fortifications. An area of 7,000 m^2 was dug up from the summit of the Lei Yue Mun headland. Eighteen casemates were then constructed to function as barrack rooms, magazines and shell and coal stores. The structures were concealed by earth. The construction was largely completed by 1887. The guns installed at Lei Yue Mun could be fired at different ranges to completely cover any approach to the Lei Yue Mun Channel (Fig. 2.18).

In December 1941, the Japanese launched their attacks on Hong Kong. Although the defense forces managed to repel several Japanese raids, they were eventually overwhelmed and the fort finally fell into enemy hands. The fort ceased to serve as a defense post in the post-war period and became a training ground for the British Forces until 1987, when it was finally vacated.

In 1993, the Urban Council decided to restore the site. The first move was to repair the fort and build a small information pavilion. After studying the site, the government architects suggested using tensile structure and covering the fortress. The indoor and outdoor heritages were adopted to form a new landscape and a new topography. These preserved and new buildings offer an interesting space in which to demonstrate the history of coastal defense over the past 600 years. The Museum of Coastal Defense was opened in 2000 to preserve the heritage of Hong Kong. It has a total area of 34,200 m^2 and cost $300 million to build. The newly installed tensile structure looks like white sails on the sea. The original underground forts are preserved as exhibition rooms. The indoor and outdoor spaces integrate organically with plants. The museum serves as a good example of environmental improvement and cultural sustainability.

Another complaint on public building is about municipal services buildings. In the late 1970s, the government began construction on municipal services buildings in various districts. A typical service building stacks a wet market, a fast food court, an indoor sports hall and a library up to 10 storeys. Although such a model saves on land in a dense city, residents are forced to move around in a compact indoor environment. In 1996, when the Urban Council sought to construct a municipal services building in the famous tourist resort of Stanley, architects conceived a new way of doing so. They suggested eliminating the function of the food market and instead concentrating on the building's entertainment and sport facilities.

Completed in 2006, the **Stanley Municipal Service Building** has a total floor area of 6,000 m^2 and surrounds an elevated courtyard. The concrete framing, cantilevered box, stairs, roof garden, opening and solid wall express indoor and outdoor spaces. Sandy glass on the garden floor provides a source of daylight to the community hall below. In the evening, the lighting from the hall penetrates through the glass and lights the garden. The bamboo pergola on the roof garden extends the lower part through an open stairway. The building opened a new direction for the design of municipal service buildings (Fig. 2.19).

The same group of architects designed a community leisure building for Tin Shui Wai district and completed it in 2011. People can enter the community building directly from the West Rail station. Most of the design methods in Tin Shui Wai have involved extending the Stanley community building. Outdoor

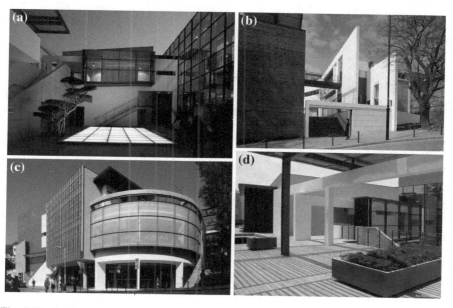

Fig. 2.19 Stanley community building, 2005. **a** The skylight of indoor sport hall below glowing lighting for the upper deck. **b** Wall and opening form planes to define space. **c** Plain and authentic materials expressed in the elevation. **d** Roof garden. Courtesy of Architectural Services Department (ASD), Hong Kong goverment

Fig. 2.20 Tin Shui Wai community leisure building, 2011. **a** Elevation facing the main road. **b** Outside landscape penetrating to the interior. **c** Outdoor reading area in library. **d** Courtyard in library

reading spaces have been created. Materials and spatial compositions change by location. Whether residents are playing sports or reading, they are immersed in a natural and beautiful environment (Fig. 2.20).

To respond to the sustainable trend, the government paid attention on the wetland between Hong Kong and mainland China border. Surrounded by tower blocks and infrastructure development, the Wetland Park stretches into the fragile wetlands north of Tin Shui Wai, which are home to thousands of migratory birds. In 1998, a feasibility study led to the recommendation for an ecological mitigation area to protect the wetlands from rapid urbanization into the area. Thus, a wetland park meeting the multiple purposes of conservation, education and ecotourism was

Fig. 2.21 Wetland Park, 2006. **a** Topography is used as part of building. **b** The public and private housing enjoy the view of Wetland Park. Courtesy of Hong Kong Wetland Park of the Agriculture, Fisheries and Conservation Department

suggested. The 61-hectare park is currently four times the size of Hong Kong's largest public open space at Victoria Park and can accommodate 500,000 visitors a year.

The Wetland Park is an ambitious project that strikes an equilibrium between architecture, landscape and ecology. Water is extensively interwoven into the development, creating harmony and integration with the natural environment (Fig. 2.21). The 10,000 m^2 visitor center contains three exhibition galleries, a swamp-themed fun area, an aquatic play space and many other amenities arranged in a semi-circular plan. The remainder of the park has been reinstated with man-made wetlands and reconstituted reserves for waterfowl. Ecological principles are the top priorities of the center's architecture and construction. For example, the visitor center is embedded in a slope and the roof is covered with lush green turf. From a bird's-eye view, the building blends imperceptibly and naturally with the wetlands, appearing to rise out of the water. The building appears part of the landscaped topography. Other green features, such as multiple shading, natural ventilation and a comprehensive geothermal system of 50-m-deep underground air ducts, have been implemented.

Unlike the other cases, the Hong Kong Wetland Park was not built for a monumental purpose. It was intended to be humble and show respect to nature. Its noble aspiration was to serve as an education-oriented building on a conservation wetland. It has enhanced and enriched public life by promoting hands-on environmental and wildlife knowledge.

2.5 Conclusion: "Public" for the Societal Betterment

After World War II, most nations and areas aspired to establish a peaceful and fair society, where citizens could have opportunity to live a decent life and display their talents. The enhanced life and ethical morale can in turn contribute to the society, create a positive cycle and bring both nation and individual people to new height and prosperity. To achieve this goal, the government subsidized low-cost housing and public building effectively balanced the greedy of free capitalist market. Hong Kong's practice in the post-war reconstruction evidenced that public housing and "collective consumption" positively supported the economic taking off, and public buildings alleviated the narrowness of daily living space and enlivened people's otherwise monotonous life. This modernization is realized by what Hilde Heynen's said of "power and money" of a resolute people-oriented government.

To build public housing and public buildings, the limited taxpayers' money must generate high social return and benefit as many people as it could. The modernist principles highly satisfy this demand—functional, pragmatic, rational, economical, fast building and efficient. Walking to any public housing estate in Hong Kong, one can vividly feel the spirit of modern architecture advocated by Le Corbusier from the 1920s to 1940s.

Public buildings in Hong Kong emerged after 1950 when people were basically sheltered with a roof. When City Hall and the town halls were built, the economy was poor and many more spaces should have been provided to correspond to the limited budget. City Hall and other excellent public buildings were outcomes not only of the modernist principles but also the skills and boldness of government architects. These examples of free plan and cubic design method had particular significance in Greater China when other parts were dominated by ideology-oriented official buildings at the same period. The government architects in the 21st century inherited their predecessors' exploration and continuously brought new ideas to Hong Kong's design. This is evident by the new civic centers, library, coastal defense museum, wetland park and cemeteries.

Across the Shenzhen River border lies the vast land of China, where public buildings have become symbols of political propaganda and evidence of government achievement in the 21st century. Taxpayers' money has been endlessly squandered to build convention/exhibition centers, museums, grand theaters, sports structures for the Olympic Games, pavilions for the World Expo and other iconic "white elephant" projects. The extravagant "public" buildings stand in the city centers far away from ordinary residents, proudly showing off the ambitions and dictatorship of China's "wise" leadership. Most of these iconic buildings are rarely used and have few patrons. In contrast, the public building practices of Hong Kong set a thrifty, democratic and responsible example in the southern part of China.

I lived in Yau Yat Chuen when I returned to Hong Kong in 1995. Located close to the City University campus, this area was zoned as green belt in the 1930s. In the 1950s, the government built Tat Chee Avenue for the industrialists, who developed low-rise houses there. The Kowloon-Canton Railway divides Kowloon Tong and Yau Yat Chuen, both of which function as districts for low-rise residential buildings, shielded behind the exuberant trees. Another City University gate opens to the Nan Shan public housing estates, most of which were built in the 1960s and 1970s. In those buildings, all of the ground floors are used as community centers, elderly housing, students' learning rooms and shops. Above the ground floor level, every family has two elevated bay windows: a big window for the habitable room and a narrow window for the kitchen. Staff guard the elderly housing, and you can see the elderly slowing moving about inside and sitting, chatting or playing chess in the public spaces. I sometimes went to the bank branches or strolled to the shops. Before construction on the Festival Walk shopping mall had finished, I walked to the shopping mall in Lok Fu, a public housing estate. Housing blocks currently stand up from the shopping mall. The mall's courtyards are located near the MTR station. Shops, restaurants and a wet market form a pleasant maze. All of the bank branches gradually withdrew from the Nan Shan district. Many shops closed and never reopened. The area is aging and its purchasing power is declining.

In 1989, the Cultural Center opened in Tsim Sha Tsui, its curved mass embracing the harbor. In its focal center stands a bronze sculpture known as "Flying French," which faces rows of palm trees in the waterfront promenade. The design of the Cultural Center has been criticized since its completion. However, its ground floor lobby and internal and external spaces demonstrate a high civic spirit. People can casually walk in and out, use the toilet, visit the exhibitions, drink at the coffee bar or enjoy free performances in the lobby on weekends. Famous architectural historian and Tsinghua University professor Chen Zhihua praised the Hong Kong Cultural Center for its public intimacy. On weekdays and weekends, the libraries in various districts are full of people. The elderly read books and newspapers, and students do their homework in the quiet rooms. Many students lack a desk at home and must do their work in the libraries. In Hung Hom, I would drop books off at the library on Floor Six and return to the ground-floor wet market, where I would pick up a live fish to take home.

References

Architectural Services Department. (2006). *Post 97 public architecture in Hong Kong*. Hong Kong: Architectural Services Department, HKSARG.

Castells, M., Goh, L., & Kwok, R. Y. W. (1991). *The Shek Kip Mei syndrome—Economic development and public housing in Hong Kong and Singapore*. London: Pion Limited.

Cheung, G. K. W. (2009). *Hong Kong's watershed: The 1967 riots*. Hong Kong: Hong Kong University Press.

Corbusier, L. (1925). *Towards a new architecture* (F. Etchells, Trans., from the French). London: Architectural Press. (1970).

Curtis, W. J. R. (1987). *Modern architecture since 1900*. Englewood Cliffs, N.J.: Prentice-Hall.

Dattner, R. (1995). *Civil architecture: The new infrastructure*. New York: McGraw-Hill.

Dijk, H. (1999). *Twentieth-century architecture in the Netherland*. Rotterdam: 010 Publishers.

Dikotter, F. (2010). *Mao's great famine—The history of China's most devastating catastrophe, 1958–1962*. New York: Bloomsbury Publishing.

Fauer, D. (2003). *Colonialism and the Hong Kong Mentality*. Hong Kong: Centre of Asian Studies, The University of Hong Kong.

Frampton, K. (1992). *Modern architecture—A critical history*. London: Thames and Hudson Ltd.

Heynen, H. (1999). *Architecture and modernity*. Cambridge, Massachusetts and London: MIT Press.

Hong Kong Government. (1972). *Report of housing board 1972*. Hong Kong: Government Printer.

Hong Kong Government. (2013). *Economic report 2013*. Hong Kong: Government Printer.

Liu, Z. P. (2010). *We all grow up in So Uk—A collective memory of public housing life in Hong Kong*. Hong Kong: Chung Hwa Book Co. 刘智鹏 (2010). 我们都在苏屋邨长大 – 香港人公屋生活的集体回忆. 香港:中华书局.

Lu, D. (Ed.). (2011). *Third World modernism—Architecture, development and identity*. New York: Routledge.

Lu, J., Rowe, P., & Zhang, J. (Ed.). (2001). *Modern urban housing in China: 1840–2000*. New York: Prestel.

Scanlon, K., Whitehead, C., & Arrigoitia, M. F. (Eds.). (2014). *Social housing in Europe*. Chichester, West Sussex: Wiley Blackwell.

Scoffham, E. R. (1984). *The shape of British housing*. London: G. Godwin.

Spence, J. (1990). *The search for modern China*. New York: Norton.

Uduku, O. (2006). Modernist architecture and 'the tropical' in West Africa: The tropical architecture movement in West Africa: 1948–1970. *Habitat International, 30*(6), 396–411.

Wang, H. (2010). A thankful life—Biography of H K Cheng, Beijing: Zhongguo tiedao chuban she. 王海文 (2010). 感恩人生 – 郑汉钧传记. 北京:中国铁道出版社.

Will, B. F. (1978). Housing design and construction methods (5). In L. S. K. Wong (Ed.), *Housing in Hong Kong—A multi-disciplinary study* (pp. 91–127). Hong Kong: Heinemann Education Books (Asia) Ltd.

Wong, L. S. K. (Ed.). (1978). *Housing in Hong Kong—A multi-disciplinary study*. Hong Kong and Singapore: Heinemann Educational Books (Asia) Ltd.

World Bank. (2015). *World development report*. New York: Oxford University Press.

Xue, C. Q. L. (2006). *Building a revolution: Chinese architecture since 1980*. Hong Kong: Hong Kong University Press.

Xue, C. Q. L., Jing, H., & Hui, K. C. (2013). Technology over public space: Study of roofed space in Osaka, Hanover, and Shanghai Expo. *Journal of Architectural and Planning Research, 30*(2), 108–126.

Chapter 3
Design Forces and Their Strategies

During the early period of colonization and plantation in Hong Kong, architects, engineers, surveyors and government officials who were predominantly from Britain and Europe undertook formal building design. Given the increasing infrastructural and new district development, qualified building designers and professionals did not always suffice. Demand for designers grew sharply after World War II.

In 1949, there were 46 Chinese architects and 42 Western architects. In 1955, 70 % of architects were ethnic Chinese In 1956, there were around 80 "Authorized Architects", listed in the Public Work Department (P.W.D.), only 24 were "pure" architects, the others had only engineering qualifications. Although ideas for organizing the professional architects were advanced in the first half of the 20th century, an organization was not founded until after the war. In the summer of 1956, some architects initiated to form an association of some kind, "incorporating a code of ethics in the association". The Provinsional Committee included J.W. Dark, N.H. Fok and G.D. Su.[1] The Hong Kong Society of Architects was founded on September 3, 1956 with 27 members, 15 of whom were expatriates and G.D. Su was the first president. This society was affiliated with the Royal Institute of British Architects (RIBA). It had 182 members in 1964, a number that grew to 243 members in 1966 and 1,026 in 1990.[2] In 1972, the organization was renamed the Hong Kong Institute of Architects (HKIA). As of 2014, it has over 4,000 individual members and 170 company members (Fig. 3.1).[3]

---

[1]The initiation and committee of the architects' association is from a news "An architectural association for Hong Kong", published in the *Hongkong and Far East Builder*, Vol. 11, No. 4, 1956, p. 21.
[2]The number of members in 1964 and 1967 is from *The Hong Kong Society of Architects Year Book* 1964, 1965, 1967. The number of founding members is from the Charter of Hong Kong Society of Architects. The number of 1990 is from Cheng (1990).
[3]From the website of HKIA, http://www.hkia.net/hk/AboutUs/AboutUs_02_01_new.htm. Accessed on 11 October 2014.

© Springer Science+Business Media Singapore 2016
C.Q.L. Xue, *Hong Kong Architecture 1945–2015*,
DOI 10.1007/978-981-10-1004-0_3

Fig. 3.1 Gathering of HKAS members in the 1950s. Courtesy of Mr. Ronald Philips

The Hong Kong government controlled building construction in many ways. For example, drawings submitted to the government had to be signed by an "authorized architect." In 1953, there were 95 authorized architects, including 35 expatriates and 11 people who started their businesses before World War II (Ng and Chu 2007). In 1967, the number of authorized architects reached 183.[4] According to the Hong Kong Annual Report published by *Wah Qiu Daily* (Overseas Chinese Daily), the number of design companies increased from 16 in 1949 to 71 in 1967. In the 1980s, 80 % of authorized architects were Chinese (Wang 2011).

Building construction usually involves thousands of hardworking people. However, architects and (schematic) design, no doubt, play leading roles. This chapter explores Hong Kong architects and companies in the post-war period. The design forces can be divided into three categories: large design companies, local Chinese architects and architects from Shanghai.

3.1 Large Design Companies

British architects founded **Palmer & Turner** (P & T) in 1868. That was in the beginning of colony and plantation. The firm was active in Hong Kong, Shanghai, Tianjin and other Chinese coastal cities in the early 20th century. **Leigh & Orange** (L & O) was founded in 1874 and did its business mainly in Hong Kong. **Spence & Robinson** (S & R) was founded in Shanghai in 1904 and moved to Hong Kong in 1947. After 1938 when Sino-Japanese war burst out, construction in Chinese cities stopped almost completely. The British companies gradually returned to Hong Kong and contributed to the post-war reconstruction after 1946. These companies were opened and mainly staffed by British or European people in the early years, but concentrated solely on building in Hong Kong. Therefore, they were considered and indeed were "local" firms.

---

[4]See *Far East Architect & Builder: 1967 Hong Kong Directory*. Hong Kong: Far East Trade Press.

In the early 20th century, **Palmer & Turner** was doubtlessly the most important design firm in Hong Kong and Shanghai. After its founding in Hong Kong in 1868, it moved its main forces to Shanghai in the 1910s after World War I to take advantage of several golden opportunities. Of the 23 heritage buildings located in the Bund, Shanghai, 12 were designed by P & T, including the prestigious Hongkong and Shanghai Banking Corporation (HSBC) (1923), Custom House (1927), Broadway Mansion (1934) and Sassoon House (Cathay and later Peace Hotel, 1928).[5] In Hong Kong, the HSBC headquarters, a spectacular building before the war, was designed by P & T and completed in 1936. With the invasion of Japanese troops in 1939, P & T closed its office in Shanghai, withdrew back to Hong Kong and persisted by working on projects in Johor Bahru, Malaysia. During the post-war reconstruction of the 1950s, P & T took on a leading role in city design. P & T designed 21 buildings along the 500-m stretch from Queen's Road to Star Ferry in old Victoria city, including the Bank of China building in 1951, Central Tower in 1997 and Chong Hing Bank Centre in 2004. During a 150-year period, the design method evolved from Victorian Gothic Revival to Neo-classical, from Art Deco to modernism, from "contemporary-classicism" to free form.[6] Some of the buildings were demolished and rebuilt on the same site, such as the two Chartered Bank headquarters buildings constructed in 1958 and 1991, respectively. Since the early colonial era, P & T's main clients have been Hong Kong Bank, Hong Kong Land and government. In the 21st century, the main clients are Sun Hong Kai, Citic and other companies associated with the Chinese economy. The design group understands the importance of powerful clients (Fig. 3.2).

P & T occupied a floor in the Hong Kong Bank after the war, and moved to Floor 19 of the Prince Building in 1970. With the rising of office rental, it retreated to Wan Chai in the 1990s. Its permanent office now occupies six floors of a building in Quarry Bay. Designed by P & T in 1960, the Prince Building was a product of 1955 building regulations that allowed developers to build a cubic volume according to the site area. Using a pedestrian bridge, people from Prince Building can walk to the second floor of the Mandarin Oriental Hotel. Both buildings were owned by Hong Kong Land, which realized the convenience of linking two of its own properties. The bridge was a precursor for the thousands of pedestrian bridges constructed in Hong Kong in later years.

P & T has designed schools, public housing, private residential towers and luxurious villas, and has won numerous design awards in Hong Kong and overseas. In a design competition for the Hong Kong Polytechnic campus in 1973, P & T won the first prize with a clean modernism design language. The campus plan uses a modular design. The ground floor consists of mechanical rooms, labs, a vehicular road and loading areas; the buildings are elevated by columns above the podium.

---

[5]Almost all buildings designed by Palmer & Turner before 1938 have been listed by Shanghai government as heritage building since 1994.

[6]The description of Palmer & Turner was referenced from P & T Group (1998); Introduction of P & T Group in Hong Kong and Shenzhen Urban Architecture Biennale (2008), Hong Kong Institute of Architects (2006) and Kwan (2015).

Fig. 3.2 Central, Hong Kong, white buildings were designed by P & T Group

The feature of the PolyU campus is an almost fully covered pedestrian floor. It is the main area for pedestrian movement, such as changing classrooms, and where students participate in activities, celebrations and ceremonies, and chat, stroll and drink coffee. In Hong Kong, nine months of the year are wet and humid, and the podium and colonnades provide a covered walkway to protect people from the rain and strong sunshine. The academic building is in the shape of wings created by modules, which can be freely divided. Lifts, stairs and toilets are packed into the "core" tubes connecting the academic areas, which are referred to by the letters of the two cores, for example BC, EF and CE.

The design of the polytechnic was partly influenced by international trends and European buildings of a similar type, such as the service space of Louis Kahn (1901–1974) and the Engineering Building of Leicester University (1967), designed by James Stirling (1926–1991). The cores and wings were designed to be endlessly expanded. According to the designer James Kinoshita, the influence might be from Kenzo Tange (1913–2005)—Kinoshita's hero.[7] To save money and construction time, the modules were repeated, creating a unified form and design language. After 30 years of expansion, the building complex moved to the other

---

[7]From Kinoshita (2005), and also from the author's interview of Mr. James Kinoshita, 2 March 2016.

(a)

(b)

(c)

(d)

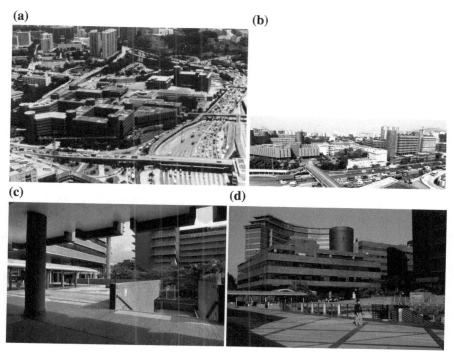

Fig. 3.3 PolyU campus. **a** and **b** Phase I completed in 1980. The service cylinder and served wings have a potential of further growth. **c** and **d** Podium for pedestrian movement, mechanical rooms and vehicles are below this floor. Courtesy of Hong Kong Polytechnic University

side of Chatham Road South. The brown tiles are a special feature of the PolyU building, a reminiscence of red brick campus.[8] The method of module repeating appears in other campus designs of P & T, for example, IVE Tsing Yi campus (1996), Lingnan University (1997) and Hong Kong Institute of Education (1998). The method of podium was also used in the Science Museum (1990) and History Museum (1998) designed by P & T. Both buildings share a podium in high level, under which is the display hall of the Science Museum (Fig. 3.3).

However, P & T's major contribution has been its designs of comprehensive development of Grade-A office towers, which have pushed the boundaries of office building studies. One example is the AIA building in Wan Chai. Completed in 1967, the building is a pre-stressed concrete structure with a five-storey podium and car park rising up from the valley. The office tower entrance is located on the roof of the podium. A 23-storey office tower rises up from the podium. The structural core is located in the center of a typical floor plan. The span from the structural core to the external wall is around 10 m, and there are no columns in the office. The

---

[8]For the description of PolyU, the author referred to the PolyU website, www.polyu.edu.hk, Wikipedia and Google Maps. The author has been investigating the others since 1989.

Fig. 3.4 AIA Building, 1967

façade of the tower clearly expresses the form, module and rhythm of the concrete structure. The tower was mainly conceived by James Kinoshita, a partner who joined P & T Group in the late 1950s (Fig. 3.4).

The Landmark was completed in Central in 1982. Two square 44-storey towers, the Gloucester and Edinburgh Towers, stand diagonally on the podium. The towers are 160 m tall and have a gross floor area of 112,500 m². The tower adopts a "tube in tube" structure. The span of the external tube is 3.75 m. The column sections are 1.5 × 0.6 m from the ground to ninth floors, and gradually decrease to 1.2 × 0.6 m at the top floor. The thickness of the internal tube changes from 0.5 m at the lower floors to 0.23 m at the top floor. The four-storey podium, which is 42.5 m long on each side, surrounds a sky-lit atrium. The pyramid-shape skylight grids project light and a sense of vitality into the atrium, which contains a fountain and high and low platforms. The atrium connects to three streets and the underground MTR station. It was the first modern atrium building in Hong Kong. Both the AIA building and Landmark adopt clear façade structures without extra decoration. Jinlin Hotel of Nanjing (1983) used the same design language and amazed their Chinese peers and users at the time of its completion. Each of the three buildings came from the pencil of James Kinoshita the director (Fig. 3.5)

P & T's corporate designs include the Jardine House completed in 1972; the Exchange Square completed in 1986 (see Chap. 6); and the office towers in Hong Kong, Macau, Singapore, Jakarta, Hanoi, Taipei, Shanghai, Nanjing and Beijing

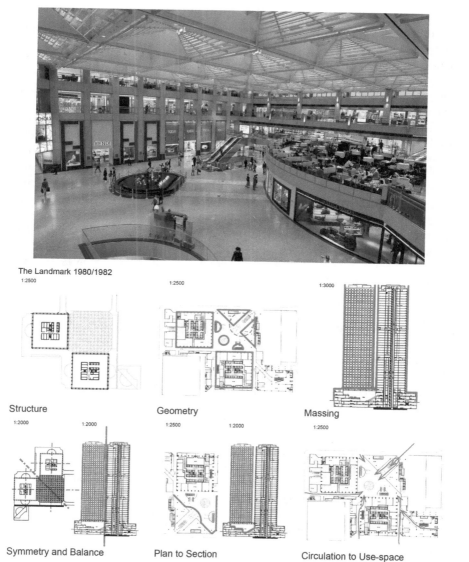

The Landmark 1980/1982

Structure   Geometry   Massing

Symmetry and Balance   Plan to Section   Circulation to Use-space

Fig. 3.5 The Landmark, 1982. People can enter the three-story atrium from three surrounding streets. Drawn by Kwan Yeung Yee

from the same period. Such grand and elegant corporate buildings redefine the quality of the Central Business Districts of Asian cities.

P & T's neo-classical design was mainly conceived by Remo Riva, the group's principal designer. Riva was raised and educated in Switzerland. In 1972, he traveled to Hong Kong, and by occasion came to work at P & T. As the principal designer of P & T and supported by a team of 40, he has designed more than 50 buildings, such as the Chartered Bank headquarters (1989), Entertainment Building (1993), Luk Kwok Hotel (1996), Bank of China in Macau (1996) and Oriental Plaza in Beijing (2000), most of which are landmarks in their respective locations. His design typifies the P & T façade. He and his team carefully elaborate the dimensions of the cladding slate, spandrel wall, vertical and horizontal gaps, gloss and rough surfaces, color cooperation, and texture. Slate size must be considered to avoid cutting the materials. In the Chartered Bank headquarters and Entertainment Building that occupy tiny land plots on Queen's Road, the designer put rotunda lobbies in the centers of the buildings, with arches open to the lobbies and stone moldings and occasional sculptures shaping balanced classical spaces. This plan is generated from such a central space and is mostly symmetrical. The slender vertical elevation is divided to several sessions. Riva called this "contemporary classicism."[9] The famous façade design brought in a great deal of business. Developers in Taiwan and mainland China sent in their plans, asking for such a grand façade design (Fig. 3.6).

P & T Group had around 30–40 staff members and three partners in 1960, 200 in 1970 and more than 600 in 1997. P & T Group changed from partnership to incorporation, and partners became directors. It has continuously developed its overseas market since 1972, mainly in Singapore, Indonesia and The Philippines. It now employs more than 2,000 people and has branch offices in Singapore, Taiwan, Macau, Bangkok, Vietnam, Malaysia, Indonesia, Dubai, Abu Dhabi, Ajman, Ras Al Khaimah, Qatar, Shanghai, Beijing, Wuhan, Dalian, Chongqing and Shenzhen. The firm's design footprints are scattered across Asia. Since 2010, its projects in mainland China and Taiwan have accounted for over 40 % of its portfolio. Five design teams located in the Hong Kong headquarters design and issue projects in Hong Kong and overseas, except those in Singapore and Thailand. Led by various directors, these teams specialize in building education, residences, commerce, hotel/service apartments and master planning. The overseas branch offices help with marketing, documentation and construction supervision.

During the 70 years' period since 1945, P & T has been recognized as the most successful firm in Hong Kong and Asia. Its works are extensively respected. This can partly attribute to its system. The most capable designers were recruited and promoted from different international education and working background. The benchmark of "good quality and service" was set high and the teams only issued design with high quality. The teams accumulated the technical data and supervised the construction work effectively. There is no "marketing" office at P & T. Its old name and portfolio are the best brand.

Before the war, **Leigh & Orange** designed St. Andrew's Church in Tsim Sha Tsui (1906), the main building of Hong Kong University (HKU) (1912) and the French Missionary Building (1917, now the Court of Final Appeal). In the early

---

[9]Description of Remo Riva's work in P & T is partly from an interview of Mr. Riva, conducted on 22 August 2014.

Fig. 3.6 Entertain Building, 1993. The sketches were drawn by the designer Remo Riva. Courtesy of Mr. Remo Riva

20th century, it designed many buildings in Sha Mian, a sandy colonial concession island in Guangzhou (Canton). After the war, the firm participated in the reconstruction of the city, including the Oriental Mandarin Hotel in Central (1963). One of its unique designs was Ocean Park, which was opened in 1977. The construction of Ocean Park was sponsored by the Hong Kong Jockey Club. The park is located on the south side of Hong Kong Island on 92 ha of land. It is zoned as "Marina World," "Summit" and "Tai Shue Wan" ("Bay"), and features a display of ocean animals, giant pandas, botanic gardens, cable cars and many "thrill" game machines. Client innovations and skillful design work make Ocean Park an appealing venue for Hong Kong tourists. The park attracts five million visitors each year. L & O has also successfully designed jockey clubs, horse racing courts and stadiums in Hong Kong and overseas. It has designed many sports facilities and institutional and comprehensive commercial buildings in Asian and Chinese cities. It has opened branch offices in Beijing, Shanghai, Fuzhou and Doha, and is

(a)

(b)

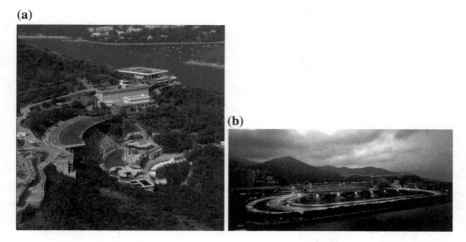

Fig. 3.7 Works of Leigh & Orange. **a** Ocean Park, 1977. **b** Shatin Jockey Club horse racing court, 1985. Courtesy of Leigh & Orange Architects

currently led by a group of directors. The firm was led by British architects in the first half of 20th century, and now most directors are ethnic Chinese, who have been trained in the firm for decades. Leigh & Orange epitomizes a process of localization for the old British firms (Fig. 3.7).

Spence & Robinson was founded in Shanghai in 1904. It designed the jockey club and racecourse building on West Nanjing Road, and completed its construction in 1932. This building adopts a British neo-classical style, and features a clock tower, a giant column and a stone podium. Over the past 80 years, the building has been used as a jockey club, a municipal library and an art gallery (Fig. 3.8). S & R moved to Hong Kong in 1947, designed the Alexandra House in Central in 1956 and remarkable Hong Kong-Macau pier and terminal in 1985. This building complex sits on the Sheung Wan MTR, bus and taxi stations. The upper floors contain a shopping mall and pier checkout in addition to many restaurants, shops and ticket booths. The terminal is busy from dawn to midnight. The ferries anchored on the pier are bound for Macau and other ports in the Pearl River Delta. A helipad is positioned on top of the pier. Two 41-storey towers rise above the podium on the pier and shopping mall, providing a home to Shun Tak Centre and the China Merchants Group Building. The refuge, top and bottom floors are made of trusses painted with an eye-catching sharp red color. The building complex uses piers to thread its shopping and transportation facilities together, and serves as an excellent example of transit-oriented-development (TOD) in Hong Kong. Christopher "Kit" Haffner, (1936–2013) of S & R was the main designer of the Hong Kong-Macau ferry pier, a TOD experiment.[10] A graduate from the University

---

[10]About early discussion of TOD complex, see Tan and Xue (2014). Haffner and his peers got the early feeling and concept of TOD and the experiment of design in this aspect was green.

Fig. 3.8 Jockey Club in Shanghai, 1934

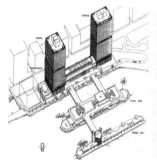 

Fig. 3.9 Hong Kong-Macau Pier and Terminal, 1985

of Liverpool, Haffner came to Hong Kong in 1961. He participated in the discussion of mega-structures and cross-street block development, and acted as president of the HKIA in 1989–90 (Fig. 3.9).

Wong Tung & Partners was founded in 1963. Founders William Wong, Jr. (1928–2012) and Albert K.H. Tung (1931–2010) received their architectural education and training in Texas in the U.S. They started their early business in the U.S. and Hong Kong. Supported by American developers, Wong Tung & Partners designed the Sheraton Hotel in Tsim Sha Tsui, which won the HKIA award in

Fig. 3.10 Wong Tung's
project: Sheraton Hotel, Tsim
Sha Tsui, 1973. The lower
part is shopping arcade, while
the upper part is guest room

1974. In this hotel, shopping mall and hotel lobby are separated, so that the podium
provides a lot of retail space. This was quite new in the 1970s.

The firm was a pioneer in planning large-scale residential areas, which will be
discussed in Chap. 5. Edward Ho steered Wong Tung & Partners for decades after
its founders moved on. He graduated from HKU in 1963 and was once a member of
the Executive Council and Legislative Council of Hong Kong. The large residential
development projects were mostly under his directorship. In the early years of
China's open-door policy, Wong Tung & Partners developed business in Shanghai
and designed the New Jingjiang Hotel in the city. The firm currently employs 210
staff members in Hong Kong, and has branch offices in Beijing, Shanghai,
Chongqing, Shenzhen and other cities around the world. Wong Tung & Partners is
successful in the design business. Its design can be seen as commerical with high
quality and some design tastes (Fig. 3.10).

Wong & Ouyang Ltd. originated out of Wong & Ng, founded in 1957. Jackson
Wong (1930–1993) and Ng Chun Men were classmates in the first cohort of
architectural graduates from HKU in 1955. Leslie Ouyang (1927–2010) graduated
from St. John's University in Shanghai in 1949. In 1964, these three people became
partners. Ng Chun Men quitted in 1972, formed his own company and evolved to
Dennis Lau and Ng Chun Men Partnership (DLN) in the 21st century. Wong and
Ouyang's business thrived in the 1980s–90s, and it excels at large-scale development and hotel design. The firm constructed the Hutchinson Building in Central
during the 1970s, the Pacific Place of Admiralty in 1988, Times Square of
Causeway Bay in 1992, Phase II of the Convention Center in 1997, Langham Place
of Mongkok in 2004, Taikoo Fong from 1990 into the 21st century, and Elements at
Kowloon Station and the Yuk Man Fong redevelopment of Kwun Tong in the 21st
century (Fig. 3.11).

Both Jackson Wong and Ng Chun Men are the HKU graduates. During the
1960s when big firms (of expatriate architects) obtained most of the design

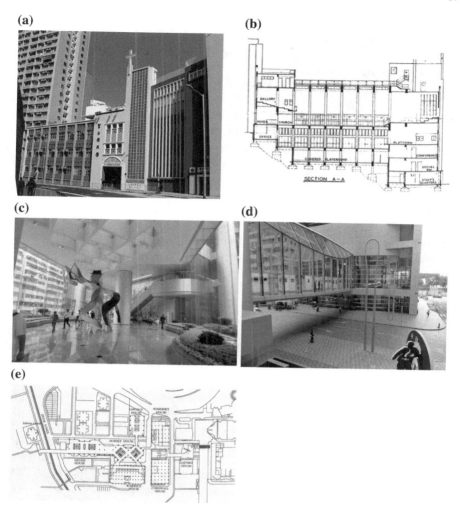

Fig. 3.11 Wong & Ouyang's works. **a** St. Stephen's Church, Wong, Ng & Ouyang, 1965. **b** Section, the church has entrance on two sides of different level. **c** Taikoo Fong, 1990–2010, Lobby linking to various tower buildings. **d** Pedestrian bridges linking high-rise blocks. **e** Master plan of Taikoo Fong

commissions, Wong and Ng broke through in the design market. The name Wong and Ouyang is closely associated with many large-scale commercial developments. The firm's progress coincided with the burgeoning economy especially the growing Chinese developers in the 1970s onward. After the first generation of founders moved on, Lam Wo Hei, a 1967 HKU graduate, led most of the group's projects and is now its leader. Wong and Ouyang was active in Shanghai in the 1980s, when China opened its doors. The firm currently employs over 250 workers in Hong Kong and has branch offices in Shanghai and Guangzhou. Wong and Ouyang's works are highly commercial, functional and friendly in construction. Some of their designed buildings become generic "background" of the districts and streets they are located. They express the machine aesthetic which typifies the city.

Andrew King-fun Lee (born in 1933) was among the second cohort of HKU architectural graduates in 1956. He went to study and work in Australia and returned to Hong Kong to run his own office in 1962. Over the past 55 years, Lee's company has designed many residential towers and school buildings and it grows to over 200 staff members in 2015. The company designed many of the academic and dormitory buildings of HKU, Chinese University of Hong Kong (CUHK), City University of Hong Kong (CityU) and Polytechnic University of Hong Kong (PolyU). In his compact plan for Hong Kong's private housing, he invented the "scissor-type" staircase and bay window. These two inventions were extensively cloned in Hong Kong and later exported to Chinese cities. In 1988, Lee and colleagues designed the Hilton Hotel, the tallest building in Shanghai. Lee is a cautious architect who always thinks of maximizing the users' benefits.

When he designed a clubhouse for Yau Yat Chuen, a low-rise residential neighborhood in the 1970s, the three-floor building was packed with restaurant and functional rooms. He put three tennis courts onto the rooftop, so that the precious backyard can serve as a lovely garden with lawn and swimming pool. The club-house has deeply loved by local residents since its completion in 1979. People read newpapers in the lobby and enjoy the garden view, while women play majohn in the upper floor rooms. Residents feel glorious to be member of this club. Andrew Lee acted as president of HKIA in 1975–76. He led Hong Kong colleagues to visit Beijing, and opened dialogue with peers in the Chinese mainland when the "Cultural Revolution" was at the end. These visits in the 1970s ushered influx of Hong Kong design in China in the 1980s (Fig. 3.12).

Ronald Lu also returned from Australia and founded his own office in 1976. Ronald Lu & Partners has designed many schools, community and cultural buildings, paying special attention to environmental sustainability and green architecture. The firm has expanded to 550 employees and more than 10 studios, and opened branch offices in Beijing, Shanghai, Guangzhou and Shenzhen. The "studio" is led by one director and staffed with 20 or more staff members. It completes projects from inception to construction drawing. The system of studio allows individual directors to display their expertise in design and production. The team will have more sense of belonging and authorship. Ronald Lu & Partners is active in both the practice and academia, and has won many awards in various places and categories (Fig. 3.13). Both Andrew Lee and Ronald Lu's companies are now managed by the second generation of their families. The new generation injects the ideas and blood of the 21st and brings the old firm to a new height.

Some other big firms include Aedas, Atkins and AECOM, which were restructured for several times. Their multi-nation practice and decades of directors ensure big projects and strong technical supporting. But their face of "authorship" is obscure. Among these big companies, **Aedas** is outstanding. Aedas was founded in Hong Kong in the beginning of the 21st century. Through merging and cooperation, Aedas grows to 13 offices with 1,450 staff members in Hong Kong, Shanghai,

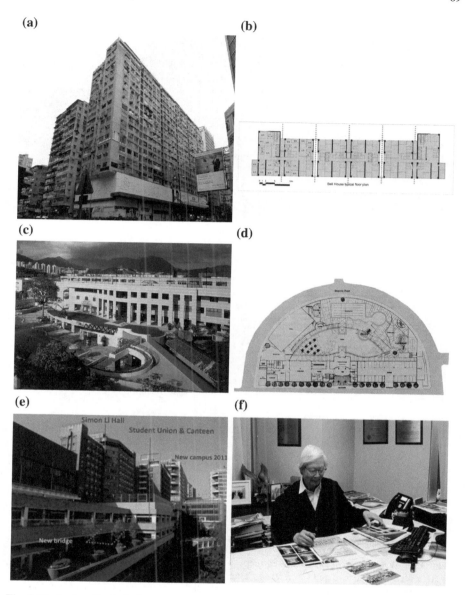

Fig. 3.12 Andrew Lee's design work. **a** and **b** Bell House in Nathan Road, Kowloon, 1964; **c** and **d** Yau Yat Chuen clubhouse, 1979. **e** Simon Li Hall, HKU, 1979. Student union and canteen linking to the rooftop garden, while students live in the tower. The bay window was used for rooms. In 2011, the university built new campus, and a pedestrian bridge penetrates the student union building. The dotted line shows the original location of staircase, where students used for various functions. **f** Mr. Andrew Lee, 83, works in the frontier of design practice, photoed in 2016

Fig. 3.13 Works of Ronald Lu & Partners. **a** Academic Building 3, City University, 2013; **b** HKYWCA Guesthouse and Conference Center, 2010; **c** Ko Shan Theatre, 2014; **d** Siu Sai Wan community building. In these buildings, natural ventilation and sustainable factors are particularly emphasized. Courtesy of Ronald Lu & Partners

Beijing, Chengdu, Macau, New Delhi, Singapore, Dubai, Abu Dhabi, Doha, London, Los Angles and Seattle. Because of its staff number and annual turnover of design fee, it has been in the top rank of World Architectural 100 since 2010. In addition to many skyscrapers and convention centers in the Middle East, Singapore and India, Aedas designed the high-speed rail station in Hong Kong (2018), the

Venetian (2007) and several other large scale casino and entertainment complexes in Macau, Fortune Square in Beijing (2003) and academic building at Xi'an Jiaotong and Liverpool University of Suzhou (2012). The projects were designed and led by various internatinal directors, who have expertise in different building types. It excels in the traffic building type like MTR station, ocean terminal and airport facilities. In these building designs, Aedas pays high attention on the sustainable part of building, convenience for the end-users and dynamic form in the city. The blurred authorship may also bring some goodness. The firm no longer relies only on a couple of names but a group of talents on revolving basis.

The scale and operation of Hong Kong design firms reflect the characteristics of the local economy and capitalism. Compared with American and Chinese companies, Hong Kong firms are relatively smaller and more flexible.

3.2   Chinese Architects

Although the population of Hong Kong reached one million before the war, the city's economic activity was not as active as that of Shanghai. The term "architectural design" applied to only a few private and government buildings. Most of the buildings on the streets were defined as "architecture without architects." Expatriate professionals dominated the design market, and Chinese architects were rarely seen. Among the few Chinese design firms was **Chau and Lee Architects and Engineers** (Chau and Lee). Chau Iu Nin was born in 1901 and graduated from HKU's Civil Engineering Department. Richard Lee studied architecture in the U.K. Chau's family was the main stockholder in Chinese banks, chamber of commerce and charity organizations, and had many businesses and connections.

Chau and Lee opened before the war and designed buildings for Tung Wah Group of Hospitals and St. Mary's Church of Causeway Bay in 1937. In the 1950s, the firm obtained more business and became the largest (Chinese) design firm in Hong Kong. The firm designed buildings in Central, the Vice-Chancellor's house at HKU. Vertical line and horizontal curves can be seen on the external walls, reflecting the taste of commercial eclecticism and modernist movement of the 1950s (Fig. 3.14).

Wai Szeto was born in 1913. A graduate of St. Paul's College in Hong Kong, he went to Shanghai to study architectural engineering at St. John's University. During 1938–1940, he received a Federation for British Industries Scholarship to study in the U.K. as a graduate engineer. In 1945, he returned to Chongqing and worked as a senior planning engineer for the national government's Water and Electricity Bureau. In 1948, he returned to Hong Kong and opened Wai Szeto Architect & Associates. In the 1950s–1960s, he designed many community and school buildings, such as Kowloon Methodist Church and School on Gascoigne Road (1951), Li Po Chun Chambers in Central, the Building Contractors' School in Tin Hau (1958), Robert Black College of HKU (1967), St. Paul's College (1969) and New Method College in Yau Ma Tei (1971).

(a)   (b)

(c)

Fig. 3.14 Works of Chau and Lee. **a** Chinese General Chamber of Commerce building, 1954.
b Vice-chancellor lodge, HKU, 1951. **c** Chapel of Chung Chi College, 1962

Kowloon Methodist Church and School were built in 1951 on the hill along
Gascoigne Road. It was the largest Methodist church in Hong Kong and also
Szeto's first design work in Hong Kong. The linear school building was inserted
into the church along the hill. The main sanctuary, with its stall and balcony,
contains 800 seats to serve the Methodist community and school. Some Methodist
churches in Wan Chai and North Point were rebuilt. The building and internal
decoration (flooring, railing and furniture) of the Kowloon Methodist Church lasted
for more than 60 years and continued to demonstrate durability and elegance. The
building complex featured a deep horizontal sunshade. It used only two colors on its
external wall, including white wash for the school and brown for the church, further
emphasizing the elevation. Many local residents continue to have fond memories of
the Kowloon Methodist Church (Fig. 3.15).

Wai Szeto & Partners was appointed to design the main CUHK campus from
1963 to 1975. CUHK was established in 1963. Before its founding, the school
comprised several colleges operating separately. Robert Fan and Chau and Lee
designed, planned and built the Chung Chi College campus in 1955. When CUHK
was founded in 1963, the campus had a land area of 273 acres. The three-college
setup was adopted from the British system of students learning and living under
college care. Chung Chi College is located at the foot of a hill, close to the sea and
train station. The mid-level of the building houses the university's administrative
center. New Asia and United Colleges are located on the higher level. The

(a)

(c)

(b)

(d)

Fig. 3.15 Wai Szeto and his design of Kowloon Methodist Church and School, 1951. **a** The white part is school, which connects to church. **b** Main hall. **c** Church and school connect together. **d** Over 60 years, the building details are durable

northwest part of the college is reserved for senior staff quarters. The level difference from the train station to the mountain peak is 70–80 m (Figs. 3.16 and 3.17).

Following its work on Chung Chi College, Wai Szeto & Partners took on the main campus, United and New Asia Colleges, including its planning, site formation, building design and construction supervision. The terrace for the main campus

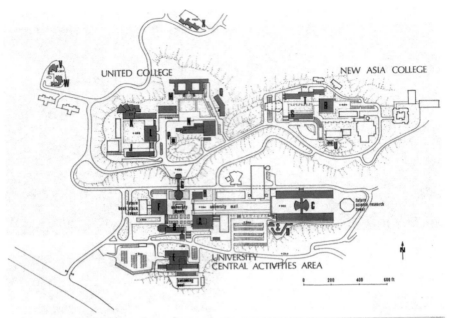

Fig. 3.16 Master plan of CUHK, central activities area, made by W. Szeto & Associates, 1960s. From W. Szeto & Associates

(a) **(b)**

Fig. 3.17 Buildings in the central area, CUHK. **a** library, **b** science Building, both were built in the 1970s

(a) **(c)**

(b)

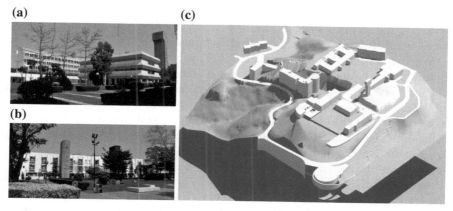

Fig. 3.18 United College, CUHK. **a** Academic building, **b** student hall, **c** buildings are spread on slopes. Picture made by CUHK students—Sze Man Tting Christy and Chow Lik Wah Joshua, under supervision of Prof. Woo Pui Leng and Zhu Jingxiang

is 250 m in the east-west direction and 40–50 m in the north-south direction. The main library and science building are positioned at the respective ends and form a plaza called the "tree lined avenue," which houses the administrative center, Research Institute of Chinese Culture and other buildings. The terrace is sizeable and carries a memorial atmosphere. Located at the top of the hill are groups of buildings belonging to United and New Asia Colleges. Each college has its own court and building group. The academic building, library and student dormitory are knitted together according to the land topography. The veranda is used in a way suitable to the southern China climate. The master plans of United and New Asia Colleges fully reflect the designers' intention to integrate the students' personal and study lives (Fig. 3.18).

From 1963 to 1975, most of the buildings at CUHK were designed by Szeto's firm, including the science building, main library, Research Institute of Chinese Culture and two colleges. The lecture hall in the science building is cantilevered over 10 m, a feature rarely seen in the 1960s. The building elevation is clad with

Fig. 3.19   Institute of Chinese Culture, CUHK, 1970

vertical and horizontal shading fins. The external wall of the staircase is cast in rough form, reflecting the "brutalism" style popular in those years.

While Wai Szeto was preparing the CUHK campus plan, he recruited a capable British architect **Alan Fitch**, who had just designed the City Hall in Central (see Chap. 2). Fitch participated in the planning of the campus and particularly designed the Research Institute of Chinese Culture (which is housed in a courtyard), the balconies surrounding the garden, and the pond. There is no extra decoration, and the building and garden form a tranquil space for contemplation. I.M. Pei visited Hong Kong in the 1960s, and made friend with Wai Szeto. During his short visit, he also gave ideas to the design of the Research Institute of Chinese Culture (Fig. 3.19).[11]

Japan held the World Expo in Osaka in 1970. It was the first time an Asian country had hosted the World Expo, and it was also the first time Hong Kong had participated in the event. Alan Fitch from Wai Szeto & Partners designed the Hong Kong pavilion. In Expo Park, the main Hong Kong pavilion exhibited products from the colony. It was surrounded by a water pond, and an auxiliary pavilion served as a restaurant. On top of the pavilion roof stood 13 masts holding junk sails made of nylon nets. The masts ranged from 10 to 22 m tall. The sails turned in different directions with the wind every day, and provided a dynamic and characteristically Hong Kong background for the performance (Fig. 3.20).[12]

Wai Szeto acted as president of the Hong Kong Society of Architects in 1960 and aspired to create new buildings with scientific attitudes. Compared with the architects who designed works in mainland China and Taiwan in the 1960s–1970s, Mr. Szeto and his colleagues were doubtlessly top-ranked designers. In addition to building design, Szeto took many jobs in the public sector. He was member of both

[11]About the description of Wai Szeto, the author took reference of *W.Szeto & Partners Architects and Engineers, Selected Works*, 1975; and interview with Mr. Chung Wah-nan in many occasions during 2010–2015. Mr. Andrew Lee King-fun told the author about I.M. Pei's giving ideas to the Chinese culture institute of CUHK, 26 February 2016.

[12]For the Hong Kong pavilion in the 1970 World Expo of Osaka, see the technical notes written by Mr. Alan Fitch, 1969; "Hong Kong will 'sail' into Expo 70", *South China Morning Post*, Feb 9, 1968; pictures provided by Victoria Fitch in 2014; and *Hong Kong Annual Report 1970*.

Fig. 3.20 Hong Kong Pavilion in the World Expo, Osaka, Japan, 1970. Courtesy of Ms. Victoria Fitch

the Legislative and Executive Councils. In his chair of transportation consultation, he and colleagues suggested to build the cross-harbor tunnel and mass transit railway. He was knighted by the Queen, and conferred honorary doctorate by the HKU and CUHK. After the open-door policy was adopted in China in 1980, the famous Hong Kong capitalist Richard Charles Lee (1905–1983) and Liao Chengzhi (1908–1983), the senior official of Communist Party in China and also a native Cantonese, jointly collaborated to develop Garden Hotel in Guangzhou. Wai Szeto was committed for design and he invited I.M. Pei to draw sketch. Two Y-shape hotel towers stand in a garden of around seven ha. It was one of the fashionable "southern style" hotels in China in the 1980s. After its completion in 1985, Szeto retired and lived in New York and Paris. He indulged in painting in the last years of his life.

3.3 From Shanghai to Hong Kong

The Communist Party took power in China in the late 1940s and early 1950s. Thousands of capitalists and professionals including a group of established architects such as Eric Cumine, Sü Gin Djih, Robert Fan, Chu Ping and Luke Him Sau escaped to Hong Kong, mainly from Shanghai. According to Wang's study, 67 architects escaped to Hong Kong. Of these architects, 22 were born in Hong Kong and 30 were descendants of Guangdong Province (Canton) (Wang 2011). Their practice was closely linked with clients moving from Shanghai to Hong Kong. During a period in which the local Hong Kong architects had not yet been fledged, these architects from Shanghai filled the gap and introduced new design ideas. Their achievements were documented in works by Wang Haoyu (2011), Ng Kai Chung and Sid Chu (2007). By citing these materials, this chapter supplements the author's own investigation and ideas.

RIBA fellow **Eric Cumine** (1905–2002) was an important architect in Hong Kong during the 1950s–1970s. He was born in 1905 in Shanghai to a family of

(a)   **(b)**

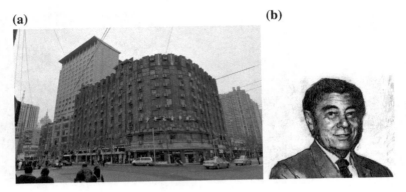

Fig. 3.21 Denis Apartment, Shanghai, 1928; Mr. Eric Cumine

Scottish and Shanghainese. His father, a Scot, was an architect. Cumine spoke fluent English, Shanghainese and Cantonese. He graduated from the Architectural Association's (AA) School of Architecture in London at the age of 20 and joined his father's firm. In 1928, Denis Apartment, which was mainly designed by Cumine, was completed in the International Settlement of Shanghai.

With a land plot of 2,563 m^2, Denis Apartment is located at the junction of Bubbling Well Road (now West Nanjing Road) and Carter Road (Shimen Er Road). The concrete-structured building has a gross floor area of 11,774 m^2 and 10 floors. The ground floor is full of shops and the upper floors comprise apartments. The curved plan turns along the road. The façade features dark brown tiles and vertical lines. Decorated with flower reliefs and sculptures, it is a typical Art Deco building, a style popular in Shanghai during the late 1920s. Cumine was 23 years old when the building was completed. The same year saw the completion of the Sassoon House (Cathay Hotel) in the Bund, Shanghai, and the Peninsula Hotel in Tsim Sha Tsui, Hong Kong. During the Pacific War, the British Cumine was imprisoned in a concentration camp in the suburb of Shanghai (Fig. 3.21).

In 1949, Cumine opened his office in Hong Kong. In 1956, his firm grew to more than 30 employees, including some capable architects such as Stanley Kwok and A. J. Brandt, who was the former professor at St. John's University, Shanghai and escaped to Hong Kong in 1949. During the 38 years from 1949 to 1987, Cumine Architect & Associates build 12 star-rated hotels, 73 residential buildings, 29 office towers and 700 other projects in Hong Kong and Macau. Most of these buildings were built in Hong Kong, including the North Point Estate of Public Housing (1957), the So Uk estate (1961), the Caroline Centre of Causeway Bay (1956), ELCHK Truth Lutheran Church in Yau Ma Tei (1962), the HKU library (1964), Hotel Lisbon Macau (1965), Excelsion Hotel (1973) and Harbor City (Fig. 3.22).

Built in 1962, ELCHK Truth Lutheran Church is located on Waterloo Road in Yau Ma Tei. The church faces the busy road, and its affiliated middle school and housing are located in the back. The ground floor of the church serves as an activity

(a) **(b)**

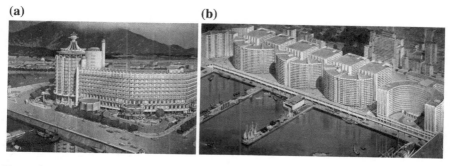

Fig. 3.22 Eric Cumine's design works. **a** Hotel Lisboa Macau, 1970. **b** Harbor City, Tsim Sha Tsui, scheme designed in 1980. From Cumine (1981)

Fig. 3.23 ELCHK Truth Lutheran Church, Kowloon, 1962

room, and the main hall is located on the upper floor. The hall can seat 750 people, with 150 in the balcony. Concrete portals with 24-m spans support the roof at a bay width of 4 m. A colored glass window is positioned behind the altar. On the façade facing Waterloo Road, the arched side wall links to the bell tower, which is painted with white wash. Two pointed arches link together, decorated by dark colored tiles. The elevation is treated differently from those of other churches in Hong Kong (Fig. 3.23).

Cumine designed Denis Apartment in Shanghai according to the Art Deco style. After he arrived in Hong Kong, he applied a more functional modernist approach to his design and only displayed his artistic skills when an opportunity arose, such as in the case of the Truth Lutheran Church. In the 1960s, he designed the HKU main library, which features mezzanine floors that serve as quiet reading corners in its tall space, and a large glass wall along its elevation. The HKU library has a simple plan, plain materials and a flexible layout. It is similar to many British university libraries of the 1960s. Cumine designed many classy apartments in the Peak and Southern Islands, such as Friston and Balmacare in 1959, Carolina Garden in 1964 and Luginsland Apartment in 1965. In these apartments, one staircase/lift serves two units. Each unit has three bedrooms. The living rooms and bedrooms have their

(a)   (b)

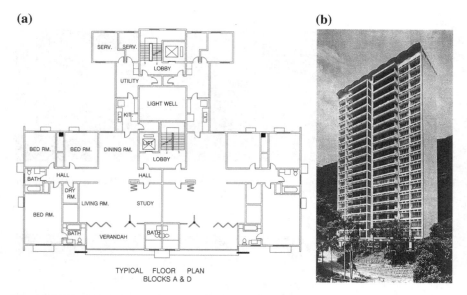

TYPICAL   FLOOR   PLAN
BLOCKS A & D

Fig. 3.24 Eric Cumine's design of residential building. **a** Floor plan of Carolina Garden, 1964. Similar plan was widely adopted in classy housing design during 1950s–1970s. **b** Luginsland Apartment, 1966

own balconies, and the bedrooms have closets. The kitchens have doors opening to the back, where working balconies, utilities and workers' bedrooms and toilets are located. In daily use, domestic helpers used their own lifts and stairways, and would not cross over into their masters' activity lines. The units were reasonably designed and shared similar characteristics with high-end apartments in Shanghai (Fig. 3.24).

Robert Fan (1893–1979) was an important figure among first-generation Chinese architects. Fan graduated with a Bachelor's degree in civil engineering from St. John's University in Shanghai in 1917, and obtained a Bachelor's degree in architecture from the University of Pennsylvania in the U.S. in 1922. In 1926, he participated the international design competition of Dr. Sun Yat-sen Mausoleum in Nanjing and his work won the second prize among more than 40 entries (Lai 2005). In 1928, he collaborated with Chao Shen and Poy G. Lee to design Nanjing Theater (now Shanghai Concert Hall). It adopts the neo-classicist approach, has excellent acoustics and has become one of the more important performing arts venue in Shanghai. In the 1930s, Fan designed a students' dormitory on the Jiaotong University campus, in addition to the Majestic Theater, Guangzhou government offices and many apartments (Fig. 3.25).

After the Communist took over the control of China in 1949, there was no architectural design works in Shanghai and nearby. Robert Fan and his wife fled to Hong Kong at the age of 56, with no money but a registered architect license to practice in Hong Kong, which he got in 1937. He designed theaters, churches, single family houses, department stores and apartments in this land. In 1954, the government allocated 10 acres land in Shatin to Chung Chi College, which was run

Fig. 3.25 Shanghai Concert Hall, 1930

by a group of ambitious immigrant educationists from the Chinese mainland. Robert Fan was appointed to plan the campus. Mountains are located to the north of the campus, roads to the west and Kowloon-Canton Railway and Tolo Harbor to the east. Declining to follow the conventional "majestic" campus plan with a central axis, Fan's design put the classrooms, students and teachers' halls on the hill and left the valley as a playground. Despite the tight budget, Fan's academic building and dormitory satisfied the functional requirements and avoided extra decoration. The building's design directly exposes its beams, columns and slabs, and its bay-and-column repetition expresses a rhythm. Local stone was used to build the walls, and the balcony and partition wall were decorated with hollowed concrete patterns. Gentle pitch was used on the roof. The building design of Chung Chi College was gradually handed over to Chau and Lee and other firms beginning in the late 1950s. However, the planning principles set out by Fan and the council were respected. Fan's design firm was located at Alexander House in Central, and lasted until the early 1970s (Fig. 3.26).[13]

Born in Shanghai, **Sü Gin Djih** (1906–1983) studied at Shanghai Baptist College and Theological Seminary during 1924–1926, after which he transferred to the University of Michigan in the U.S. and obtained a Bachelor's degree in 1929 and a Master's degree in 1930. Returning to Shanghai, Sü Gin Djih, Lei Wei-Paak and Yang Renjun jointly opened a design firm called Hsin Yieh Architects & Associates. They won first prize in the Nanjing museum design competition, and part of the building complex was completed in 1934. In 1949, Sü Gin Djih brought the firm to Hong Kong, and it continues to run to this day. Hsin Yieh designed a church in North Point, a sports facility at MacPherson Playground in Mongkok and a church school in Central. However, most of these buildings no longer exist. In 1933, Sü and colleagues launched the Chinese Architects' Society in Shanghai. In 1956, he and other architects founded the Hong Kong Society of Architects, with Sü acting as founding president. The society aimed "for the general advancement of Civil Architecture and for promoting and facilitating the acquirement of the

---

[13]About the Chung Chi College, see Gu (2011). Most description in this chapter is from the author's invesigation.

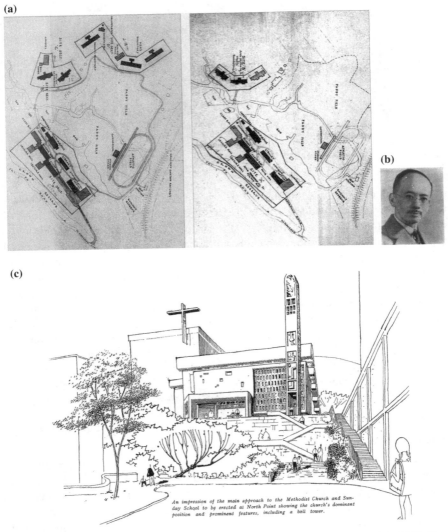

(a)

(b)

(c)

An impression of the main approach to the Methodist Church and Sunday School to be erected at North Point showing the church's dominant position and prominent features, including a bell tower.

Fig. 3.26 Robert Fan's design in Hong Kong. **a** Chung Chi College master plan, 1955. From D. Gu, 2011. **b** Mr. Robert Fan. **c** Methodist Church in North Point, 1960

knowledge of the various Arts and Sciences connected therewith (Figs. 3.27 and 3.28)."[14]

In 1964, Sü published a book entitled *Chinese Architecture: Past and Contemporary*, which depicted his generation's approach to "national form" and

---

[14]Quoted from Deed of Constitution, Hong Kong Society of Architects, September 3, 1956.

(a)

(b)

Fig. 3.27 Design works of Sü and Hsin Yieh Architects & Associates, Chung Chi College in Glenealy, The National Cash Register Building, New Asia College in Farm Road, completed 1951–1955

the "Chinese Renaissance." In that book, he made the following observation: "as an architect, I am very proud of our masters who had achieved such brilliant results in architecture throughout our history. To make a study of Chinese architecture comprehensive is our responsibility." Sü wrote about traditional Chinese architecture and relics in the book. In analyzing the "Chinese Renaissance," he reviewed the design works of his peers in Taiwan and China from the 1920s to 1950s. Some architects and scholars of his generation such as Liang Sicheng (Liang Szu-Ch'eng) investigated and wrote about traditional Chinese architecture through the Society for Research in Chinese Architecture. However, very few commented on their contemporary peers. Sü introduced the new development of the "Chinese national form" on the two sides of the Taiwan Strait. He praised the achievements of architects who had been exiled to Taiwan by the national government. He also criticized communist Chinese policies, but included no word about Hong Kong.

Fig. 3.28 Central Museum, 1st prize in design competition, partly completed, designed by Hsin Yieh Architects & Associates, 1934. From D. Su, 1964

His book remains a rare and valuable early work about architecture in Greater China (Sü 1964).

Luke Him Sau (1904–1992) was born and raised in Hong Kong. Educated deeply in Chinese tradition, he worked as an apprentice at a British architect's firm for four years. In 1927, he attended Year 3 (due to his intern experience) at the AA's School of Architecture in London. During his study in Britain, he met Bank of China Director Chang Kongquan, who invited him to work for the bank. Luke graduated in 1930 and traveled to Europe and the U.S. to investigate bank buildings (Fig. 3.29).

Fig. 3.29 Luke Him Sau's works in Shanghai, Bank of China, Bund, 1934

After returning to Shanghai and working as a building director at the Bank of China, Luke designed Kin Cheng Bank in Qingdao, and the building was completed in 1934. He cooperated with P & T to design the headquarters building of the Bank of China in the Bund, Shanghai, which was completed in 1936. The building design was influenced by Art Deco, and took the form of the Chinese word *Zhong* (middle). The gentle pitched roof is completed by a top and decorated with shallow *dougong* (brackets in Chinese wood building). A relief of Confucius is located above the entrance gate. During World War II, Luke withdrew along with the bank to Chongqing. In 1945, he returned to Shanghai and taught at St. John's University. He and other four British graduates, including Ta-hung Wong, Chen Chan-siang, Henry Wong (Huang Zuoshen) and Arthur Kun-Shuan Cheang, jointly opened a firm called Five United. Less than 20 years later, Luke participated in bank construction in several cities and designed apartment buildings to house bank staff members in Shanghai, Qingdao, Nanjing and Chongqing. After the war, the municipal government of Shanghai initiated Greater Shanghai Plan, Luke was a major mind in drawing the future blueprint for Shanghai. Eric Cumine, Robert Fan and other architects were also in the committee. However, with the changing political situation, Luke and Cumine did not finish the plan. Luke, Cumine and other committee members/commentators A.J. Brandt, Arthur Cheang and Robert Fan escaped from Shanghai and contributed their last career years to the colony. Ta-hung Wang went to Taiwan and became "father" of modernist architecture in the island.[15]

In 1949, at the age of 45 Luke gave up all of his belongings and traveled to Hong Kong to find opportunities (Fig. 3.30). After a year, encouraged by his friend Liang Sicheng, he returned to Shanghai and disappointed. He cooperated with P & T once again and designed the Bank of China building, which was completed in Central in 1951. This building was almost a "recycled" version of the Bank of China in Shanghai. In the 1950s, he participated in the building design of the So Uk public housing estate, Ritz Garden Apartment in North Point, chapel at Wah Yan College, Repulse Bay Apartment and several other housing and factory projects. Many clients were entrepreneurial businessmen who had escaped from communist-ruled Shanghai. They were also the main economic force in Hong Kong in the 1950s, and were naturally served by highly skilled designers from Shanghai such as Luke (Fig. 3.31).

In designing those classy apartment buildings, Luke adopted a typical plan involving one staircase/lift serving two units, and it was mirrored in the back of the building, with four units sharing a back stair. These four units formed a module that

---

[15]In 1946, the Shanghai government started to prepare the Greater Shanghai Plan, a signal of ambitious post-war construction. The Greater Shanghai Plan was prepared for three rounds and approved in the autumn of 1949. It can be compared with the Abercrombie's Hong Kong plan described in Chap. 1. The mayor of Shanghai and the director of Public Works led the work. Master planning committee of the Greater Shanghai Plan consisted of eight people, Luke Him Sau, Richard Paulick (professor of St. John's University), Eric Cumine, Zhang Jun Kuen, Huang Zuoxin (graduated from AA and Harvard, professor of St. John's University), A.J. Brandt (professor of St. John's University), Zhong Yaohua and Mei Guochao. See *Greater Shanghai Plan*, Shanghai: Tongji University Press, 2014.

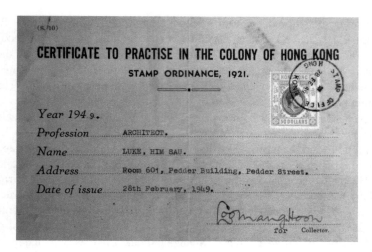

Fig. 3.30 Luke's certificate of practice in Hong Kong, 1949

repeated along a street. In the Ritz Garden Apartment, the unit modules form a long elevation along King's Road. A lane was left between the blocks and led people around to the back. Many residents of the Ritz Garden Apartment went on to become billionaires (Shen 2013) (Fig. 3.32).

Among commitments from Society of Jesus, Luke designed St. Ignatius Chapel of Wah Yan College, Kowloon in 1958. An English school run by the Chinese in 1924, Wah Yan College set up its Kowloon campus and moved to Ho Man Tin in 1952. School buildings were designed decently with simple geometry and plain materials. The vertical and horizontal sunshades and wide balcony feature the building. Following the context, Luke's design wraps the chapel with cloister, which is the same height as main hall. Breeze and landscape penetrate to the corridor. Activity rooms and clergies' dormitory are pact in the back side of chapel. Hollowed in circular and cross shape, the patterned blocks fill the span between columns. This hollowed pattern blocks appear as screen wall in the corridor. Hollowed pattern screen wall was popular in the 1950s and the technique was almost forgotten in the era of air-conditioning (Fig. 3.33).

Luke's drawings were archived by the HKU library in 2008. From those drawings and sketches, one can find his exploration of lighting, ventilation, topography and comfortable interior/furniture for human dimension. In 1968, street turmoil forced Luke to close his Hong Kong office and travel to the U.S., where he worked temporarily at a firm in New York City. In 1972, he returned to Hong Kong and retired. In his last 20 years, he lived a peaceful life and wrote more than 1,700 poems.[16]

---

[16]About the facts of Luke Him Sau, the author took reference of Wang (2007), Dension and Guang (2014); and Luke Him Sau Archive, University of Hong Kong Library.

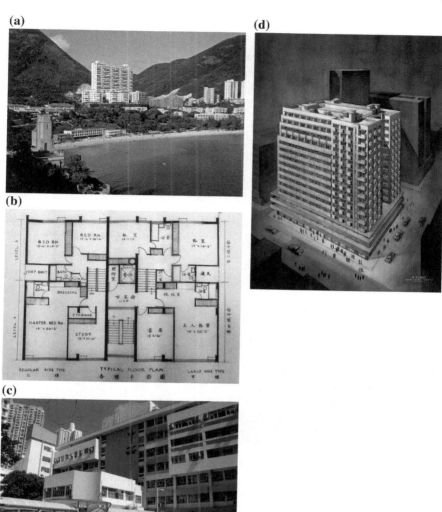

Fig. 3.31 Luke Him Sau's works in Hong Kong. **a** Repulse Bay Apartment, 1963. **b** Plan of Repulse Bay Apartment. **c** Our Lady of Maryknoll Hospital, Wong Tai Sin, 1958. **d** Apartment in Des Voeux Road, 1960s. (**a**), (**b**) and (**d**), courtesy of Luke Him Sau Archive, HKU Library

Chang Chao Kang (1922–1992) graduated from St. John's University in 1946 and went on to obtain a Master's degree at Illinois Institute of Technology, MIT and Harvard University in the U.S. He worked in New York City in the 1950s. In 1954, I.M. Pei invited Chang to Taiwan, and together they designed the campus of Tunghai University. The campus planning and building are highly regarded as the

(a) (b)

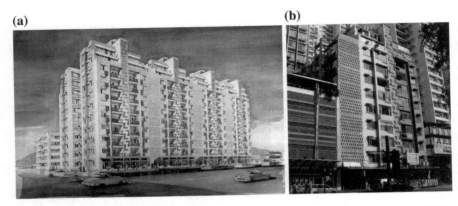

Fig. 3.32 Ritz Garden Apartment, King's Road, 1958. **a** Perspective drawing. Courtesy of Luke Him Sau Archive, HKU Library. **b** Part of the building shot in 2013. The central part was replaced by a taller apartment

(a) (b)

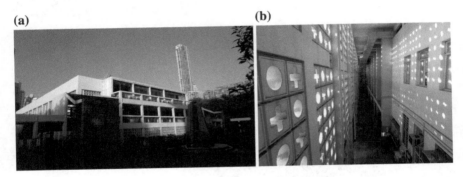

Fig. 3.33 Chapel at Wah Yan College, 1958. **a** The back side. **b** Corridor of chapel. The hollowed wall brings in breeze

seeds of modernit architecture in Taiwan, where Chang designed some academic buildings. In 1961–1965, Chang worked for Eric Cumine, and then traveled to the U.S. In the 1970s, Chang returned to Hong Kong again and taught part time at HKU. In 1978, he was one of the first Hong Kong architects to design and lecture in mainland China. He traveled over 70 times to various provinces in China and traced the Chinese traditions, which he crystalized in his 1987 book entitled *China: Tao in Architecture* (Chang and Blaser 1987).

Not every architect from China received such opportunities. In 1934, famous Guangzhou architect Chan Wing-Gee designed the first steel-structured high-rise building: the 17-storey Aiqun Building. In 1948, he was appointed director of construction in the Public Work Bureau of Guangzhou. In the 1950s, he escaped to Hong Kong and his life took a downturn. Although he worked for Chau and Lee for a short period, he did not continue to develop his career. When Luke Him Sau arrived in Hong Kong, he had to live under the care of his brother.[17]

The post-war Hong Kong architects pursued the spirit of functionalism. Various design forces and firms used their own methods to meet tasks and challenges. Designers were mainly educated overseas. The 1960s were formative years for the local educated architects.

The Shanghai architects were mostly born around the turn of the 20th century. They were typically the first generation of Chinese architects. More than half remained in mainland China after 1949. Although they were affected by political movements, Liang Sicheng, Yang Ting-po, Tong Jun, Chao Shen, Chen Zhi and other architects of the same generation enjoyed high esteem and prominent social status, especially after 1978. Their works have attracted great attention and in-depth study.[18]

One army exiled to Hong Kong was almost forgotten. When the soldiers arrived in Hong Kong, they were around 50 years old. In the 1950s, the situation in Hong Kong was different from that of Shanghai. The soldiers applied their experience and devoted themselves to the post-war reconstruction in Hong Kong. Against the abnormal turmoil of mainland China, Hong Kong fortunately received management, professional talent and money from Shanghai. Given the explosion of population pressure and the laissez-faire policy, Hong Kong architecture grew up in a special way.

With the passing away of this group of architects, most of the firms folded except for Hsin Yieh. Opened by Sü Gin Djih in 1930, Hsin Yieh has become an ordinary company name given its personnel and stockholder changes over time. The local Hong Kong architects did not have many encounters with the Chinese masters, whose influences were mainly reflected in the buildings they produced in the 1950s–1960s. Most of those buildings were demolished in the wave of property updating. In the 1950s, a design force from the Chinese mainland facilitated the construction of Hong Kong, and forcefully pushed back along the wave caused by the open-door policy in mainland China. This effort, which took place over a span of 30 years, is worth noting.

3.4 Injecting New Blood

HKU already had its Department of Engineering at the time of its founding in 1912, and it has trained a lot of engineers over time. In 1950, HKU opened its Department of Architecture, and the first group of students graduated in 1955. HKU graduates

---

[17]Chan Wing-Gee's situation in Hong Kong was told by Mr. Chung Wah-nan, meeting on 16 January 2013.

[18]About the first generation of Chinese architects, see Cody et al. (2011), Lai (2007), Zhang (1999).

such as Jackson Wong, Ng Chun Men and Andrew King-fun Lee started their own firms in the late 1950s and early 1960s. The early graduates benefited from the education of Professor Gordon Brown (1912–1962), the first dean. In 1944, Brown was appointed as Principle of the Architectural Association School of Architecture in London, at the age of 31. The school rose from 100 to 550 students with 50 teaching staff. He organized summer school in Sweden, Denmark and Italy, so that students could work under the guidence of foreign professors and architects. In 1948, he became the first Professor of Architecture at the University of Edinburgh. As the Govenor Sir Alexander W.G.H. Grantham (1899–1978) couple appreciated him, Brown was invited to Hong Kong.

When assuming the duty of school dean, he noted that regional architecture instead of international style formed due to the war, "any school in Asia must have a regional outlook and aim to train young architects who are able to meet the social, economic and technical requirements of their own people. I think it would be a loss of a very great opportunity if we were to become nothing more than a reflection of the architectureal schools of Europe and America ... The development of the student does not depend so much on the number of subjects which he is taught as on the qualities which already exists in the student and which are developed by his training. The most important of these qualities are sensitivity and imagination, logical thinking, technical sense, administrative ability and the power of self-expression."[19]

He was engaged in both education and practice. The other teachers were from the UK, Swedon, South Africa and other European countries, where modernist ideas were successfully spread after the war. The teachers taught Aalva Aalto's designs, and also invited modernist master Richard Neutra (1892–1970) to give lecture. Naturally, the HKU students' works in the 1950s reflected a popular modernist taste. Students were encouraged to work as apprentice in the design firm even in Year 1. Student learnt from the practicing architects and engineers and visited the site in Hong Kong and Macau. The architectural education at HKU basically followed the curriculum of Britain, but added with architectural history of China and Asia, and Chinese ink painting. The B.Arch degree was accredited by the RIBA in the 1960s (Fig. 3.34).[20]

Brown's successor, W.G. Gregory, was originally a teacher at HKU. Gregory also paid attention to teaching and practice. In the 1960s, he wrote many articles in *Architects and Builders of Far East*, a bi-monthly magazine published in Hong Kong. In these articles, he praised the architecture nurtured by local culture and conditions, such as City Hall, the American Consulate and Elizabeth Hospital; and buildings expressed by their structure, such as the works of Pier Luigi Nervi, Oscar Niemeyer and Kenzo Tange. He applauded the scale and courage of public housing

---

[19]"Professor Gordon Brown's notes on the new department of architecture", *Hongkong and Far East Builder*, October 1951, p. 13.

[20]The career of Professor Gordon Brown is written based on the news at *Hongkong and Far East Builder*, October 1951, p.13; HKIA 2006, chapter about Donald Liao; and conversation with Mr. Andrew Lee King-fun, 26 February 2016.

Fig. 3.34 Professor Gordon
Brown, 1912–1962, the
founder of architectural
education in Hong Kong

and thought it comparable with the best buildings in the world (such as Seagram in New York). He held that architecture was imbued with social arts and environmental science. Meanwhile, he criticized that many Hong Kong architects took building regulation as a design guideline: "They only know how to utilize the plot ratio and forget arts of design and comfortable functions. These can only be called 'Bylaw buildings', instead of architecture." These viewpoints were embodied in his teaching and leadership at HKU.[21] Gregory implemented a practical curriculum in education. Construction drawings took a considerable weight in assignment.

Professor Eric K.C. Lye (1934–2007) became the chair of the Department of Architecture at HKU in 1976 and stepped down in 1996. Malaysian Chinese in ethnicity, Lye graduated from Princeton University and worked in the U.S. and Canada. From 1970 to 1976, he was the architectural department chair at the University of Manitoba in Canada. After he arrived at HKU, he integrated American education into the purely British system. He gave priority to conceptual design and thought of his roots, as he confessed "for some time I perceived 'culture' as something solely embedded in English literature. As a consequence I did not have the urge to engage myself in any serious discussion with others regarding our own culture except when it concerned/touched upon the Taoist rituals, which our parents performed and in which we dutifully took part. We came away, not so much mystified by, as ignorant of our roots: our identity still remained fuzzy (Lye 2006, p. 11)."

Although he did not personally understand Chinese language, Lye advocated local culture and vernacular architecture. In the 1980s, HKU became a bridge between the architectural circles of the two sides of the Taiwan Strait. It produced over 20 architectural graduates in the 1950s, a number that increased to 30–40 in the 1970s. Since the 1980s, more than 70 students have graduated with professional degrees each year. Architecture education benefits from neighboring disciplines such as urban planning, urban design, landscape architecture and conservation.

---

[21]Words of W.H. Gregory are concluded from *Far East Architect & Builder* (Editor: A.G. Barnett), 1963: 65.

HKU provides the benchmark of architectural education in Hong Kong. Many professionals in government and the design industry come from HKU.[22]

In 1988, City Polytechnic opened its higher diploma course in architectural studies. Its mission was to train technical personnel at the sub-degree level. In 1994, City Polytechnic was renamed City University of Hong Kong. In 2000, its architectural course became an associate degree program. The same year, CityU collaborated with Queensland University of Technology of Australia to run a degree course. In 2005, CityU opened its Bachelor's degree program in architectural studies, which the government financially supported in 2012. Over the past 25 years, CityU has trained more than 2,000 architectural graduates to work in design, construction, management and government. Its architectural program is nestled in the College of Science and Engineering, and emphasizes technology and practice.

In 1991, CUHK opened its Department of Architecture under the Faculty of Social Science. Its first cohort of students graduated in 1998. In 2012, the School of Architecture moved into a new purpose-built building. It is currently the only architectural school to have its own home building in Hong Kong. CUHK education pays attention to both the design and research sides, such as sustainable architecture, heritage preservation and tectonic study. These sides both relate to the faculty's research interests.

Some old British and French colonies do not have architectural education even today. Urban construction is driven by the tourism and booming economy. However, the designers come or are trained from the suzerain or neighboring countries.[23] HKU's opening of architectural course in 1950 is epochal for this city. The year 1950 saw sprawling shantytowns and rugged refugees, however, aurora appeared in the HKU campus of Mid-level. The architectural design and thinking was able to be systematically forwarded from generation to generation.

Although the teachers at Hong Kong's higher education institutes come from locations around the world, the majority of students are recruited from the local pool. Architectural education operates between "internationalized" and "localized" tendencies. Students are able to absorb information from the various sides. However, the schools find it difficult to form their own areas of excellence. Moreover, professional education is subject to the accreditation of professional bodies and the university's general guide to higher education. These frames make all of the architectural schools work in largely the same way. In addition to the aforementioned schools, other institutes provide various levels of architectural education. For example, HKU's School of Professional and Continuing Education

---

[22]About the education of HKU, see part of K C Lye from Hong Kong Institute of Architects (2006). The other materials are from the author's investigation. The teaching of Aalva Aalto method and Richard Neutra was told by Mr. Andrew Lee King-fun, 26 February 2016.

[23]See Taylor and Conner (2014). The book describes how the architectural design helped the development of Pacific Ocean nations from European colony to modern tourist paradise. Same as a colonized island, Hong Kong's development path was completely different, education played a key role in Hong Kong's transition and progress.

runs a higher diploma program in architecture. Students can obtain a top-up degree via collaboration with universities overseas. Chu Hai College and Hong Kong Design Institute are currently running Bachelor's degree, higher diploma and/or top-up degree programs. These programs prepare students at different levels to enter the building industry in Hong Kong.

3.5 Conclusion: Filling the Gap in the Post-War Reconstruction

For the colony, the 1950s was chaotic, tough but with hope. Hong Kong survived with the immigrant labors and talents. The existing and newly arrived architects settled in the territory and benefited with commitments from the public and private sectors. The architects from Shanghai left their motherland and worked in a strange environment. They designed relatively smaller projects, compared with their peers in China, and contributed to the field uniquely and adaptively in the port city. The modern Chinese history records a splitting of the country in different governance. The separation with the Chinese mainland and physical distance with Britain allow Hong Kong to walk a unique way and set up its paradigm both in architectural practice and education, which accumulated energy for its heyday decades later.

The Bank of China building stood shoulder to shoulder with the Cathy Building (Peace Hotel) at the junction of Bund and Nanjing Road in Shanghai. Along the road to the west, you will see Shanghai Concert Hall (Nanking Theater) and Majestic Theater, designed in the 1930s. These performance buildings exhibit the glamorous art deco, modern and classical styles of the years between the wars. They are symbols of Shanghai's glorious past. I passed by the Bund numerous times and was fascinated by these precedent masterpieces, especially after I became engaged in building design, but never thought that the designers had such a deep association with Hong Kong. The designer of Bank of China, Luke Him Sau, worked at its headquarters in 1946 and lived in the Denis Apartment of Nanking Road, which was designed by his friend Eric Cumine in 1923. The municipal government appointed Luke and Cumine as the main planners for the Greater Shanghai Plan. On weekdays after 5 p.m., Luke left the bank office and walked down Nanking Road to the Shanghai Public Works Department on Hankow Road, a walking journey of around 10 min. This part of downtown Shanghai was preserved after 1990 and has undergone little alteration. What did he see and think about during that after-work walk? Although Luke's name was signed first in the Greater Shanghai Plan, he did not finish the planning work. He and several other committee members escaped to Hong Kong when the cannon of the People's Liberation Army took aim at Suzhou Creek. Luke finally left Shanghai in 1950. In the following 40 and 50 years, did he or Cumine ever return?

In 2006, I listened to a Hong Kong University PhD student discuss her study of a Chinese architects army "branch" exiled in Hong Kong. Details of the architects' careers gradually became known through publications. Cumine's career in Shanghai and Hong Kong was legendary. His office designed many impressive buildings in Hong Kong and Macau. However, his two books mentioned little about his architecture and included mostly "trivial" folklore about Hong Kong. The drawings in the Buildings Department indicate that Cumine had many partners and directors in his firm. Where are his colleagues now? Where are his office documents and sketches?

One member of this exiled army was Mr. Chang Chao-kang, who graduated from St. John's University of Shanghai in 1946. He went on to study at Harvard University and helped I.M. Pei to design the university campus in Taiwan in the 1950s while travelling frequently to and from Hong Kong and the U.S. I met Chang three times in 1989. He spoke fluent English, Putonghua, Cantonese and Shanghainese. My professors in Shanghai were schoolmates of his. A talkative man, Chang spoke with me in Shanghainese about his friendships with his schoolmates in Shanghai, his cooperation with Pei and the people of Hong Kong. Walking gently with a stick, he insisted on sending me back via taxi after a party on Pokfulam Road. Unfortunately, the party would be my last meeting with Chang. Twenty-three years after his death, I found and read his book on Chinese architecture, published by a German publishing house in 1987.

At the time, Chang occasionally taught at Hong Kong University, where Professor Lye was serving as a department head. In some institutions, some department heads or "key" professors possess personal charisma and supreme power and command authority and respect in both the academic and professional spheres. Lye was such a head and professor. In 1985, he visited Shanghai, and I was among the people who met with him. In 1989, I had several occasions to talk and listen to his philosophy. He puffed on a thick cigar while talking in English across the big table in his office, exuding charisma and intensifying his myth. However, Lye produced few written works. We can track his ideas only through other people's memoirs and his commentary article on Macau architect Manual Vincente.

References

Chang, C. K., & Blaser, W. (1987). *China: Tao in architecture*. Basel, Boston: Birkhauser Verlag.

Cheng, J. Y. S. (Ed.). (1990). *The other Hong Kong report*. Hong Kong: Chinese University Press.

Cumine, E. (1981). *Hong Kong: ways & byways—A miscellany of trivia*. Hong Kong: Belongers Publications.

Cody, J. W., Steinhardt, N. S., & Atkin, T. (Eds.). (2011). *Chinese architecture and the Beaux-Arts*. Honolulu: University of Hawaii Press.

Denison, E., & Guang, Y. R. (2014). *Luke Him Sau, architect: China's missing modern*. Chichester, West Sussex: Wiley.

Gu, D. (Ed.). (2011). *Chung Chi original campus architecture—Hong Kong Chinese architect's practice of modern architecture*. Chung Chi College. Hong Kong: The Chinese University of Hong Kong.

Hong Kong Institute of Architects. (2006). *Deeply loving architecture—Dialogue with 15 senior architects in Hong Kong*. Hong Kong: Hong Kong Institute of Architects. 香港建筑师学会. (2006). 热恋建筑 -与拾伍香港资深建筑师的对话. 香港建筑师学会出版.

Hong Kong Society of Architects. (1956). *Deed of constitution*. Hong Kong: Hong Kong Society of Architects. September 3 1956.

Kinoshita, J. H. (2005). *From Slocan to Hong Kong—An architect's journey*. Victoria, BC.: Trafford Publishing.

Kwan, Y. Y. (2015). *The trajectory of office design in central, Hong Kong by the Palmer & Turner (P&T Group)*. Bachelor Degree thesis, City University of Hong Kong.

Lai, D. (2005). Searching for a modern Chinese monument—The design of the Sun Yat-sen Mausoleum in Nanjing. *Journal of the Society of Architectural Historian, 64*(1), 22–55.

Lai, D. (2007). *Study on the modern history of Chinese architecture*. Beijing: Tsinghua University Press. 赖德霖 (2007). 中国近代建筑史研究. 北京: 清华大学出版社.

Lye, E. K. C. (2006). *Manuel Vicente: Caressing trivia*. Hong Kong: MCCM Creations.

Ng, K. C., Chu, S. C. H. (2007). Story of the first generation of Chinese architects in Hong Kong. Hong Kong: Hong Kong Economic Journal Press. 吴启聪, 朱卓雄 (2007). 建闻筑绩 - 香港第一代华人建筑师的故事. 香港: 经济日报出版社.

P & T Group. (1998). *P & T group*. Hong Kong: Pace Publishing Ltd.

Shanghai Institute of Urban Planning and Research. (2014). *Greater Shanghai plan (1946-1950)*. Shanghai: Tongji University Press. 上海城市规划设计研究院编. (2014). 大上海计划. 上海: 同济大学出版社.

Shen, X. C. (2013, December 28). Ritz Garden, a good Fengshui place. *Apple Daily* (Hong Kong), D18. 沈西城 (2013). 丽池风水地. 香港 苹果日报.

Sü, G. D. (1964). *Chinese architecture: past and contemporary*. Hong Kong: Sin Poh Amalgamated (H.K.) Limited.

Talyor, J., & Conner, J. (2014). *Architecture in the South Pacific—The Ocean of Islands*. Honolulu: University of Hawaii Press.

Tan, Z., & Xue, C. Q. L. (2014). Walking as a planned activity—Elevated pedestrian network and urban design regulation in Hong Kong. *Journal of Urban Design, 19*(5), 722–744.

W. Szeto & Partners Architects and Engineers (1975). *Selected works*. Hong Kong: W. Szeto & Partners Architects and Engineers.

Wang, H. (2007). Interviewing Mr. Luke Him Sau's descendants in Hong Kong: A case study of a pioneer modern Chinese architect. In *Proceedings of the International Conference on Chinese Architectural History*. Shanghai: Tongji University. 王浩娱 (2007). 陆谦受后人访问记 – 中国现代建筑师案例研究. 中国建筑史国际会议论文集. 上海:同济大学建筑学院.

Wang, H. (2011). Chinese migrant architects in Hong Kong: 1948-1955. In Gu, D. (Ed.), *Chung Chi original campus architecture—Hong Kong Chinese architect's practice of modern architecture* (pp. 48–55). Hong Kong: Chung Chi College, The Chinese University of Hong Kong.

Zhang, F. (Ed.). (1999). *Study and preservation of Chinese modern architecture*. Beijing: Tsinghua University Press. 张复合主编 (1999). 中国近代建筑研究与保护. 北京: 清华大学出版社.

Chapter 4
Government Control, Building Regulations and Their Implications

Building regulations and government control have always constrained and influenced the development of Hong Kong architecture. The government holds most of the land in Hong Kong (Crown hold), except for the villages in the New Territories and some special areas. In the mid-nineteenth century, the government divided the land on Hong Kong Island and leased it to interested people. Plots of land were quickly leased at every auction. The scarcity of land has always frustrated the territory and strict land and construction control have long been essential. Building regulations and control, as an "intangible hand", powerfully shape the urban architecture in the territory. Any discussion of Hong Kong architecture needs to be conducted in the context of the evolution of building control and regulation to provide a comprehensive picture of its formation and mechanism.[1]

4.1 The Origin of Building Control in Hong Kong

In the nineteenth century, British and European colonists built villas on Victoria Peak, whereas Chinese residents were confined to the foot of the hill, the so-called Tai Ping Shan area. The continuous influx of refugees stimulated the endless sprawling of squatter sheds. In 1882, Osbert Chadwick, a British hygiene engineer invited by the Hong Kong government to investigate Hong Kong, pointed out the appalling hygiene conditions of the Chinese settlement. Chadwick advised the government to control the building density and leave space between buildings to provide necessary ventilation. In 1883, the government issued a Public Health Ordinance, which was amended in 1887 to include back yard open spaces.

---

[1]The description in this chapter is partly referenced from a working paper by Han Zou and Charlie Xue, Shaping the city with an "intangible hand"—a review of the building control system of Hong Kong. Working paper at City University of Hong Kong, 2014.

© Springer Science+Business Media Singapore 2016
C.Q.L. Xue, *Hong Kong Architecture 1945–2015*,
DOI 10.1007/978-981-10-1004-0_4

Fig. 4.1 Buildings of various stages in the 20th century mix in the Tai Ping Shan area, Hong Kong Island

Buildings could be occupied only after obtaining a permit from the public health authority, in an attempt to avoid epidemics such as cholera.

The government enacted the first Building Ordinance in 1889. An amendment of 1901 stated that buildings should be no higher than four stories and that the open space at the back of buildings should be at least eight feet wide. This space was called the service lane, which was later augmented to three meters wide when metric system was used. Residential houses at the time used bricks as the load bearing material. The amendment of the ordinance stated that the lower part should use high-quality bricks and only the top floor could use blue bricks of lower quality. In 1903, a public health and building ordinance was issued, which was valid for the next 30 years. Few buildings from the early twentieth century are still in existence. However, the widths of roads and land plots were not altered. For example, the Queen's Road and roads perpendicular to it, leading to the hill and old district of Wan Chai, are all products of the early twentieth century (Fig. 4.1).[2]

During the twentieth century, Hong Kong occasionally received refugees. The Building and Hygiene Ordinance was difficult to implement in full. The Building Ordinance of 1935 raised the requirements for day-lighting, ventilation and fire proofing. This ordinance was followed until 1955. In the 1930s, Hong Kong was geared towards a busy port city. Public transportation reached to the various corners of the city. Houses for low-income residents were built in Kowloon Peninsula. From Sai Wan to Wanchai, most buildings along the main streets were four-story high. However, all building activities were halted at the end of 1941, when Japanese troops invaded Hong Kong.

---

[2]For further details on the role of British hygiene engineers in Hong Kong, see Xue et al. 2012.

4.2 Control of Density

Many people fled from Hong Kong during the Pacific War and the population was only 600,000 by the time it ended in 1945. By 1950, it had surged to three million. The newly arrived refugees needed housing and the city needed to accommodate more people. In 1955, the Buildings Ordinance was amended significantly, relaxing the building height control. Previously, the height of the buildings along a street could not exceed 1.25 times the street width and could be no higher than 35 feet, which meant that buildings were only two or three stories. The revision of the ordinance extended the maximum building height to three times the street width. The ordinance also controlled the volume of buildings, for instance, the site's area x the street's width x a coefficient (which could be two, three or more). In urban areas, buildings had to grow upwards toward the sky. In the 1950s, many private buildings were built to the maximum volume allowed. Many private buildings built between 1958 and 1961 that still exist in To Kwa Wan, Tai Kok Tsui and Sham Shui Po were the products of the 1955 Buildings Ordinance. They can be described as "volumetric". These buildings did not have lifts and some were nine floors high, or even 10 or 11, given the illegal structures added on top. Now they are generally referred to as *Tong Lou* or tenement houses.[3] In Hong Kong, where vernacular architecture with artistic value is relatively scarce, *Tong Lou* is considered to have its own distinctive indigenous characteristics (Fig. 4.2).[4]

The Buildings Ordinance is Chapter 123 of the Laws of Hong Kong. The Buildings Ordinance that was revised and implemented in 1955 consisted of three regulations: "Building (Administration) Regulations," "Building (Construction) Regulations" and "Building (Planning) Regulations," the aim of which was to provide instructions for design, management and construction activities. Building (Planning) Regulations direct how to plan and design. Later, the ordinance included regulations on private streets and roads, garbage rooms, sanitary equipment standards, toilets, ventilation systems, energy efficiency, demolition and inspection repair, etc. The revision of the Buildings Ordinance in 1955 can be regarded as a milestone in the management of Hong Kong development and construction.

Meanwhile, the government began to promulgate "Practice Notes for Authorized Persons" (PNAPs). Due to the complexity of structural technology, "authorized persons" such as architects and surveyors could not handle the job unaided. The first structural engineer was registered in 1970. In 1980, the "Practice Notes" were extended to "Practice Notes for Authorized Persons and Registered Structural Engineers." The authorities produced a timely update for a variety of circumstances. These notes were intended to become regulations or laws following the approval of

---

[3]According to the Buildings Regulations (Standards of Sanitary Fitments, Plumbing, Drainage and Toilets), *Tang Lou* (tenement house) refers to any building in which part of any living room is intended or adapted for more than one tenant or sub-tenant. April 1999.
[4]For more about Tang Lou, see Chan (2005).

Fig. 4.2 Buildings following 1955 regulations in Hung Hom

the Legislative Council. Therefore, PNAPs guide the design and sometimes act as new trend setter.

A building's volume in the 1955 Building Ordinance was based on the site area multiplied by the height, which meant the streets were filled with buildings. The revised "Architecture (Planning) Regulations" of 1964 introduced concepts such as "site coverage," "plot ratio" and "gross floor area." These indicators are related to residential and non-residential buildings. The plot ratio is related to the number of streets on which the site is located. There are three kinds of sites: facing one street, two streets or three streets. Sites facing three streets reach the maximum plot ratio. The situation is complicated for urban blocks, as sites may be irregular or triangular. Here "street" refers to roads that are more than 4.5 m in width and can be used by fire engines.

Under the dual conditions of the plot ratio and site coverage, it is acceptable for a building less than 15 m high to cover 100 % of a site, whereas for buildings above 15 m, the volume is determined as a percentage. For residential or office towers, there is a provision for "open space" (Buildings Department 1998). These concepts comprehensively describe, regulate and control developers' three-dimensional development of a piece of land. The concepts are not only still in use, but are spreading to mainland China and have become important indicators for controlling

Fig. 4.3 Podium and towers above. Courtesy of Mr. Raymond Wong

land development. The introduction of density control resulted from the population explosion and residents' increasing housing requirements. Office and residential buildings have risen to 20 floors and above, although the development of concrete and steel structures means that the buildings' growth toward the sky is not a problem. In addition, because of this provision, the shops along a street are connected, but three floors above, the tower becomes slender, like the candle holders on a birthday cake. This is particularly obvious in the properties above and abut the MTR stations, developed mainly since the 1990s (Fig. 4.3).

In Hong Kong Island, the plot ratio for residential development can reach 1:10, in Kowloon, 1:7.5. As a result, a lot of public and private housing estates have a density of 1,000–1,600 units per hectare. The average household size in Hong Kong is three people. Therefore, 3,000–4,500 people live in a land plot of one hectare. In the inner city London, the residential density can reach 350 homes which is called "super density" and not recommended. In the subdivision of most US states, a hectare may be lived by eight to 16 families.[5] In several urban districts, residential density is over 50,000 per km^2 in 2013.[6]

Royal Peninsula in Hung Hom, developed by Sun Hong Kai and designed by Wong Tung & Partners, may be read as an example of such "super density" in Hong Kong. Completed in 2001, the estate has five blocks and 1,669 units, among which one and two-bedroom account for over 80 %. In a land plot of 1.5 ha, five blocks ranging from 43–47 stories stand together with club house, swimming pool, garden and internal road for vehicle drop off. More than 300 parking lots are located in basement. A chunk of land is built for hostel for moderately mentally handicapped and sheltered workshop so that the developer was awarded for building more units. The building blocks divide the garden into two parts. The north part is

---

[5]For the density in London, see a report jointly written by HTA 2015. For the density in the United States, it is the author's experiences for most of the subdivisions in the Mid-west states.

[6]Density varies and increases in many urban areas of Hong Kong. The current number is available from the website of Planning Department, Hong Kong Government. See www.pland.gov.hk.

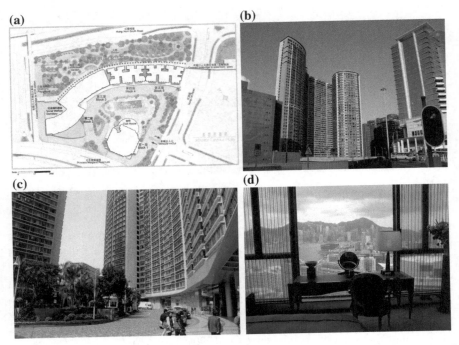

Fig. 4.4 Royal Peninsula, Hung Hom. **a** Master plan, the north side garden is for public use and passage to the other buildings. **b** The 47-storey high residential towers standing together with nearby buildings. **c** Internal circulation road of the estate. **d** Penthouse. Drawn by Zang Peng

used by public, making the real garden for residents even smaller. In such a tiny common area, the residents' association runs activities like Christmas party, new year's banquet, children's class, sport match and collection of recycled materials, almost in every week (Fig. 4.4).[7]

In 1998, the government issued a new regulation, relaxing the podium height to 20 m if there is a public transport terminus or the increase in podium height would give a better aesthetic or environmental effect.[8] Entering the 21st century, the voice of criticizing the "screen wall" building was high in the society. Many high-rise estate developments form continuous high wall to block the breeze in districts and produce heat islands. To break the "screen wall", the government issued regulations in 2011 to improve the environmental quality in three aspects. (1) Building separation. For building's length over 60 m, 20 % permeability should be allowed. For a bigger site and taller building, such a permeability can be up to 33.3 %. (2) Building set back. No part of the building, up to a level of 15 m above the street

---

[7]The material of Royal Peninsula is from the author's investigation from 2001 to 2015, and also from the "Particulars and conditions of sale", made on 18 March 1996 by Land's Department, Hong Kong government.

[8]Practice Note 223, 1998.

level, shall be within 7.5 m from the centreline of the street. This means that a street should normally be 15 m wide or above. For building with a communal podium garden, no part of the first 15 m shall protrude maximum 45° inclined plane from the boundary line of opposite site. This will prevent the street from too enclosed effect. (3) Site coverage of greenery. For different size of site area, the greenery coverage should reach 10–30 %. Of course, garden on the podium roof is also counted.[9]

4.3   The Annoyance of Small Areas

In studies of high-rise buildings, the international community generally agrees that the standard floor area of 1,500–2,000 m^2 is the most economical and maintains maximum efficiency. In the old districts of Hong Kong, due to the past land division, many high-rise residential or office buildings have a standard floor area of only 200–300 m^2, while stairs, elevators, toilets and piping ducts occupy a considerable area (about 50–60 m^2). To save space, Hong Kong architects in the 1960s invented the scissors staircase, in which one shaft accommodates two intersecting fire-fighting stairs separated by a wall. People on the same floor can independently use the two sets of stairs to go up and down without meeting each other. Later, scissor stairs appeared in a large number of residential buildings with cross plans. In 2008, a scissor staircase was displayed at the Venice Architecture Biennale as a characteristic of Hong Kong architecture (Fig. 4.5).

When setting the plot ratio, the government also calculated the shadows that buildings cast on the street. This legislation was derived from Manhattan in New York City in 1916, in the hope that the canyon-like streets formed by high-rise buildings would still receive sunshine; the shaded area on the street cannot exceed 62 % of the street area. This restriction was added to the Building Regulations in 1969. A control line was drawn at an angle of 76° from the center to the side of the street and all buildings had to be under the control line. Between 1964 and 1970, eight 14-floor buildings were built on the Mandarin Estate, Ferry Street, Jordan. The tops of the buildings appear cone-shaped with an angle of 76°, designed in accordance with this legislation. In 1979, the Hong Kong and Shanghai Banking Corporation held an invited competition to design its new headquarters (see Chap. 7). All of the submitted proposals included computations for the street shadow. As it is not cold in Hong Kong and the streets should accommodate a greater floor area, the regulation was abandoned in 1987. In Macau, the government introduced the same street shadow regulation in 1980, but re-examined the rationale behind it in 2014, which aroused protests from the public. Most voices expressed

---

[9]Practice Note for Authorized Persons, Registered Structural Engineers and Registered Geotechnical Engineers, APP-152. 2011. See (Hong Kong Government 2011).

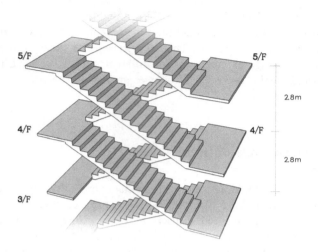

Fig. 4.5 "Scissor" staircase saves floor area of stair shaft in a typical floor. Drawn by Zang Peng

(a)   **(b)**

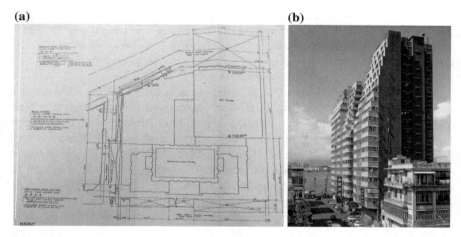

Fig. 4.6 Street shadow control. **a** Residential building in Causeway Bay. From HK Government archive. **b** Design drawing for the HSBC design competition, street shadow calculation is included. Courtesy of HSBC Asia and Pacific Archives

the hope that Macau would not follow the lead of Hong Kong and let the streets become dark canyons (Fig. 4.6).[10]

---

[10]Like Hong Kong, Macau suffers from a small territory area and insufficient construction land. In 2004, the government wanted to reconsider the street shadow regulation, but it was strongly protected by the public; see the *Macau Daily*, 4 Sep 2014. http://www.macaodaily.com/html/2014-09/04/content_932665.htm. Accessed 1 Dec 2014.

In 1965, the government issued a planning outline for the whole territory: the first part comprised the Hong Kong planning standards and guidelines and the second part the regional development strategies. The planning standards and guidelines emphasized that the Building Regulations and Building (Planning) Regulations were the only legal regulatory documents for high-density development. The regulations of 1967 contained additional regulations for the New Territories. By the early 1970s, the building control system in operation today had been substantially completed. The Building (Planning) Regulations formulated the allowed plot ratio and site coverage of residential and non-residential buildings with different heights. The maximum plot ratio of commercial buildings reached 1:15. A built project's plot ratio today does not depend entirely on the Building Regulations. The developmental potential of a project is subject to three provisions: the land lease conditions issued by the Lands Department, which overrides other regulations; the Outlined Zoning Plan formulated by the Town Planning Board, which is stricter than the Building Regulations; and the Building Regulations. When the Lands Department is writing the lease condition, it will take reference of the Outlined Zoning Plan. And the zoning plan will not violate the building regulations.

In the 1950s and 60s, many of the private apartments built in Causeway Bay, Repulse Bay and Mid-Levels were of the slab type with natural ventilation, in which two or three households shared a staircase. In the late 1970s, to fit more residential buildings on a limited piece of land, the cross-shaped plane was invented and adopted for both public and private housing, including Mei Foo Sun Chuen in 1979 and Taikoo Shing, Island East and City One, Sha Tin in the 1980s. When residential buildings reached 30, 50, 70 or even 80 floors, the cross-shaped plane in the overall layout appeared to be a point. To create as many residential units as possible in a limited site area, architects and developers tended to place a few cross-shaped buildings together, left only a narrow gap, so that the buildings created a screen or arranged them independently. The above-mentioned scissor stairs not only met the fire safety requirements for two sets of stairs, but also saved space. They were extensively used in cross-shaped planes in which elevators, stair shafts, meter boxes and pipe ducts occupied the center and the four wings housed four or eight apartment units. In the case of eight units, each wing contained two units. The allowed minimum distance between the two units (2.3 m) enabled the kitchen window to be opened onto this "open space." However, in reality, the smell from one kitchen often affected the neighborhood (Fig. 4.7).

According to PNAP 68 of 1980, the area of a bay window does not count as part of the floor area when calculating the site coverage and plot ratio. To be exempted from the calculation, bay windows must meet the following conditions: the bay should protrude from the exterior wall by less than 500 mm, rise more than 500 mm above the floor and finish at least 500 mm below the ceiling. The principle of this regulation is to encourage a greater area of natural lighting. Over the following 10–20 years, new private residential buildings had only bay windows, while balconies disappeared. Although the bay window is exempted from the calculation of the plot ratio and site coverage, it is included in the category of *shiyong mianji*

(a) **(b)**

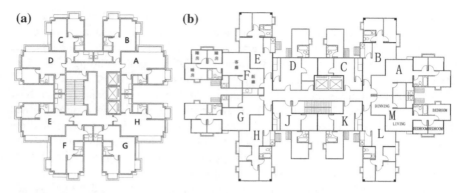

Fig. 4.7 Typical floor plans of private housing, small unit type in the 1980s. Drawn by Zang Peng. **a** Gold Lion Garden, Tai Wai, 1987. **b** Grandway Garden, Tai Wai, 1989

Fig. 4.8 Cantilevered bay window for exemption of gross floor area calculation

(literally usable area). The English version of the term *shiyong mianji* is salable area, which includes the area of the interior and exterior walls and structural walls. The floor area allocated to every household includes the public corridors, lobbies, clubs, machine rooms, etc. (Fig. 4.8).

In 2001, the Planning Department, Buildings Department and Environmental Protection Department jointly issued a PNAP to encourage the design of comfortable living areas. The "green terrace" and the "working platform," a total of approximately 2.24 m², can be exempted from the calculation of the site coverage and plot ratio. From 2001 onward, small or narrow balconies, with an area of up to 2.24 m², mushroomed in many new private residences. A 2.24 m² balcony looks tiny and strange, compared with a so-called luxury apartment of 1,000 ft² (which has a usable area of about 700 ft²). These incentives to encourage comfortable living have been used by developers to build larger floor areas and to gain more commercial profit, while the property price and the actual usable area for residents are disproportionate. By 2010, the public was criticizing these buildings as *fashuilou* (inflated buildings), leading the government to once again tighten these measures in 2011. The result is that balcony disappears from residential units again.

4.4 Conclusion: Making High-Density Reasonable and Effective

From 1989 to 1995, the government improved and refined three regulations: the Means of Access, the Means of Escape and Fire Resisting Construction. These regulations provide strict conditions for the standard floor design of high-rise office and residential buildings. For instance, in the standard floor of an office building, the distance between the outer wall and the core tube cannot be too long due to the limit on the distance to an escape exit (15 m). Of course, it will not be too short either, as too short a distance would be uneconomical. In the old districts of Hong Kong, the length of a building's side is commonly 20 m or less. In a 300–400 m^2 plot (a typical land sale division in the nineteenth century), the standard floor is only 150–200 m^2. After deducting the area of two fire-fighting stairs, two elevators and toilets, some buildings have a usable area of only 100 m^2, just enough for a small company or a "mini" clinic (Fig. 4.9).

The Methodist Church originally built in Wan Chai in the 1930s with a Chinese-style pavilion occupied a 486 m^2 triangular plot formed by three surrounding streets. Such a tiny piece of land is too small for even a garden in the city, but after the church's demolition it was occupied by a 23-storey building with an area 15 times the area of the plot. A 200–300 seat assembly hall, a church with a balcony and a small chapel respectively occupy the basement, first and second floor. An axis linking the triangle's tip with the bottom helps to lay out the stairs and other key components. The church occupies a circular space in the center of the triangle and the circle is tangential to the three sides of the triangle. The staircases and elevators through which people can reach the building's 4–23 floors are at the bottom of the triangle. A bell tower similar to the original church is placed at the triangle's tip and is lower in the front than the rear. The architects attempted to arrange the plan perfectly and to enrich the facade. This building epitomizes numerous small skyscrapers in Hong Kong.

In 1997, the government launched barrier-free guidelines in a move to generate social goodwill. The purpose of building regulations is to protect users' safety and

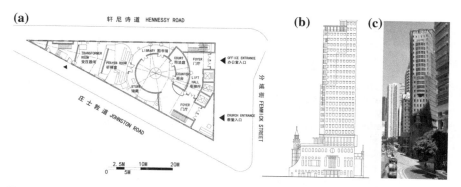

Fig. 4.9 Methodist Church in Wan Chai, 1996. **a** Plan **b** Elevation **c** View in the street. Drawn by Zang Peng

health and to restrict intemperate development that might endanger public safety. With the land shortage in Hong Kong, many design companies have become "experts" on researching building regulations, boundary conditions or possible loopholes. W.G. Gregory, a professor and head of the Department of Architecture at the University of Hong Kong, wrote a number of magazine articles in the 1960s, criticizing the lack of innovation and tendency to create larger floor areas through the study of regulations.[11]

However, the consequences can be very serious if designs do not reach the maximum plot ratio or the architect violates the contract. One well-known example is the case of Eric Cumine, who was sued by his client Wharf Properties Ltd. in the late 1980s over the Harbor City project. The client argued that the architect's failure to maximize the allowed plot ratio and to supervise construction to the best of his abilities caused them to lose interest on loans and the amount of rental income that the owners could generate. They asked the architect to compensate their related financial losses (hundreds of millions of HK dollars). The lawsuit was protracted over a decade and the architect employed a British Queen's Counsel to fight his case. Finally, the architect gained a tragic victory, as he also lost his assets and had to close his firm.[12] Construction management is also subject to government laws. Those who violate the law may find themselves embroiled in a lawsuit. For example, the owner, architects and engineers involved in the excavation of the basement in the former Hong Kong Chief Secretary for Administration Henry Tang's house in Kowloon Tong were subject to court interrogation for failing to declare the work to the Buildings Department (Fig. 4.10).[13]

Before the Pacific War, the Hong Kong government built few buildings. Public investment in housing and building only began after 1950. The Building Regulations were repeatedly updated to regulate the development of private houses. The construction of public buildings and housing estates funded by the government was executed and supervised by the internal organizations of the Housing Department and the Architectural Services Department. Of course, whether for private or public housing, the requirements for ventilation, lighting, fire-fighting and others followed the same principles.

---

[11]For further discussion of Gregory, see *Far East Architect & Builder* (Editor: A.G. Barnett), 1963–1965.

[12]For more details on Wharf Properties Ltd.'s lawsuit against Eric Cumine, see Wu Qicong and Zhu Zhuoxiong, Jianwen zuji: Xianggang diyidai huaren jianzhushi de gushi (Hong Kong: Jingji ribao chubanshe, 2007); the title of the lawsuit was Wharf Properties Ltd. versus Eric Cumine Associates (1991) 52 BLR 1, see online http://www.aeberli.com/uploads/articles/wharf1.pdf, http://www.aeberli.com/uploads/articles/wharf2.pdf; Although it was widely spread that the plot ratio of Harbor City did not reach the maximum allowed by the authorities, this reference only mentions the issues of schedule delay and the architect's supervision of construction.

[13]Henry Tang's residential basement in Kowloon Tong was exposed by the media during his 2012 election campaign for Chief Executive, as the construction of the basement had not been reported to the Buildings Department. The BD checked his house and took the case to court. See Hong Kong's *Ming Pao Daily News*, *Metro* and other newspapers, July 31, 2013.

Fig. 4.10 Buildings were continuously redeveloped on the street grid of 19th century

The evolution of the buildings ordinances and regulations in Hong Kong were driven by social and economic developments. Although the adjustments tended to lag, they eventually reflected, in part, social needs and changes. Any change in regulations will soon shape different buildings and townscape. For a city with limited land, desperate demands on building and rampant capitalist greedy, the building regulations and control are necessary and imperative. In the study of post-war architecture in Hong Kong, it is clear that the Buildings Ordinances played a crucial role in the development of the architecture of the city. Hong Kong surveyors who knew the ordinances very well often played a much more positive and authoritative role than architects.

Although building regulations are practical and necessary for practice, they are difficult for students to learn. In 1996, I was assigned to teach Y2 and Y3 design studios, in which students produced high-rise residential and office towers. The exercises related to development potential, ventilation and lighting regulation, means of escape and fire-fighting construction. Hong Kong's regulations and building controls dictate design decisions in complicated dense and high-rise environments. They are stricter than those of China and the U.S. The regulations and practical notes were written in British legal language, with some paragraphs comprising only one sentence. The lengthy regulations sometimes intimidate even the native English speakers. They had to be read and comprehended carefully, better with graphics. As teaching is the best way of learning, I read the regulations, drew sketches according to their descriptions and made myself understand them before teaching. I also taught a course entitled "Building Practice in China." Comparing China and Hong Kong's regulations allowed me to understand more about legal and control issues.

References

Buildings Department. (1998, April). Practice Note for Authorized Persons and Registered Structural Engineers 223, *Podium Height Restriction under Building (Planning) Regulation 20 (3)*. Hong Kong: Buildings Department, Hong Kong government.

Buildings Department. (2011, January). Practice Note for Authorized Persons, Registered Structural Engineers and Registered Geotechnical Engineers, APP-152. *Sustainable Building Design Guidelines*. Hong Kong: Buildings Department, Hong Kong government.

Chan, C. (2005). Tenement house in a city without memory. In C. Chan & H. Choi (Eds.), *A trip in space: Hundred years of Hong Kong architecture* (pp. 50–57). Hong Kong: Joint Publishing Ltd. 陈翠儿(2005). 没有记忆的城市:花样年华的唐楼. 陈翠儿、蔡宏兴主编. 空间之旅:香港建筑百年. 香港:三联书店.

HTA, Levitt Bernstein, Pollard/Thomas/Edwards and PRP. (2015). *Super density—The sequel*. London: HTA, Levitt Bernstein, Pollard/Thomas/Edwards and PRP.

Xue, C. Q. L., Zou, H., Li, B., & Hui, K. C. (2012). The shaping of early Hong Kong: Transplantation and adaptation by the British professions, 1841–1941. *Planning Perspective*, *27*(4), 549–568.

Part II
Private Forces Command

Through a series of government support and channeling, the economy of Hong Kong picked up in the 1970s. The private developer had opportunity to provide large-scale residential estates for the burgeoning middle class. The development has been integrated with the rail station construction and took the form of mega-structure. Transit-oriented development got full growth in the crowded Hong Kong. To facilitate the transformation of Hong Kong into a service and financial center, the skyscrapers proudly stood up in the central business district to symbolize the coming of global era. Together with the arrival of celebrity international architects, the local designers cultivated and explored the architecture which belongs to this context.

Chapter 5
Serving the Middle Class—Private Housing and Shopping Mall

5.1 Emergence of Chinese Developers

In 1967, ignited by the "Cultural Revolution" in the Chinese mainland, the left wing in Hong Kong launched a series of demonstration and destructive strike in streets and factories. Most citizens in Hong Kong were once political and economic refugees, who were eager to live in an affluent and peaceful life. The violence and conflict could not win supports from the majority of people. The riot lasted for half a year, and gradually died down (Welsh 2010; Cheung 2009). To keep the society stable, the government was more convinced by the importance of providing social housing and keeping the high employment rate so that people will love their own land and be far away from unlawful commitments. The business and life gradually turned to thriving in the 1970s.

After the war, the capitalists in Hong Kong were first engaged in family-based "cottage industry". When the property market was increasingly hot, more money was invested. For example, some business people first did jewelry making and selling. When they got fortune, they invested money to the property development in Causeway Bay and other city areas. In the list of Real Estate Developers Association of Hong Kong in 1966, there were over 300 member companies and individuals.[1] The 1967 riot blew the trading, economy and real estate property for a while. Some insightful capitalists grabbed the opportunity to absorb property and land in a cheap price. When the economy picked up, they soon became winners and acquired more small companies. In the 1970s, several Chinese property development companies were listed in the stock market and they accumulated sufficient funding from society for large scale development. After 20 years, in the mid-1990s,

---

[1]Booklet of "Property Model Exhibition", The Real Estate Developers Association of Hong Kong (1966).

© Springer Science+Business Media Singapore 2016
C.Q.L. Xue, *Hong Kong Architecture 1945–2015*,
DOI 10.1007/978-981-10-1004-0_5

80 % of private housing development was concentrated to and controlled by five to six property tycoons, for example, Cheung Kong, Sun Hong Kai, Henderson and Sino.[2]

Sun Hong Kai was once one of the 300+ small development companies in the early 1960s. After two generations of operation, Mr. Kwok Tak-seng and his three sons run the company and expanded to a property group worth 10 billion US dollars in 2013.[3] In 2000, *World Architecture* of UK ranked it No. 1 housing developer in terms of living unit quantity.[4] In addition to housing, the company also developed office complex, hotel, factory and shopping mall in Hong Kong, Chinese mainland and overseas, including the tallest landmark skyscrapers on two sides of the Victoria Harbor—IFC of 415 m and ICC of 484 m. They run financial company to loan mortgage for the home buyers, and operate bus and ferry companies to serve their properties in remote area. Another tycoon Sir Li Ka-shing started his career from making plastic flower in 1950 and shifted to the real estate property in the early 1960s. Through real estate, he conquered the other business fields like energy, electricity power, gas, mobile communication, port facilities, supermarket, drugstore, bio-technology, TV channel, newspaper and information industry in Hong Kong, Chinese mainland and other countries in five continents. For a long time, Li was Asia's richest person and a famous philanthropist, who generously supported university development, science and society in Hong Kong, Chinese mainland and overseas. According to *Forbes* magazine in 2013, Mr. Li was ranked No. 8 in the world's richest list with a portfolio valued 31 billion US dollars.[5] Kwok and Li are among many people from rag to rich through property fables.

The local property developers arose because they had seen clearly the strong demands of housing and Chinese people's psychology of owning a roof over the head. In the early 1970s, most residents were originally political or economic refugees escaped from China. They were eager to live in a decent life. After government's intensive resettlement, people could find a job in flourishing manufacturing industry. Many people were gradually moving up to "middle class." Through overwhelming commercial advertisement and societal collective consciousness, owning a property was a symbol of being "middle class", no matter how small the flat unit was. Therefore, the residential unit size of condominium popularized in the 1970s and 80s was around 40 m², buildings were mostly built in new towns for the cheaper land premium, so that they are affordable for many people.

---

[2]About the monopoly of property market in Hong Kong, see A. Poon (2010). Poon is more critical. Fung Banyan's book (2001) gives statistics and facts of real estate development in Hong Kong in the 20th century.

[3]Data of Sun Hong Kai, see its company website, http://www.shkp.com/en-US/. Accessed 27 May 2015.

[4]*World Architecture*, London: The Builder Group, Issue No. 81, January 2000. The ranking is mainly for design firms, and in some years it also ranked the building related industry.

[5]The worlds' billionaires, *Forbes*, http://www.forbes.com/billionaires/list/. Accessed 27 May 2015.

The 1960s was the early years of preparing large amount of private housing projects. *The Hongkong & Far East Builder*, a bi-monthly periodical, reported 110 building projects during 1960–1969, 55 were residential buildings. The next main type is school building (26 projects).[6]

Large scale private housing development is the outcome of growing property giants and the strong demand from end-users. Such housing development surrounds shopping mall with controlled indoor air. The arrival of internationalization and globalization pushes forward the wave of individuals' consumption. On one hand, people are easy to find and buy goods to stimulate production; on the other hand, the shopping malls provide another kind of "public" space for the crowded city. The building type shopping mall naturally follows the pace of large scale housing estates.

5.2 Large Scale Private Residential Estates

On the demand side, the post-war years saw the influx of migrants and baby boom. Their children reached marriage age in the 1970s and 80s. From 1970 to 1980, population in Hong Kong increased from four million to five million. Every year, 50,000 couples got married and the demand for proper housing was high (Feng 2001). After the intensive development of public housing estates, residents could find a place to live and work. In the early 1970s, with the industry updating and economic progress, Hong Kong residents generally had more disposable income, and higher demand of owning the property. The original public housing residents bought their own property, or moved to home ownership housing or private housing. Their old public housing units could be filled by new applicants in the pipeline.

From the 1950s, the private developers usually found plot of land, which could accommodate one or several building blocks. Facing the surging demand of comfortable and affordable housing, traditional private development model could no longer satisfy. Moreover, the government developed large scale public housing which could house tens of thousands people. This inspired the society and showcased a possible life style. In the late 1960s, the new trend arose.

The first large scale private residential estate is Mei Foo Sun Chuen, which is located in Lai Chi Kok Bay. Mei Foo is the old brand oil dealer Mobil from New York, which entered Hong Kong in 1906 to sell its petroleum and petrol lamp. Viewing the escalating of land and property price, Mobil moved its oil tank warehouse to Tsing Yi Island and collaborated with Galbreath Ruffin Corporation, a US property developer and Turner Construction Co. to develop the old waterfront warehouse to a private "suburbanized" housing estate in New Kowloon (Fig. 5.1).

---

[6]We count from the ten years' publication of the magazine *The Hongkong & Far East Builder*. For the detailed counting, see Chan (2016).

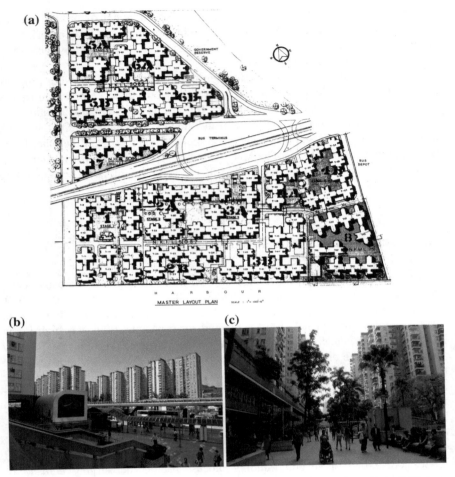

Fig. 5.1 Mei Foo Sun Chuen, 1969–1976. **a** Master plan. Courtesy of Wong Tung & Partners. **b** Main road going through the estate. **c** Internal space for shopping and leisure

Mei Foo Sun Chuen, literally means "Shell Oil residential estate", was planned and designed by Wong Tung & Partners. The 99 towers with 13,149 housing units arranged on a site of 17 ha, including gardens, terraces, lower floor shops and traffic interexchange. It was conceived as an autonomous town in the edge of city. The development was divided to eight phases. Towers stand on the common podium garden and vehicular traffic on the ground level, which has shops and roads. Fountains, sculptures, trees and flowers decorate the podium garden. People can stroll on the garden, without the interference from vehicles below (Will 1978).

The unit size ranges from 450 to 1,400 ft^2, one to four bedrooms in a flat. The unit number Mei Foo provided was over any public housing estate. The cruciform was used in typical floor plan. The point block form made the master plan compact to accommodate more flats. Wong Tung pioneered in planning large-scale residential areas. The last phase of Mei Foo Sun Chuen was completed in 1976. It received warm responses in the housing market. Some home buyers were public housing residents of nearby So Uk. For them, this is a real updating in life quality.

Mei Foo residential estate was built on the old dock. This might inspire another old enterprise in Hong Kong, Swire Group. The main business of Swire was ocean shipping, airline, newspaper and trading. Swire had owned Taikoo sugar factory since the 19th century. With the declining of ocean shipping, Swire established a property development company in 1972 and hoped to share a pie in this promising business. The first big project is on its old shipyard and sugar factory of 20 ha. Swire Property invited Wong Tung & Partners to design a similar large estate—Taikoo Shing (city). Taikoo Shing is located in the east Hong Kong Island, and features 69 residential towers of 28 to 32-storey high, office buildings and a large shopping mall. Housing blocks adopted cruciform—lift, staircase, trash chute and meter room are in the core while living units are in the four wings (Fig. 5.2).

Pedestrian bridges, shopping malls that cover several street blocks, podiums, pedestrian arcades and central parks are extensively adopted in large-scale residential areas. A skating rink was designed in the atrium space of Taikoo Shing Plaza, this is the first time indoor skating appearing in Hong Kong. The office towers were developed in several phases close to the MTR stations. When Taikoo Shing was being prepared, a comprehensive complex—Barbican Centre in London —made its name known. Barbican Centre consists of high class condominium, concert hall, theater and art galleries, garden and artificial lake. The living, art, performance and landscape are subtly interwoven in the City of London center connected to the underground railway. The development of Barbican inspired many city revival plans including Taikoo Shing in Hong Kong. From its inception, Taikoo Shing is a typical middle class community. According to the 2011 census, the median monthly income is HK$ 62,370, only after the richest Mid-level (Census and Statistics Department 2011). After more than 30 years, Taikoo Shing is still coveted by many white-collar residents because of its professional upkeep.

While Mei Foo Sun Chuen and Taikoo Shing were being constructed in the 1980s, Wong & Ouyang designed Whampoa Garden in the old Hung Hom shipyard

Fig. 5.2 Taikoo Shing, 1976–1986. Courtesy of Wong Tung & Partners

for Hutchison Whampoa led by Sir Li Ka-shing. The firm planned 88 towers, each around 20 storeys high, in 12 phases. Some towers contain units sized around 35–40 m² in floor area; some towers 70–100 m². Guided by the idea of garden city, each phase is a street block, with a retail shopping mall covering the ground, basement and a car park located under the podium. Gardens and basketball courts can be found above the commercial podium. Residential towers stand on the garden. The blocks are linked with pedestrian bridges to allow vehicles to pass through smoothly. The clubhouse and bus terminal in addition to a ship-shape retail building can be found at the center of the estate (Fig. 5.3).

In 1978, Li acquired Hutchison Whampoa, an old British corporation, and its whole shipyard site in Hung Hom, an old district in Kowloon Peninsula. In addition to Whampoa Garden, Li's family built the other residential estates, headquarters of Hutchison Whampoa, five-star Harbor Grand Hotel, 59-storey luxury condominium with curtain wall and serviced apartments with over thousand units in the same

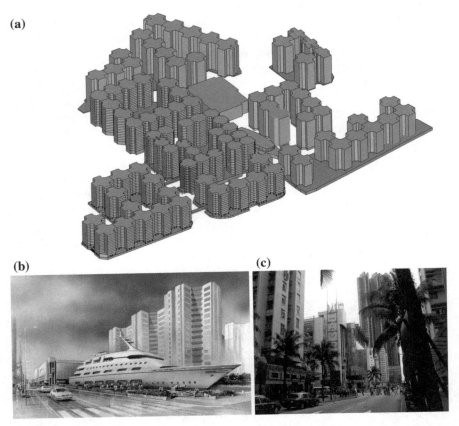

(a)

(b)   **(c)**

Fig. 5.3 Whampoa Garden, 1980s. **a** The estate was developed through 14 phases. All towers stand on podium (*red color*). Drawn by Au Yeung Hiu Yan. **b** Perspective drawing showing the central shopping part, drawn by Wong Suen Kwok in 1986. **c** Street in Whampoa Garden

district. The construction lasted from the 1970s to 2016. Although residential units were sold to the home-owners, Cheung Kong manages all residential and commercial properties, and decides to what kind of shops they will lease out. Hung Hom area is part of Li Family's kingdom. The shops, brands, trades and streetscapes are organized by virtually one company. Such big development companies lead and set the trend for lifestyle. Such phenomenon was criticized by scholars like David Harvey, "We have largely surrendered our own individual right to make the city after our heart's desire to the rights of property owners, landlords, developers, finance capitalists and the state. We have abrogated our right to make ourselves to the rights of capital to make us through the passive acceptance or mindless embrace of the restructuring of daily life by the projects of capitalist class interests." Harvey gives prescription as, "Critical and dialectical method is vital to understand not only where we have been and how we have been re-made but also to understand where we might go and what we might collectively aspire to become (Harvey 2006, p. 89)" (Fig. 5.4).

The above three large scale estates were completed in the 1970s and 80s. Mei Foo was the first experiment while Taikoo Shing and Whampoa Garden share more common characteristics. They presented new models of residential development in the following aspects:

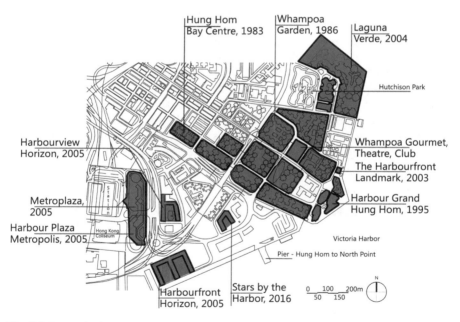

Fig. 5.4 Properties in Hung Hom owned by Cheung Kong Holdings Ltd. (Li's Family). Hung Hom Bay Centre, 1983. 814 units, GFA 74,000 ft². Whampoa Garden, 1986. 10,519 units, GFA 9.33 million ft². The Harborfront Landmark, 2003. 324 units, 59 stories high. Laguna Verde, 2004. 4,735 units. Harborview Horizon serviced apartment, 2006. 1,980 units. Harborfront Horizon serviced apartment, 2006. 1,662 units. Metropolis Residence (above the shopping mall Metroplaza), 2005, 662 units. Drawn by Zang Peng

- large tract of land with grid streets and many (around 10) phases;
- separation of pedestrian and vehicle in different levels;
- towers of over 20 stories above the podium to achieve targeted density so that more people can be accommodated, and
- podium garden for the residential tower entrance and podium itself containing many retail shops.

For Mei Foo, shops are in the ground and street level of podium; for Taikoo Shing, a big central shopping mall with skating and for Whampoa, six-storey high central shopping mall and cinema, plus two-storey high shopping mall in each phase and street block. These methods were absorbed more or less in the other development projects in years ahead. Table 5.1 summarizes the three pioneering private residential estates. Through the table, one can find that the prevailing "high" density in the 1980s was around 500–700 dwellings per hectare. This is two times the top of the London Plan Density Matrix in 2015 (HTA, Levitt Bernstein, Pollard/Thomas/Edwards and PRP 2015). In the 21st century, the density in Hong Kong is doubled of its 1980s' figure (see Chap. 2).

The large scale private housing development in the 1980s inspired and stimulated many followers. The city proper in the Hong Kong Island and Kowloon Peninsula were saturated. The urban renewal in the old city area was piecemeal. The developers had to search the land in the New Territories. Through cooperation with the Mass Transit Railway (MTR) and other transportation arrangement, remote areas became new town and large tract of land was site-formed for luxurious estates, for example, Kong Lok Yuen (1993), Constellation Cove (2004) and estates along Ma An Shan in Tolo Harbor. In the above mentioned projects, shops are located on the podium.

From 1991 to 1998, Cheung Kong Property Ltd. developed Kingswood Villas in Tin Shui Wai in seven phases. The site was originally fish pond, several miles away from the China border. 58 residential towers with 15,800 living units were built on a tract of 40 ha land, 10 % of the land is covered by building, the rest is for park

Table 5.1 Summary of three private residential estates in the 1980s

	Mei Foo Sun Chuen	Taikoo Shing	Whampoa Garden
Construction period	1965–1976	1973–1986	1983–1991
Designer	Wong Tung & Partners	Wong Tung & Partners	Wong & Ouyang
Location	Border between "New Kowloon" and the New Territories, outskirt of city	Old shipyard and sugar factory in the east Hong Kong Island	Old shipyard in Hung Hom Bay
Site area	17 ha	20 ha	19 ha
Living units	13,149	12,698	10,519
Habitants	70,000–80,000	Over 60,000	Over 40,000
Density	773.5 units/ha	634.9 units/ha	553.6 units/ha

Fig. 5.5 Kingwood Villas, 1998. Photoed by Henry Kwok

and lake. Rows of residential towers overlook the vast expanse of trees, greeneries, fountain and lake. In Kingswood Villas, shopping mall, five star hotel and traffic interexchange stand together, while housing blocks are arranged in curved V-shape, surrounding the park. The development of Kingswood cooperated with the public housing and thoroughly changed the face of an otherwise unknown rural area. Because of its remote location, the Kingswood Villas is often one of the lowest priced private housing in Hong Kong and attracts lower middle class residents to join the rank of home owners. Kingswood Villas is a successful project in terms of both finance and planning (Fig. 5.5).

5.3   Living in the Island

Mei Foo Sun Chuen is located at the edge of "New Kowloon"; Taikoo Shing in the east Hong Kong Island, once industrial town outside Victoria City; while Whampoa was boat repair yard in Hung Hom Bay. All three sites are away from the traditional town center, where one could not find such large plot of land. When developers found land in the outskirt, some other business people were exploring the outlying island. In 1970, people started to build villas in Pearl Island outside Tuen Mun. Link with the mainland by a narrow dam, the Pearl Island of less than two hectare was soon occupied by four estates. After 45 years, there are still no retail shops in the small island. It is an early example of developing island living, but its too small size does not set role model for the others. In Hong Kong's territory, there are 240 big and small islands and islets. The largest is Lantau Island, its size is even larger than that of Hong Kong Island of around 78.5 km². In 1973, a merchant planned to build a resort in Lantau Island including luxury hotel and golf course. But the plan was not successful. After several rounds of business merge and acquisition, a new formed company started to develop residential area there, it was named Discovery Bay (Fig. 5.6).

Discovery Bay is an American-type condominium located on an outlying island and linked to the city by ferry with 12 km waterway. People who commute to Central, the major location of office work, will take boat for 45 min one way. Occupying a site of 650 ha, Discovery Bay includes several bays and was developed through 15 phases. There are garden houses, low-rise, multi-story and high-rise apartments, shopping mall and international schools. The multi-story (5–6 storeys)

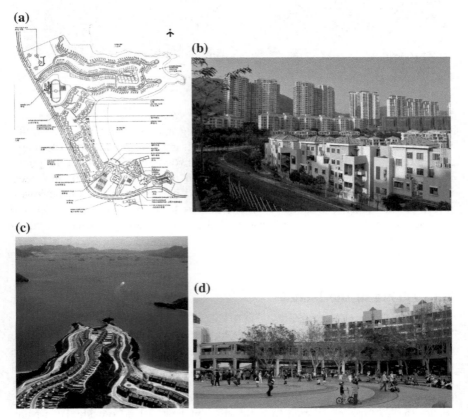

Fig. 5.6 Discovery Bay. **a** Master plan, Courtesy of Wong Tung & Partners. **b**, **c** The combination of high-rise, middle-rise and low-rise residential buildings surrounding the central landscape and sea view. **c** HK Government archive. **d** Town center

and high-rise apartment (20 storeys) stand in the outer ring. There are buses serving the estate. Golf cart for family usage is allowed but not private car. The town center is a pedestrianized landscaped circle, similar to the shopping arcade in Californian towns of the US. The life style in Discovery Bay has attracted many expatriates and white collar workers. 18,000 residents are from over 30 countries. All of these design methods were the predecessors to later developments of similar scale and created an island living lifestyle in Hong Kong. Since the completion of Phase I in 1983, the developer continuously built housing and expanded new phases in its land of 650 ha. Primary and secondary international schools were built to cater for increasing residents (Fig. 5.7).

The development of Discovery Bay greatly inspired the peers to find large tract of land. In the early 1990s, the government launched a "Rose Garden" plan of building ten "core projects", including new airport in Chek Lap Kok and the Tsing Ma Bridge leading to Lantau Island and new airport. The Tsing Ma Bridge is a

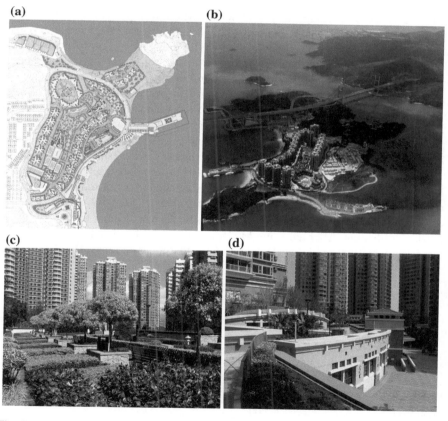

Fig. 5.7 Ma Wan Island development. **a** Master plan. Courtesy of Dr. Simon Kwan. **b** Living in island gives a way for Hong Kong's development. **c** Roof garden above the clubhouse. **d** Land topography is fully used

suspension bridge which spans 1,377 m across channel. One group of piers of the Tsing Ma Bridge falls upon Ma Wan Island. For several centuries, the island residents made a living by fishing. In 1997, Sun Hong Kai Property bid the land in Ma Wan Island and built an approaching ramp bridge from the island to the Tsing Ma Bridge, linking the island to the Tsing Yi MTR by bus (9 km), and to Central (around 13 km) and Tsuen Wan (6 km) by ferry. In a slope of 13 ha on Ma Wan Island, a residential area called Park Island was planned. The planning and design of Ma Wan Island were handed to Simon Kwan & Associates (also see Chap. 8). Phase I of Park Island was completed in 2002.

The master plan for the residential building respected the land topography, with the road surrounding Phase I on low land and later phases on high land. The development is divided into six phases with 32 residential towers, lived in by over 10,000 people. The main area is a big ring of towers. Phases 5 and 6 are grouped separately. On the south side of the island there is a waterfront promenade, Shell Square, a shopping arcade and a ferry pier. On the north side are local fishermen's new village houses (provided by the developer for old house compensation), a water reservoir and sewage treatment works. The developer created an environmental park and Noah's Ark and renovated the old streets into an artists' village. There are many large-scale residential estates in Hong Kong; however, the challenges and opportunities offered by the sophisticated topography and landscape in Ma Wan are rare. Simon Kwan's planning and design of Park Island satisfies the demands of commerce, usage and environment. It pushes the boundaries of residential planning and design. Comparing the Park Island with Discovery Bay, we can find that the density of Park Island keeps similar with the other residential projects in the city area. As it is located in island surrounded by sea, the real feeling is airy and less depressed. Table 5.2 summarizes the private estates in two islands.

In the hustle and bustle city area, people have to cramp themselves in small size living and working space. The island living is labelled as a relaxed lifestyle and a retreat from the city frontier. When the government leased the island land for residential usage, an assumption was that residents would most take ferry to the outside destination. After the Tsing Ma Bridge was completed and connected to the two islands in 1998, more residents preferred shuttle bus to ferry. The demand for

Table 5.2 Comparison of two island estates

	Park Island	Discovery Bay
Construction period	1997–2009	1975–2013
Designer	Simon Kwan & Partners	Wong Tung & Partners
Location	Ma Wan Island	Lantau Island, rural and fishing area
Site area	13 ha	650 ha
Living units	5,281	8,329
Habitants	Around 15,000	Around 18,000
Density	407.7 units/ha	12.8 units/ha

Source Centaline Property Research Department, Hong Kong. http://www1.centadata.com/eptest. aspx?type=3&code=WDPPWPPEPB&info=basicinfo&code2=&page=0

(a) **(b)**

Fig. 5.8 The Gold Coast in Tuen Mun, 1990. **a** Housing blocks behind the shopping arcade. **b** The shopping arcade takes the form of American country style

bus and taxi was high, which was against the government earlier intention. The island traffic to external destinations was often criticized by residents. However, this does not hamper people's admiring the serenity of living. In our investigation of the two islands, most residents selected the island living because of their high quality environment. Environment, community facilities and traffic were ranked three top things in their satisfaction. Most people accepted an hour of one way traffic to work and ten minutes walk to the shopping center.[7]

In addition to the development of island, the remote waterfront areas are planned for similar retreat. Such estates sometimes become acupuncture points to stimulate the remote districts. Along this line, we can find Gold Coast in Tuen Mun and Double Cove in Ma An Shan. Developed by Sino in 1991, the Gold Coast consists of marine club, shopping piazza, residence and five-star hotel. The complex faces Lantau Island across a vast water of at least 5 km. The designers from Wong & Ouyang made the building form, courtyard, openings and windows American country taste and pleasant yellow tone. Before development, this area of Tuen Mun was deserted and forgotten. After the Gold Coast was constructed, the Tuen Mun part of Castle Peak Road was gradually known and busy. More developments were attracted in the nearby. Architecturally, imitating foreign style has little (academic) value. However, the Gold Coast is popular and loved by local people, expatriates and yacht players (Fig. 5.8).

Mei Foo, Taikoo Shing, Whampoa Garden and Discovery Bay were completed in the mid-1980s. They are all "blue chip," middle-class residential areas in Hong Kong. Most later private estates are gated communities and occupied considerable part of city. The higher management fee paid by the residents mean more gardening, club house facilities and heavy security guards. They seem exclusive within

---

[7]Our investigation was conducted in February 2016. 40 residents from each island of Discovery Bay and Park Island were surveyed, totally 80 people. Around half of the subjects lived in the area less than five years, one quarter lived longer than ten years. See Yuan (2016). Before 2009, no taxi was allowed in Ma Wan Island. The criticism of external traffic existed for a long time. The outcome is that government gradually allows more buses and taxi to enter the island. This is from the author's investigation during 2006–2010.

the estates, and may bring some vanity for the home owners and tenants, as a symbol of "middle or upper-middle class". However, too many gated communities only occupy the valuable urban land. The five estates introduced in this chapter are open and actively contribute to the city life. Their gardens are literally open. Most ground floors are retail shops and malls open to the general public, the security guard only keep the building gate. In the holidays, many people tour the Discovery Bay and Park Island, strolling along the waterfront promenade, hanging in the shopping arcade or playing on the beach.

These estates epitomized decades of similar residential projects during the same period, they are the physical symbol of bulging middle class in the 1980s in this once refugee—ridden port city. From the 1970s to 21st century, the housing price and annual income ratio increase from 6 to 19 in Hong Kong.[8] That means buying a unit is more difficult for salary-earners now than before. This forces building design to delicately elaborate every square inch of usable area. In the following decades, more pretentious luxury condominiums and large scale residential areas emerged in the city area and the New Territories. They were decorated with classical architectural vocabularies, for example Roman columns, Ironic capitals and charming clubhouse with marble, sculpture and fountain. Beautiful European young women images appeared in the housing sales advertisement. Compared with those later commercial projects, the estates mentioned above are original, frank, healthy and full of modernist taste. They represent people's upward-looking attitudes in the 1980s.

As discussed above, private housing development shapes the middle class community. The marketing means of the developers is easily associated with "upper class", "consumerism" and "vulgar taste". The using of young white female model is a typical image of such psychological and conceptual construction. In the architectural and academic circle, it is generally disdained. In the 21st century, some foreign (star) architects were invited to give ideas in private housing design. For example, Foster Partners designed residential towers in the Cyberport in 2003 and Providence Bay in 2012. Both above mentioned residential buildings do not demonstrate any taste of "Foster" and attract little interest. When DLN (Dennis Lau and Ng Chun Man) Architects & Engineers (HK) Ltd. designed Double Cove, a residential estate of 21 towers in the terminal station of Ma An Shan Line, Lord Richard Rogers was invited in 2008. In most residential buildings in Hong Kong, the ground floor is only for lobby, facilities, machine room and shops. Rogers designed duplex units on the ground and first floor with garden. The lobby for the upper floors is arranged in a high level of open podium. Rogers also suggested to use black and sharp orange colors for the external wall, making the housing building visually impactful in waterfront. Double Cove has particular quality in its common space, landscape integrated with sea view (Fig. 5.9).

---

[8]The housing affordability data was issued by Demographia in the US, see http://www.guancha.cn/local/2014_01_23_201666.shtml. Accessed 31 May 2015. For the figure in Hong Kong in 2015, that means a family can buy a unit of average size and quality with 19 years' income without any other expenditure. That unit may be 50–60 m^2 in gross floor area. In most states of the US, this ratio is around 3, and the house size is around three times that of Hong Kong.

Fig. 5.9 Double Cove—high density living in natural and artificial landscape. Phase I completed in 2013. Pictures **a** and **c**, courtesy of Henderson Land Development Company Limited. Picture **b**, View from the living unit

These joint-designs are significant for the residential design in Hong Kong. First, for a long time, the typical floor design in Hong Kong is driven by developers' old speculative format and they are by and large the same. The joint designs have modified and improves the typical plan. The joint design brings new ideas on master plan, which include how to link the many towers to the commercial, clubhouse, parking and public transportation, and how to separate and integrate the pedestrian and vehicular circulations. The new unit form, master plan and public transportation facilities are the selling points in addition to the size of living unit. In this trend, Frank Gehry also designed housing for the Swire Property in the Victoria Peak. Completed in 2013, the building consists of 12 floors, each whole floor is devoted for one home. However, the idiosyncratic non-linear design of housing tower is difficult to be applied to other mass housing production (Fig. 5.10).

5.4 Shopping Malls

In the post-industrial and globalization era, the economy is driven by consumption instead of manufacturing. Consumerism encourages more spending from customers, citizens, visitors and society, so that more products can be manufactured

Fig. 5.10 Model of Opus in Hong Kong, Frank Gehry & Associates, 2011

and sold to enhance the economy or GDP. This trend is reflected in the ubiquitous shopping malls in big cities like Tokyo, Singapore and Hong Kong, where shopping is a kind of major leisure activity in the "limited public space" provided by private-owned shopping malls.

In his book *Urban Space*, Rob Krier mentions: "The aesthetic quality of each element of urban space is characterized by the structural interrelation of detail. I shall attempt to discern this quality wherever we are dealing with physical features of a spatial nature. The two basic elements are the street and the square" (Krier 1979, p. 15). The public nature of urban space is closely associated with human and social activities. Both square and street are considered as components of urban public space as they accommodate frequent urban and social activities. Public space is also the "eye" of a city, revealing its genius loci, people and culture in a tangible and condensed way (Miao 2001).

In Hong Kong, outdoor public space consists of waterfront promenades, parks, and pocket parks within the urban districts and large swathes of open space in the New Territories. As a large proportion of land use is occupied by buildings and transportation right of way, the supply of public space in the urban center is believed insufficient, especially in the old districts like Mongkok, Sai Wan and Wanchai (Xue and Manuel 2001).

In Hong Kong, social interaction is partly taken place through consumerism. Most buildings with atrium design have comprehensive functions. With several retail clusters organized by atriums of different shapes, these atrium spaces act as nodes of routes and functions. They accommodate activities and become active places in the city. In these buildings, escalators and lifts are extensively positioned along circulation space to make the upper floors accessible. The atrium is usually surrounded by balconies and corridors, forming the parts of an indoor street system.

This design benefits shop owners as it provides shoppers with an interesting, safe, air-conditioned and well lit environment free from vehicular traffic and adverse weather. Within such buildings, people can easily find the way to the atrium, where various retail types such as furniture, electronics, clothes, food, recreation and entertainment are readily visible and accessible.

Some atrium space opens 24-hour a day as if traditional outdoor space, acting as focal points of urban life in high-density Hong Kong. This space not only provides efficiency in way-finding for customers, but can be altered for different occasions to enrich shopping experience and satisfaction; such as Christmas decorations during Christmas and live broadcast of world cup match. Urban plazas, which were given way to high-density development, reincarnate in the atriums of these types of comprehensive mega-structure buildings and flourish in a colourful and vibrant interior manner. The spacious atriums become essential nodes of pedestrian movement, act as a new spiritual place and boost the civic pride of the commercial city. Most of the shopping malls are located within buffer zone of metro station, say 800 m radius. So shopping and casual meeting happen on the way people going to home.

As discussed above, the commercial atriums of shopping mall display social functions in citizens' daily life. They improve the life quality in the old derelict and dense city area, where public space is generally in shortage and poor quality. Nevertheless, such an enlarged indoor space described in this chapter is not equivalent to the "genuine" public space of conventional definition. A public space should be accessed by all residents in a city through 24 h. Because of their open nature, public space is often the most inexpensive social and recreational facilities for the majority of urban residents who cannot afford private amenities such as clubs and golf courses. This mass-placating role of urban public space can be observed in societies ranging from ancient Rome to modern capitalist cities. In Hong Kong, the meagre public spaces in the city areas are heavily used. In the holidays, people walking dogs, whole family outing and the Pilipino domestic helpers praying and singing songs are commonly seen.

In the shopping malls of Hong Kong, the indoor "urban" space is controlled and supervised by private owners. They have to offset the cost and earn profits efficiently by building high density properties with plot ratio 1:10 or even higher. Apparently, the purpose of building shopping mall with atrium does not originate from philanthropy, but from commercial consideration. Some activities, which are commonly conducted in traditional public space, may not be allowed in these spaces without prior permission from the building management, while passage by foot, chatting, meeting, sitting (in some dedicated places) and, especially shopping are encouraged. There are overwhelming criticisms such as "public space, private interests", "gentrification and evicting the deprived class" and "government colluding with developers" in academic articles and mass media (Cuthbert and McKinnell 2001).

As a democratic society, picky criticism and sensitivity to capitalist tycoons are part of civic life. Arguments against the big corporations gaining huge amount of profit through developing high density properties are not uncommon. However, the application of this development model partly alleviates the plight of public space shortage, when more than 50 % of Hong Kong people live in flats less than 45 m^2.

In those shopping malls and atriums, poor people, even in rags, are not denied from window shopping. Underprivileged children, who live in the public housing estates, can stroll along the mall after school, can enjoy cool air and burgers, or watch the promotion activities and festival decorations from Christmas to Chinese New Year. Strolling in the shopping mall is part of Hong Kong's lifestyle.

Popular stars are often invited to stage in the shopping mall atrium, as a common strategy to attract large amount of audience and media coverage. During the World Cup of football season, large TV screens in the atrium broadcast the live matches in some shopping malls with seats and hot water bath arranged for people who watch the match overnight. Brand shops, expensive restaurants and lower-priced food court, grocery stores co-exist around atriums. These are the most common strategies to utilize societal value of atrium by mall management, attracting a lot of potential customers of different classes and thus making a lot more revenue from shop rents.

Some commentators might have pointed out that in gentrified shopping malls, the quiet environment contrasts drastically with traditional busy streets with hawkers and stalls. In Hong Kong, most of shopping malls are same busy and crowded as the streets outside. Moreover, the hot and rainy weathers of Hong Kong last for about seven months in a year. Some local people prefer to stay in the air-conditioned indoor space rather than being exposed in the hot and humid streets. The "semi-public" space in the shopping mall atriums has its community value.

The design with atriums in the mega-structures is not originally driven by design theories such as interior urbanism, but the spontaneous evolution of urban context, and ever-rising consciousness about the commercial value of it by developers and designers. Most of the shopping malls were developed together with the residential properties and adjacent to the metro stations. Some features of atrium are categorized according to their corresponding functions, urban contexts and building types above and/or near the stations. In fact, most atriums have one or two, or all features, some obvious, some not. The selected cases bear distinctive features which are clearly understandable through illustrations and description. They also possess significant impact in the formation of locals' daily life and regional urban development.

In its inception, shopping malls with atriums were designed to provide a better shopping environment and protect shoppers from harsh climates. The first malls with atriums were built in cold regions, such as the Eaton Center in Toronto and the arcades in Minneapolis, USA, in the 1970s (Saxon 1986). In the 1970s, John Portman's design of hotel influenced the peers in the US and Asia, and it was introduced in design magazines in Hong Kong. The Sheraton Hotel in Tsim Sha Tsui was designed with atrium in 1974. In 1982, when the Landmark was rebuilt in Central, Hong Kong gained a decent shopping mall with an atrium (see Chap. 3). The Landmark's two square towers hold a square atrium. In addition to its grand design, the Landmark connects to the MTR and other buildings in Central and plays an active role in urban life. With the rise in consumerism, shopping malls with atriums have continuously appeared in Hong Kong. Times Square, built in 1992, was a milestone, with an atrium nine floors high. Times Square, The Pacific Place and Landmark can be seen as the first generation of shopping malls in Hong Kong.

In 1993, Swire Property developed Festival Walk in Kowloon Tong, with a gross floor area of 100,000 m^2. It was designed by Arquitectonica from Miami, with help from Dennis Lau, Ng Chun Men & Associates as the local architect and Arup as the structural designer. Opened in 1998, Festival Walk formed a slanting cross in plan. Although six to seven stories high, it provides a clear layout for shoppers to find their way around. The shopping mall consists of a big open space without beams and posts. The floor slabs span 20 m or more. Skylights and side lighting make the interior bright and structure looked light-weight. Escalators interlock at various angles and lighting flows gently in the atrium, expressing the sense of a "river" and light-hearted (Fig. 5.11).

The Festival Walk connects to Tat Chee Avenue, East Rail, MTR and CityU campus, and sets an example for TOD complexes. After Festival Walk, Arquitectonica designed Cyberport in Pokfulam, Hong Kong Island, which is a type of science park run by the private sector (Fig. 5.12).

Shopping malls in overseas are not usually more than two stories high. The nine stories of Times Square broke this rule first. In 2004, Langham Place stood in the old area of Mongkok. Its shopping mall reached 12 stories. According to the coverage rate of Building Regulations, a podium should be open to the sky, but the client applied to cover it. When visitors arrive from the MTR station and ascend the three floors in the basement and three floors within the podium, they are exposed to a 60 m high glass atrium. The long escalator brings them to the eighth floor. There is a spiral walkway from the eighth to the twelfth floor, designed to make shoppers feel as though they are exploring a cave. Festival Walk and Langham Place feature stunning, large central spaces, with clear way-finding. These examples can be seen as Hong Kong's second generation of shopping malls (Fig. 5.13).

The Langham Place shopping mall was designed by the Jerde Partnership, which also designed many festival shopping malls in Los Angeles, San Diego, San Francesco, Tokyo and Shanghai. In high-density Hong Kong, Jerde further exploited the possibilities of the vertical dimension. In 2007, the MegaBox opened in Kowloon Bay. This vertical mall of over 20 stories is divided into several sections. Each section, three to five stories high, has its own atrium and motif. There

Study of pedestrian movement.

Fig. 5.11 Festival Walk, 1998. Interweaving of escalators and irregular floor plans make space complicated, but way-finding is clearly defined by the atrium. Study of pedestrian movement

Fig. 5.12 Cyberport, 2002. **a** Master plan. **b** Shopping mall

are lifts leading to the upper floors and escalators for each or several floors. This mixed vertical circulation caters for a variety of high and low spaces. Jerde's design highlights a celebratory atmosphere and is loved by local people (Fig. 5.14).

MegaBox is a high-rise shopping mall. Rather than having a central atrium dominating the whole building, it has several atriums, each linking several floors. There are escalators crossing several floors and also from floor to floor. This makes the space more sophisticated, but difficult for customers to find their way around. Other buildings, such as iSquare (see Chap. 8), The One in Tsim Sha Tsui (2010) and Hysan Place in Causeway Bay (2012), follow a similar design.

The One, built by Chinese Estates Holdings Ltd., stands on one side of Granville Road, Tsim Sha Tsui. The building plate of around 20×90 m sits on a site of 3,000 m^2. It has 29 floors covering 40,000 m^2, filled with shops and restaurants. The big anchor shops are in the basement and lower floors, Floor 16 is a sky garden

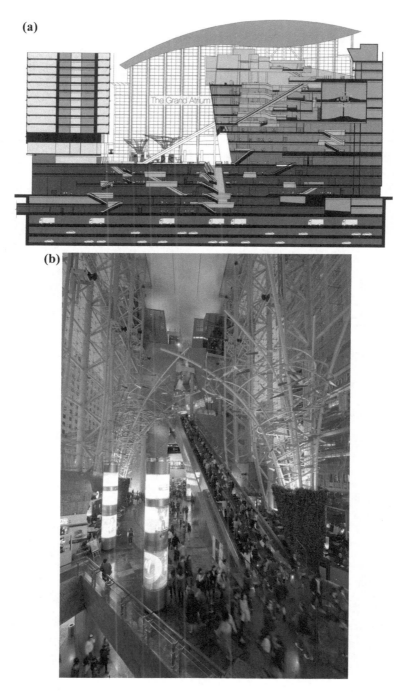

Fig. 5.13 Langham Place, 2004. **a** Section **b** The original open space is covered with atrium, it stands out in the old Mongkok area. Courtesy of Jerde Partnership

(a)   **(b)**

(c)

(d)

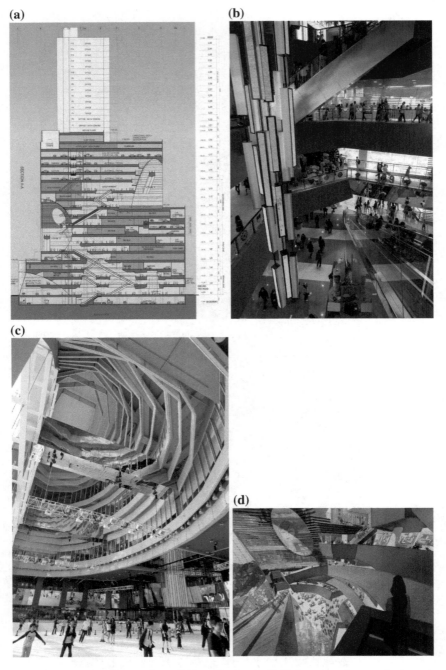

Fig. 5.14 MegaBox, Kowloon Bay, 2007. **a** Section is divided to several zones. **b** An atrium dominates several floors. **c** Ice rink. **d** Design perspective. Courtesy of Jerde Partnership

Fig. 5.15 The One, 2010. The long and narrow shape is wrapped with different pattern of curtain wall

and above Floor 16 there are high class restaurants. The One was designed by Tange Associates of Japan, founded by Kenzo Tange (1913–2005), a Japanese master and Pritzker Architecture Prize laureate. The escalators and traffic flows are arranged at the two ends, while parts of the lower floors are hollowed into side atriums. The plan is narrow, with some areas left for light wells and a sky garden. The delicate interior design gives it the feel of the Ginza boutique shops in Tokyo. Patterned windows clad the different floors. It is a long plate and the design emphasizes the feeling of a "thin slab (Fig. 5.15)."

Hysan Place in Lee Garden was developed by the Lee Family, which has been doing business in the Causeway Bay for hundreds of years. Seventeen of the 40 stories contribute to the shopping mall. The lower floors link the tramway on Hennessey Road with the back roads up to the hill. Double decker lifts and long and short escalators busily weave into the traffic net, sending people to the upper floors.

(a)   **(b)**   **(c)**

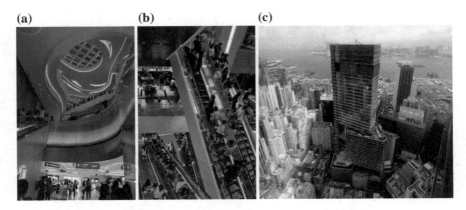

Fig. 5.16 Hysan Place, Causeway Bay, 2012. The tower-type shopping mall is divided to several zones, each led by an atrium. **c** Courtesy of Dr. Chan Lai Kiu

Some of the long escalators follow the external glass wall. Sky gardens on various floors serve as "urban window", so that the tall building will not block the neighboring buildings. The customers can take a rest in these areas. Hysan Place was designed by KPF, Dennis Lau & Ng Chun Men and Benoy. The interior design was by various designers, all of them innovative, with some floors for women's goods, some for bookshops and some for brand shops. The different plans, instead of same stacked floors, intricate escalator locations and roof garden are characteristic of this group of shopping malls like The One, iSquare and Hysan Place. We can see them as the third generation of shopping malls (Fig. 5.16).[9]

5.5 Conclusion: Settling Down and Quasi "Public Space"

Under the government's favorable policies, Chinese entrepreneurs and capitalists swelled quickly in Hong Kong in the 1970s. Their business shifted from family-based industry to real estate property for thicker and quicker profits. Large scale private housing is an outcome of the intensive development. It appeared on time when the society and citizens were eager to live in a well-to-do life. The government-led public housing and private developers' housing partly satisfied residents' demand. From public housing, government subsidized ownership housing to private housing, people climb up, jump into new life and the rank of middle class. The design of private housing has long been constrained in the developers' speculative plans. The modernist vigor once shown in the 1980s is gradually replaced by more commercial and vogue cliché. The fake "Beverly Hill", "royal

---

[9]The description of the shopping malls in this section is from the author's own investigation. The floor area and site area data are from Wikipedia or the owners' websites.

garden" and "little Venice" plus Baroque fountain and sculptures form the main design stream of private housing in the 21st century. They reflect the general taste of developers and housing market.

When people are settled, they have higher demand on leisure activity. Public buildings discussed in Chap. 2 provide venue for such activities. But public buildings are usually formal and some are far away from home and daily life. Consumerist trend stepped into the society when the industrial era was phased out in the 1980s. Shopping mall with atrium provides a "public space" for certain kinds of public activity, although some people accused that shopping mall destroys the traditional market and streets. In the hot and humid climate, the shopping malls provide a cozy and enjoyable environment for people indeed. It is a progress of civilization for human being. Through the analysis of Chap. 6, one can see these shopping malls are mostly associated with the transit-oriented (TOD) megastructure projects and act as a focal center of building complex and daily life in town. Through government proper channeling, private development can also contribute to the betterment of society.

In 1995, I returned to Hong Kong and rented a 725-ft^2 condominium unit on Tat Chee Avenue, a 3-min walk to the campus where I worked. The rent was HK $18,600 (US$ 2,400). The "usable area" within the internal wall totaled around 40 m^2. The master bedroom was 2 × 3 m, and two other bedrooms measured 2 × 2 m each. The estate was located in the aviation zone. When an airplane soared down toward Kai Tak Airport, you could see the screws on the airplane body. If you were talking on a phone, you had to stop and wait for the airplane noise to quiet down. Such a unit was priced at US$1 million in 1997 and US$1.5 million in 2015. In 1997, the stock and property markets went crazy. People had to queue overnight to buy property, most of which was still under construction. They began to pay mortgages two to three years before their buildings were completed. After the Asian financial crisis in 1998, the stock and property market plummeted. In 2003, the properties were only 30 % of their value in 1997. Many private house owners including my colleagues and friends entered into "negative equity." This "negative equity" disappeared after 2011, and in 2015 the property value was 150 % that of its 1997 level, far above the incomes of most middle-class salary earners.

I plunged into the property buyer ranks in 2001. After viewing many places, I chose Hung Hom, a near-harbor location two stations away from my workplace. The price was 20 % higher than my budget and I accepted the heavy burden of paying for it. Most private developers were decorating living estates like multi-star hotels. This was reflected in the entrances, lobbies and clubhouses of the residences, which seemed to justify the rocket-high prices and partly balance the smaller-sized living units. The plans for these properties had some merit. They were compact and could house more families and social functions. I also lived on Ma Wan Island for four years, a location that possessed all of the standard tourist attractions including forests, beaches, club houses, temples, swimming pools, shops, restaurants, clinics and sea views. Less than 1 km^2 in size, the island hosted *fifteen thousand residents, and half of its land was covered by greenery. I could not stay in this relaxed setting for too long, as I found the* 50-min *commute (each way) exhausting.*

Our university campus is adjacent to the Festival Walk. When the shopping mall of GFA 100,000 m² *was completed in 1998, the CityU campus had similar gross floor area. Most students and staff arrive at the campus by MTR and East Rail. They will usually pass through the shopping mall and be elevated to floor and floor by many intricate-overlapping escalators. The university's motto of "in the city, of the city and for the city" is no more obvious than this proximity with commerce. In any working day, I walk through the mall at least twice a day. The column-less internal space, irregular floor shape, atriums on two sides, skylight and artificial light never make me boring.*

References

Census and Statistics Department. (2011). Population census. Thematic Report: *Household Income Distribution in Hong Kong*. Hong Kong: Hong Kong Government.

Chan, C. K. (2016). *Architectural publication in Hong Kong: A study of Hong Kong's architectural history in the 1960s*. Undergraduate graduation thesis, City University of Hong Kong, Hong Kong.

Cheung, G. K. W. (2009). *Hong Kong's watershed: The 1967 riots*. Hong Kong: Hong Kong University Press.

Cuthbert, A., & McKinnell, K. (2001). Public domain, private interest—Social space in Hong Kong. In P. Miao (Ed.), *Public places of Asia Pacific countries: Current issues and strategies* (pp. 191–214). The Netherlands: Kluwer Academic Publishers.

Feng, B. (2001). *Hundred years of real estate property in Hong Kong*. Hong Kong: Joint Publishing Ltd. 冯邦彦 (2001). 香港地产业百年. 香港:三联书店.

Harvey, D. (2006). *Spaces of global capitalism—Towards a theory of uneven geographical development*. London and New York: Verso.

HTA, Levitt Bernstein, Pollard/Thomas/Edwards & PRP. (2015). *Super density—The sequel*. London: HTA, Levitt Bernstein, Pollard/Thomas/Edwards and PRP.

Krier, R. (1979). *Urban space*. New York: Rizzoli International Publications Inc.

Miao, P. (Ed.). (2001). *Public places of Asia Pacific countries: Current issues and strategies*. The Netherlands: Kluwer Academic Publishers.

Poon, A. (2010). *Land and ruling class in Hong Kong*. Hong Kong: Tian Chuan Chubanshe.

Saxon, R. (1986). *Atrium building: Development and design*. London: Architectural Press.

The Real Estate Developers Association of Hong Kong. (1966). *Property model exhibition*. Hong Kong: The Real Estate Developers Association of Hong Kong.

Welsh, F. (2010). *A history of Hong Kong*. London: HarperCollins Press.

Will, B.F. (1978). Chapter 5: Housing design and construction methods. In L. S. K. Wong (Ed.), *Housing in Hong Kong—A multi-disciplinary study* (pp. 91–127). Hong Kong: Heinemann Education Books (Asia) Ltd.

Xue, C. Q. L., & Manuel, K. K. K. (2001). Chapter 8: The quest for better public space: A critical review of urban Hong Kong. In P. Miao (Ed.), *Public places of Asia Pacific countries: Current issues and strategies* (pp. 171–190). The Netherlands: Kluwer Academic Publishers.

Yuan, W. T. (2016). *Living in the island—A study of Discovery Bay and Park Island*. Bachelor degree thesis, City University of Hong Kong.

Chapter 6
Rail Village and Mega-Structure

6.1 Rail Village

Facing the increasing population and survival pressure in the 1960s and 70s, the Hong Kong government and planning professionals thought of decentralization and setting up new towns. Similar ideas were raised half a century or even earlier in the other parts of the world.

Foreseeing the sharp increase of population in the city, Le Corbusier conceived "le Plan Voison 1925 of Paris", the historical town center was replaced by a matrix of similar towers. This could arguably be seen as the first step of exploring the high-rise megastructure in the modern era. While Le Corbusier's plan exists only on paper, his lofty ideas on urbanism were to be largely absorbed in La Défense in Paris in the 1970s, and perhaps more significantly in developing countries several decades later. The new town movement engulfed Britain and Northern Europe in the 1950s. Large developments spanning several street blocks became the norm. In the UK, Alison and Peter Smithson designed large-scale social housing developments, linked by "sky bridges" crossing the street. These visionary examples were soon echoed in Hong Kong (Tan and Xue 2014).

In the 1960s urbanization in Japan came to the forefront, as the nation faced problems of scarce land and increasing urban population. The situation pushed Japanese architects and urbanists to rethink urban structure and architectural form and search for new possible solutions. The metabolists were the first to acknowledge the potential of vast structures in addressing aspects of Asia's urbanism, and they were responsible for several megastructure proposals, especially in Tokyo Bay (Kikutake et al. 1960). Fumihiko Maki's *Investigation in Collective Form* in 1964 defines "Mega-Structure" as "a large frame in which all the functions of a city or part of a city are housed" (Maki 1964). It has been made possible by present day technology, for example, the mega-structure buildings in Tokyo Bay and near the subway and railway stations in Tokyo and Osaka.

© Springer Science+Business Media Singapore 2016
C.Q.L. Xue, *Hong Kong Architecture 1945–2015*,
DOI 10.1007/978-981-10-1004-0_6

All these foreign ideas and inventive prototypes inspired the professionals and government in Hong Kong. The discussions could be found in magazines and media in the 1960s and 70s (Xue et al. 2016). To develop more land for building homes, the Hong Kong government looked at the possibility of building new towns; Kwun Tong and Tsuen Wan were first formed as industrial districts. At the end of the 1960s, the government employed a consultant to study the feasibility of a mass transit railway (MTR) so that the city could be linked to the remote new towns. The consultant's report considered that as 80 % of Hong Kong's population lived in the narrow linear area between the mountain and the sea, it was very suitable for building an MTR (Freeman Fox and Partners 1970).

The Kowloon-Canton Railway (KCR) starts from Guangzhou, passes through Luohu and arrives in Kowloon. It began operating in 1913. The first MTR line, the Kwun Tong Line, opened in 1979 and the Tsuen Wan Line in 1982. In 1985, the Island Line was built through the east and west sides of north Hong Kong Island. The KCR and MTR lines spread through the territory like vessels, and the train stations were surrounded by clusters of offices and residential buildings. In the US, this was first termed a transit-oriented development (TOD)[1] (Fig. 6.1).

Most of these TODs used high-rise and high-density architectural designs. Because of the number of people, narrow roads and accessible public transportation, 90 % of Hong Kong residents use public transportation, according to statistics from the Transportation Department in 2010. One third of public transport passengers travel by rail and only 6.6 % people drive a private car. The growth rate of private cars in Hong Kong is much lower than that of Beijing and Shanghai.[2] In the world statistics of gasoline consumption per capita, Hong Kong is at the low end and American cities such as Houston are found at the high end.[3]

In the 1970s, the government proposed the "ten year housing construction." A large amount of land in the New Territories was converted for a new town, including Shatin and Tun Men. The MTR network was formed in the 1980s to serve

---

[1]For more about transit-oriented-development (TOD), see Cervero (1998), Bernick and Cervero (1997), Dittmar and Ohland (2004). These books define the TOD theory and practice mainly in North America.

[2]In 2010, the Transportation Department of Hong Kong counted 12 million people using public transportation, about 90 % of the population. This compares with 36 % in Beijing. From *Beijing shi jianshe renwen jiaotong keji jiaotong lvse jiaotong xingdong jihua* (Constructing a green traffic plan in Beijing 2009–2015). In Hong Kong, one third of public transport journeys are undertaken by rail; the figure for Beijing was 12 % in 2004 and for Shanghai 24 % in 2009. Public transportation and policy controlled the growth of private cars. In April 2010, there were 589,951 private vehicles in Hong Kong, less than 100,000 more than 10 years ago. From 2004 to 2008, the number of private cars in Shanghai grew from 317 to 613 thousand (http://www.stats-sh.gov.cn/tjnj/nj10.htm?d1=2010tjnj/C1313.htm. Accessed 3 March 2014). From 2001 to 2009, the number of private cars in Beijing grew from 624 thousand to 2.8 million. (http://www.bjtrc.org.cn/PageLayout/IndexReleased/Evaluation.aspx?menuid=li3. Accessed 3 March 2014). The above data demonstrate the effect of public transportation on urban development.

[3]For more information about the gasoline consumption and car ownership per capita, see Knaap (2006). The materials are mainly up to 2000.

Fig. 6.1 Rail development in Hong Kong. **a** Clustered "rail village" is linked by rail. **b** MTR Tung Chung Line and its stations

the old residential and industrial areas. The rehabilitation of older areas usually took place around the metro stations. In the 1990s, when the MTRC planned the Tung Chung Line, Airport Express Line and Tseung Kwan O Line, every station was integrated with the land development in the vicinity. These sites were designated as "rail + property" (R + P) or transit villages. During the 21st century construction of the West Rail, Ma An Shan Line and South Island Line, planning was conducted in a more scientific and precise way. In the 1990s, the cost of railway construction was HK$500 thousand per meter, whereas the construction of the Shatin–Central Line in 2012 cost HK$5 million.[4] Building one kilometer of railway costs HK$5 billion, which is equivalent to eight times the cost of the Olympic stadium in London in 2012. Only by serving more people can such an expensive railway produce economic and social value. The densely built residential towers, offices and commercial buildings bring large numbers of passengers and consumers and high revenues. The train station in turn brings convenience to people living nearby. TOD was first referred to in the US and was applied in Hong Kong on a larger and denser scale.

For TOD projects, the current study uses 5D principles to measure: Density, Diversity, Design, Distance to transit and Destination accessibility.[5] Density: there must be a sufficient number of residents, office workers and consumers (shoppers) near to the station to ensure a high capacity of passengers for the railway. Diversity: the land use, building type and neighborhood transportation network must be diverse and mixed. Design: the site, building and passageway design should be comfortable and enjoyable for pedestrians and cyclists and should encourage people to use the railway. Distance to transit: the walking distance from homes/work places to the train station should be adequate. Foreign research suggests that a reasonable distance is a quarter (400 m) to half a mile (800 m). When returning home from work, people will accept a longer walking distance (900 m). In Hong Kong, people are willing to walk 500–1,000 m to the station. Destination accessibility: residents within a reasonable radius of the train station can use the rail network to reach

---

[4]For more about the cost of metro construction in Hong Kong, see *Wenwai Pao*, 2 April 2012, A5.

[5]The 5D principles are from Cervero and Murakami (2009). The principles are used to measure the effectiveness of TOD projects.

various destinations, such as workplaces, shopping, activities and other places. The 5Ds demonstrate the effectiveness of a TOD.

Since 1979, the metro rail in Hong Kong has served the old community and new reclamation land. The planning of rail lines and property developments generally follows the principles of the 5Ds. Currently, there are 84 stations along the 187-km metro line. Apart from some special stations, such as Luo Wu, Lok Ma Chau, Sunny Bay and Disneyland, 74 stations contain residential buildings and commercial offices within a reasonable radius. About 42 % of the territory's households, 43 % of the employed population and 75 % of the commercial and office floor areas are located within a 500-m radius of train stations.[6] The author's team employed "Depthmap" approach of Space Syntax on the entire street network in Hong Kong, and the segment model has been built based on the axis of all streets. We find that MTR lines and entrances of station are heavily overlapped with the top 5 % highest accessible streets. That means that MTR stations are located in most convenient and accessible locations.[7] The rail villages profoundly influence the city planning of the territory. MTRC is a listed corporation, of which the government takes large percentage of stock share. The infrastructure and public buildings are invested by the public fund, while the office and residential towers are built by private companies. Therefore, all rail villages are results of public and private partnership.

This chapter selects one station on the East Rail (Shatin) Line, an early MTR station (Kowloon Bay), five stations on the Tung Chung Line and typical stations in Tseung Kwan O Line. The first two examples are the results of TOD in the early 1980s. The Tung Chung Line was the first example of the MTRC's spontaneous use of the R + P mode. Tseung Kwan O Line is short but built later than the Tung Chung Line. Each station represents a type of different role in city or suburb. The South Island Line and Ma On Shan Line follow the similar principles. The stations on the Tung Chung Line include those in the central business district, new reclamation land and new towns. Therefore, the Tung Chung Line epitomizes the development of the railway since the 1990s. Moreover, when a station is built, new development will follow in the nearby land lots. The station catchment and its configuration will vary in different years. The description of this chapter is mainly on the situation after 2010.

6.2 Experiment in the 1980s

When the Kwun Tong Line, the first metro line, opened in 1979, the MTRC and private developers cooperated to build residential buildings adjacent to the **Kowloon Bay station**. It was the first TOD of a residential estate to be developed by the

---

[6]For more about the data on the MTR, see Yin (2014); and 'The Public Transport-oriented Development' Approach in Hong Kong, on the website "Study on the Action Plan for Livable Bay Area of Pearl River Estuary," http://www.prdbay.com/UploadFile/20110330140011e.pdf. Accessed 25 October 2014.
[7]See Yin (2014). The method of Space Syntax, see Hillier (1999) and the website of Space Syntax company.

MTRC in the 1980s. It helped to transform the area from an industrial area into a mixed commercial and residential area. The whole development consists of 41 residential towers above a podium, which also houses the Telford Plaza shopping center and the MTRC headquarters office building. Bus and taxi terminals are on the ground floor, the shopping center is on the first and second floors and the train station is elevated above. The podium acts as a central garden with a train depot below.

Telford Plaza Phase I (52,171 m^2 gross floor area), designed by P & T, completed in 1980, was the largest shopping mall in East Kowloon at the time. Inside the shopping mall, there are six square atriums along the north-south axis. The building is rectangular with a regular structural grid. The six atriums face six entrances onto the garden and five pedestrian bridges link the building complex to the offices, Phase II and MTR headquarters and nearby facilities. A 300 m bridge links the Plaza to the Choi Hung Estate, a large-scale public housing estate. The connection with the external pedestrian system makes the atrium an interexchange point. Telford Plaza Phase II, completed in 1997, is six stories high with a gross floor area of 21,030 m^2 (Fig. 6.2).

Compared with Phase I, Phase II of the shopping center has a more compact and vertical layout. The podium of Telford Garden connects and radiates in different directions to office towers, factories and private and public housing estates. The podium also connects to every part of the rail development, including Phases I and II of Telford Plaza, the residential towers, cinemas, post office, community center, music and dance schools, a kindergarten, university annex and clinics. A variety of people walk through the atriums, heading home or to the office, for leisure or study. Above the station podium there are 15,000 residents. Including the residential areas opposite Kwun Tong Road, the station serves over 200,000 people (Xue et al. 2012).

While constructing the first metro line, the government was engaged in the infrastructure construction of **Shatin New Town**. Early in the 1960s, the government planning department conducted a study on the dispersion of people to the outskirts. The Hong Kong Society of Architects commented on the Shatin planning report and suggested learning from the planning examples of Cumbernauld in Scotland and Vallingby in Sweden, where the new town centers were located above the main traffic thoroughfares. This method of grade separation made the new town center a mega-structure with a multi-level podium and functions.[8] Before the train was upgraded to electric system, Handerson Property initiated housing in Shatin in 1977. Andrew Lee King-fun and Associates designed the Shatin Centre, with shopping mall and bus stations in the podium and eight residential towers above the podium. The Shatin Centre was completed in 1981 and set an example of podium + tower for the later development (Fig. 6.3).

Shatin Station on the East Rail Line is integrated with the new town facilities. Citylink, above the station platform, contains offices with a floor area of over 20,000 m^2 and a small shopping mall of 5,000 m^2. The passenger exit faces New Town Plaza, with a 9-floor shopping mall and a floor area of 200,000 m^2. New

---

[8]The documents from the Hong Kong Society of Architects are cited in Bristow (1989). When Bristow's book was written in the 1980s, such practice was just in the beginning stage.

Fig. 6.2 Kowloon Bay Station. **a** Towers plugged into the elevated pedestrian system. **b** Platform is used as public space, roof top of the shopping mall is garden of residents. **c** Platform leading to office towers and factories. Below the platform are vehicle road, depot and station. **d** Telford Garden built on top of the train depot, which is under the basket ball court

① Sha Tin Station 沙田站
② New Town Plaza 新城市廣場
③ Hilton Plaza 希爾頓中心
④ Sha Tin Town Hall 沙田大會堂
⑤ Sha Tin Centre 沙田中心

Fig. 6.3 Shatin town center and MTR station (Picture shot in 1992). Drawn by Dr. Tan Zheng

Town Plaza straddles several highways and main roads. Its 5,000 m² rooftop is paved with a wooden deck and fountains with several levels. The shopping mall, designed by the in-house architects of Sun Hong Kai Property, opened in January 1985, when mega-structures of this type were still rare. The central axis of New Town Plaza is several hundred meters long. Outside the shopping mall, the podium terrace continues, with cartoon figures and a children's playground linking the Shatin town hall, library, wedding registry, restaurant, central park and Shing Mun River. The shopping mall starts from 1st floor and straddles several street blocks, the ground is left for road and bus terminals. Passengers are transported to the shopping mall of upper floor by escalators and stairs. Phases II and III of New Town Plaza extend to and embrace the central park.

Like Hong Kong City Hall, the town halls were built as local-oriented centers and offer cultural amenities and facilities such as concert halls, libraries, performance venues and marriage registries. All of the town halls are located in traffic junctions or town centers and enjoy heavy patronage on weekdays and weekends. People go to see performances in the evenings and on weekends, children visit to attend various extra-mural art courses and the elderly engage in dance exercises at the podium. The building designs are plain, but meticulously serve the daily lives of the local citizens.

New Town Plaza and the station have become the axis of Shatin town center. To the east of the station are bus and mini-bus stations. The residents of the other estates and villages of Shatin rely on buses and mini-buses to connect to the station. To the east is another large commercial building, New Town Central Plaza, developed by Sun Hong Kai as a "home-square" for furniture and household utensils. Residents along the Shing Mun River, office workers and hotel passengers mainly use New Town Plaza as a passageway to and from the train station. The distance from the far end of Phase III to the station is around 400 m. From dawn to night, passengers crowd the shopping mall. When it opened in 1985, no shop wanted to open in this "remote" and sparsely populated area. Twenty years later, New Town Plaza was the busiest and densest shopping mall in the world.[9] When Shatin was developed in 1973, the population was around 20,000, but by 2014 it had increased to 648,200.[10] According to contemporary terminology, Shatin New

---

[9]The data on Shatin station and New Town Plaza are from http://www.newtownplaza.com.hk/chi/about.html, http://www.mtr.com.hk/chi/properties/mtrshopping_centres.html#citylink. Accessed 25 June 2012. According to the pedestrian count of Experian FootFall in 2010–12, Shatin New Town Plaza was the busiest shopping mall in the world. This can be observed and felt through its daily operation.

[10]For more about the population growth of Shatin, see the article, *Xin Shizhen de qishi* (The enlightenment of a new town—a case study of Shatin and Tian Shui Wai) http://wk.baidu.com/view/fb29ca086c85ec3a87c2c51b?ssid=&from=&bd_page_type=1&uid=bk_1344223402_501&pu=sl@1, pw@1000,sz@224_220,pd@1,fz@2,lp@1,tpl@color,&st=1&wk=sh&dt=doc&md=sax_2, and also the materials from Shatin District Council, http://www.districtcouncils.gov.hk/st/tc/dchighlights.html. Accessed 6 December 2012; and also the Government Statistics 2014, *Mingpao Daily News*, 1 April 2015.

Fig. 6.4 Shatin town center. **a** Seen from the high level of New Town Plaza. **b** Public space in front of New Town Plaza. **c** Shopping malls are connected above the street. **d** Atrium of shopping mall

Town was a good example of the "New Urbanism" practice in Hong Kong. It was compact, lively, convenient, pedestrian friendly, beautiful and close to public transportation and the town center[11] (Fig. 6.4).

[11]For details on the new town construction of Hong Kong, see Bristow (1989). For details on the public housing in Hong Kong, see Yeung and Wong (2003).

6.3   Linking the Rail Villages

In 1992, the Hong Kong government launched "ten core infrastructure projects" for the new international airport, including Chek Lap Kok International Airport, Tung Chung new town, North Lantau Highway, Lantau Link, Route 3, West Kowloon Highway, West Kowloon reclamation area, West Cross Harbor Tunnel and the Central reclamation plan. The **Tung Chung Line** and Airport Express use the same main railway line, but different entrances to the station. The 31.3 km line runs along the west part of Hong Kong Island, Kowloon Peninsula and the west part of the New Territories—Tsing Yi, Lantau, Sunny Bay, Tung Chung and Chek Lap Kok airport (Fig. 6.5).

When the airport plan was confirmed, the government filled 20 ha of sea near to Exchange Square in Central. The costal line was pushed 350 m outward. The reclaimed land was used as the terminal for the Tung Chung Line. Above the station is the IFC (International Financial Center) complex, with a shopping mall, office towers, hotel and serviced apartments on a 5.71 ha plot of land. In the Airport Express station, passengers can check in their bags and travel to the airport terminal in 30 min: "bringing the airport back to the city." This Tung Chung Line terminal is several hundred meters away from the old Central metro station.

The podium of the IFC is in the shape of an oval, with vehicles passing through the ring. The building complex is plugged into the pedestrian bridge web of Central and eight piers serving outlying islands. The pedestrian bridge system of Central originated in 1970, when Hong Kong Land built it to connect its own properties, and extends several hundred meters. The central pedestrian bridge starts from the Mid-level and ends at the waterfront, where the IFC complex is located. At the center of the IFC ring plan is the taxi and bus stop, surrounded by the train station and a three-story high shopping mall with a floor area of 59,460 m^2.[12] On the rooftop of the shopping mall there are bars, coffee shops and a public garden. According to the MTRC, the IFC shopping mall enjoys the highest patronage in Central.[13] Two office towers, the five-star Four Season hotel and the "Four Seasons Place" serviced apartments rise up from the podium. Phase II of the IFC is a tower of 480 m. The total floor area of the complex is 436,000 m^2, with offices, a hotel and retail, but no housing. This development of 20,000 m^2 was generated as a result of the Hong Kong station. The ratio of the station floor area to the development floor area is around 1:21. The ratio of Kyoto station, the second-largest station development in Japan, to nearby buildings is 1:20.[14] This ratio shows how effectively a station can generate development in the surrounding area (Fig. 6.6).

---

[12]For all five stations on the Tung Chung Line, the building floor area, residential towers and units, distance and other data were counted and calculated from general building plans, the Centaline Map and relevant property websites. The work was undertaken by the author's research assistant Yang Ke in 2014.

[13]The description of Central and Shatin stations are partly from Tan and Xue (2014).

[14]The ratio of Kyoto Station is from Hui (2011).

Fig. 6.5 Composition of IFC
complex in central. Drawn by
Dr. Tan Zheng

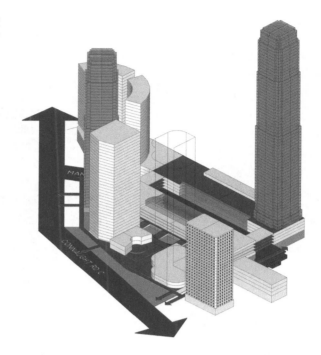

In Kowloon Peninsula, Yau Ma Tei, Mong Kok and Tsim Sha Tsui were the earliest developed areas, and as such they have been the most crowded areas in Hong Kong since the early twentieth century. Located in the heart of the Kowloon Peninsula and surrounded by Victoria Harbor, the growing population in this area has dramatically exhausted the land resources and caused massive traffic problems for continued urban development. As one of the core projects of Hong Kong Airport, the West Kowloon reclamation project has the direct objective of providing land for the expansion of the Yau Tsim Mong quarter. The development of this reclamation area has largely been led by the metro lines, and therefore also by the distribution of stations. **Kowloon Station** was planned as an important local node with a certain density and mixture.

Although developments encircling the station are connected to each other by roads and metro lines, these developments are mainly accessed through the metro stations as there are few pedestrian routes between them. The well-organized elevated pedestrian bridges, which connect the train station to the nearby housing and commercial arcades, also encourage users to travel by underground metro. Consequently, the ground is left almost entirely for vehicular use. This urban design strategy has shaped the expansion of West Kowloon into an isolated urban form, in stark contrast with the continuous "mat-like" urban blocks of the Yau Tsim Mong areas and, even more notably, the IFC and Pacific Place developments on Hong

(a)

(c)

(d)

(b)

(e)

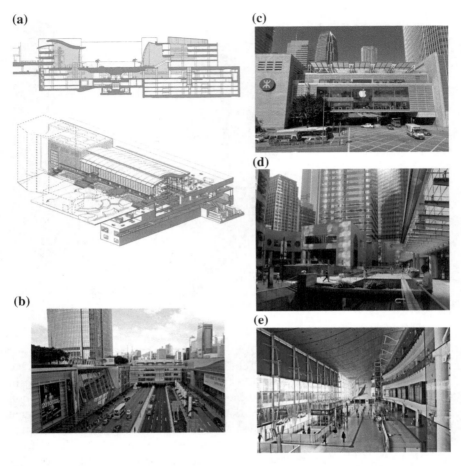

Fig. 6.6 IFC and Hong Kong Station. **a** Section showing station, road and superstructure. Courtesy of Rocco Design. **b** Traffic transition in the central part of IFC complex. **c** The opening allows vehicles entering to the complex center. **d** Pedestrian bridges linking the IFC to the central elevated walking network. **e** Lobby for the Airport Express terminal

Kong Island, which benefited from their connections to a network of pedestrian sky bridges, the Mid-level escalator and the Central ferry piers (Fig. 6.7).

The urban fabric of West Kowloon has been transformed in comparison with the older parts of Kowloon. First, the road systems are designed for fast transport, regardless of the relations between or within the blocks. In essence, the typical street-block pattern of Yau Tsim Mong has entirely disappeared in West Kowloon. Second, the street blocks are vastly enlarged compared with the older section of Kowloon. The huge dimensions encourage urban life to take place inside rather than outside on the public streets. The metro station was designed and constructed together with the entire block. Its location in the center of the block undoubtedly

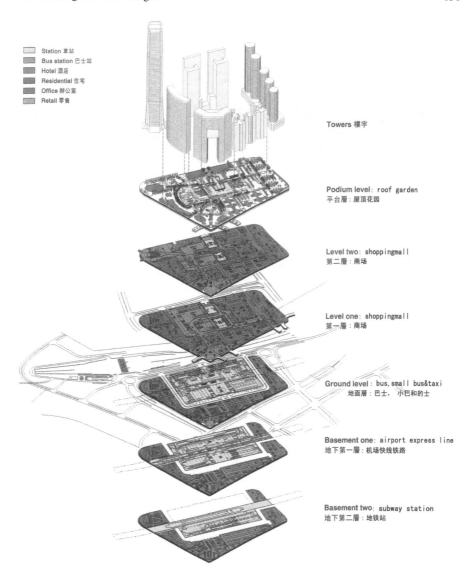

Station 車站
Bus station 巴士站
Hotel 酒店
Residential 住宅
Office 辦公室
Retail 零售

Towers 樓宇

Podium level: roof garden
平台層：屋顶花园

Level two: shopping mall
第二層：商场

Level one: shopping mall
第一層：商场

Ground level: bus, small bus&taxi
地面層：巴士，小巴和的士

Basement one: airport express line
地下第一層：机场快线铁路

Basement two: subway station
地下第二層：地铁站

Fig. 6.7 Relationship of various floors in the Kowloon Station development, master planned in 1992. Courtesy of Terry Farrell and Partners

intensifies the level of activity in the air-conditioned commercial spaces. Third, the traditional street-block has been replaced by a megastructure of towers on a 13 ha plot with a 1.7 million m² floor area.

The development includes 14 residential skyscrapers and two hotel and office buildings. The ICC tower is 483 m high, designed by KPF from the US. The floor area of the station is around 20,000 m². The ratio of the station and the

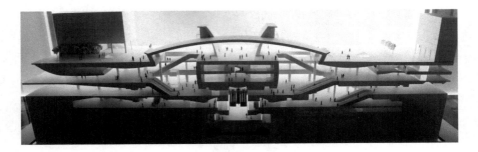

Fig. 6.8 Section of Kowloon Station and shopping mall

development area above is 1:80—three times higher than that of Hong Kong and Kyoto stations (Fig. 6.8).

The real estate development of Union Square, attached to Kowloon Station, was contracted to four main developers, Hang Lung Group, Sun Hung Kei Properties, Wharf Holdings and Wing Tai Asia, organized by the Hong Kong SAR government through the coordination and participation of the MTRC. Terry Farrell and Partners was appointed to produce the design for the station and a workable master plan for the whole block. Based on studies of the projects in the literature and an analysis of the built form in a historical context, the design strategy can be summarized as follows.

West Kowloon comprises a three-dimensional city with different functions, spreading out in diverse layers to achieve the maximum density and mix without sacrificing transportation efficiency. The main traffic circulation routes are organized along the ground floor to facilitate easy access from the roads surrounding the development, while also maintaining preferred connections with the underground stations. Shopping arcades and pedestrian routes can be found on the first and second floors, mainly to avoid conflicts with ground-level traffic at peak times. Bridges extend the pedestrian routes to the blocks and other interchanges nearby. On the podium floor, 18 m above ground, the towers share a common terrace, which serves as a traditional ground floor with controlled access for vehicles and pedestrians.

The city has a diverse mix of functions, reflecting all of the uses that are needed to grow into a complete and self-sufficient city. Located on reclaimed land far away from the older urban areas of Kowloon Peninsula, the success of the real estate development depends largely on the capability and performance of the project; that is, whether it can provide the correct or proper diversity of uses while still meeting the needs of all types of inhabitants and visitors, and thereby performing as a micro-city (Fig. 6.9).

High-rise towers represent the factual protagonists in real estate development projects. The Hong Kong skyline is well known for its contiguous high-rises of iconic value, and it is hoped that the towers of the West Kowloon project will contribute to the creation of new landmarks for Kowloon and Hong Kong overall.

Fig. 6.9 Kowloon station complex. **a** A floating island. **b** From roof garden to MTR station. **c** Station. **d** Shopping mall. **e** Podium roof garden

For quite some time, the towers along Hong Kong Island's waterfront have been an icon of the Asian metropolis, whereas on the opposite side of Victoria Harbor, due to the height limit restrictions necessitated by the city-center location of the old Kai Tak Airport, there was no such comparable urban scenario in Kowloon until the arrival of the West Kowloon project. The formation of the prototype for the West Kowloon megastructure can be discussed through four sub-topics, which range from the analysis of the prototype to the verification of its elements.[15]

Olympic Station can be found 1,000 m north of Kowloon Station. If Kowloon Station is an enclosed floating island, Olympic Station is like an octopus stretching out to the old area of Tai Kok Tsui and Mong Kok. During the early initiation stage, the station was named Tai Kok Tsui. However, it was renamed after the 1996 Olympic Games to honor the achievements of the Hong Kong athletics. Olympic Station's 16 ha plot mainly came from the reclamation of West Kowloon. In this

---

[15]Some of these materials are from Xue et al. (2010). The designer's description gives a detailed technical data for the Kowloon station, see Terry Farrell & Partners (1998).

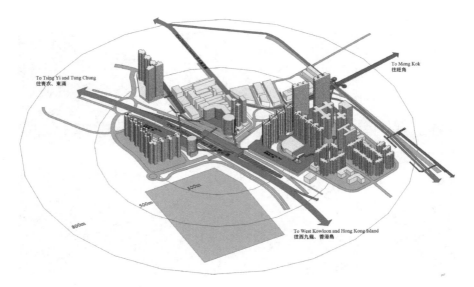

Fig. 6.10 Olympic Station—the catchment area of station. Drawn by Yang Ke

area, traffic accounts for 34 %, a higher percentage than in the other projects. The plan in the early 1990s set up the station location, connected to the neighborhood by six pedestrian bridges crossing West Kowloon highway and other busy streets. Within a radius of 600–800 m, old buildings and new estates all enjoy the concept of the Olympic Station (Fig. 6.10).

According to our calculation, the gross floor area of Olympic Station is around 15,660 m². The nearby projects that were developed directly as a result of the station development include Island Harbor View, Park Avenue, Olympian City, Central Park and Harbor Green,—a total of 23 blocks with 6,764 residential units—four office towers belonging to Hong Kong Bank and Bank of China and the Olympian City shopping mall Phases I and II. The total gross floor area of these properties is 667,652 m². The ratio of the station floor area to that of nearby developments is 1:43 (Fig. 6.11).

Within a 500-m radius, in addition to the properties developed by the MTRC, there are other communities and commercial buildings with a total floor area of 889,800 m², including The Long Beach, Imperial Cullinan, One Silver Sea, Hoi Fu Court and Charming Garden. From 1998 to 2011, 11 residential estates were built, providing 18,692 residential units for over 50,000 people. Housing accounts for more than a quarter of the total development. In this station-led area, the ratio of the reclaimed area to the old area is 1:2.6. There are public spaces with a floor area of tens of thousands of square meters, including a roof garden, park and sport courts[16] (Fig. 6.12).

---

[16]The information on Olympic Station are partly from Hui (2011) and the subsequent investigation by the author's research team.

(a)   (b)

Fig. 6.11 Residential estates and commercial buildings surrounding the Olympic Station. People mainly move on bridge instead of on ground. **a** Courtesy of Raymond Wong. **b** Street level of the Olympic Station area

(a)   (b)

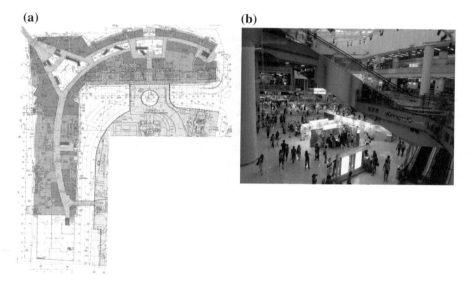

Fig. 6.12 Plan of Olympian City shopping mall. One circular route threading the shopping. **a** Drawn By Hui Ka Chun. **b** Interior of the shopping mall

In daily usage, the three-phase Olympian City shopping mall acts as a physical and psychological center. Phase I of the Olympian City is located in the west part of the development, mainly serving nearby estates. Phase II is in the center of the area, connecting to more housing estates and the bus terminal. However, the shopping mall of Phase II is just an L-shaped corridor, making the shopping space monotonous. Phase III crosses Hoi Wang Road by a pedestrian bridge. Its shape and functions are defined by the private housing towers above. The linear shape means that the station extends to the old area of Mong Kok. The walk from Mong Kok MTR to Olympic Station is more than 800 m. To attract people, the Olympian City management often hosts events such as live broadcasts of the World Cup football, appearances by movie stars, etc.

The Tung Chung Line and Airport Express emphasize speed, hence there are few stations on this line. The first station in the New Territories is **Tsing Yi**, after which the Airport Express heads straight for the airport. The Tsing Yi complex contains the station and Maritime Square shopping mall. The bus, shuttle and mini-bus stations are on the ground floor. The first floor is connected to the park and the open bus terminal by several pedestrian bridges. The east- and west-bound Tung Chung Line platforms are on the second and third floors and the Airport Express is on the fourth. All of these station facilities link to Maritime Square shopping mall, with a gross floor area of 46,000 m². Every day, 200,000 people pass through the building complex and Maritime Square is constantly crowded. Above the shopping mall is Tierra Verde, with 12 residential towers of over 35-stories providing 3,500 homes. There is parking for 920 vehicles in the basement of the shopping mall. The ground floor is a bus terminal, the first and second floors are linked to the Tung Chung Line and the fourth floor serves the Airport Express line. The podium and towers have a gross floor area of 291,879 m² on a plot of 5.4 ha, thus the plot ratio is 1:5.4.[17] The lobbies of Tierra Verde residential towers are within the shopping mall, so the residents can shop on their way home (Fig. 6.13).

Another large private development next to Maritime Square is Villa Esplanada, which is connected to the station and shopping mall by a footbridge. Developed by Cheung Kong Property, Sun Hong Kei Property and China Resources, Villa Esplanada comprises 10 towers of 35–40 stories containing 3,000 living units. The two large estates house more than 20,000 residents. In a 500-m radius, apart from the sea and parks, there are other properties, private or home ownership towers, all above 30 floors. No matter where they live, most of the 200,000 residents of Tsing Yi Island rely on the railway to commute. They arrive at the station by foot or mini-bus. At the end of the working day, the grocery store and restaurants in Maritime Square enjoy heavy patronage from commuters on their way home.

Tsing Yi station also houses a shopping mall and traffic exchange in the same building, similar to Kowloon Station. In Tsing Yi Station, the ground floor has a closer relationship with the nearby streets. The shopping mall opens onto the seashore park and promenade. The Tsing Yi complex only has a shopping mall and residential buildings, and does not provide office space. Residents of nearby public and private housing estates take the MTR to commute to Kowloon and Hong Kong Island, which conforms to the "destination accessibility." Using the "development rate" concept, within a radius of 500 m, other building developments with a total floor area of 336,900 m² were led by Tsing Yi Station. The ratio of the station area to the nearby direct developments is 1:3.5. Including the other developments in the 500-m radius, the ratio reaches 1:10. The 500-m radius includes large areas of sea and park, therefore the ratio is lower than that of other stations (Fig. 6.14).

Tung Chung is a new town that emerged from the airport construction in the 1990s. There are four phases of development and it is planned to accommodate

---

[17]The data on Tsing Yi Station in this chapter are from the MTRC website, http://www.mtr.com. hk/chi/properties/prop_dev_ty.html. Accessed 26 June 2012.

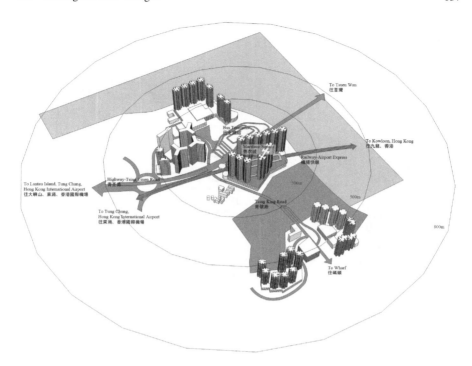

Fig. 6.13 Catchment area of Tsing Yi Station. Drawn by Yang Ke

(a) **(b)**

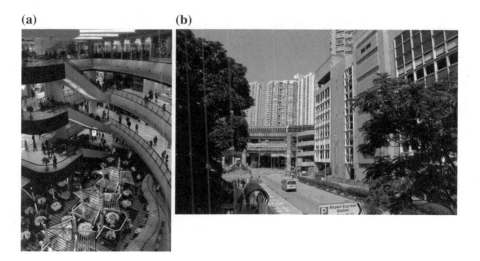

Fig. 6.14 Tsing Yi Station **a** Tsing Yi shopping mall; **b** Station on the right hand side

(a)

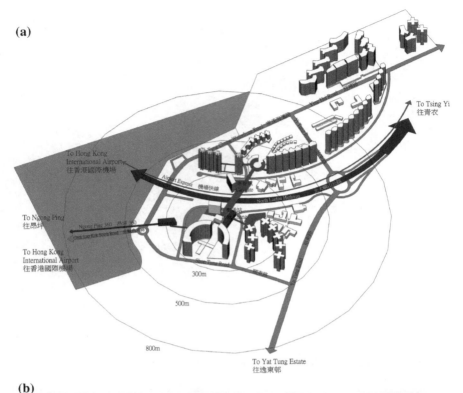

(b)

Fig. 6.15 Tung Chung Station **a** Catchment area of Tung Chung; **b** Residential estates arranged near the Tung Chung Station **c** Constructing Tung Chung in 2008. (**a**) Drawn by Yang Ke and Kwok Shing Yan

250,000 people. The population was 19,000 by 2000; 34,000 by 2006 and 100,000 by 2010 (Fig. 6.15).

Tung Chung Station is the terminal of the Tung Chung Line. The North Lantau Highway and railway run along the seashore, from Tung Chung Station turning to the airport. Tung Chung Station is located at the turning point of the road and railway. The station and cross-highway Citygate shopping mall surround the residential estates on two sides. The TOD site is 21.7 ha. To the east of Citygate there are hotels and the residential estates of La Rossa, Coastal Skyline and Caribbean Coast. To the west is Tung Chung Crescent. These private estates include 32 towers and low-rise town houses, with a total of 12,400 residential units. There are office towers with 15,000 m² of floor area, the Citygate shopping mall and a 440-room hotel, four kindergartens, primary and secondary schools and a wet market. The GFA of these developments is 1,028,910 m², with a plot ratio of 1:5. The ratio of the train station to its related development is around 1:66. The rail village displays the station's function in leading the new town development. The train station is not in the center, but is around 200 m from the west end of Tung Chung Crescent and 1,200 m from the east end of Caribbean Coast. People can walk from Caribbean Coast to the station through a covered foot bridge or take a mini-bus.[18]

Tung Chung Station was the catalyst for Tung Chung new town. The government subsidized home ownership and public housing prospered as a result of the railway. To reach the goal of 250,000 residents, the government has continued land formation and public housing construction along the seafront and at the foot of the mountain; 110 ha of land has been claimed from the sea[19] (Fig. 6.16).

The rail village in Tung Chung is mainly residential, with a small portion of office space. The shopping mall serves the residents. The central public space is surrounded by the shopping mall and the bus and train stations. There are roadside coffee shops and a fountain. In a high-density development with 100,000 residents, it is still possible to find many pleasant places, with natural mountain and ocean views. These beautiful sights are due to insightful planning and delicate design. In response to the appeal to find more housing land, the Tung Chung plan was augmented, doubling its current size. The new master plan stretches the development along the seafront, with high- and low-rise buildings around the sub-center and parks (Fig. 6.17).

Chapter 4 introduces the development of podium after the 1965 amendment of building regulations. A multi-story podium fully covers the site. Landscape is installed on rooftop and encourages leisure activities, where building towers grow up. The initial idea is to fully use the conditions allowed by building regulation. It gradually evolves to a trend in development and design. When the **Tseung Kwan O Line** was planned and constructed at the turn of the century, the pattern of podium was applied to almost all street blocks reclaimed from the Junk Bay. Take Tiu Keng Leng and Tseung Kwan O stations as examples. The two stations are distanced around one kilometer. Along the underground rail line, street blocks are divided, approximately 130 × 200 m each. Except one block is for design institute, swimming pool, indoor sport hall and library, the other blocks are all shopping mall in podium, and residential towers on rooftop. The housing belongs to middle class

---

[18]The data on Tung Chung Station in this chapter are from the MTRC website, http://www.mtr. com.hk/chi/properties/prop_dev_tc.html. Accessed on June 26, 2012.

[19]For the new Tung Chung development plan, see *Am730*, June 20, 2012, p. 8.

Fig. 6.16 Tung Chung Station. **a** Train, bus station and shopping mall. **b** Shopping mall. **c** Station house

Fig. 6.17 Master plan of Tung Chung Town, 2014. The opposite (near) side is the man-made island for Hong Kong-Macau-Zhuhai Bridge

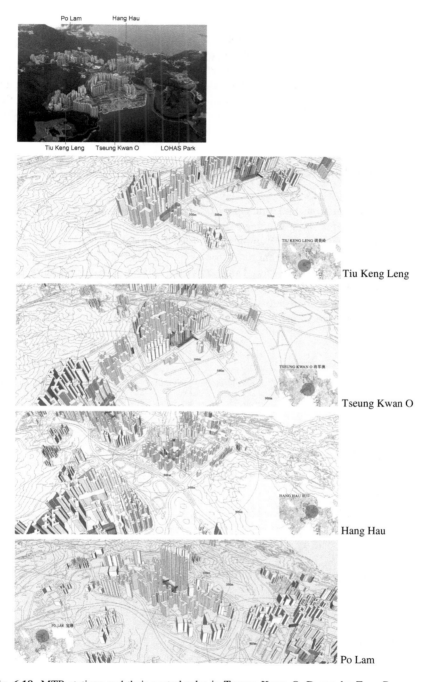

Fig. 6.18 MTR stations and their central roles in Tseung Kwan O. Drawn by Zang Peng

private residential estates, homeownership estates and public housing. Therefore, the shopping malls below gather shops in different classes. In Tseung Kwan O Station, the shopping mall is connected to two high-rise hotels, Holiday Inn and Dragon Crown. The two hotels flank a central green pedestrian bridge, leading to park and shopping mall and residential estates of the opposite street. The bridge is 50 m wide and 150 m long, covered with greenery and opened with hole, so that the road and park on ground can also receive daylight (Fig. 6.18).

6.4 Concluding Remarks: Mega-Structure as a Solution

To compare the functions and efficiency of MTR stations, we summarize the data of stations along Tung Chung Line as listed in Table 6.1.

Tung Chung, Tsing Yi and Olympic can be seen as typical residential "rail village". From Table 6.1, the development ratios for Tsing Yi, Olympic and Tung Chung are 1:6.7, 1:43 and 1:66 respectively. Tsing Yi is the lowest. The surrounding public housing was built in the 1970s, long before the MTR station was erected. Within an area of 500 m radius, there are waterfront park and Tsing Yi Park. The Olympic Station was built on reclaimed land, many new residential estates were planned and

Table 6.1 Summary of sample rail villages

Location	Hong Kong	Kowloon	Olympic	Tsing Yi	Tung Chung
	City	Reclaimed city area	Reclaimed city area	New Territories	New Territories
Building type and function in the rail village	Shopping mall, office, hotel	Shopping mall, residential, hotel	Shopping mall, residential, office	Shopping mall, residential	Shopping mall, residential, hotel
Rail village area (ha)	74.7	13.5	77.2	5.4	97.4
Approximate catchment radius (m)	200–300	Podium 369 × 503	500–800	300–800	300–1200
Floor area of train station (m²)	20,000	18,000	15,660	50,000	15,500
Floor area of buildings in the catchment (m²)	415,900	1,090,000	784,300	291,870 (immediate 300 m) 336,900 (800 m)	1,028,910
Development ratio	1:21	1:60	1:43	1:5.8–6.7	1:66

The data is obtained from drawing and map, and calculated by the author

constructed after the train station operated. The Tung Chung Station is in the new town center. There is a variety of high-rise and low-rise residential buildings. Hong Kong and Kowloon Stations are megastructure, with towers standing on the podium. The method will be further discussed, as we summarize in the following points.

6.4.1   Adapted Mega-Structure Prototype

Driven by the real estate economy, the Hong Kong, Kowloon and Tsing Yi stations adopted the mega-structure concept. The Olympic and Tung Chung station buildings each link to a large shopping mall and rail village.

Wilcoxon (1968) offers a helpful definition of a mega-structure as a construction of modular units that can be considerably, or even unlimitedly, extended. Using this definition, a mega-structure should be a structural framework into which smaller, modular units can be built or added to—or even "plugged in" or "clipped on" after having been prefabricated elsewhere—to create a structural framework that should have a useful life expectancy much longer than that of the smaller units that it might support. Wilcoxon's definition reveals the central concept of a mega-structure as an architectural organism that exists somewhere at the margins between permanence and temporariness and between simplicity and complexity. Various projects have emerged based on these concepts, typified by Habitat 67 in Montreal by Moshe Safdie, Centre Pompidou in Paris by Richard Rogers and Renzo Piano, and the Yamanishi Centre in Kofu by Kenzo Tange, among other examples. Most of these were constructed using a number of standard modules for the main structure with the capability for further adjustment. Significantly, however, none of them has ever been significantly modified using "plug-in" volumetric extensions or through replacement of the attached units.

Driven by the land-scarce economy of Hong Kong, the West Kowloon and Tsing Yi development certainly deploys all of the concepts of a megastructure as elucidated by Maki: "a large frame in which all the functions of a city or part of a city are housed" (Maki 1964). Therefore, in these terms, the development can be considered a mega-structure, albeit one that differs significantly from the historical precedents due to the unique constraints and local context that gave it shape. For example, as the block has been subdivided into several plots, each given over to different developers, the architectural and structural grids that should be uniform to facilitate future design and construction have been abandoned. The current gird dimensions do not welcome any further modular design. Furthermore, the Hong Kong, West Kowloon and Tsing Yi station developments do not fully comply with Wilcoxon's definition.

6.4.2   A Station as an Integrated Transport Interchange

Like the Airport Express and the stations on the Tung Chung Line, the principal aim of Hong Kong, Kowloon and Tsing Yi stations is to bring the airport back to the city. The location of the old Kai Tak Airport, along the harbor and almost directly in the center, was highly convenient. Kowloon Station aims to provide an extended airport service, similar to a remote airport, complete with in-town check-in and an express train that takes passengers to the terminals in just 30 min.

Based on this groundbreaking idea, Hong Kong, Kowloon and Tsing Yi stations were designed and built in a manner far removed from the usual image of the modern train station. Serving as an integrated transport interchange, the stations are well organized using different layers to maximize efficiency. Instead of a giant plaza in front of the station to collect the flow of passengers from all directions, the giant foyer on the ground floor has direct access to traffic nodes such as taxi areas, coaches, franchises and public bus stops. Pedestrians enter the foyer from the upper floor, where the commercial arcades and pedestrian networks are integrated. Underground, the Airport Express Line and Tung Chung Line are separated into overlapping platforms that share some vertical connections for direct interchanges. Owing to the clear zoning of the different modes of transport, these mega stations provide maximum convenience for the maximum number of passengers. These stations not only provide the best experience for departing travelers, but also present a new gateway for those arriving in Hong Kong. Highly efficient MTR trains transport passengers underground and the line works as an extension of the plane to take them directly downtown. However, compared with the well-integrated transport modes, the pedestrian routes from the ground floor are limited and leaving on foot is not encouraged.

Shatin, Kowloon Bay, Tsing Yi and West Kowloon stations use the station and shopping mall as a podium, upon which stand clusters of skyscrapers. Designed by Ronald Lu and Partners and completed in 2006, 8 Clear Water Bay Road provides another model: a slender "pencil building" convenient for bus stops, MTR stations and retail outlets, with a clubhouse and apartments in the tower. The podium consists of 12 stories and the traffic hall floor is around 25×30 m. The core contains escalators and lifts linking the rooftop to the basement MTR station. Restaurants, coffee shops, convenience shops and clinics are scattered around the podium floors. Through a long vehicular ramp, cars, minibuses and buses enter the Mid-level bus terminal, which is at the same level as the lobby of the residential tower. Residents alight from the bus, with an easy walk to the lobby to return home. The slender building is linked to the old public housing estate, wet market and community building on the opposite street. People's daily needs for food, living, entertainment and access to public transport are all within a 100-m radius covered areas. 8 Clear Water Bay Road is a typical TOD "pencil tower." Le Corbusier invented cluster of towers in the city center, the 20th century urban planning of Hong Kong, Tokyo and Singapore anchor the stations inside the complex of towers (Fig. 6.19).

(a)   (c)

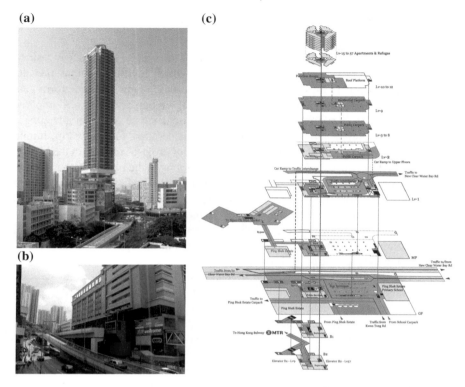

(b)

Fig. 6.19 8 Clear Water Bay Road, 2006. MTR, bus, mini-bus transition, daily shops, clinics and leisure activities all solved in a "pencil building". **a** Tower. Courtesy of Ronald Lu and Partners. **b** Ramp leading cars and mini-bus to the upper floor, while double deck bus stop is on ground floor. **c** Diagram. Drawn by Dr. Xiao Jing

6.4.3   *Elevated Ground Floor*

In Shatin town center, Telford Garden and the podiums of the Tung Chung Line stations, office or residential towers stand on the roof garden. The towers share closed-circulation routes for vehicles and pedestrians, and the entrances are connected to different levels according to their specific privacy requirements. In Shatin town center, Telford Garden, Hong Kong, Kowloon, Olympic and Tsing Yi stations were designed with semi-private gardens and squares on top in an attempt to create a coherent relationship between private properties and the public realm. In Kowloon Station, the podium is elevated 18 m off the ground (the maximum height allowed by the Hong Kong Building Regulations for 100 % coverage of the site). Although it still serves as the traditional ground floor of the towers, the mega-structure that has been lifted to the top of this podium level is fundamentally different in terms of its spatial structure and relationship with the elevated public streets and vehicular traffic on the ground.

6.4.4 Towers and Real Estate Properties

As an urban development project involving several of the biggest real estate investors, tower-block housing became the main means by which building designs met the market requirements. In the 1990s, the central symmetric, eight-unit cruciform plan became popular and now dominates high-rise housing layouts and design. Compared with high-rise "slab" buildings, a centralized high-rise design has greater advantages in terms of ventilation and daylight, a crucial consideration for the warm, humid climate of Hong Kong. During our interview, the Chief Project Manager of the MTRC also confirmed this as one of the decisive considerations in the planning phase of the West Kowloon project. Consequently, several towers based on this design were inserted into the north and west sides of the West Kowloon, Olympic and Tsing Yi projects, with the entrance lobbies connected to the commercial arcades and podium floors. Situated alongside Victoria Harbor, these towers form the silhouette of the skyline in Hong Kong and can be considered "smaller units plugged in or clipped on," as opposed to the main structural framework.

Skyscrapers are expensive to build. Because of their proximity to train stations, the skyscrapers described here conform to market expectations and bring in plenty of revenue. In the sequence of construction, housing is usually built before shopping malls, to quickly generate revenue from selling the residential units. The residential towers of Kowloon Station have been occupied since 2001, although the shopping mall, "The Element," only opened in 2007. In the IFC at Hong Kong Station, the tenants include the Hong Kong Monetary Authority, foreign currency settlement companies and the Henderson Property headquarters. The Four Seasons Hotel and up-market serviced apartments also sit on the podium of Hong Kong Station. In the ICC of Kowloon Station, the Ritz Carlton, Credit Suisse AG, Morgan Stanley, ABN and AMRO are the main tenants. These companies are an active part of the financial center and international metropolis of Hong Kong. In the economic boom years, property sale and rental prices sky-rocketed. In 2015, the selling price of a residential flat in Kowloon station was above HK\$40,000 per ft^2.

Mega-structures and high towers are attractive features of the rail village. The stations in Tung Chung and other lines have generated various types of developments, far bigger than the stations themselves, for example, 20 times bigger for Hong Kong Station, 66 times for Tung Chung Station and 80 times for Kowloon Station, as mentioned above.

6.4.5 New Experiences of a High Density City

The height, span and density of a "rail village" are completely different from those of classical cities and most people's conventional spatial experiences. For example, the tower jungle above Kowloon Station, the continuous commercial and public buildings in Shatin, the underground concourses between Central and Hong Kong stations and various linking spaces and roof gardens are pleasant places for users to linger and look at, both inside and out. Externally, these building complexes form a unique townscape. When people view the Kowloon and Olympic stations from the West Kowloon Highway or look at the IFC complex from Tsim Sha Tsui, they are astonished by the panorama revealed between the sky and the sea. This man-made miracle was brought about by infrastructure and transportation. The practice in Hong Kong enriches the "infrastructural urbanism" that prevails in Western countries.

In addition to the examples described above, almost all MTR stations, during their construction or afterwards, serve a kind of "rail village." In the area surrounding a station, the price of housing is far higher than it is further away. The different performances and forms of rail villages generate experiences in high-density living. Today, populous mega-cities are mostly concentrated in Asia. The unlimited sprawl generates city problems such as traffic jams, long commuting times, a worsening living environment and high crime rate. The concept of separating vehicles from people, mega-structures and rail villages first emerged overseas, but was soon adopted in Hong Kong, Singapore and other Asian cities, where the new town and rail system partly alleviates the problems caused by the increasing population. Hong Kong demonstrates that living conditions can be maintained at a civilized level even with the highest density in the world. There is no doubt that this is the right direction for sustainable development.

According to a map, my home is located four kilometers away from my work-place. With five to eight minutes spent walking on both sides plus six minutes in the running MTR cabin, the journey takes about twenty minutes door to door. I never bring an umbrella, as the entire walk is covered by building canopies, pedestrian bridges, the MTR station, an air-conditioned shopping mall and covered walkways. No umbrella is required when traveling to most destinations in Mongkok, Tsim Sha Tsui, Central or Causeway Bay. Our university campus comprises a small city of classrooms, lecture halls, large theaters, offices, libraries, banks, bookshops, canteens, restaurants and coffee shops, and has a gross floor area of 150,000 m². Before the hill part was built, one could reach any destination without need of an umbrella. Such were the conveniences that accompanied the "rail villages," MTR and mega-structure. Properties close to the MTR station were more expensive than those in other locations. The properties within a radius of 1,000 m are labelled with "MTR" proximity as a main selling point.

References

Bernick, M., & Cervero, R. (1997). *Transit villages in the 21st century*. New York: McGraw-Hill.
Bristow, R. (1989). *Hong Kong's new town: A selective review*. Hong Kong: Oxford University Press.
Cervero, R. (1998). *The transit metropolis—A global inquiry*. Washington DC: Island Press.
Cervero, R., & Murakami, J. (2009). Rail and property development in Hong Kong: Experiences and extensions. *Urban Studies, 46*(10), 2019–2043.

Dittmar, H., & Ohland, G. (2004). *The new transit town: Best practices in transit-oriented development*. Washington, DC: Island Press.

Freeman Fox and Partners. (1970). *Hong Kong mass transit further studies: Final report*. Hong Kong: Government Documents.

Hillier, B. (1999). *Space is the machine: A configurational theory of architecture*. Cambridge and New York: Cambridge University Press.

Hui, K. C. (2011). *Station complex mega-structure: Olympic station/olympian city—A study in urban and architectural perspectives*. Hong Kong: City University of Hong Kong, Bachelor's degree dissertation.

Kikutake, K., Otaka, M., Maki, F. & Kurokawa, K. (1960). Metabolism 1960—A proposal for new urbanism. In *The proceeding of 1960 World Design Conference*. Tokyo.

Knaap, G. (2006). Smart growth and urbanization in China: Can an American tonic treat the growing pains of Asia? In *Guangzhou: 2nd Megacities International Conference*.

Maki, F. (1964). *Investigations in collective form*. St Louis: School of Architecture, Washington University.

Tan, Z., & Xue, C. Q. L. (2014). Walking as a planned activity—elevated pedestrian network and urban design regulation in Hong Kong. *Journal of Urban Design, 19*(5), 722–744.

Terry Farrell & Partners. (1998). *Kowloon transport super city*. Hong Kong: Pace Publishing Ltd.

Wilcoxon, R. (1968). Council of planning librarians exchange bibliography. *Monticello, 66*, 2.

Xue, C. Q. L., Ma, L., & Hui, K. C. (2012). Indoor 'public' space—A study of atriums in MTR complexes of Hong Kong. *Urban Design International, 17*(2), 87–105.

Xue, C. Q. L., Tan, Z. & Xiao, Y. (2016). Architecural magazine in Hong Kong for a century. *World Architecture, 36*(1), 40–44. 薛求理、谭峥、肖映博 (2016). 香港建筑杂志百年. 世界建筑. 2016年第1期.

Xue, C. Q. L., Zhai, H., & Roberts, J. (2010). An Urban Island floating on the MTR station: A case study of the West Kowloon development in Hong Kong. *Urban Design International, 15*(4), 191–207.

Yeung, Y. M., & Wong, T. K. Y. (Eds.). (2003). *Fifty years of public housing in Hong Kong: A golden jubilee review and appraisal*. Hong Kong: Chinese University Press.

Yin, Z. (2014). *Study on relationship between catchment and built environment of metro station in Hong Kong and Shenzhen*. Hong Kong: City University of Hong Kong, Ph.D. dissertation.

Chapter 7
From Commercial to Global

In the 1970s, under the rule of Governor Murray MacLehose, Hong Kong society presented a thriving scene. More than a million people lived in public rental or government subsidized ownership houses. Social problems were gradually ironed out and people envisaged a peaceful life and rosy tomorrow. At the beginning of the 1980s, Hong Kong took off economically due to its unique position in the open-door policy of the Chinese mainland. In 1981, the gross domestic product per capita reached HK$26,530, and the colony entered the ranks of rich Asian countries, only behind Japan and Singapore.[1] Development and (de-)colonialization converged in an interesting and special way within shifting global and local connections (McDonogh and Wong 2005). Hong Kong stood at the convergence of globalized trend and emergent Asia. The city demonstrated its power by building skyscrapers to project its world vision. In addition to skyscrapers, many other projects were either digging the earth or in construction. These include metro subway, rail station, infrastructure in new towns, institution campus, land reclaiming and underground projects. The port city presented a thriving scene and set up an example for the Chinese mainland, a once closed land just opened its window and door. The Hong Kong architects, engineers and professionals were busily sought after in the Greater China area (Xue 2014).

At the end of the 1970s, the manufacturing industry accounted for 35 % of Hong Kong's economy and the service industry for 62 %. The demand for high-quality offices and their serving facilities was strong (McDonogh and Wong 2005). Capitals and investment displayed their role in shaping the city. In his book *Hong Kong: Culture and the politics of disappearance*, Ackbar Abbas declared that "buildings in Hong Kong suffer the fate of any other commodity, an insight that Walter Benjiamin arrived at more than half a century ago: 'In the convulsions of the commodity economy we begin to recognize the monuments of the bourgeoisie as ruins even before they have crumbled.' … Property speculation means that every building in Hong Kong, however new or monumental, faces imminent ruin, on the

---

[1]For more on Hong Kong's economy in the 1980s, see Cheng (1977) and Enright et al. (1997).

© Springer Science+Business Media Singapore 2016
C.Q.L. Xue, *Hong Kong Architecture 1945–2015*,
DOI 10.1007/978-981-10-1004-0_7

premise of here today, gone tomorrow—a logistics that, by contracting time, dispenses even with the pathos of decay" (Abbas 1997). Before describing the glamorous buildings shining the central business district as (post)card of city, this chapter first discusses several "disappearing" cases in the capitalist economic wave, and then how buildings competed to become spectacles in the consumerist and global era.

7.1 Giving Way to the Commercial Interests

Between Central (Victoria City) and Wanchai is Admiralty. Because it was occupied by military barracks since the 19th century, it was quiet for a long time. The conversion of the Victoria Barracks started in 1977. The early stage of its redevelopment showed by three rounds of zoning plans was claimed by the prestige planning theorist Roger Bristow as a set-back in the system of public participatory planning that may never recover ever since (Bristow 1984). It envisioned the future Hong Kong Park at the center of a high-density commercial district, which is a rare case of such military redevelopment. This park design has multiple relations to the architectural projects within the site, but neither the making of this park nor the architecture nearby has been seriously challenged by the conservation strategy of historical landscape. Indeed, the park receives overwhelming positive feedbacks. However, if with careful examination, the whole process of transformation indicates a hidden contestation in the concept of preserving military landscape.

The Governor-in-Council commissioned a special committee to conduct the development research,[2] and a preliminary planning proposal was submitted in June 1977. In the introduction of this proposal, it said that three aspects would be taken into consideration of redevelopment: amenity to commercial growth of the central area, direct or indirect return to public revenue, and the retention of existing buildings if with proposals for use "which are generally acceptable to the public and compatible *with [first two aspects]* above" (Victoria Barracks Planning Committee 1977). In a site of about 16.8 ha, the committee basically allocated four sectors with different functions: commercial/residential development squeezed in the northeast corner, a new Supreme Court building in the northwest, medium-density residences in the middle, and space for government, institution and community in the east and west ends.

In light of these comments, the special committee was ordered to revise the land uses and to implement schematic recommendations for each military building to be protected. The final report with major changes was submitted in September 1977. On one hand, there would be no more medium-density residential development in

---

[2]The committee comprises eight members, including the Honourable Szeto Wai as Chairman, Doctor S.M. Bard, William L. Chan, the Honourable D.W. McDonald, G.R. Ross, George C. Tso, G.L. Mortimer, and K.C. Lye, the then professor of architecture at the University of Hong Kong.

the central area. It maintained the successive levels of platforms where Block C, D, E once occupied. This would make available an interaction between two open areas in the middle and west by means of a hillside corridor in-between. It would also provide a larger boundary for the Hong Kong Park of more than 13 hectares, an open space being doubled for public uses. On the other hand however, the proposal had no scheme of urban design as detailed as the previous one.

However, due to unclear reasons, this revised report was not approved by the Executive and Legislative Council. A new zoning plan was required later to be made by another body of consultancy (Executive and Legislative Council Office 1977). The Yuncken Freeman Ltd., a company in architecture and planning, was then commissioned by the Urban Council and the Public Works Department.[3] The submission of this new plan (Plan No.LH4/49) was prepared in August 1978 and finally approved in 1979.

All the landscape features of these platforms from the level of +20 m down to ground zero were therefore doomed. Technical problems followed when building caisson walls and land excavation. The situation was much serious when building towers of the Pacific Place I & II. After the plot of nearly 20,000 m^2 was sold to the Swire properties in the public auction, it was required to build no less than 960,000 m^2 of gross floor area within a six-year covenant allowed by the Crown Lease.[4] It envisioned a cluster of commercial towers, including the Marriott Hotel, Conrad Hotel, and Shangri-La Hotel. The architectural design was made by Wong & Ouyang, whose fame rose during its collaboration with architect Paul Rudolf in the project of the Bond Center at Admiralty by the other side of Queensway. The design includes a massive podium of 118,000 m^2 under the towers, rising from −4 MPD (mean principle datum) to +55 MPD. It contains twelve levels of shops and carparks (Fig. 7.1).

Pacific Place was owned by Swire Property, which is renowned for its consistently high quality in building. The two ends of the shopping mall are enlarged to receive more people from the streets, and act as a circulation hub. The central part is a linear space for shops. Lit by a skylight, the three-story high atrium is slightly curved along the street. Wong & Ouyang had rarely used curvilinear shape before. After the success of Pacific Place, the designers at Wong & Ouyang were convinced by this form. In 2010, the owner invited Thomas Heatherwick from London to remodel the interior. The white tone, wood decoration, waterfall-like glass lift, glass

---

[3]Yuncken Freeman H.K., later called Denton Corker Marshall HK, was then a branch office of its main base in Australia. The project budget list of the Urban Council up to 1986 indicates that this company was the second largest architectural company that received commissions from the Urban Council, with a list of nine projects worth $63,846 million HKD in total. By contrast, Wong & Ouyang Architects received only three projects worth $2,000 million HKD (Urban Council, 1986: 70).

[4]BJHKC, Historical barracks site sold to Swire Properties. May.1982: 20; 1985: 30 "1985 To strengthen the company's investment portfolio, Swire Properties purchased the Victoria Barracks site on Queensway at a land auction. The site was planned to be redeveloped into a commercial and hotel project." http://www.swireproperties.com/en/about-us/history-milestones.aspx.

(a)

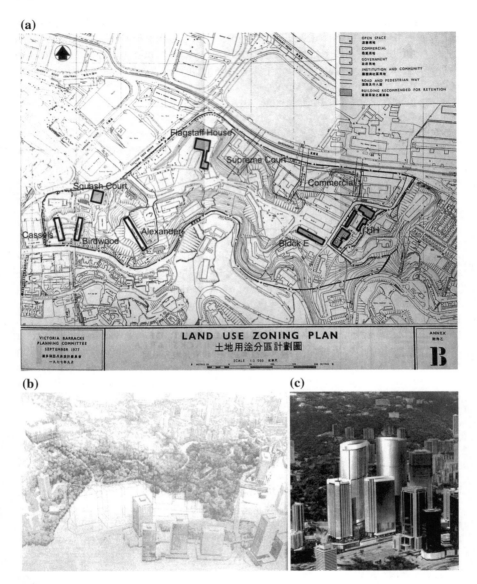

(b)   **(c)**

Fig. 7.1 From military barrack to commercial complex. **a** Zoning plan of Admiralty in 1979. **b** In the 1970s, the consultant Yuncken Freeman studied the urban design of Admiralty when the military barracks were removed. The pencil line shows the location of Pacific Place. Courtesy of Hong Kong Government. **c** The commercial complex replaces the old barracks on Admiralty

balustrade and variously textured wall slate make the building classy and elegant. The vehicular road to the hotel and offices is at the level of the podium top and hill. The lobby and many restaurants and rest spaces in the hotels and offices face the

Fig. 7.2 Pacific Place as shopping mall, venue of public events and transition of traffic (MTR, bus, street and mountain levels)

mountain or sea. In the past 30 years, many more shopping malls and complex buildings have emerged in Hong Kong. Compared with later buildings, Pacific Place has never looked out of date. It set the prototype for classy shopping malls, commercial complexes and transit oriented developments (TOD) (Fig. 7.2).

Both the Hong Kong Park and Pacific Place are good design by themselves. However, these are at the expense of old military heritage and disappearance of (colonial) history.

Victoria Barracks is not an isolated case. The Central Post Office, an English Renaissance building built in 1911, was demolished for the higher price commercial development in 1976. Alexander House in Central, a 16-storey "high-rise" built in 1953, was demolished 20 years later for a 34 storey skyscraper. Just a couple of years after the Ritz-Carlton Hotel in Central was completed in 1993, the client considered to rebuild it into office building for a higher revenue. It was down to ruin in 2008. Upon the land, a curtain wall office building was built. Such frequent cycles of demolishing and rebuilding happen in Central and other districts year after year. Sustainability and durability all give way to the commercial profits and the figures of corporations' annual report.

7.2   Creating Spectacles

According to French scholar Guy Debord, for the present day, which prefers the sign to the thing signified, representation to reality, the appearance to the essence… illusion is sacred. "Images detached from every aspect of life merge into a common stream, and the former unity of life is lost forever… the spectacle is both the outcome and the goal of the dominant mode of production. It is the heart of society's real unreality—the spectacle epitomizes the prevailing model of social life" (Debord 1994). When Hong Kong gradually moved to consumers' society, building and spatial production transcended the mere pragmatism. Some buildings in the central business district were constructed more as spectacles in this consumerist society.

In the limited Central and on the ruins of old buildings, the new spectacles are staging for spotlight. The 1970s–80s saw a group of such spectacular mansions rising up in Central.

There has always been a shortage of land for building in Hong Kong. After the war, the government became more aggressive in reclaiming land from the sea. On June 1, 1970, the government auctioned a 5,000 m^2 plot of the "land of the king" in the Central reclamation area. Eighteen groups competed for the land, which was finally bought by Hong Kong Land, the oldest and biggest landlord in Central, for HK$258 million. This was the highest price ever paid per square meter of land in Hong Kong. The owner decided to build public space in front of the building although it has distance with the central business district. To reward the public usage, the government allowed a "bonus" floor area so that the plot ratio could reach 18. The project named **Jardine House** was designed by Palmer and Turner, mainly penned by James Kinoshita. To speed up the construction, the external wall was designed to be a smooth tube shape, so that a sliding form could move up it. In addition to the central core, the external wall was also load-bearing. Kinoshita decided to use a circular window, as it would protect the window opening and place the stress on the external wall continuous. When presented two schemes to the client, one with conventional rectangular windows, one with circular windows, Mr. Henry Keswich, the chairman of Hong Kong Land and Jardine, approved the circular windows, "Why not? We might as well try something different" (Kinoshita 2005, p. 146). The building was constructed by Gammon Construction Ltd. and took only 16 months from breaking ground to completing the roof structure on top of Floor 52 (Fig. 7.3).

The building is a square tube shape, with no podium. The four corners and the external walls firmly support the structure. The circular window is 1.8 m in

(a)   (b)

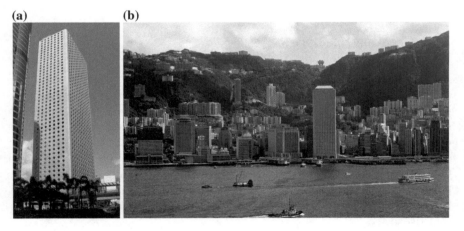

Fig. 7.3 Jardine House, 1973. **a** Cladding changed to metal due to the falling of tile. **b** Standing on the waterfront in the early 1970s, Peak Tower (1972) is on its remote top

diameter and the spandrel wall is the same size horizontally and vertically. The concrete external wall was first clad with mosaic, but was changed to metal in 1978 when some of the mosaic peeled away and fell off. The building was completed at the end of 1973. In the 1970s, Jardine House was the tallest building in Hong Kong and Asia. Capitalism in a city is always associated with land speculation and skyscrapers. During the economic boom years, Jardine House stood proudly on the Central seaside and became the symbol of Hong Kong.[5] In addition to the Jardine and Hong Kong Land offices, the building housed investment banks and law firms. Class A office towers such as Jardine House provided a suitable symbol for Hong Kong as a globalized city.

In 1980, seven years after Jardine House was built, the 66-storey, 216 m high Hopewell Center was completed in Queen's Road East, Wanchai. The ground floor opens onto Queen's Road and the 15 lower floors house shops, restaurants and parking. Floor 17 connects to Kennedy Road on the hill. Its top floor is a rotating restaurant. The Hopewell Center is 30 m taller than Jardine House. The design and construction were both conducted by Hopewell itself. The foundations were constructed with 330 piles pushed into the rock and the construction adopted sliding form technology. The Hopewell Center was the tallest building in Hong Kong until 1989, when the Bank of China building was constructed. One characteristic of Hopewell is that the building connects Queen's Road with Kennedy Road, which have a considerable height difference. Many residents on the hill take the lift down to Queen's Road and the MTR, offering great convenience to the community. As the tallest building in the 1980s, many companies were proud to be located there (Fig. 7.4).

The Hopewell Center was designed by Sir Gordon Wu, Chairman of the Hopewell Group. Sir Gordon's father, Wu Chung, started his business running a taxi company and speculating on taxi licenses. Sir Gordon graduated with a civil engineering degree from Princeton University.[6] Based in Wanchai, his Hopewell Group developed real estate property and infrastructure in Hong Kong, the Chinese mainland and Asian cities. In the early 1980s, he invested in the first expressway from Shenzhen to Guangzhou and the construction of Shenzhen's city center. When the Hopewell Center was in preparation, the project only had permission to build housing. Wu found a loophole in the outline zoning plan and sued the Town Planning Board. He eventually won the legal battle and built the center as offices. The plot ratio was raised to 1:15 and the floor area was increased by 30,000 m^2. The building rose to 66 floors.[7] Among the examples discussed in this chapter, the Hopewell Center is the most "localized," with local investment and design. Other Chinese enterprises were building their headquarters at this time, such as the Sun

---

[5]The description of Jardine House is referenced see Wikipedia (2013). For more about its design, see Hong Kong Institute of Architects (2007).

[6]Sir Gordon Wu is a major donor to his alma mater Princeton University. In the early 1980s, the Gordon Wu Hall was constructed on the campus of Princeton University, designed by Robert Venturi as a typical post-modernist work.

[7]For more about the Hopewell lawsuit, see Jianzhuyouren (2013).

(a)   (b)

Fig. 7.4 Hopewell Center, 1980. **a** Lobby of 17th floor, serving for the entrance of Kennedy Road. **b** Cylinder-shaped building

Hong Kei Center (1982) and Great Eagle (1983). An international metropolis should have a compatible image and design, which brought the arrival of overseas designers.

From its inception in the mid-nineteenth century, Central (Victoria City) was a heavily used commercial town. After the war, most office buildings in Central were classified as Grade A offices. They were mostly developed by Hong Kong Land, founded in 1889, and its parent company, Jardine & Matheson Co, which has been active in Central since 1844. A strategy of Hong Kong Land was to rebuild its own buildings in Central. Due to Hong Kong Land's taste and operation, many buildings in Central present a corporate and elite atmosphere.

Located at the junction of Queen's Road and D'Aguilar Street, the first-generation Hong Kong Club provided a social venue for rich expatriates. It is still only open to members today. The second-generation Hong Kong Club, in Edinburgh Square, was four-stories high and built in the Renaissance style with elegant decoration in 1895. At the end of the 1970s, the owner planned to demolish it and build a new building, but the proposal was met with protests from civil organizations. However, the nineteenth century building was old and dirty, and the owner could see no particular value in keeping it. Moreover, the colonial building had always had a "high status" and was never accessed by ordinary citizens. A newspaper commented that "in terms of architectural art, this building might have some value. However, politically, this building should disappear, as early as it can (Fig. 7.5)."[8]

The Hong Kong Club and Hong Kong Land jointly developed the new club-house. The lower part belonged to the Hong Kong Club and the upper part to Hong

---

[8]The comment on the Hong Kong Club is quoted from Lui Ta Lok's book *Na shiceng xiangshi de qishi niandai* (The 1970s we might know), Zhonghua Shuju 2012.

Fig. 7.5 Hong Kong Club, 1895

Kong Land, which retained ownership for 25 years. An international design competition was held for the building, which was won by Harry Seidler & Associates (1923–2006), an Australian firm associated with Palmer & Turner. Completed in 1983, the building's lower six floors and two basement floors are for club use, while floors 7–25 are offices with a separate entrance.

Seidler graduated from Graduate School of Design (GSD) Harvard University in 1946 and, as a student of Walter Gropius (1883–1969) and assistant to Marcel Breuer (1902–1981), introduced modernism to Australia. The design of the Hong Kong Club was a natural extension of the method he consistently followed in other projects—curves dividing the square plan and interlocking planes in the Baroque style. The clubhouse fully covers the site. The four corner column-walls stand firmly on the ground, with curvilinear planes spilling out from the square frame. The podium floor is used as a garden. Structurally designed by famous Italian engineer Pier Luigi Nervi (1891–1979), the beam changes section from rectangle on two sides to T-shape in the center. It conforms with the change in stress and expresses the elevation with an elegant rhythm. In the 1970s, Seidler and Nervi cooperated in several projects including Australian Embassy in Paris and used similar structural method. The beautiful variable-section main and secondary beams free the interior from column. The use of structure as decoration was popular in the 1970s and 80s. Seidler's design presented a more delicate and elegant shape. The staircase in the entrance lobby spirals up, inviting visitors to gaze upward. The curved beams are well integrated with the lighting channel and the beam-slab structure is the best decoration on the ceiling. Most of Seidler's designs used prefabricated T-shaped beams. A worker's wage in Hong Kong was half that in Europe and Australia at the time and all of the structure was poured in situ (Figs. 7.6 and 7.7).

The arch gate and column capital from the old building were used as decoration in the new building, which commemorated its predecessor. The construction of the new Hong Kong Club was led by Roy Munden, President of the Hong Kong Club that year. At that time, he was busy with the construction of both the Hong Kong

Fig. 7.6 Hong Kong Club, 1984. **a** The elevation reflects the structural features. **b** Beams are natural decoration in the dinning hall. **c** The old portico is left as decoration. **d** Staircase, the curve is signature of Seidler's design

Club and the Hong Kong Bank.[9] Originated from the colonial period, Hong Kong Club is for members only. Most people can appreciate the building only from its outside.

In 1978, the **Hong Kong Bank** (**HSBC**, Hong Kong and Shanghai Banking Corporation) initiated the expansion of its headquarters on its own site. The estate officials of the bank asked Mr. Gordon Graham, then President of the Royal Institute of British Architects, to act as a consultant on the project regarding a

---

[9]The data on the Hong Kong Club are partly taken from *Vision–Architecture, Design*, June 1983. Some parts are taken from an interview with Mr. Ronald Lau, Deputy Manager of the Hong Kong Club, 14 August 2013.

(a)   (b)

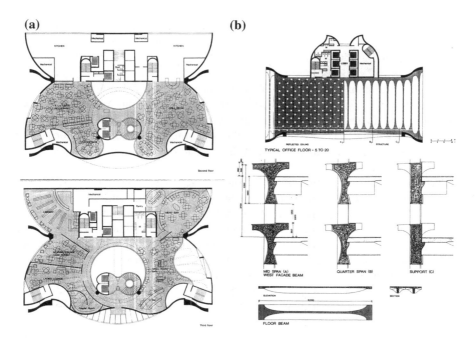

Fig. 7.7 Design of Hong Kong Club **a** Plan **b** Reflected ceiling plan of dinning hall and beam details

proper scheme and designer. In June 1979, HSBC invited seven design firms to present a scheme for the project, called 1QRC (1 Queen's Road Central). The designers could either provide a scheme for extending the old building, or for a new building covering the whole site. The brief gave the participants ideas for a better solution. The participants included Foster Associates and Yorke Rosenberg Mardall of the UK, SOM and Hugh Stubbins Associates of the USA, Harry Seidler and Yuncken Freeman Pty Ltd. of Australia and Palmer & Turner of Hong Kong. Each firm received HK$150,000 as compensation. HKBC's estate officials visited the firms and their representative works to gain experience.

The schemes were submitted in October 1979. Stubbins, based in Boston and Dean of the GSD at Harvard University, had designed Citicorp's headquarters in New York city in 1977. The building consisted of four huge columns supporting the tower so that an old church could remain under the tower. His design for HSBC was similar. The tower of the HSBC building was supported by a huge column and the external wall was clad with white strips. A podium straddled Des Voeux Road and extended to Statue Square, so that people could walk to the bank without being interrupted by the busy Des Voeux Road. Seidler's design included a twisted spandrel wall and was reminiscent of the Hong Kong Club. Yuncken Freeman's design consisted of a cannonball-shaped tower. Palmer & Turner's design highlighted the stair shaft and the floors were typically in the shape of a flower petal.

Palmer & Turner used the staircase as a node, a similar design to that used in the design of the Hong Kong Polytechnic campus. Another of Palmer & Turner's designs featured a tower in the south and kept the old building. The new building adopted similar vertical lines to the 1936 building. All of the schemes were reviewed by a team consisting of Roy Munden of HSBC, Gordon Graham the consultant and David Thornburrow from Spence & Robinson. Munden was convinced by the flexibility of the design presented by Norman Foster. He persuaded the other consultants and recommended the design to the board of directors. After undergoing an interview and defense at the end of 1979, Norman Foster's design was approved (Fig. 7.8).

This building was the fourth generation of HSBC's headquarters. HSBC was a top-ranking bank in the world, and had been based in Hong Kong for more than a century. In 1865, HSBC rented the Wardley Building in Wardley Street (now Bank Street) as its offices. In 1866, HSBC bought the land plot and built a Victorian style building. In 1933, Palmer & Turner designed its third-generation building in the Art Deco style. Opened in 1935, the building had 13 floors and was 70 m high. Once the largest building in the Far East, the symmetrical building was the first to use air-conditioning in Hong Kong. During the Japanese occupation, the building was used as the government's headquarters. The central gate was rather small to receive

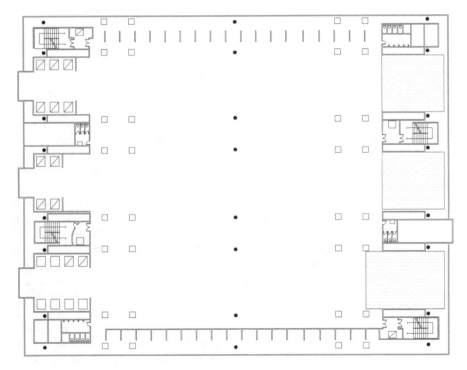

Fig. 7.8 Plan of HSBC headquarters, foster scheme

(a) **(b)**

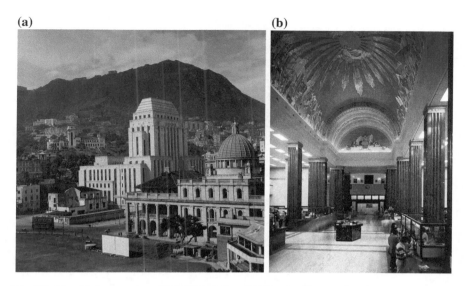

Fig. 7.9 The third generation of HSBC building, 1936. **a** Art Deco style helping the grandiose gesture. **b** Bank hall, the color mosaic was from an Egyptian temple. Courtesy of HSBC Asia Pacific Archives

a large influx of people. The external stone wall looked solid, but felt enclosed to the eyes of the 1980s (Fig. 7.9).

The fourth-generation HSBC building faced Statue Square and the Star Ferry. Ove Arup was responsible for the structural design and J Roger Preston for the mechanical design, while Levett & Bailey was appointed as the quantity surveyor and John Lok/Wimpey Joint Venture as the constructor. The building has a superstructure of 48 upper floors and 4 basement floors, with a height of 180 m and a gross floor area of 70,398 m^2. The design used eight groups of columns and five groups of V-shaped horizontal trusses to undertake all of the loadings. The floors are suspended by the structure, with traffic towers on two sides and an atrium in the center. A preliminary idea was to keep the old entrance lobby in the center, but finally the old building was demolished. Every group of vertical structures consists of four huge steel tubes. Between the columns are prefabricated floor slabs with an 11 m span. The five horizontal trusses are located in Floors 11, 20, 28, 35 and 41. The suspended steel tubes hold the floor slabs. The structure and loading conveying systems are exposed in elevation. The steel components were soaked in special chemical paint nine times so that they would keep their color for 50 years. The vertical traffic and auxiliary facilities are on two sides, which gives great flexibility to the central functional part of the building. A conventional office tower has the core in the center with typical floor stacking. The HSBC building broke this convention. From the side view, the building comprises three parts, the tall central part and the low south and north parts. This satisfied the street shadow calculation of the 1970s Building Regulations (Fig. 7.10).

Fig. 7.10 HSBC Bank headquarters completed in 1985. Courtesy of HSBC Asia Pacific Archives

The ground floor lobby has a headroom equivalent to three stories, open to the south and north. A couple of 20 m long escalators lead customers to the upper floors. The lobby has a curved glass ceiling to separate the public space from the bank hall above. Going through the glass ceiling, a visitor sees a bank hall with a 52 m high atrium. At the height of Floor 11, there is a row of huge mirrors to reflect daylight into the interior. The offices all open onto the atrium. Although considered in the design, the daylight is insufficient for such a high atrium and deep plan. The bank building was traditionally enclosed and solid. The open (and landscaped) plan of office and atrium delivered a grand new view for banking business (Fig. 7.11).

All of the bank files are conveyed by 80 electric carts. The air-conducts, power, telephone and computer wires are hidden in the raised floor 60 cm above the structural slab. The floor is formed by a 600 × 600 light-weight aluminum panel, covered with carpet. The floor panel can easily be opened for the maintenance or installation of facilities. Although raised floors have become popular in the 21st century, they were rare in the early 1980s. Twenty-three lifts run through the transparent shafts. The building used 30,000 tons of steel and 4,500 tons of aluminum. The engineers of J Roger Preston brought the revolution in building services. Most of the components were manufactured in the factory and assembled on site. In the early 1980s, China's industrial standards had not yet reached a

Fig. 7.11 Interior of HSBC building. The ground floor and upper atrium is separated by a glass soffit. Perspective drawn by famous architectural renderer Helmut Jacoby (1926–2005)

satisfactory level, so all of the components were made overseas. The structural steel was from the UK, the glass, aluminum shell and floor from the US and the service components from Japan. The large amount of prefabrication reduced the number of wet jobs on site and contributed to the buildability of the construction.

The construction of the foundations took a lot of effort as it was related to the seawall, cooling water and salt water systems. The construction of the super-structure took less than three years. In the summer of 1985, the first eleven levels and four basements were open for use. It cost HK$5,200 million (US$ 645 million) and was the most expensive building in the world at the time. An outcome of concerted efforts from elite professional teams in design, consultancy and con-struction, the building is scientific, rational and stern. The internal modules and many details demonstrate the beauty of accuracy and the poetry of technology. The angle of the escalator and the installation of the bronze lion, according to Feng Shui, added to the legend of Hong Kong.

In April 1986, the HSBC building held a grand opening ceremony hosted by Sir Edward Youde (1924–1986), the Governor of Hong Kong.[10] The building astonished the world. It was used as the cover photo for a classical architectural history book, *Modern Architecture since 1900*, and the author, William Curtis, called it a "building of the Pacific era" (Curtis 1996). HSBC was originated in Hong Kong and Shanghai for the British trading in China. Its early emblem demonstrated obvious British and "colonial" flavor, which seems outdated in contemporary view. In Hong Kong's transition from colonial to global, HSBC rebranded itself as "world's local bank". The new HSBC headquarters building is a physical symbol and statement of the rebranding. It was also a clear manifesto for Hong Kong's intention to join the modern world. When Norman Foster acquired the job in 1979, he was 44 years old, the youngest among all of the tenderers. Before HSBC, the tallest building he had designed was only four stories high and he had no experience in designing a bank. As he recalled, the competition of Hong Kong bank for the firm was "like a gambling, if we lost, we will go bankrupt..." But they still decided to gamble.[11] The HSBC building was a turning point in his career. This British local high-tech architect was in the spotlight and became an international master and celebrity. The independent consultant Gordon Graham recommended Foster to participate in the competition. During the bank's construction, he was employed as a director of Foster Associates.[12]

Every day, more than 4,000 people work in the HSBC building and tens of thousands of people walk through the ground floor lobby. At weekends, the open

---

[10]Hong Kong Governor Sir Edward Youde hosted the opening ceremony of Hong Kong Bank in April 1986 and passed away in December during an official visit to Beijing.

[11]About Norman Foster's talking, see documentary movie *How much does your building weigh, Mr. Foster?*, directed by Norberto Lopez Amado and Carlos Carcas, produced by Elena Ochoa 2010.

[12]The details on the construction of Hong Kong Bank and Foster & Partners are from the HSBC, Asian and Pacific Archive; and from Stephanie Williams, *Hong Kong Bank—The Building of Norman Foster's Masterpiece*, Jonathan Cape, London, 1989; *Vision*, No. 20, 1985; *Asian Architect & Contractor*, Vol. XV, No.11, December 1985.

ground floor is occupied by overseas domestic helpers, which makes an interesting townscape in Hong Kong. The anti-capitalism "occupy Central" movement started by occupying the ground floor of HSBC building. In the past 30 years, the HSBC building has enlightened the technical trend in world architecture. Thirty years later, it is still regarded as pioneering.

In the 1980s, the economy in Hong Kong was gradually focusing on the service and financial industries. Dozens of banks scattered thousands of branches across Hong Kong Island, Kowloon and the New Territories; as locals said, there were "more banks than rice shops." If HSBC reflected the capital of big British business, the Bank of China no doubt represented the wealth and power of China. The success of the HSBC building inspired other corporates that an excellent head-quarters building could not only provide office space, but also tremendous social effects. Although corporates in Hong Kong, including the Bank of China, had accumulated considerable capital, none of them had such a prominent building.

Mr. Pei Chuyi was the first manager of the Hong Kong branch of the Bank of China in the 1920s. After WWII, he was promoted to General Manager of Bank of China. His name was printed on the Chinese bank notes. For the design of the Bank of China building, it was natural to invite Pei's famous architect son—I. M. Pei. In 1983, Pei, Cobb, Fred & Partners of New York was engaged to design the Bank of China building in Hong Kong. At the same time, I. M. Pei designed the alteration project of the Louvre Palace in Paris and the Morton H. Meyerson Symphony Center in Dallas, USA.

The Bank of China building is located at the junction of Garden Road and Queensway, 300 m away from its old headquarters built in 1951. The tower is 70 stories high, with two 52 m antennas. The total height is 368 m, 150 m higher than the Hopewell Center, the record holder in the 1980s. The plate of the tower is square with each side 52 m long. The diagonal lines divide the plate into four triangles. These triangles rise and stop at different heights and are cut obliquely, which makes the tower appear like a shining polygon. The tower is supported by huge steel columns, 12 stories high, at the four corners. Steel rods cross over the elevation and internal space, so there are no columns in the interior. This design saved steel compared with a conventional structure. When a visitor ascends to the banking hall on the second floor, he can look up through the atrium shaped by different triangles. The building reflects the Chinese saying of "ascending bamboo section by section." The area of the site is 6,700 m^2, with a gross floor area of 128,600 m^2. By tapering the plan, the architect dragged the tower to 70 stories, much higher and shinier than its neighbor, HSBC. Granite covers the lower external wall, symbolizing the Great Wall. The main building is covered with aluminum and silver glass. Looking from Tsim Sha Tsui across the harbor or the Peak, the Bank of China building is the most eye-catching item (Fig. 7.12).

There are 45 lifts serving low Zone 1 and high Zone 2. Floor 43 is a transfer floor, on which people can transfer lifts to reach the higher floors. In conventional buildings, the rooftop is usually a mechanical floor. In the Bank of China building, the mechanical floor is set in Floor 69 and Floor 70 is designed as a "heavenly hall" for banquets and viewing the city. The tall, oblique steel skylight sheds sunshine into the hall. The building was completed in 1989 and cost HK$1 billion, one fifth of the cost

(a)   **(b)**

(c)

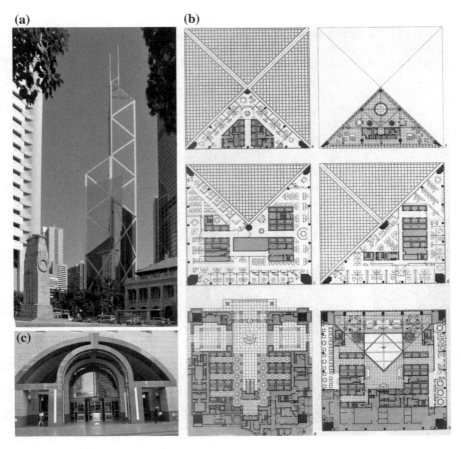

Fig. 7.12 Bank of China headquarters, 1990. **a** "Sprouting bamboo". **b** Plan. **c** Entrance facing the tram way

of the HSBC building. When it opened in 1990, the building gave confidence to society when a pessimistic attitude loomed over the future of Hong Kong.

The square and diamond pattern used in the Bank of China building appeared later in the Bank of China Beijing headquarters building (1998), an office tower in Manila (1991), Suzhou Museum (2006), the Science Museum in Macau (2009) and the Museum of Islamic Art, Doha (2008). After completing the Bank of China building, Pei retired from Pei, Cobb, Fred & Partners and helped his two sons to run Pei Architects and Associates. The examples mentioned above are all from his sons' firm. Before the sovereignty handover, Bank of China was one of the presences in Hong Kong by the Chinese central government. Its vicinity with the HSBC forms a subtle competition. However, Chinese born architect I. M. Pei fulfilled the mission brilliantly with his distinguished modernist gesture.

Fig. 7.13 Lobby of
Chartered Bank, 1990, next to
the HSBC building

While HSBC and the Bank of China were building their new mansions, Chartered Bank and Hang Seng Bank were also constructing their new generation offices. The Chartered Bank building (Fig. 7.13) was designed by Palmer & Turner and the Hang Seng Bank building by Wong & Ouyang, both completed in 1990. The two old buildings were built in the 1960s and were demolished after 30 years, reflecting both the land shortage and the rapid business expansion/upgrading of the 1980s.

The **Bond Center** (now the **Lippo Center**) is located on the west side of Admiralty MTR station and comprises two towers of 42 and 46 stories high. Its gross floor area is 110,554 m². The curtain walled tower is divided into three sections, each of which is cantilevered from the shaft, rather like a koala climbing a tree. The two towers are linked by a four-story podium, with an interior square and corridor. Above the podium, the high and low columns push the tower to the sky. The Bond Center was designed by American architect Paul Rudolph (1918–1997) in the 1970s when the MTR Island Line was planned, in cooperation with local architect Wong & Ouyang. The same interlocking plan is found in other designs by Rudolph. The architect proposed that the bottom 30 m of the skyscraper should correspond to the dimensions of people—it should have a delicate design that could be appreciated by pedestrians. When people walk along Queensway or the

(a)   **(b)**

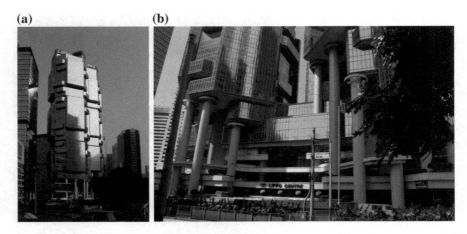

Fig. 7.14 Lippo Center, 1986. **a** Twin towers **b** The design gives more details and interactions with people's dimension and feeling. Required by the government, the podium part is used as a passage way to MTR station

pedestrian bridge, they can clearly see the fountain and interlocking floors and columns. The typical floor of the Bond Center is smaller than 1,000 m², which is not an economical design. The cantilever walls make it difficult to operate a conventional window cleaning gondola. For this purpose, a cleaning company invented a special facility for cleaning the indented curtain wall. However, it takes twice as long to the clean windows as it does in a conventional building (Lee 1988) (Fig. 7.14).

When HSBC and the Bond Center were completed in 1986, **Exchange Square** was built on the Central seaside. Exchange Square was developed by Hong Kong Land and designed by Palmer & Turner. The project includes three commercial towers and a garden podium, under which there is a car park and bus terminal. The area of the Exchange Square site is 13,400 m² on a reclaimed land and the gross floor area of the building is 144,500 m². Two L-shaped towers of 52 stories connect at 45°. The designer conceived the interaction of circular and straight lines in the plan. The escalator, squeezed into a colorful valley with a granite wall and a waterfall, is set at the entrance and leads people to the upper floor lobby and terrace, which provides space for exhibitions and looking at the sea (Fig. 7.15).

The first two floors house the stock exchange hall with a floor area of 2,500 m². Phase III is a 32 story commercial building with a garden platform and retail shops. The curtain wall and windows are made of silicon sealant reflective glass from the USA. The stainless steel window frame was from Germany. The spandrel is covered by Spanish rosy granite. The components were made in the factory and shipped to the site in the evening. Hong Kong Exchange deals with large amount of stock trading daily, and is a pillar of economy. The grandeur of the building partly achieved its intended purpose to accommodate wealth and wisdom. Palmer & Turner had designed more than 20 notable buildings in Central, including the

Fig. 7.15 Exchange Square, 1985. **a** Granite and glass form the curtain wall. **b** Sculpture and fountain on podium level. **c** From stock exchange to the office tower lobby. **d** Office workers and public can view the sea and occasional exhibition in the lobby

nearby Jardine House. Exchange Square was no doubt the best design produced by the firm in the 1980s. During this period, Palmer & Turner designed several bank and corporate buildings in Hong Kong, Singapore and Macau, all of which tended toward a grand and classical design. These projects were also closely associated with the schematic design of Remo Riva (Fig. 7.16).

The podium of Exchange Square connects with the buildings opposite Connaught Road, the bus terminal below and the IFC podium in the busy Central pedestrian network. The area is crowded with people, on the paths of the podium, the benches next to the flower planters and in front of the coffee shops. Only stock exchange staff can enter the exchange hall. However, the citizens can use most parts of podium and

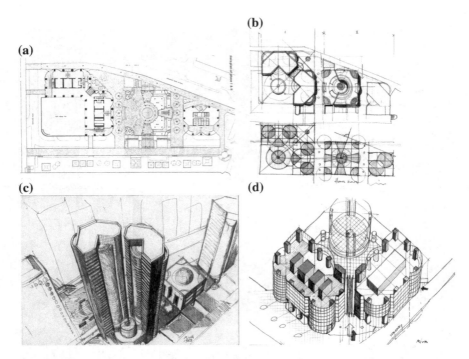

Fig. 7.16 Design of Exchange Square. **a** Plan of podium level. **b–d** Design sketch of Remo Riva, who loves curvilinear form

building. In 2014, Shenzhen stock exchange building was completed in the city center. The OMA designed skyscraper rises singularly in the plaza. Citizens are not allowed to enter the huge lobby. Compared with its Shenzhen counterpart, the Hong Kong Exchange Square built 30 years earlier is much more intimate.

7.3 Boosting Confidence

In 1984 when the Sino-Britain Joint Declaration was issued, the Hong Kong society was dominated by a panic. The completion of a series of buildings in Central, The Landmark, HSBC headquarters, Bond Center and Exchange Square revitalized the city center and symbolized confidence of investment. In 1989 when the June 4th Tiananmen Square Incident took place in Beijing, (Encyclopedia Britannica 1990) more people in Hong Kong felt the imminence of communist rule. A wave of immigration flooded the territory. The capitalists and middle class citizens, bringing massive money, emigrated to foreign countries. To restore the business confidence and ensure the smooth transition of seven years before the sovereignty handover, in October 1989, four months after the Tiananmen Square Incident, the governor Sir David Wilson announced a "Rose Garden Project" to build a new airport in Chek

Lap Kok, including flattening a couple of islands, dredging the seabed, building link railway, expressway, port and suspension bridge across the channel. This Keynesian exercise cost HK\$ 160 billion (US\$21 billion). However, the Rose Garden Project was criticized by the Chinese government as an insidious plan. The last colonial government would spend huge foreign reserves and leave a bankrupt territory to China. Meanwhile, the British companies and merchants could over-charge fee from their "Rolls-Royced" civil and architectural engineering projects. Despite disputes, the Rose Garden project was carried out on plan. It provided plenty of working opportunities for many Hong Kong people and foreign compa-nies, and boosted the confidence of Hong Kong society.[13] The architectural and civil engineering projects again became the arena of international designers and contractors. Convention Center and international airport are two obvious examples.

The new **Chek Lap Kok Airport** was located in the north of Lantau Island. More than half of its 12.5 km^2 land was reclaimed from the sea. After the master plan, the Hong Kong Airport Authority started to solicit terminal building design. Before the Hong Kong airport, Norman Foster & Partners designed Stansted Airport in London from 1981 to 1991, its specially designed steel components repeat and form a light-hearted structure. Foster's team accumulated experiences of airport terminal design, from functional planning to organization of large, open plan spaces. With the Foster's design skill and British Airport Authority (BAA)'s management, they jointly bid the job in Hong Kong. The other six design teams are international experts of airport design including HOK and Leo A. Daly from the US. Neither the design teams nor public were informed till the last minute of the press conference on March 3, 1992. Foster & Partners was announced to win the terminal building design. Seven years after the Hong Kong bank, Foster & Partners set up office in Hong Kong again.[14]

The terminal's full length measured at its center is over 1.8 km, a third of the building is constructed below ground. In Hong Kong airport, the designer used a module of 1.5 m, span grid of 36 m and standard spatial barrel vault to make the double Y-shape terminal building of 570,000 m^2. The terminal building has a sophisticated and dimensionally precise steel roof, comprising 129 modules, each with an average weight of 140 tons. It was once the largest airport terminal in the world when it was completed in 1998. The main structure is only responsible for roofing and building shell. Many shops and decks were built and structurally supported by themselves. Renovation, addition and alternation can be made without influencing the building. Passengers take MTR or bus to the airport, they move from the check-in counter through custom and to the gate almost in the same level without inconvenient up and down. In the huge volume, the different levels are skillfully interlocked and interwoven, forming many interesting and intimate spaces for the waiting area, custom check, retails, coffee shops and restaurants.

---

[13]For the last years before Hong Kong's sovereignty handover, see Patten (1994, 1998).

[14]Some information about the competition and design of the Hong Kong airport is from the chief architect Winston T. Shu, interviewed on 4 March 2016.

In the Kai Tak and other old airport terminals, air-conditioning came from the ceiling, and made the ceiling heavy. Foster's design arranged the cabinet of retail shops and toilets as air outlet and return register, leaving the high ceiling light-weighted and delightful. The temperature is comfortable in the height of human activity, but may be very high in the ceiling part. Clad with glass, metal and clear panels of 46,000 m^2, and facilitated with many functional devices, the Hong Kong airport terminal delivers a feeling of speed, high-tech and modern comfort. The high curtain wall is supported by light-weight bow-back mullion. Foster's design of airport terminal and Hung Hom train station (1998) used a modular span and repeated the module for making large space. Without delicately designed details and clarity in the light-weight structural form, such kind of modular buildings could easily fall to a feel of "warehouse." The airport terminal itself is a complicated machine with high efficiency. However, it presents a light-hearted face for the passengers. The Hong Kong airport is highly regarded by various world airport ranking.[15] This partly attributes to its forward-looking and high-tech design (Fig. 7.17).

For a long time, Hong Kong acted as a broker and trading agent for China, Asia and the world. When the economy took off in the 1980s, a convention and exhibition center was urgently needed. The task went to the Hong Kong Trade Development Council. A convention center was designed for the Wanchai waterfront by Ng Chun Men & Associates, which was completed in 1988. With a huge glass front facing the sea, it was the biggest curtain wall in the world at the time. Visitors arrive at the convention center from the street and are dropped off in the circular plaza. Walking into the lobby and preparing to take the escalator to the upper floors, the blue harbor and azure sky over Kowloon draw the eye. There are two five-star hotels on two sides of the convention center.

It was not long before the convention center, once famous in Asia, was not big enough. Close to the sovereignty handover in 1997, 1.8 million m^3 of sand and stone were poured into the sea to create an island of 6.5 ha. Phase II of the **Convention Center** was designed by SOM of the USA. Taking inspiration from birds and a piece of porcelain, the designer created a shell that covers the multi-story oval hall and projects into the sea. Clad with a curtain wall 60 m high and containing 7,000 m^2 of glass, the lobby allows visitors to view Central and west Kowloon across the harbor before entering the exhibition hall. The shell has an area of more than 4,000 m^2 and is made of aluminum. Costing HK$ 4.8 billion, the project was managed and supervised by Wong & Ouyang, who sent hundreds of people on site, working day and night to complete the job. On June 30, 1997, the half-completed convention center became the venue for the solemn sovereignty handover ceremony[16] (Fig. 7.18).

---

[15]Hong Kong airport was ranked No. 1 in the world for eight years. After 2011, it was in No. 3–4. See SKYTRAX (2015). The technical data of the Hong Kong airport is from HKIA (1998).

[16]For details of Phase II of the convention center, see the website of HKCEC (2016) and Wong (1998).

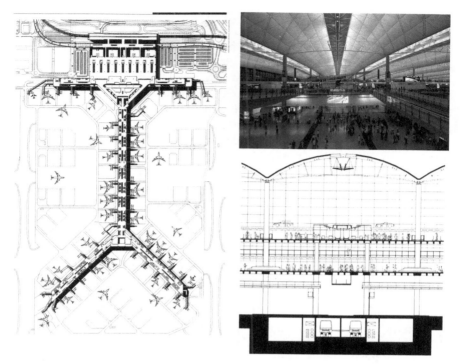

Fig. 7.17   Hong Kong airport

Fig. 7.18   Convention and Exhibition Center, 1989 and 2007. **a** The bird gesture in the waterfront. **b**, **c** Lobby to the exhibition halls

The man-made island and Phase I convention center are linked by a steel bridge 110 m long, which is part of the internal hall. In 1992, before Phase II was built, Central Plaza was built on a plot behind the convention center. Central Plaza, one of the tallest buildings at the time, was developed by Sun Hong Kei and designed by Dennis Lau, Ng Chun Men & Associates. The typical floors of the Central Plaza are triangular, clad with grey and with gold curtained walls. Its upward gesture, together with the bird (turtle) shaped convention center, became a classical picture of the harbor city of Hong Kong and the best background for the festival fireworks.

Because of the projecting man-made island, the line of the seashore from Admiralty to Wanchai is indented. This soon induced a new round of reclamation. Over the past 150 years, the first reclamation in Hong Kong took place in the bay; when the bay was filled, a new "peninsula" projected out to form a new "bay," which was subsequently filled, making the harbor narrower year after year. The newly filled land was easily acquired with little resistance and the government reaped a huge amount of revenue from auctioning the waterfront land. In 1997, the Legislative Council passed an ordinance for the protection of the harbor and introduced public participation. Reclamation was strongly opposed by society. Despite such resistance, the government decided to build the Wanchai to Central bypass, the government headquarters and a seaside park. Half of the bay from Admiralty to Central was filled in 2012 (also see Chap. 9).

In the twenty-first century, the competition from neighboring cities is keen. In 2003, Guangzhou built a convention and exhibition center in Pazhou, with a gross floor area of 400,000 m². In 2008, an international convention center was built near Baiyunshan, on a scale much larger than that of Hong Kong's convention center. Shenzhen also built an exhibition center in the heart of the city, designed by gmp from Germany. In Hong Kong, an Asian World Expo pavilion had to be built on the airport island in 2005, to provide 70,000 m² exhibition space. The bridge between Phases I and II of the convention center was also refurbished to make it part of the exhibition hall. Even after so many extensions, the gross floor area of the Hong Kong convention center is still only 80,000 m², one fifth of the center in Pazhou, Guangzhou. There is a plan to convert the nearby swimming pool and playground into a convention center. However, in a civic society, it is by no means easy to convince the public to yield public land in this way.

7.4 Conclusion: Architecture of Globalization

The 1980s saw substantial changes in Hong Kong's economy and urban architecture. Hong Kong jumped to the leading position in the harbor and financial industries. No matter old and new, cheap and expensive, buildings can be demolished at any time when the clients and corporates' interests want. During the process Hong Kong was moving on from an industrial base to a node in global network, the buildings of the 1980s and 90s in the CBD projected a new image of Hong Kong and injected confidence for business and society. According to scholars Bell and de-Shalit, "globalization is often a synonym for the free movement of capital, humans and goods and an open-minded attitude to foreigners and the 'other'" (Bell and De-Shalit 2011). Accepted by the local merchants and bankers, the HSBC headquarters was the turning point in the shift to globalization. The Hong Kong bank building and other new edifices laid down the standard for buildings in Central. New buildings had to strive to reach this level, with its high design standards, glamorous interiors and quality maintenance. The rapid rising of so many high-rise and comprehensive buildings challenged the traditional way of construction. A revolution was brought to the construction management, technology and production. The skyscrapers of Central were erected on narrow land, which is a normal phenomenon in Hong Kong. The skillful design of high-rise buildings on limited waterfront land shapes part of the Hong Kong characteristics, which resist or enrich the homogeneity of globalization.

With rapid gentrification, the CBD became populated by financial, multi-national, listed corporations and associated services such as law and accountancy firms and clinics. Between the 1950s and 70s, the majority of architectural design firms were in Central. Since the 1980s, most design firms have had to move east or west, to Wanchai, Causeway Bay, North Point or Quarry Bay. The buildings in Central provide a "globalized space," only serving the global commercial elite and attracting classy serviced apartments (for example in West Kowloon) and pub streets (Lan Kwai Fong, SOHO and Lockhart Road in Wanchai). Ordinary consumers have been forced out to the peripheries by the high prices (Sassen 2000).

Since the 19th century, design businesses have been run by British professionals. By the end of the war, most British firms had served Hong Kong for more than half a century. The change in staff brought in a new culture and these "British" firms became localized—they were born in Hong Kong and only did Hong Kong projects. In the 1980s, private clients started to welcome designs from overseas, rather than from these "British" but local firms. The "colonial" emblem and past seemed outdated. Some international firms opened their offices in Hong Kong. In the design competitions of the 1980s, it was clear that local firms were still some way off the international level. The international design firms stepped into the Hong Kong and Chinese mainland market.

During its construction of the Hong Kong Bank and the new airport terminal, Foster & Partners ran an office in Hong Kong with over a hundred staff. Once the projects ended, the staff members opened up their own offices and spread their high-tech ideas. Foster's former partner Lord Richard Rogers is also a Pritzker Architectural Award Laurette. He won the first prize in the international design competition for Lujiazui master plan in Pudong, Shanghai in 1992, which was highly appreciated and widely reported. However, he never has any project realized

Fig. 7.19 Maggie's Cancer Caring Centre in Hong Kong, 2013. Every component is "non-standard", which made the construction difficult. Thanks to the BIM system, the size, location and joints could be coordinated in the construction. Courtesy of Ronald Lu & Partners

in the Chinese mainland. Through cooperating with DLN Architects & Engineers, Rogers had opportunity to contribute to the residential estate design in Hong Kong (see Chap. 5).

OMA of the Netherlands used Hong Kong as its experimental base for the "culture of congestion" and undertook projects in neighboring areas. KPF (Kohn Pedersen Fox Associates), made its name known in super high-rise building, is applying its knowledge to the Chinese frontier via both its Hong Kong and Shanghai offices. KPF designed the tallest buildings in the two cities—ICC in Hong Kong and GFC in Shanghai. Terry Farrell & Partners (TFP) won the design for Peak Tower, the super Kowloon Station in 1992 and started its journey of "ten years, ten cities." After London, Hong Kong is Farrell's most important base for his "urban experiment" ideas. Based in Hong Kong, TFP has participated in many large projects in Shenzhen, Guangzhou and Shanghai.[17] The same can be said for Arquitectonica, from Miami, USA. The company was founded in 1977 and has won numerous awards and projects in the US and overseas. After designing the Festival Walk in Hong Kong in 1993, the firm stepped into Greater China and designed many bold projects in Macau, Shenzhen, Shanghai and other Chinese cities.[18] Frank Gehry Partnership has engaged in Hong Kong project since 2000. In addition to his housing design in the Mid-level (see Chap. 5), his office designed a small

---

[17]For more about Terrell Farrell's practice in Hong Kong and Asian cities, see Tobin (2002) and Rosi and Erasmus (2008).

[18]For more about the career of Arquitectonica, see Arquitectonica (2014).

"non-linear" building for the Maggie's Cancer Caring Centre in Tuen Men Hospital,[19] assisted by the Ronald Lu & Partnership and Arup in 2013 (Fig. 7.19).

In the 1990s, globalization permeated every corner of the world. Hong Kong, an old colonial port, was transformed into an Asian global metropolis. Colonization and globalization both involve the influence of foreign culture on local culture, while colonial city was forerunner of global city today. If colonization was realized by force and power, globalization is driven by multi-national business and a strong economy. Moreover, the de-colonization process from the 1950s made Hong Kong determined to be self-reliant and shine in the international stage. The large construction projects in Central and Wanchai were the physical symbols of this process. The Hong Kong airport, with designers and contractors from multi countries, states the city's international status. In a quarter century from 1990 to 2015, more infill or big projects will and have taken place, improving the infrastructure. However, substantial changes took place in urban architecture actually in the 1980s, which created the Hong Kong townscape we know today.

When I was in Shanghai in the 1980s, I heard Hong Kong described as both a colorful and evil capitalist heaven. The myth about the "four Asian dragons" spread throughout the Chinese newspapers. I went to the University of Hong Kong as a visiting graduate student in March 1989. It was during an economic heyday of the territory, when China still issued food, oil, pork, egg and textile ration coupons to its city residents. I took the train from Guangzhou to Hong Kong, where it slid into the terminal station at Hung Hom. A teacher from Hong Kong University collected me at the train station and we took a taxi to Chi Fu Garden where we had lunch at Maxim Fast Food. Outside the window, a white boat was plowing through the blue sea. The fast food shop was located in the Chi Fu mini shopping mall. It was the first time I had seen such a building and restaurant. After I left my baggage in the student hall, I went to Central, strolled over to Admiralty and visited the HSBC headquarters and Bond (now Lippo) Center, which I had read about in architectural magazines and admired. Bank of China was in the last stages of construction. Bound by ropes, workers were cleaning the big slanting glass wall. At street level, the workers appeared to move like ants across a massive shining surface. Queensway Plaza was linked to the newly completed Pacific Center via a pedestrian bridge crossing the tram road. Walking across the bridge, you could see the profiles of the Central skyscrapers. Being from Shanghai, I was completely overwhelmed by the materialistic quality of this capitalist city. I could not contain my excitement and wrote letters to my parents and professor in Shanghai the same night, reporting what I had seen and whom I had met. Over the next nine months, I was frequently struck by the huge differences between Shanghai and Hong Kong.

---

[19]Maggie's Cancer Caring Centre was founded by Maggie Keswick Jencks (1941–1995) and Charles Jencks in 1996. The first centre was located in Edinburgh, and the other 17 centres are scattered in the UK. Buildings were designed by famous architects free of charge. See https://www.maggiescentres.org/about-maggies/. Accessed 2 February 2016.

The University of Hong Kong was an international institution that exhibited an élite ethos. Many of the lecturers were gentle and elegant expatriates who lived in the senior staff quarters, which had an ample ocean view. Even some of the clinic doctors and staff lounge bartenders were expatriates. The teachers, students and staff members spoke fluent English. Notes and handouts were written in English, following the British courtesy and format. Some of the design firms' drawings and documents were annotated in English. I had to train myself in earnest by talking with teachers and students and reading articles from journals and newspapers.

After working in the U.K. and U.S. for a couple of years, I landed in Hong Kong again at the end of August 1995 and temporarily lived in a small hostel in Causeway Bay. After my years of experience driving across the Texas ranges and through southern cities such as Houston and Dallas, I found Causeway Bay extremely cramped and ugly. The humid summer air mixed with the pollution, making it difficult to breathe. Two years later, my wife and daughter traveled to Hong Kong from the U.S. My wife did not feel the shock I had experienced in 1989. As one of my colleagues overtly confessed, the main reason foreigners came to Hong Kong was money.

From 1996 to 1998, I had several opportunities to visit the Convention Center and airport construction sites. Tsing Ma Bridge had not yet been connected, so we took the ferry from Wanchai to Chek Lap Kok. An outsider would have seen only a massive and busy construction site. Looking at the blueprints, whether it was a master plan, a general plan or a detailed tender drawing, you were dazzled by the many lines, signs, dimensions and abbreviations. These projects were truly engineering miracles in the 1990s.

References

Abbas, A. (1997). *Hong Kong* (p. 64). Minneapolis: University of Minnesota Press.

Arquitectonica. (2014). The company website. *Arquitectonica.com.* http://arquitectonica.com/portfolio/. Accessed December 1, 2014.

Bell, D., & De-Shalit, A. (2011). *The spirit of cities—Why the identity of a city matters in a global age* (p. 6). Princeton: Princeton University Press.

Bristow, R. (1984). *Land use planning in Hong Kong: History, policies and procedures* (p. 239). Hong Kong: Oxford University Press.

Cheng, T. (1977). *The economy of Hong Kong.* Hong Kong: Far East Publications.

Curtis, W. (1996). *Modern architecture since 1900.* London: Phaidon.

Debord, G. (1994). *The society of the spectacle* (pp. 12–13). New York: Zone Books.

Encyclopedia Britannica. (1990). Tiananmen Square incident. *Encyclopedia Britannica.* http://global.britannica.com/EBchecked/topic/594820/Tiananmen-Square-incident. Accessed June 6, 2015.

Enright, M., Scott, E., & Dodwell, D. (1997). *The Hong Kong advantage.* Hong Kong: Oxford University Press.

Executive and Legislative Council Office. (1977). *Seventh annual report of the Unofficial Members of the Executive and Legislative Council Office (UMELCO)* (p. 16). Hong Kong: Government Printer.

HKCEC. (2016). Hong Kong Convention and Exhibition Centre. *Hkcec.com*. https://www.hkcec.com/cn. Accessed January 5, 2016.

HKIA. (1998). *The New Hong Kong International Airport*. Hong Kong: China Trend Building Press.

Hong Kong Institute of Architects. (2007). *Deeply loving architecture—Dialogue with 15 senior architects in Hong Kong*. Hong Kong: Hong Kong Institute of Architects. 香港建筑师学会. (2006). 热恋建筑 -与拾伍香港资深建筑师的对话. 香港:香港建筑师学会出版.

Jianzhuyouren. (2013). *Building feeling*. Hong Kong: Joint Publication. 建筑游人. (2013). 筑觉: 阅读香港建筑. 香港:三联书店.

Kinoshita, J. H. (2005). *From Slocan to Hong Kong—An architect's journey*. Victoria, BC: Trafford Publishing.

Lee, Z. (1988). Hang'em high. *Asian Architect and Contractor, 3*, 18.

McDonogh, G., & Wong, C. (2005). *Global Hong Kong*. New York: Routledge.

Patten, C. (1994). *Hong Kong, a thousand days and beyond*. Hong Kong: Government Printer.

Patten, C. (1998). *East and west: The last governor of Hong Kong on power, freedom and the future*. Basingstoke: Macmillan.

Rosi, A., & Erasmus, G. (2008). *UK>HK Farrells placemaking. From London to Hong Kong and beyond*. Hong Kong: MCCM Creations.

Sassen, S. (2000). *Cities in a world economy*. Thousand Oaks, California: Pine Forge Press.

SKYTRAX. (2015). The World's top 100 airports in 2015. *Worldairportawards.com*. http://www.worldairportawards.com/Awards/world_airport_rating.html. Accessed July 13, 2015.

Tobin, J. (2002). *Ten years, ten cities—The work of Terry Farrell & Partners*. London: Laurence King Publishing.

Victoria Barracks Planning Committee. (1977). *Planning proposals for the Victoria Barracks are*. Hong Kong: Government Printer.

Wong, R. (1998). *15 most outstanding projects in Hong Kong*. Hong Kong: China Trend Building Press Ltd.

Xue, C. (2014). *Contextualizing modernity: Hong Kong architecture 1946–2011*. Hong Kong: Commercial Press. 薛求理 (2014). 城境:香港建筑1946–2011. 香港:商务印书馆.

Chapter 8
"Being Chinese in Architecture"—The Growth of Local Architects

8.1 Introduction

Chapter 3 of this book discusses the situation in the 1950s and 60s and the rise of local designers. During that period, many professionals who had escaped from China were cultivating in the colony. By the 1970s, HKU graduates had matured with years of practice. Students from overseas returned to Hong Kong and plunged into the increasingly booming construction industry. In 1990, there were around 1,000 registered architects; in 1997, this number jumped to 1,700.[1] The economy was resurging, providing ample opportunities both in the public and private sectors for these new practitioners. In the decades before the handover, the old British development companies tended to be conservative while the main building developers were emerging local Chinese capitalists who demanded exclusive, high-quality buildings. As a result of the highly commercial market and dense urban development, many new buildings were in-fills in the street blocks and projects tended to be big and pragmatic. In many projects, design was only one part of the long chain from development to construction to operation; hence, the designers remained anonymous behind these grand mansions.

At the same time, there was increasing awareness in society of the need to find roots. This situation enabled architects to consider the Hong Kong problem, face the local conditions and create architecture that belonged to this land. Several people and firms stood out in this wave. "Being Chinese in architecture" is a title for Rocco Design works' monograph (Rocco Design 2004). I borrow it to summarize the characteristics of these architects, who are consciously searching for identity. They were trained in English in Hong Kong or overseas. They speak, read and write fluent English, while they chat or may sometimes think in Chinese (Cantonese). They grow up in the Hong Kong community, are familiar with local society, people's habits and preference, and practice on the general conditions and market of

---

[1]The number of architects is from Wong and Cheng (1990) and Ho (2000).

© Springer Science+Business Media Singapore 2016
C.Q.L. Xue, *Hong Kong Architecture 1945–2015*,
DOI 10.1007/978-981-10-1004-0_8

Hong Kong in the 1970s onward. Sometimes, they are Hongkongers; some other times, they are "Chinese in architecture". They connect not only to the ruling and elite class in the CBD Central, but also grass-root citizens in the marketplace. The local feeling and intuition sprung out naturally from their pens.

This chapter investigates these prominent people, links architects with the unique architectural projects that have evolved since the 1970s and explores how Modernism was applied in Hong Kong. The selected architects were prominent in different years from 1970 to the 21st century. Their design works have clear authorship and personal imprints, instead of obscure corporate products. They each won design awards and influenced their peers in many ways during their time. In the 21st century, a new generation emerged with different method and strategies. The author has followed their work for decades and has made acquaintance with most of them. This chapter depicts the spectrum of designers and will hopefully contribute to the forum on contemporary Hong Kong and Asian architecture.

8.2   Masters Since 1970

Chung Wah-nan (born in 1931) grew up in Hong Kong. The environment of Lingnan[2] and the New Territories nurtured his love of local culture. His father was a building contractor who once built the tallest building in Guangzhou—17 stories high steel structured Aiqun Building in 1934. During the Japanese invasion, Chung and his parents fled to Xinhui in Guangdong Province, the family's hometown. Living in the Cantonese countryside, he understood the cultural importance of country and nation. After the war, he studied undergraduate and Master's courses in the UK and graduated from the Bartlett School of Architecture at University College London in 1959. After working for three years in London, he returned to Hong Kong with his Swiss wife. In 1964, he opened his own office and in 1971 partnered with Alan Fitch, the designer of City Hall (see Chap. 2). The practice was named Fitch and Chung till 1985 when Fitch left. The firm Chung and Partners has run up to now. In the 1980s and early 1990s, Chung frequently traveled to the Chinese mainland, where he investigated heritage buildings and lectured in Beijing and other cities. During the early period of the open-door policy, his books and articles greatly enlightened his Chinese peers. He introduced the latest development of western modern architecture to the Chinese audience. In Hong Kong and traveling abroad, he is an enthusiastic advocator of Chinese culture (Fig. 8.1).

Chung's design activities were concentrated in the 1960s to the 1980s. Based on the analysis of clients' requirements, he tried to find solutions with a meaningful form. At the end of the 1960s, the Kadoorie brothers offered him the opportunity to

---

[2]"Lingnan" literally means "south of the mountain". It generally ranges in the Pearl River Delta. Several mountains in its north side block the cold air from the north. Its climate is very different from the north neighboring province Hunan.

Fig. 8.1 Mr. Chung
Wah-nan, pictured in the
1980s

design the Peak Tower above the tram station for Hong Kong and Shanghai Hotels
Ltd.[3] Drawing on his experience of ancient Chinese city walls and towers, he
developed the principle of "solid bottom and floating top" and applied it to the
design of the Peak Tower. In Chinese, Peak Tower is written *lu-feng*, which means
the peak of a stove. Chung designed the tower in the shape of a stove supported by
columns, floating in the sky, which can be seen through the column. Hong Kong
people felt an emotional intimacy with the tower and gave it the name Peak Tower,
which accompanied Hong Kong into the temporary looming years (Fig. 8.2).

The end of the 1970s saw a high wave of public housing construction. During
this wave, Fitch and Chung designed the shopping arcade of the Lok Fu public
housing estate. The shopping arcade was designed to sit within the housing blocks.
There is a courtyard in the center and the housing blocks rise above the retail
buildings. The entrance of the courtyard is decorated with a traditional portal
(*pailou*) (Fig. 8.3).

In the municipal services building of Lockhart Road, Wanchai, designed by
Fitch and Chung, car parking is in the basement, the first four floors are a market,
followed by a library. The top floor houses an indoor basketball court. This design
created the prototype for municipal services buildings and tried to make changes in
the sections in a narrow land (Fig. 8.4).

Chung's largest and most sophisticated project was the City Polytechnic
building, which he was awarded after winning a design competition intensely
fought by six joint teams of local and overseas firms. In 1984, the second

---

[3]Kadoorie, a Jewish family, arrived in China in 1880 and made a fortune in Shanghai, following
the Jewish capitalist Victor Sassoon. After the Pacific War, the family withdrew to Hong Kong and
ran electric companies, hotels and real estate. It is one of the richest families in Hong Kong. See
"Kadoorie—legendary   family",   http://info.ceo.hc360.com/2006/03/13101222267-2.shtml.
Accessed 17 May 2015.

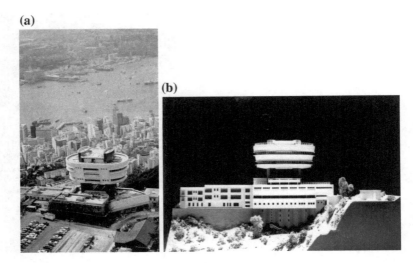

Fig. 8.2 Peak Tower, 1972. **a** Overlooking the harbor and Mid-level. **b** Model of Peak Tower. Courtesy of Mr. W.N. Chung

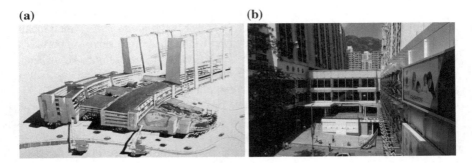

Fig. 8.3 Lok Fu shopping arcade, 1982. **a** Design perspective. Courtesy of Mr. W.N. Chung. **b** Public events taking place in the courtyard of arcade

polytechnic, City Polytechnic, opened (renamed City University of Hong Kong [CityU] in 1994). At its inception, City Polytechnic rented an office tower in Mongkok, while running a campus design competition. In 1985, Percy Thomas of London and Fitch and Chung of Hong Kong jointly won the design. Fitch and Chung had participated unsuccessfully in the design competition for the Hong Kong Polytechnic campus (1973). Chung Wah-nan was the Authorized Person for the City Polytechnic project[4] (Fig. 8.5).

---

[4]The competition to design the Kowloon Tong campus for City Polytechnic started in January 1983 and was reviewed on June 6–10. Six teams were shortlisted from more than 40 companies, including Alan Fitch and W.N. Chung in association with the Percy Thomas Partnership; Hsin Yieh Architects in association with the Colin St John Wilson Partnership; Ng Chun Men and

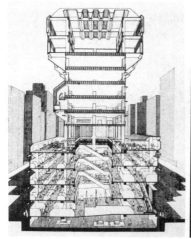

Fig. 8.4 Municipal service building, Lockhard Road, Wanchai, 1986. Courtesy of Mr. W.N. Chung

Fig. 8.5 CityU design competition, Percy Thomas and Fitch and Chung's winning scheme. The building complex sitting on the valley can effectively avoid wind blow and create many platforms permeated with natural surroundings. Courtesy of Mr. W.N. Chung

The CityU campus, with a gross floor area of over 100,000 m², is located in the valley of Kowloon Tong. The designer used a grid and modular design to control the large building mass. The building complex is horizontally zoned with atriums

---

(Footnote 4 continued)

Associates in association with Shepheard Epstein and Hunter; Kwan Ng Wong and Associates; Russell and Poon Group Partnership in association with Denys Lasdun, Redhouse and Softley of London; and YRM International (HK). The jury was chaired by D.W. McDonald, director of Land and Public Work; Director Sir Flowers from Imperial College London; Prof. D.J. Jones, Director of City Polytechnic; Prof. Eric Lye of HKU; Peter Y.S. Pun, Chair of Government Projects and Housing; and J. Lei, acting Director of the Buildings Department. The jury recommended Fitch-Chung and Percy Thomas for the work and the Planning Committee of City Polytechnic approved the decision. *Vision*, No. 9, 1983.

(a)   (b)

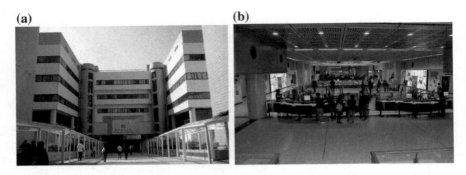

Fig. 8.6 CityU campus. **a** Pedestrian entrance. **b** Concourse is flanked by lecture theaters

and different colors. The seven story building is vertically divided by function. The whole of the third floor is the library (once the largest single-floor library in Asia). The fourth floor comprises the concourse and lecture theaters, with shops and flexible spaces for activities. In the mountain valley, the pedestrian and vehicular entrances are arranged in different levels. Therefore, the fourth level is used as circulation thoroughfare (Fig. 8.6).

In the traditional college, knowledge was delivered one-way from teacher to student. Classrooms with six-plane enclosure are enough. The big sky-lit space within building blocks encourages students to communicate out of class. The concourse is busy for students' daily life, exhibition and activities. The designer used huge skylight to illuminate the common space. Chung sees this as a modern adaption of traditional courtyard house. When the CityU campus was completed in the early 1990s, this type of concourse design had rarely been seen in Hong Kong and the Chinese mainland. It became a prototype, copied by Chinese peers when building new campuses.[5]

The functional areas of CityU take up the full volume, while the staircases, lifts and toilets are packed into semi-circular tubes. This is similar to the design of PolyU and Louis Kahn's concept of "served and service" space.[6] For the past 20 years, the building has served over 20,000 students and staff, and is run all year round with high efficiency and at capacity (Fig. 8.7).

---

[5]Since 1999, Chinese government has rapidly expanded higher education and built more than 300 new campuses, funded by provincial and municipal government. From 2003, there are 5–7 million university graduates every year. The expansion of higher education has high demand on campus planning and academic building design. See Yuan Wei, Zhonghuo gaodeng jiaoyu dazonghua de xianzhuang, wenti he zhanwang (China's higher education: status, problems and prospect), Sino-Europe Social Forum, http://www.china-europa-forum.net/bdfdoc-996_zh.html. Accessed 21 May 2015.

[6]Louis Kahn's design method of "service and served" space was obviously adopted in the Hong Kong PolyU (completed 1980) and CityU's campus (completed 1990) building design. For the concept, see Goldhagen (2001).

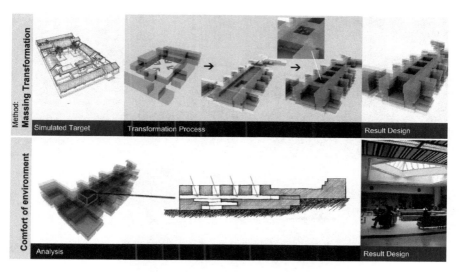

Fig. 8.7   Analysis of CityU academic building. Drawn by Vivian Lo

In the 1970s and 80s, Chung designed various park pavilions for the Urban Council. Traditional Chinese pavilion wan made by wood. Chung used concrete to design different symmetrical pavilions with either flying or long cantilevered eaves. This group of pavilions inherited the Chinese tradition, while also experimenting with modern materials. Chung presented the built and unbuilt schemes in an article and a seminal book, *Ting de jicheng* (Inheritance of pavilion). In the book, Chung considered that Chinese pavilion is a starting point to recall the Chinese taste. Peak Tower can be seen as the prologue to this set of pavilions (Chung 1989) (Fig. 8.8).

In the early 1980s, the Tsim Sha Tsui train station was demolished to give land for new construction. The clock tower, built in the early twentieth century, was also threatened by the bulldozer. Society was not yet aware of the importance of "conservation." Chung Wah-nan, David Russell, a lecturer in the Department of Architecture, and William Meacham, a lecturer in the Anthropology Department at HKU, carried on a marathon dialogue with the officials from the Urban Council. They suggested keeping the clock tower but building a new cultural center. Their suggestion was eventually adopted. At the beginning of the twenty-first century, the clock tower is still bustling with activity inside and outside the cultural center. After a hundred years, the clock tower still stands, silently telling the story of this land (Fig. 8.9).

The design by Chung Wah-nan and his colleagues faithfully followed the principles of Modernism and absorbed the Chinese tradition, upon which Chung built a local culture. In Hong Kong, 95 % population is ethnic Chinese, but prevailing media in institutions, professionals and government is English. The voice of learning from indigenous traditions is frequently heard, but practiced superficially. Chung is among few people who dig deeply into the indigenous stratum and overtly voice out. He is a cultural architect and public intellectual. Philosophical, literate and with

Fig. 8.8 Inheritance of Chinese pavilion, 1970s–80s. **a** Elaboration the form. Courtesy of Mr. W.N. Chung. **b** Pavilion in Wanchai. **c** Pavilion in Lok Fu

Fig. 8.9 Train station in Tsim Sha Tsui was demolished in the early 1980s. Only the clock tower was *left*. From HK Government Archive

broad horizons, his writings interrogate the reality in Hong Kong and China and look toward the future. Chung's books and writings have greatly influenced his peers and students for decades, and have moistened the once "cultural desert" (Chung 1982, 1991; Chung and Zhang 2007). He bravely criticizes capitalism which strangles the cultural growth and indigenous identity. However, the echo is few. He wrote

Fig. 8.10 Dr. Tao Ho, pictured in 1999

calligraphy with a brush, which was widely appreciated.[7] Chung made an appeal to strengthen architectural theory, localization and regional architecture, for three reasons: "First, we must understand our own cultural tradition. We can study foreign culture, but also know the culture of our ancestors. Second, relying less on other countries and reducing the economic erosion from outside. The third is identity and self-esteem, which is the most important. I hope that we can nurture our regional architectural culture and set up an example for the world"[8].

Dr. **Tao Ho** was born in Shanghai in 1936 and moved to Hong Kong to escape from the Communist rule in the 1950s (Fig. 8.10). He studied in the United States and graduated as a Bachelor of Art History from Williams College and as a Master of Architecture from Harvard University in 1964. In 1979, he was conferred an honorary doctorate from Williams College. During his study at Harvard, he was educated by Walter Gropius (1883–1969), a pioneer of Modernist architecture, and worked as a research assistant for Sigfried Giedion (1888–1968), a historian of Modernist architecture. At the end of 1964, he returned to Hong Kong and taught basic design with Bauhaus theory. In 1968, he opened his own office, Taoho Design, and was awarded commissions in architectural, interior and industrial design. Tao Ho's designs embraced Modernist ideas, expressed in his use of structure and materials.

---

[7]The description of Chung Wah-nan in this chapter is based on the author's communication with Mr. Chung since 1989 and Lo (2011). For more details on the preservation of the Tsim Sha Tsui clock tower, see Chung Wah-nan, Preservation of the clock tower—Kowloon Canton Railway Terminal, *Hong Kong Institute of Architects Journal*, No. 1, 2013. Apart from *Ting de jicheng*, representative books written by Chung include *The art of Chinese garden*, 1982; *Chao yu chao, jianzhu sheji chengshi guihua sanlun* (Copy or surpass: on architectural design and urban planning), 1991; *Contemporary architecture in Hong Kong*, Hong Kong: Joint Publishing Ltd., 1989; *Quan qiu hua, ke chixu fazhan, kuawenhua sheji* (Globalization, sustainability and cross-culture design), Beijing: China Architecture and Building Press, 2007; *Chengshihua weiji* (Crisis of urbanization), Hong Kong: Commercial Press, 2008. See the references of this chapter.

[8]Chung Wah-nan, *Regional Culture and Modernity*. Keynote speech at the Architectural Symposium of Hong Kong, Taipei, Macau and Shenzhen. Hong Kong, 16 March 2013.

At the beginning of the 1970s, aware of the lack of cultural venues, Tao Ho and his friends set up the Hong Kong Arts Center, which was later supported by the Governor, Sir Murray MacLehose. The government allocated a plot of land on the Wanchai seafront, but the budget was only five million dollars.[9] The arts center is located on a street corner. The new building closely abuts older buildings and the two sides are cut at 45 degrees to reduce the bulkiness and follow the site coverage requirement. A theater, music hall, gallery and classroom are stacked from the basement to the fifth floor. On top of the theater, the gallery makes use of the height difference by splitting the space to create half a floor. This concept was quite new in the 1970s. In the center of the building there is a five story atrium. The big staircase spirals up the wall, linking to various floors and half-floor platforms. The box office and lift lobby are on the ground floor. Tuck stores and coffee shops are set in the open space of the upper floors. Art works or banners are hung on the railings of the stairs. This central space with a big staircase is light-hearted. Tao Ho designed the staircase carpet and ordered it to be made by a factory. The air-return tube was originally suspended from the tall ceiling. However, the carpet and tube were removed in the later refurbishment. The building volume and details are formed by a clearly edged triangle structure.

Over the past 38 years, the arts center has held numerous arts exhibitions of high and indigenous arts. The arts center school has run many visual and performing arts classes. The tower houses the offices for arts and cultural organizations. In the cultural desert of Hong Kong, a small tower in the downtown hustle sprays water droplets of Muse (Fig. 8.11). At the time of designing arts center, Tao Ho submitted scheme to the design competition of Pompidou Center in Paris, France.[10] Both Pompidou Center and Hong Kong arts center were completed in 1977. Piano and Rogers' design for Paris astonished the world with a frank high-tech gesture, while Tao Ho's design became a manifesto of Modernist architecture in Hong Kong.

St. Stephen's College on the Stanley seafront was a church-run school in the early twentieth century. The school was damaged in the Japanese invasion during WWII, but returned to tranquility after the war. In the early 1980s, Tao Ho was commissioned to design an arts and culture building, a school hall and an academic building. The group of buildings near the entrance forms a U-shape. The arts and culture building is a long strip-shaped building in the center, linked with the semi-circular open staircase. The buildings are in an upward trapezoid-shape, while the cantilevered balcony is at a reverse angle, making the form strong. Rooms are linked by long verandas and attract a breeze. The external walls are either fair-faced

---

[9]To visualize how much was five million dollars in 1972, a university graduate could earn 700–1000 Hong Kong dollars a month at the time. See Zhang (2005). A new unit of two bedrooms, 585 ft.[2], in Taikoo Shing asked for HK$124,500 in 1976, according to the Archive of Swire Group.

[10]In 1972, the design competition of Pompidou Center in Paris received 681 entries from all over the world. Tao Ho's design was published in *Asian Architect and Builder*, Hong Kong, March 1972.

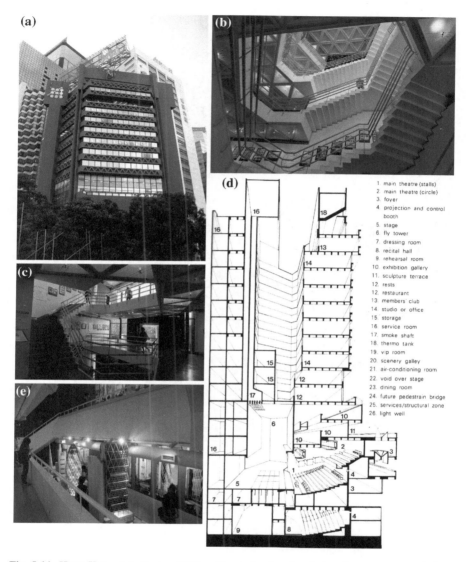

Fig. 8.11 Hong Kong Arts Center, 1977. **a** The main elevation facing the street corner. **b** Stair along the wall is the main feature of design. **c** The staircase dialogues with inside and outside. **d** Section showing the flexible usage of level heights. **e** Gallery. **f** Design sketch. Drawings courtesy of Dr. Tao Ho

concrete or brick. The form, materials and texture are reminiscent of the buildings of Le Corbusier, Louis Kahn and Paul Rudolph (Fig. 8.12).

With the rising of his fame, Tao Ho was awarded more big jobs later and adopted eclectic and decorative methods in some projects. Compared with his later works, Hong Kong Arts Center and St. Stephen College both explored structural

(f)

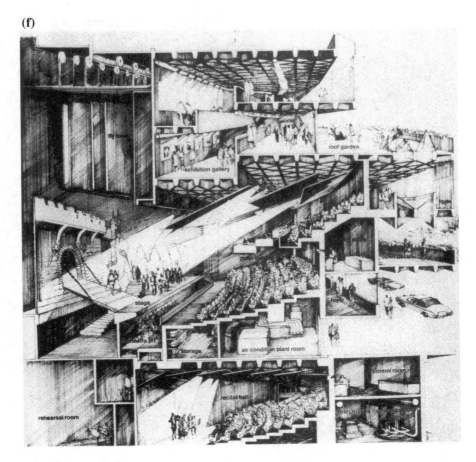

Fig. 8.11 (continued)

and material expression. These two early woks keep a robust modernist spirit from his teachers like Walter Groupius, Kenzo Tange and Fumihiko Maki. Few of his contemporary peers used modernist method so resolutely except the expatriate architects in the government.

In 1986, Hong Kong participated in the World Expo in Vancouver, Canada. Tao Ho's design for the Hong Kong pavilion won over 40 competitors. His scheme used bamboo to wrap the exhibition box, in a modular order. The details were delicately designed and later applied to his other projects. The implementation of Hong Kong pavilion was helped by Bing Thom, a Chinese Canadian architect in Vancouver (see Chap. 10). In the late 1980s, as colonial rule was coming to an end, there was a rising awareness of conserving local traditions. Tao Ho collaborated with the Land Development Corporation (the predecessor of the Urban Renewal Authority) on two projects—Sheung Wan Market and Li Chit Street. Completed in 1905, Sheung Wan Market was an Edwardian style building with a brick arch and patterned brick

Fig. 8.12 St. Stephen's College, 1983. **a** Arts and cultural building. **b** Design sketch. **c** Design drawings showing the relationship of parts. **d** Sport building with fair-faced concrete. Drawings courtesy of Dr. Tao Ho

wall. The renovation repaired and kept the external wall. All of the original internal floors were removed and replaced with three floors of steel structure. The atrium and internal stairway were designed to cooperate with the skylight from the roof truss. The old building became a landmark of Sheung Wan (Fig. 8.13). Li Chit Street is an old part of Wanchai. High-rise residential towers occupy the street. In the small garden, Tao Ho designed a "shop-house" facade, to remind people of the

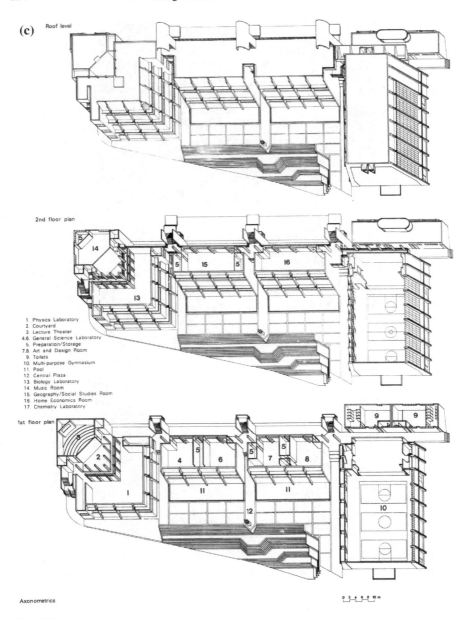

1. Physics Laboratory
2. Courtyard
3. Lecture Theater
4,6. General Science Laboratory
5. Preparation/Storage
7,8. Art and Design Room
9. Toilets
10. Multi-purpose Gymnasium
11. Pool
12. Central Plaza
13. Biology Laboratory
14. Music Room
15. Geography/Social Studies Room
16. Home Economics Room
17. Chemistry Laboratory

Fig. 8.12 (continued)

indigenous tradition in the area (Fig. 8.14). The two projects set examples for the conservation movement in Hong Kong, which attracted more enthusiasm and involved more projects in the 21st century, and were loved by local people.

Fig. 8.13 Sheung Wan
Market, 1905, renovated in
1992. The interior was
completely remodeled

Fig. 8.14 Li Chit Street, only
a "façade" of shop-house is
left

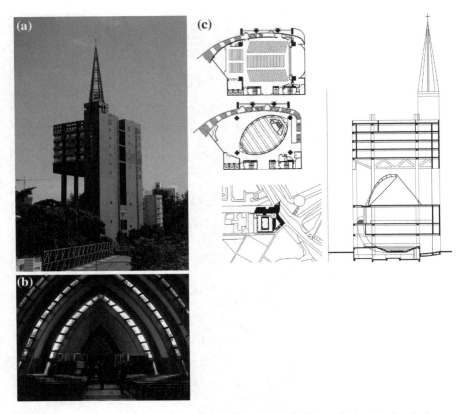

Fig. 8.15 Wing Kwong Pentecostal Holiness Church, 2000. **a** In a small site, the church rises up with a "bookshelf" manner. **b** Inside the church. **c** Drawings by Kwok Wing Sang

At the end of the 1990s, the Christian Church invited Tao Ho to design Wing Kwong Pentecostal Holiness Church. The site is located on the public housing estate of Lok Fu, with a plot area of 1,500 m^2. On this limited site, Tao Ho stacked an activity room, chapel, classroom and office in a 10 story tower, and designed the structure like a bookshelf. This structure allows the roof of the chapel to be free form. A "pilgrimage" external staircase leads to the chapel. A color striped skylight was embedded in the structure. Tao Ho drew the colored windows himself. Part of the offices and classrooms are on the upper floor. Only in land-short Hong Kong could such a church be produced; Tao Ho found inspiration from the constraints (Fig. 8.15).

In addition to the above projects, Tao Ho designed the campus and academic building at Baptist University (1989), the Ho Sin Hang Engineering Building at CUHK (1994), the Construction Bank headquarters in Beijing (1998), the Gold Bridge Building, Pudong, Shanghai (1997) and other important buildings. He consulted for the governments of several Chinese cities and private firms, introduced the technology and experts for the construction of Shanghai's metro subway.

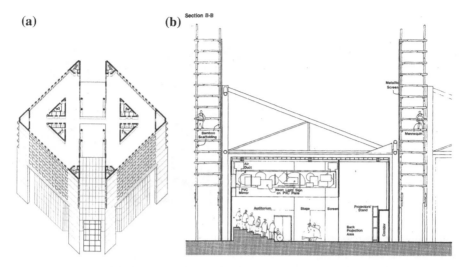

Fig. 8.16 Other works of Taoho. **a** Construction Bank of China, Beijing, 1997. **b** Hong Kong Pavilion, World Expo, Vancouver, 1986. Drawings courtesy of Dr. Tao Ho

In particular, when the open door policy was implemented in China in the early 1980s, Tao Ho contributed to the establishment of "Great Earth," an experimental incorporated design firm in Beijing, at a time when state-owned design institutes were prevailing.

In architectural design, Tao Ho remained rooted in modernism. He was fond of using structure and technology to express his buildings. These methods contrast sharply with many mediocre and compromised buildings in Hong Kong. Besides architectural design, Tao Ho created many art works. In the 1980s, he used containers to construct his office in Kowloon Tong, which was full of artistic atmosphere (Fig. 8.16). His steel sculpture was hung in the terminal of Hong Kong airport. In 1997, Hong Kong's sovereignty was returned to China, and Tao Ho designed the Bauhinia flag of the Special Administrative Region. His "Explosion" sculpture, made from crystal and optical fiber, was collected by the World Economic Forum in Geneva, Switzerland. His sculptures, paintings and installations were displayed and collected in airport, university campus and museums in China and abroad. With his talent and hard work, Tao Ho practiced the integration of architecture, interior, product and art design like a Renaissance master, which has often amazed and energized the society.

Apart from his design work and business, Tao Ho was an active thinker and social activist. After his formative years in the United States, he met and was influenced by the great thinkers and scholars in the 20th century, for example, Greek urban planner C. Doxiadis (1914–1975), anthropologist Margaret Mead (1901–1978), geographer Jean Gottman (1915–1994), social scientist Barbera Ward (1914–1981) and architect Buckminster Fuller (1895–1983). He lectured in Hong Kong, the Chinese mainland, Europe and the United States, and made presence in

Fig. 8.17 Dr. Simon Kwan
(*right*), with Prince Charles,
in the construction site of
HKUST, 1989

magazines, newspapers, TV and radio talks. He advocated the integration of Chinese traditional thinking, modernity and cosmological theory, and criticized the capitalist greedy. Through his relationship with Harvard University, Tao Ho introduced the famous Japanese architect Fumihiko Maki to Hong Kong and collaborated with William Lim of Singapore and Sumet Jumsai of Thailand. Together, they pushed forward modernity in Asia.[11] In terms of introducing macro theory and communicating with the Western world, Tao Ho's ideas and actions were similar to those of the Japanese architect Kisho Kurokawa (1934–2007), who worked during the same period. They both knew and influenced each other. Through design practice and social activities, Tao Ho realized his life goal of "Renaissance man".[12] Unfortunately, Tao Ho suffered a stroke while busily working in Wuhan in 2002. Otherwise, his contribution to the design in Hong Kong and China would have been even greater[13].

Unlike the first two architects, **Simon Kwa**n is a local trained architect. He graduated from HKU in 1967 and opened his own firm in 1973. Later, he was awarded a Ph.D. in Chinese fine art history from HKU. Kwan is not only an architect but also an artist, art historian and collector. His sketches and perspective drawings vitally convey his imagination of the buildings and atmosphere of the future ambience. The appreciation of Chinese arts lends him a tool of conceiving architectural design, especially the relationship of figure and ground (Fig. 8.17).

In 1981, the government allocated a plot of land in Wanchai and the Jockey Club donated a sum for the development of an Academy for Performing Arts. Simon Kwan's design won first prize. Beneath the site lay sewage pipes that drained into

---

[11]William Lim particularly calls his and Asian peers' practice as "non-western" modernity, see Lim and Chang (Ed.), 2012. For the relationship of Tao Ho with his Asian peers, see Xue and Xiao (2014).

[12]The term "Renaissance man" repeatedly appears in Tao Ho's speeches, see Ho (2000).

[13]The description of Tao Ho's career in this chapter is based on the author's communication with Dr. Ho during 1985–2001, Ho (2000), Kwok (2010), Lim et al. (1980) and Khan (1995).

(a)   (c)

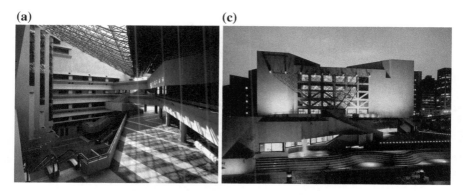

Fig. 8.18 Hong Kong Academy of Performing Arts, 1985. **a** The atrium gathers waiting and social functions for all theaters. **b** Plan drawings. **c** The outdoor space serves for open performance and social events. Courtesy of Dr. Simon Kwan

the harbor. The buildable area consisted of only two triangles. The design placed a vehicular drop-off area between these two triangles. Entering the lobby, visitors take the escalator and arrive at the huge atrium, from where they can reach the concert hall, grand theater, chamber hall, dancing hall, recording studio and experimental theater. According to the program brief, all of these performing venues were to have their own lobby. The design gathers them together and lets them share a big atrium, which expresses the spatial order and sequence, and also provides a social and communication area. The variously sized performing spaces are all woven into the modular grids of a triangle. The acute angles are used for stair shafts or storage, while the functional parts are rectangular. The building was completed in 1985 and echoed with I.M. Pei's design for the East Building of the National Gallery in Washington, 1978 (Fig. 8.18).

Kwan's design for the Hong Kong University of Science and Technology (HKUST) campus was a brilliant milestone in his career. In 1987, the government decided to establish a third university, the Hong Kong University of Science and Technology (HKUST). The government allocated a plot of mountain land in Clear Water Bay, Sai Kung, and the Jockey Club donated money for the construction. Five teams participated in the campus design competition, judged by a committee consisting of presidents/provosts of US and other universities. Fifteen jury members recommended the scheme proposed by Simon Kwan Architect and Associates and Percy Thomas Partnership Ltd.[14] The HKUST campus sits on a hill and faces the sea. The level difference from the hill top to the sea is around 100 meters. The buildings were built according to the varying topography. The main academic

---

[14]The design competition committee of the HKUST campus first announced that the first prize went to a rectangular plan designed by Eric Lye, Patrick Lau and other HKU faculty members. But for some reasons, Simon Kwan's plan was recommended for implementation. See Hong Kong Institute of Architects, 2007, the part of Patrick Lau; and also from the interview with Professor Patrick Lau, 9 May 2013.

(b)

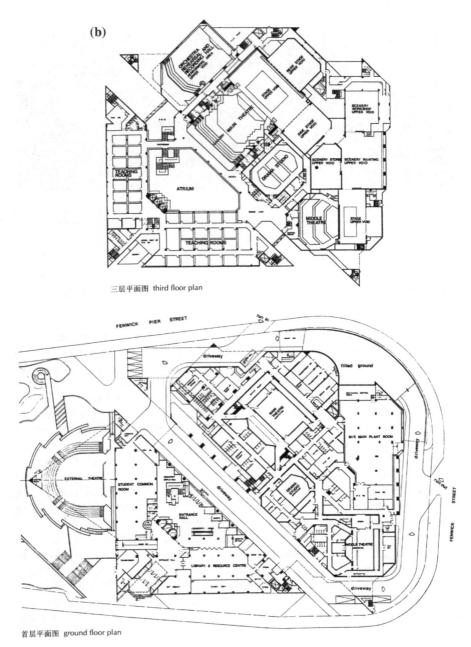

三层平面图 third floor plan

首层平面图 ground floor plan

Fig. 8.18 (continued)

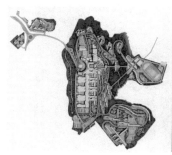

Fig. 8.19 HKUST campus, 1991. *Left* master plan. *Right* entrance plaza. Courtesy of Dr. Simon Kwan

building is situated along the ridge to reduce the level difference. When students change class, they can easily get to their next classroom (Fig. 8.19).

The campus entrance features a semi-circular plaza, like the prologue to a grand symphony. Walking through the semi-open lobby and standing on the balcony, a visitor is faced with a spectacular view of the sea and the sky, with islets appearing indistinctly in the sea like a Chinese ink painting. From the central axis, people can go down to the student halls on the east side through a series of corridors and pavilions, flanked by the green mountain and blue sky. The route from an academic building to a dormitory becomes a poetic journey. The academic blocks are linked by a north-south axis, frequently enriched by rest areas and plenty of light from the glass wall. The academic and student-staff quarters cascade to the sea from the east and north (Fig. 8.20).

The huge HKUST complex comprises three design vocabularies: square, equilateral triangle and semi-circle. Through the composition and contrast between these primary forms, the designer facilitated the perception of various spaces and sequences. The openings and windows, aligned along the solid shadowed wall, produce a strong effect. The whole building uses 6 × 6 inch grey tiles, mingled with a few white tiles. Some areas are highlighted by primary red, blue and yellow coloring. From a distance, the light-grey appears to be white, which creates an obvious shadow effect. The few white tiles are a reminder of the graduation between grey and white. Window openings are adjusted to fit with the integers of tiles, thus avoiding the need to cut the tiles. The design of HKUST was a milestone in the design of Hong Kong campuses. The entrance plaza, with its big red sundial, presents a typical picture postcard of Hong Kong's new generation of higher education buildings.[15]

---

[15]The description of the HKUST campus is taken from the author's own investigation, ongoing since 1995; an interview with Simon Kwan, December 5, 2011; and Charlie Q.L. Xue, Modernism is coming to Hong Kong—A Tale of Four Architects, *The Architect*, No. 156, April 2012, pp. 69–75.

Fig. 8.20 Volume, geometry, solid and void manipulate the spatial effects. **a** Semi-open hall as a pausing spot in the long corridor. **c** Transition between building and plaza. **d** Long corridor linking the academic building and students' halls. Courtesy of Dr. Simon Kwan

Following that project, between 1988 and 1997 Kwan's firm designed three buildings in Tat Chee Avenue in Kowloon Tong for semi-government organizations—the Hong Kong Productivity Council, the Inno Center of the Hong Kong Science Park and the Jockey Club environmental building. These buildings range from 5,000 to 15,000 m². In these buildings, Kwan's design dug a tall atrium within the building bulk and used the crisp geometry of a square and a circle. The various functional usages were unified in tidy modules and window openings. There is a level difference between the street front and the back of the buildings. In the Inno

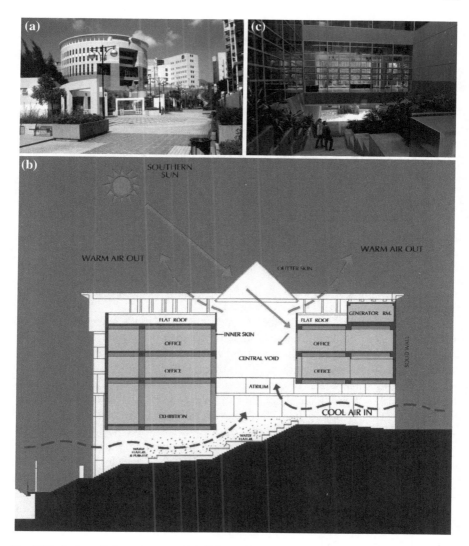

Fig. 8.21 Jockey Club environmental building, 1997. **a** Seen from street park. **b** Diagram of green measurements. Courtesy of Dr. Simon Kwan. **c** From street down to the garden

Center, the lower part at the back is a machine room and sunken exhibition space. In the Jockey Club environmental building, under a semi-open atrium, a big central landscaped staircase leads people from Tat Chee Avenue down to the park through lush trees and shrubs. The circular building is rooted in the earth and draws energy from the ground to the upper-level entrance (Figs. 8.21 and 8.22).

Kwan's designs for public and office buildings are always clear, crisp and tend to be minimal. The atrium space is comforting to people inside. The long glass atrium

(a)   (b)

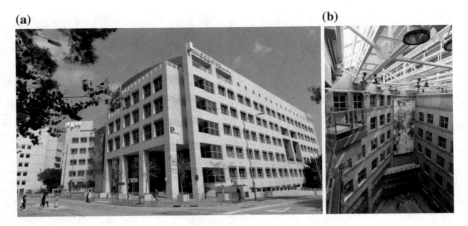

Fig. 8.22 Inno Center, Kowloon Tong, 1995. **a** Square and alignment are the main elevation treatments. **b** Atrium

in the Science Park links many building blocks and forms pleasant indoor and outdoor leisure spaces (Figs. 8.23 and 8.24).

As gentle as Dr. Kwan is, artistic creativity upsurges in his heart. He is fond of painting and using modern (abstract) language to express concepts. Although loving the tradition, Dr. Kwan never directly uses symbols like pitched roof or pavilion. He studies tradition and understands the importance of "line" in the Chinese arts. Most of his designs manipulate geometry or form a curvilinear plane (the HKUST entrance and Ma Wan Parken Shop, for example, see Chap. 5). Many vertical lines appear in the Hong Kong Custom Headquarters building. He studies calligraphy and seal cutting, which elaborates the stroke of the cutter in white jade. "Minimal" and structural layout is the spirit of Chinese seal. Applying the same principles to architecture, he treasures every movement in the design of a facade. In key parts such as the entrance, his use of one or two big openings highlights the hierarchy. Kwan's design is spectacular, delicate, modern, elegant and thoughtful[16].

Patrick Lau graduated from the University of Manitoba in 1969. During his studies, he was deeply influenced by Professor Gustavo da Roza, who was among the first cohort of graduates from HKU in 1955 and later taught in North America. The University of Manitoba is located in Winnipeg, Canada, where it is cold for almost half of the year. One of the educational concepts of Manitoba was to design according to the climate. Lau was trained with this climate-sensitive idea in school. After graduation, Patrick Lau worked in a design firm and later on the planning committee of the Vancouver municipal government. He participated in the renovation of an old industrial area. Amid the rising movement of the local community, he prevented an

---

[16]The description of Simon Kwan in this chapter is partly based on an interview conducted on 5 December 2011 and *Rhythm of Space, Selected Works by Simon Kwan & Associates Ltd.*, Jiangxi Fine Arts Publishing House, 2001.

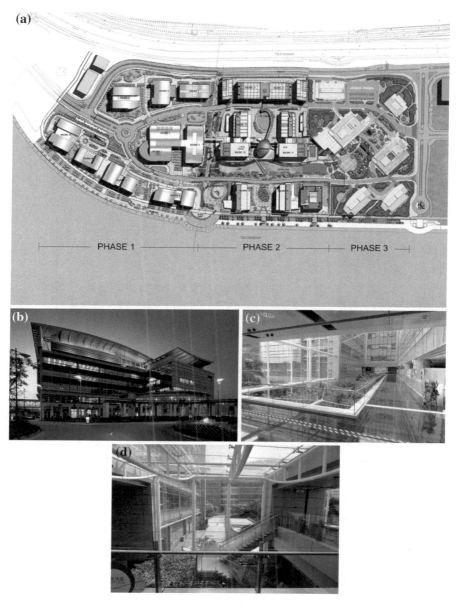

Fig. 8.23 Hong Kong Science Park **a** Master plan. Courtesy of Dr. Simon Kwan. **b** Management building. **c, d** Lobby of management building

expressway from cutting through China Town. He and the China Town community built Dr. Sun Yat-sen Park and the Chinese garden in Vancouver (Fig. 8.25).

In 1973, Patrick Lau returned to Hong Kong and taught at HKU, where he has been head of the architectural department since 1996. He worked as vice-chairman

(a)

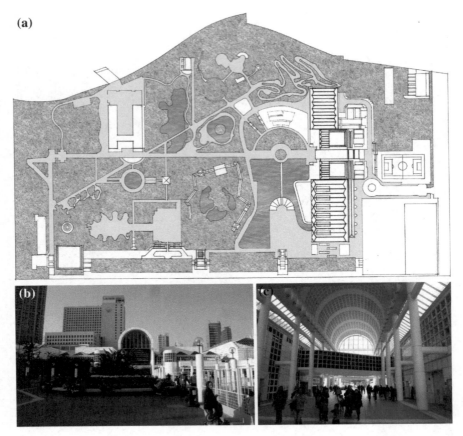

Fig. 8.24 Kowloon Park, 1989. **a** Master plan. Courtesy of Dr. Simon Kwan. **b** Park building, mainly for sport and swimming. **c** Park building acting as a passenger route from Austin Road to the Kowloon Park

of the town planning board and Legislative Council member, organized the professional green building council and appealed for the protection of the harbor and the creation of sustainable building.

Lau continues to find questions through his practice and brings these inquiries to architectural education. Besides his busy teaching, administrative and societal duties, he has continued his building design and practice. Although he has only a couple of employees, he has fulfilled a series of impressive projects, especially school buildings, and reaped many awards.[17]

---

[17]The information about Patrick Lau is based on the author's communication with Lau since 1999; Hong Kong Institute of Architects, 2007; Patrick Lau, Future Architecture, *Hong Kong Institute of Architects Journal*, No. 2, 2013. pp. 88–89; and an interview conducted on 9 May 2013.

Fig. 8.25 Professor Patrick
Lau, pictured in 2013

In 1975, Lau restored Sam Tung Uk, a clan house during the Qing Dynasty (1644–1911), to a vernacular life museum. In 1979, he planned the first university campus in Macau—East Asia University (now Macau University). Its academic and administrative buildings stand above the mountain of Taipa and face the sea. He designed the buildings and courtyard and laid down the skeleton of the campus. Some buildings are fare-faced concrete with ventilated openings, reminiscent of the CUHK buildings constructed at the same time.

For a long time, all schools in Hong Kong were designed according to government standards, so they were almost all the same. In the 1980s, several international schools located on the hill found that their small hilly sites could not accommodate the standard plan. For the new buildings of these schools, Lau's design used columns to support the building block. The large, elevated deck is light and breezy, with a long vista of mountain and sea. The public spaces are in the arms of building. Students can carry out activities on the high and low podiums. The buildings are faithful to their structure without extra decoration, but with contrast in their shape, size and geometry. These methods are reflected in several school projects— the French School, the International School at Tai Tam and West Island School of ESF (English School Foundation) (Figs. 8.26, 8.27 and 8.28).

At the end of the twentieth century, Lau designed the Australian International School in Kowloon Tong. In this school, classrooms open on to the veranda. The ends of the veranda vary on each floor. The different sizes and openings create spatial interest and airy holes. There is a swimming pool on top of the roof. A big metal umbrella covers the atrium opening, both symbolic and functional. The Australian school and the above-mentioned international school buildings won awards from the HKIA (Fig. 8.29).

In the 21st century, the government allocated land for social organizations to run private college. The HKU SPACE community college gained a plot of land in the industrial area of Kowloon Bay and commissioned Lau to design the building. HKU community college is larger than an ordinary primary or secondary school. The central sky-lit atrium is surrounded by classrooms, the library and various other rooms. Outdoor terraces on each floor are linked to the atrium, which creates natural

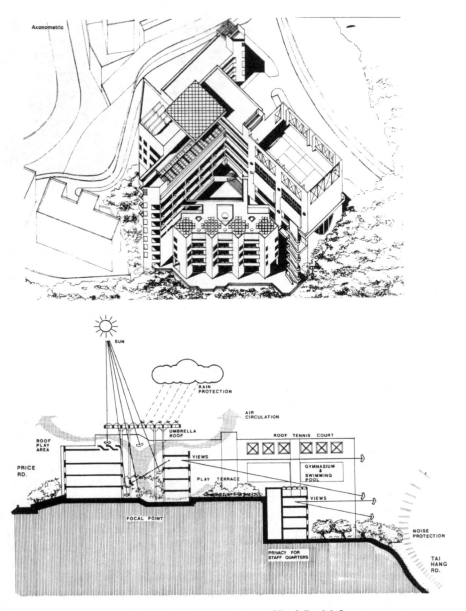

Fig. 8.26 French International School, 1984. Courtesy of Prof. Patrick Lau

ventilation. Unlike other school buildings, this atrium is naturally ventilated without air-con, allowing a breeze to be felt in the summer. Most building complexes in Hong Kong—deep plan shopping malls and academic buildings—are like huge refrigerators and only rely on artificial lighting and ventilation. Buildings like HKU community college, with a naturally ventilated atrium and indoor public space, are

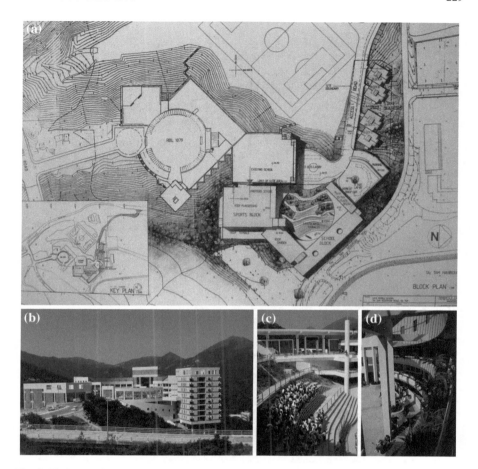

Fig. 8.27 International School of Tai Tam, 1986. **a** Master plan. **b** The school standing from valley. **c, d** Playground skillfully uses hilly topography. Courtesy of Prof. Patrick Lau

rarely seen. For decades, Professor Lau has responded sensitively to the climate in his building designs. In the 21st century, this sustainable concern is expressed in a new technology and fresh form (Fig. 8.30).

Anthony Ng received a Bachelor of Architecture degree from HKU in 1972 and later studied in Rome and the UK. In 1977, he returned to Hong Kong and in 1979 became a partner at Kwan, Ng and Wong. The company grew from around 10 to 230 staff, and in 1991, Ng led 27 people to found Anthony Ng and Associates.

St. John's Building in Garden Road, Central, is the property of Hong Kong and Shanghai Hotels Ltd. Its ground floor is the tram station. In the early 1980s, Ng produced the design for its reconstruction. The site's buildable area is 47 × 14 meters and is surrounded by roads. The design is a regular plan sitting on a slope. Its aluminum-clad facade is made up of a window frame, spandrel wall, corner

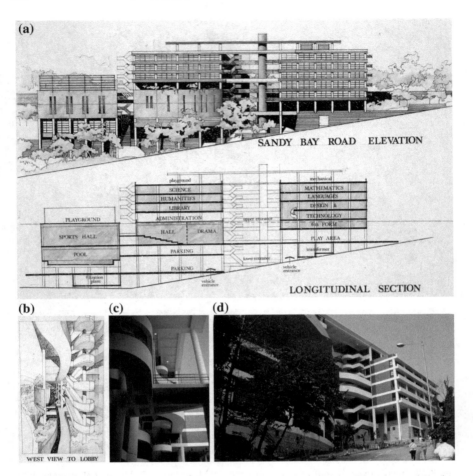

Fig. 8.28 Western Island School, English School Foundation, 1990s. **a** Elevation and section. **b** Curvilinear interests in staircase and corridor. **c** Semi-open public space. **d** Street view. Courtesy of Prof. Patrick Lau

window, corner spandrel and other prefabricated components. The aluminum slab is 6 cm thick and the aluminum slabs are set in dark colored silicon. The window frame sits on the corner of the building, which is rounded. The ground floor is the entrance lobby, and the ceiling and six round columns are clad with stainless steel sheets. A circular fountain and granite steps are in front of the entrance. Although constructed in the early 1980s, 30 years later, people still feel its exquisite quality and sleek gesture (Figs. 8.31 and 8.32).

Hong Kong and Shanghai Hotels Limited built the Repulse Bay Hotel in 1920 and it once attracted foreign celebrities and artists. In 1982, the owner planned to build an apartment block on the site. The original hotel podium was kept for shops, restaurants and a club house. The huge flag-shaped apartment building, "The

Fig. 8.29   Australia International School, Kowloon Tong, 2000. Courtesy of Prof. Patrick Lau

Repulse Bay," sits above the podium with the units cascading down toward the bay. Every ten stories there are terraces and large holes through which the green mountain and blue sea can be viewed. The external walls are clad with a wavy horizontal frame, which unifies the windows, balconies and holes behind. The first apartment buildings with large openings were designed by Arquitectonic in Miami, USA, in the 1980s. Borrowing from their experiences, The Repulse Bay created a new prototype in Hong Kong. The architect started to pay attention to ventilation. The external frame found its early use in Hong Kong (Fig. 8.33).

In 1997, Verbena Heights, a Housing Society project, was completed in Tseung Kwan O. The development comprises six 35–50 story blocks for sale, a 36 story building for rental and six facilities for the community. This was the first project completed by Anthony Ng and Associates. It was also an experiment in green architecture: influenced by the "eco skyscraper" designed by Ken Yeang of Malaysia, Ng and his colleagues aimed to respond to the climate of Hong Kong.

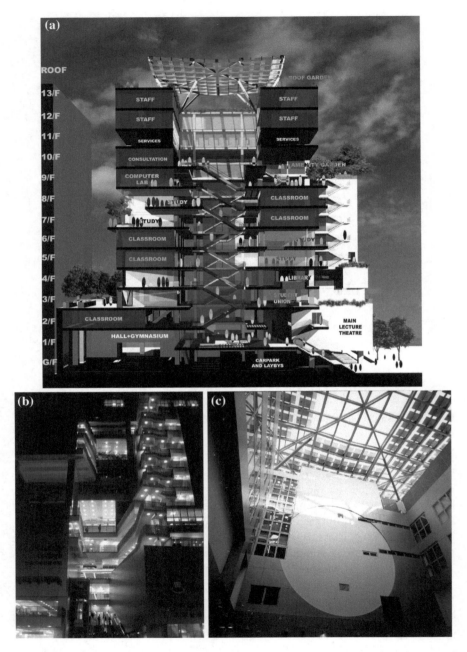

Fig. 8.30 HKU SPACE, Kowloon Bay, 2006. **a** Sectional view. **b** Entrance **c** Atrium. Courtesy of Prof. Patrick Lau

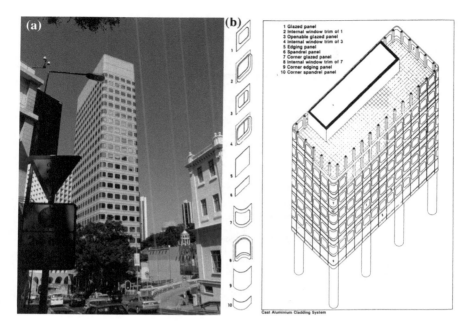

Fig. 8.31 St. John's Building, Garden Road, 1982. **a** View in the Garden Road; **b** Components of cladding; **c** Plan. Drawigs from Vision, 1982

K.S. Wong of Anthony Ng and Associates was the project architect.[18] In completing this design, the architect referred to wind tunnel tests and the solar path. The buildings are set high or low according to the view and the noise from street. A noise barrier is installed on the external wall and a tensile fabric wind canopy was erected. Low-flush water tanks are installed in every unit (Fig. 8.33).

For better ventilation, the floor plan uses a linear form rather than a cruciform. Blocks are hollowed to enable the wind to flow naturally through the building. Sky gardens are installed on every third floor, which were sold to the flat buyers.[19]

Verbena Heights was an early experiment in the use of green technology for mass housing. In subsequent developments, Ng and his colleagues introduced other green features, such as in Tung Chung Crescent, completed in 1999. The estate comprises two crescent towers, with the units arranged from high to low to welcome the dominant wind. The two crescents are connected by a bridge with a

---

[18]K.S. Wong became a leading figure in the green architecture movement in the twenty-first century. He was appointed Director of the Environmental Protection Department of the Hong Kong government in 2012.

[19]The description of the design of Verbena Heights is based on materials from the Hong Kong Institutes of Architects, http://www.hkia.net/en/Events/action.do?method=detail&mappingName= AnnualAwards&id=4028813c24c36d2d0124c3ba5304001b; and Wikipedia http://zh.wikipedia. org/wiki/%E8%8C%B5%E6%80%A1%E8%8A%B1%E5%9C%92. Accessed 8 March 2015.

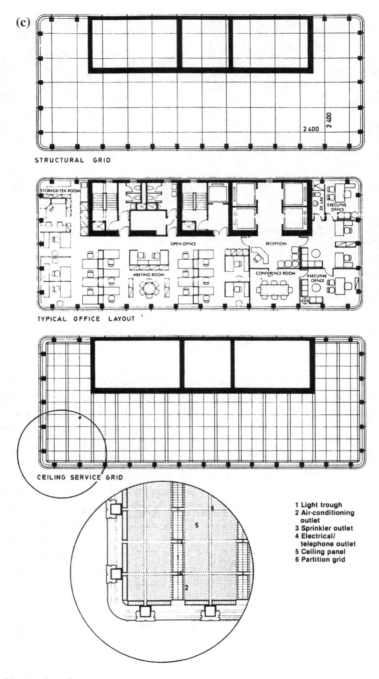

Fig. 8.31 (continued)

Fig. 8.32 The Repulse Bay apartment, 1989

Fig. 8.33 Verbena Heights, Tseung Kwan O, 1997

pedestrian road underneath, leading to the estate. These housing projects created a new architectural language for high-density conditions.

In the Tsing Yi community building, Ng and colleagues attempted to give a new form to this type of building. The ground floor houses a wet market. The podium is a broad platform for people to transit from the residential estates to the street opposite and the MTR. The sports hall and library on the upper floors provide a contrast in space and volume and generate beautiful scenes.[20]

Anthony Ng's design method transformed from sleek wrapping in the 1970s to more concerns on ventilation in the 1990s, which changed his design languages and building form. Compared with Patrick Lau who also emphasizes the response to

---

[20]The description of Anthony Ng is partly based on Kvan et al. (2000).

Fig. 8.34 Dr. Rocco Yim,
pictured in the early 1990s

climate, Ng designed in a larger scale and broader building types—apartment blocks, office buildings, shopping malls and MTR stations, with the support of his company and capable colleagues. His modernist aesthetic vision is fully implemented in plan, space and structure. In the early 1990s, his office experimented paper-less operation and electronic filing, which made the first step in the information age.

Rocco Yim graduated from the University of Hong Kong in 1976, and was conferred an honorary doctorate by the HKU in 2013. The architectural education at HKU emphasized technology in the 1970s, therefore Yim was trained with a pragmatic attitude. In 1979, he and his schoolmates opened Rocco Design, which has grown from several employees to more than 200 (Fig. 8.34).

In 1983, Yim's design was one of three shortlisted schemes in the international design competition for the opera house in the Bastille, Paris. His design dialogued with the street context of Paris (Fig. 8.35). Carlos Ott from Canada eventually won the competition and his design was built. However, through his debut in Paris, Yim was commissioned to design the Tianjin Exhibition Center. At the same time, he designed Park Lane and the gate of Kowloon Park along Nathan Road, the north-south thoroughfare of the Kowloon peninsula (Fig. 8.36). The design emphasized the portal form of a gate. In these designs, Yim elaborated building geometries and volumes. In the early 1980s, Postmodernism prevailed around the world and also permeated Hong Kong. Yim felt that although the US and Japan had culture and context that architects could tap, Hong Kong was not sensitive to history and culture. When the Japanese and American masters considered stylish "-ism" in their designs, Hong Kong architects had to work out how to produce more residential units and saleable floor areas on a small plate. The chaotic and dense city had little interest in culture and history. There was a huge distance between the ideal and the reality, which made him feel helpless. He was influenced by Japanese

Fig. 8.35 Competition scheme for Paris Opera House, Bastille, Paris, 1983

Fig. 8.36 Park Lane,
Kowloon Park, 1986
Courtesy of Dr. Rocco Yim

architects, especially Kisho Kurokawa, and was eager to cultivate seductive fruit in the barren land of Hong Kong.[21]

Yim's designs pay close attention to circulation and traffic—how people arrive at a building, how people move from the building to other places and how the building connects to other buildings. Yim's work has continuously tested these questions. The twin towers of the Citibank headquarters (1992) sit on the podium, the upper and lower floors of which contain various restaurants and coffee shops. When people arrive at the building, they can see the artistic waterfall and the Mid-level landscape through the curtain wall. From the Citibank building, people can cross the street or walk to Hong Kong Park using pedestrian bridges (Fig. 8.37).

Hollywood Terrace (1999) was designed for the Hong Kong Housing Society. The design includes stairs and a lift for passers-by from Queen's Road to

---

[21]Rocco Yim's words on Hong Kong and overseas; see Rocco Yim, Architalk, *Vision*, No. 7, 1983.

Hollywood Road on the upper level. Passers-by arrive at the higher level and walk across the pedestrian bridge to Hollywood Terrace. They can see the courtyard of the residential estate without disturbing the residents. The design creates the pleasure of passing by and viewing other people's lives, but with no interference (Fig. 8.37). The new addition to the Lok Fu shopping mall (1991), designed by Yim, connects on the fourth floor to the old part, designed by Chung Wah-nan in 1981. The new part links to the MTR and Junction Road at the higher level (Fig. 8.38). The International Finance Center is located in Central. People can arrive at the building from the MTR, Airport Express, bus station, piers and pedestrian system of Central. The podium part is designed in a circular form, with a central opening for the bus station and traffic to pass through (Fig. 8.39).

Compared with other cities, Hong Kong has a severe shortage of buildable land and 80 % of residents use public transportation in their daily lives. High-rise and high-density are the main solutions. Rocco Yim grew up in Hong Kong and deeply understands the importance of pedestrian and vehicular traffic. When designing a building, he always integrates the functional aspects with various pedestrian routes. The circulations inside and outside his buildings weave an artistic pattern and end-users appreciate the convenience and the intimate and relaxed feel of the space.

Convenient circulation and pedestrian accessibility make such buildings an organic part of the city. Based on a rational circulation design, Yim pays more attention to the elaboration of the building's form—the juxtaposition of solid and void, high and low, horizontal and vertical, and exposed and shaded. A cantilevered glass box (or clad on one side with metal or tiles), horizontal sun-shading fins and a long, thin single column often feature, in different versions, in his designs, such as the Shek Kip Mei Sports Center (1997), the new wing of Lok Fu (1991) and the Far East Mansion on Nathan Road (1998).

The Peninsula Hotel was built in 1928 in Tsim Sha Tsui to accompany the train terminal of the Kowloon-Canton Railway. The hotel saw the surrender of the Hong Kong governor to Japanese troops in 1941. It has long been one of the landmarks of colonial Hong Kong. Yim was engaged to design the alterations and add a tower. He elaborated the proportion of the new tower while respecting the original symmetrical form. In adding the new tower, he aimed to embody a classical composition. The window openings, division of wall lines and other details were derived from the old building. This was partly learnt from the Postmodernist method. The alteration of the Peninsula Hotel respects the old building, adds the colors and values of a new era and graces the Tsim Sha Tsui area (Fig. 8.40).

The podium of Hong Kong University's Graduate House (1998) contains a lecture theater at the lower level and a lobby/activity room on the higher level. The rise in the lecture theater floor echoes the hilly topography outside (Fig. 8.41). The two directional axes meet in the lobby of Graduate House, creating dynamically interesting spaces. His several academic building designs in the CUHK and other institutions experiment many spatial effects. The Icon Hotel of Polytechnic University (2011) used the method of hollowing volume and pushing in glass box. The building allows circulation from two sides, with a separate entrance for school teaching (Fig. 8.42). iSquare (2009) is a shopping mall focusing on young

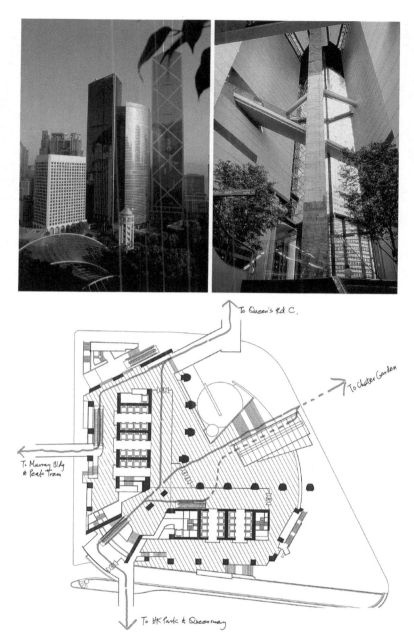

Fig. 8.37 Citibank headquarters building, 1992. The lower part acts as a traffic transition from street to the hill and park. Courtesy of Dr. Rocco Yim

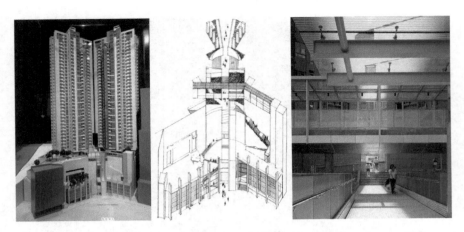

Fig. 8.38 In Hollywood Terrace, passers-by can go from Queen's Road up to the Hollywood Road through the building. Courtesy of Dr. Rocco Yim

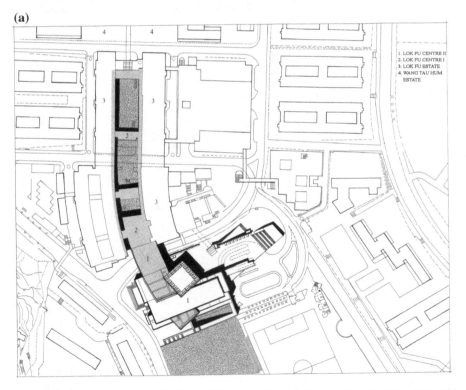

Fig. 8.39 Lok Fu Shopping Mall, 1991. **a** Master plan showing the new "head" adding to the old linear shopping arcade. **b** Big platform and steps leading to the upper floor of shopping mall. **c** The old and new parts connect above the road. Courtesy of Dr. Rocco Yim

Fig. 8.39 (continued)

Fig. 8.40 New addition to the Peninsula Hotel, 1994. The proportion of shape and windows was elaborated. Courtesy of Dr. Rocco Yim

customers. The design places a long escalator crossing three floors adjacent to the external glass wall. In addition to several big escalators climbing three floors, and one directly piercing the busy MTR station of Tsim Sha Tsui, there are many

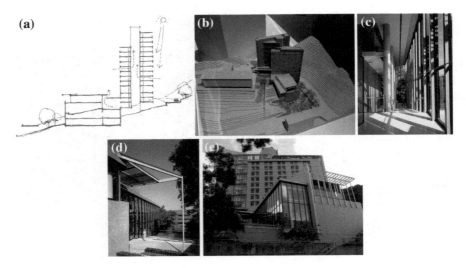

Fig. 8.41 Graduate Hall, HKU, 1998. **a** Ideas on sketch. Courtesy of Dr. Rocco Yim. **b** Model shows how the buildings work with the hilly site. **c** Corridor next to the theater. **d** Hall entrance. **e** Building mass

Fig. 8.42 Icon Hotel, PolyU, 2011. **a** The building in Hung Hom. **b** Manipulating the mass. Courtesy of Dr. Rocco Yim. **c** Interior. **d** Hotel entrance

Fig. 8.43 iSquare, Tsim Sha Tsui, 2009. **a** Building mass. **b** Interaction of traffic space. Courtesy of Dr. Rocco Yim. **c** Long escalator rises along the glass wall

escalators between floors. The nine-floor podium and the upper tower are skillfully integrated. The designer exposed the long escalator and thus implied the characteristics of Hong Kong architecture. However, the escalators are located in different places from floor to floor, making it difficult for visitors to find their way around (Fig. 8.43).

Since 1983, Rocco Design has engaged in design projects in the Chinese mainland, where "design creation" is encouraged and many public buildings are also provincial or municipal landmarks. Practicing in China has given Yim the opportunity to contemplate "Chinese-ness" and "being Chinese in architecture." He poses questions for himself and the peers, "What is expected of a Chinese person in his work? Will 'Chinese-ness' come about by the architect being Chinese, or by the context being Chinese? Is 'Chinese-ness genuinely discernable, a quality that can be consciously pursued? Or is it something that comes from within, a subtle reflection of personality conditioned by ancestral mentality and taste, and therefore incidental rather than intentional? While I put forward my belief, back in 1989, that in order to ponder the future of Asian (Chinese) architecture, we have to come to terms with who the modern Asian (Chinese) is" (Rocco Design 2004, p. 1). This query shows his concerns of local end-users.

In the compact city of Hong Kong, the physical environment is the main context, whereas in the Chinese mainland, cultural context is the crucial consideration. In the design of the Boao housing estate on Hainan Island (2002), the building blocks extend from high to low. Many gaps are generated between the blocks to provide a narrow or open sea view. Yim's design of a single family mansion in "Nine Houses" in Shanghai (2006) demonstrates his taste for a "Chinese lifestyle." Moving to the multi-family scale, "17 Mile" is a high-class residential area on Shenzhen's east coast. The terraced houses face the sea and the penthouse is highlighted. The slab-wrapped penthouse is reminiscent of Yim's design for the IFC in Hong Kong. The Guangdong Museum (2010) uses a "treasure box" as its motif and holes were dug in the building facade. The box sits on a supporting cube and exhibits a floating gesture. The designer anticipated visitors' interactions with those holes; however, the management of the museum locked all of the openings for safety reasons, so Yim's idea was not realized. The Guangdong Museum is located on the central axis of Pearl River New City and faces the Guangzhou Opera House, designed by Zaha Hadid. There is no dialogue between either the buildings or the physical context. The designers of these landmark buildings spoke only to themselves. Using the similar method of Guangdong Museum, Rocco Design made Yunnan Museum in 2014 and paid tribute to the famous "stone forest" in Yunnan. These buildings on the Chinese mainland embody Yim's sensitivity to "Chinese-ness" and cultural symbolization. The beauty glowing from these buildings is also related to the tastes of the clients and the architect[22] (Figs. 8.44 and 8.45).

Rocco Yim works hard and has had tremendous opportunities in practice and business, which are coveted by his peers. His designs add a modern sense to the streets of Hong Kong and express a possible delicacy in a high-rise, high-density environment. Since 1981, Rocco Design has won around 20 awards from the Hong Kong Institute of Architects (HKIA) and the company has won the most awards since the award system was established in 1965. In addition to design, Yim is involved in many seminars and events in Hong Kong and China. His explorations push the boundaries of architecture and reinterpret the meaning of Chinese architecture.

According to Fumihiko Maki, Rocco Yim sensitively responds to the density of Hong Kong and Chinese culture. Maki himself focuses on the density and proposed collective form and mega-structures since the 1960s (see Chap. 6). Kenneth Frampton describes Yim's design as coinciding with the dramatic pioneers of the Modern Movement, especially Le Corbusier and Hannes Meyer. Yim's design in dense Hong Kong "totally surpasses Koolhaas's more limited notion of the 'culture of congestion', a term that he coined to characterize the post facto polemic of his *Delirious New York* of 1978." The task in the city of Hong Kong is denser and more complicated than the situation of New York in the 1970w. For the new Chinese architecture represented by Yim, Frampton continued, "we will have to recognize that there will be no truly authentic new Chinese architecture without acknowledging the brilliant yet fragile triumph of Japanese modern architecture, dating back to the second quarter of the last century."[23]

---

[22]The description of Rocco Yim in this chapter is based on the author's communication with Yim since 1989, Rocco Design (2004, 2012), DeHoff (2013), and an exhibition of Yim's work at the HKICC Lee Shau Kei School of Creativity, June 2009.

[23]For more comments on Rocco Yim by Fumihiko Maki and Frampton, see Fumihiko Maki, "Globalization and floating modernism," and Kenneth Frampton, "Beneath the radar: Rocco Yim and the new Chinese architecture," in DeHoff (2013), pp. 8–13. For the "Culture of congestion," see Koolhaas (1994).

Fig. 8.44 Guangdong Museum, Guangzhou, 2010. **a** The building is shaped like a jewelry box. **b**, **c** Interior atrium is partitioned by steel net, creating a translucent effect. **d** Model. **e** Yim (*left*) and colleagues on the site. Courtesy of Dr. Rocco Yim

Fig. 8.45 Yunnan Museum, 2014. Courtesy of Dr. Rocco Yim

8.3 Generation of the 21st Century

Generations are evolving like surf. In addition to these highlighted architects, a new group has emerged that possesses a strong desire for creativity, keeping indigenous characteristics and discovering new potential, including Chris Law (Oval Partnership and Integer), Winston Shu (IDA), Bernard Lim (AD + RG), Gary Chang, Weijen Wang, Vincent Ng (AGC Design), William Lim (CL3 Architects), Barrie Ho and Gravity Partnership. Compared to their predecessors, the generation in the 21st century was born in a relatively wealthier, open and less-bumpy society. They absorb the prevailing design method in the world. They are more influenced by the democratic and sustainable trend, and are more accustomed to face the society and public. Many people themselves are involved in promoting civic movement. They prepare drawings in office and also appear in public forums. They design buildings not only in Hong Kong, but in Greater China and other places. This gives them opportunity to explore different method and design language.

Graduated from Bartlett School of Architecture, University College London in 1983, **Chris Law** has actively contributed to the urban, architectural, interior design and social movement. He established Oval Partnership in 1992, an "elite" firm focusing on the delicate quality of design, and purchased Integer of London, a green-design-oriented firm. His design of Taikoo Li Sanlitun, Beijing (2010), created a new shopping landscape in addition to mall complex. Following the success in Beijing, Swire Property continued the "Taikoo Li" model in Chengdu of Southwest China, which was also designed by Law and his team. Taikoo Li in Chengdu integrated more southwest China flavor. In Star Street of Wanchai, Law designed buildings and street improvements, making the dilapidated community a lovely living and SOHO environment in the old Mid-level (Fig. 8.46).

Winston T. Shu (born in 1955) studied at Kingston University and AA in London. Under Terry Farrell and Bernard Tschumi's tutorship he was particularly

Fig. 8.46 Works of Chris Law and Oval Partnership. **a** New performing space for the Academy of Performing Arts. **b** Renovation of Star Street, Wanchai. Courtesy of Mr. Chris Law. **c** Sanlitun Taikoo Li, Beijing

influenced by the free-thinking of the school and Tschumi's manifesto on space and human behavior. From 1980 to 1999 Shu worked at Foster and Partners. Through Stansted Airport of London, Shu learnt the skills in the design of highly serviced buildings, a holistic approach to integration of building technologies, systems and functions In 1992 he played a pivotal role in bidding the job and designing the Hong Kong airport. In 1999, supported by the brilliant achievements and lessons gained from leading large scale projects and Foster, Shu opened his own firm Integrated Design Associates Ltd. (IDA).

In the 21st century, IDA designed projects in Hong Kong, Chinese mainland, India and Middle East, but none of the projects can be compared with the Parkview Green in Beijing, whose design and construction lasted for 12 years. Shu helped the client to initiate the program in the business center of Beijing. Over 120,000 sq.m. office and hotel space and a 55,000 m^2 retail mall are packed in four buildings sited in a sunken garden to the surrounding street level. All buildings are designed with atria spaces, sky-gardens, terraces, and link bridges, and together are shielded from the external environment by an outer building envelope that is constructed of steel, glass and ETFE cushions. The skin is essentially the weather protection layer that controls the microclimate of the entire development by way of a thermal insulation layer formed in the airspace between the skin of the internal buildings and the outer skin. Therefore air-con is not needed in the atrium. The building mass is two triangles cut from a square cube with a slanted top. This on the one hand allows daylight to reach every window in the neighborhood, and on the other hand creates a sharp image in the city center.

The boutique hotel is located at the highest floors of the development accessed exclusively via glass shuttle lifts from the hotel entrance foyer at street level. The hotel has 44 luxury rooms, each ranging from 72 to 100 m^2 in area, and a presidential suite which is 500 m^2 in area. Each room has its own expansive terrace, individual swimming pool, jacuzzi, sauna and entertaining facilities. A Sky-lounge is located at the pinnacle of the whole development. A wonderful stroke in design is a suspended pedestrian bridge, connecting the opposite site, piercing diagonally through the atrium. Visitors can stroll on bridge and watch the atrium and building complex in an optimal angle. The bridge has little "commercial function" except occasional fashion and sculpture shows. But the client generously supported this design with hundred millions of dollar to erect the bridge. In traditional atrium, such a location is usually void, but Parkview Green provides such a vantage trail of watching and being watched.

The unique space stimulates diverse activities inside: shopping, office working, eating, dating, taking escalators and lifts … According to Shu, easily comprehend layout, well oriented circulation, visible people activity and unobstructed line of sights are basic strategies for shopping mall space. "We set up the movements by locating activities so that people transgress space, and the activities are clearly visible from inside as well as outside of the building. We want the building to come alive, so we make sure the activities that create the movements are places people want to go." In the tide of E-commerce, most shopping malls in Beijing suffer from quiet business. Parkview Green stands out with its hustle and bustle "urbanity" scenes all year around.[24] Architects in Beijing visited the building by fulfilling their needs of continuing and professional development (CPD).

---

[24]The situation of IDA and Parkview Green project is from an interview of Winston T. Shu on 4 March 2016, and from special issue of Parkview Green, Beijing, *Architectural Creation*, No. 1, 2015.

In Shu's career, the first decade was involved in Stansted Airport; the second decade dedicated to the Hong Kong airport; and in the third decade he set up the milestone work—Parkview Green in the capital city of China. From this "defining project", Shu received commitments from other airports and institutional clients, for example the Cebu airport in The Philippines, airports in India and the Maldives, and mixed-use developments in countries from Asia to Europe (Fig. 8.47).

Bernard Lim (born in 1956) is scholar, architect and organizer of various social activities. Through his teaching at CUHK and leadership of HKIA and HKIUD (Hong Kong Institute of Urban Design), Lim advocated high-quality building for the society and public engagement in urban redevelopment. Lim has long surveyed the living environment and actual needs for elderly and created new details to facilitate the ideal indoor and outdoor space.[25] He and colleagues found that the round corner in corridor can avoid clash. People in wheelchair or pushing cart will have more confidence in moving in such round-corner area. This has been applied to the interior of several hospital and health facility designs. His practice AD + RG aims to integrate design with research to improve the community architectural design. These ideas are reflected in his design of Hong Kong Community College in West Kowloon (2007, collaborated with AGC Design Ltd.), rehabilitation of Mei Ho Building (2013, see Chap. 9), Bishop Walsh Primary School at Kowloon City and many other school and community buildings. In the school buildings, he extensively uses sharp color; while in the elderly caring houses, he still uses color, but sedate. The Learning Common of Institute of Education is light-hearted by color, lighting and smooth flowing of line and plane (Fig. 8.48).

Weijen Wang (born in 1958) designed buildings in Taiwan, Hong Kong and the Chinese mainland in addition to his teaching at the University of Hong Kong. Through the practice in high density Asian city context, Wang develops an idea of "sectional or vertical courtyard", where public patio space is created outdoor, indoor or in-between in the multi-level tall buildings through interlocking, offsetting and overlapping building blocks. This is particularly reflected in his design of Hong Kong Community College building in Hung Hom Bay (2005, collaborated with AD + RG and AGC Design). In a tower of over 20 stories, every four floors of classroom cluster are organized into modular blocks to create their own semi-outdoor public/activity spaces linked by the open stair. The changing volume of such public spaces is expressed in the building facade as a sequence of rotating vertical voids and also a movement system. Such a small indoor-outdoor "public" space is morphed and enriched in other projects, for example, Community College Building of Lingnan University (2007), Taiwan Merchants' School in Dongguang (2008) and Shenzhen Campus design of CUHK (2014, collaborated with Rocco Design and Gravity) (Fig. 8.49).

---

[25]Professor Bernard Lim's study on public engagement and community buildings is reflected in the following books, Lim et al. (2005), Department of Architecture, The Chinese University of Hong Kong (2003).

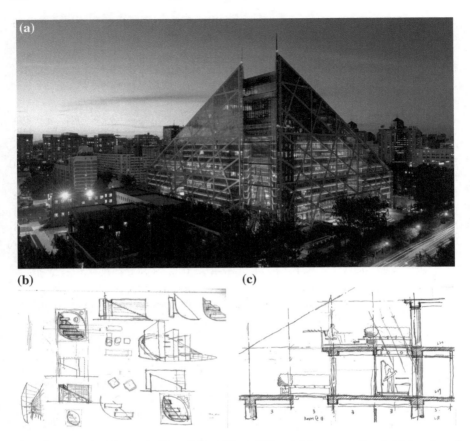

Fig. 8.47 Parkview Green, Beijing, 2012. **a** The building and its surrounding; **b** Elaboration of building mass; **c** Concept on hotel; **d, e** Pedestrian bridge piercing the atrium; **f** Winston T. Shu. Courtesy of IDA

Barrie Ho was trained at Polytechnic University and University of Hong Kong (M.Arch, 1996). He started his career from interior design. Details and materials are given more attention in his projects. His designs of "pencil" apartment building and community building under the flyover bridge are tasteful (Fig. 8.50).

Some architects in this generation consider the new model of practice. For example, Gravity Partnership abandons the conventional model of top designers served by job-running team. In Gravity Partnership, staff members are motivated by participating competition, scheme, design development and running job for their own designs. Some academics contribute to design with their expertise niches, for example, Zhu Jingxiang's light-weight assembled building for disaster-relief site and Jia Beisi's exploration of energy conservation especially in building envelop. The above mentioned architects and their works account for only a small

Fig. 8.47   (continued)

percentage of building practice in Hong Kong, but they are trying to push the boundary of architecture.

Compared with the architects grown up in the 1970s, the generation of the 21st century is inevitably influenced by its era, when democratic, sustainable and fair-society oriented trends dominate the society. More contemplation voices were issued, evidenced in TV documents (RTHK 2000), newspaper/magazine articles and books written by architects themselves, as mentioned in Preface (Chan and Choi 2005; Ng and Chu 2007) and the publication of a quarterly magazine *Hong Kong Institute of Architects Journal* (starting from 1996). The *HKIA Journal* is run by architects in their spare time, and remains as building report and the organization's bulletin. Ideally, it should shoulder both the professional and academical tasks.

Fig. 8.48 Works of Bernard Lim and AD + RG. **a** Hong Kong Community College in West Kowloon, 2007. **b** Institute of Education, Learning Common, 2014. Courtesy of Prof. Bernard Lim. **c, d** Polytechnic University, Phase 8 academic building, 2013. **d** Professor Bernard Lim

Fig. 8.49 Hong Kong Community College building in Hung Hom, 2005. Courtesy of Prof. W.J. Wang

Fig. 8.50 Works of Barrie Ho Architecture Interiors Ltd.—Mercer serviced apartment. Courtesy of Mr. Barrie Ho

In 2005, Hong Kong Architecture Centre was founded to create interaction between architecture and the general public. The organizer believes that an enhanced appreciation of the built-environment around people from various aspects can help cultivate a deeper understanding of the art of architecture, culture, and subsequently to build collectively for the betterment of the city. The activities launched by the centre concentrate on preservation of city's collective memory and engage many members of the public. It is a professional consciousness of appealing for total quality of society and environment.

Moreover, Shenzhen-Hongkong bi-city urban architecture bienalle has been run since 2007. The old Central Police Station (built in 1915), West Kowloon Cultural District, Kwun Tong Pier and Kowloon Park were used as event venue in the past years. The bienalle serves as a incubator for fresh ideas of young people and firm.

8.4   Conclusion: Different Directions

The architects introduced in this chapter typify the architectural trends in Hong Kong since the 1970s. Their works represent landmarks in this process. Chung Wah-nan's Chinese concept, Tao Ho's expression of structure, the space and volume of Simon Kwan, the climatic responses of Patrick Lau and Anthony Ng, and the circulation and geometry manipulation of Rocco Yim hold tightly onto the rationale of Modernism, but personal expressions are varied and have a human touch. In the 1960s, Modernist architecture had a colorful development in the US and Europe. Architects designed many masterpieces with the available materials, local context and personal skills. Tao Ho's design coincided with the works of the second generation of Modernist architects in the US and Europe. Ho was also pivotal to link Hong Kong with the overseas peers. Simon Kwan further developed the geometric forms with a simplified aesthetics. Patrick Lau and Anthony Ng discovered new ways of attracting ventilation in high-rise buildings. Rocco Yim's design emphasized lightness and slimness and the contrast between solid and void. Yim's designed buildings, no matter how proudly standing in the skyline, humbly connect to the city's vehicular and pedestrian transportation systems. Except Chung and Ho, the other four architects were active in practice and continuously refining designs in the 21st century.

As Hong Kong is an integral part of China after 1997, the generation in the new millennium faces competition not only in Hong Kong, but also from their motherland. They could tap sources not only from this southern China island but also the vast hinterland. They should not only run business in Hong Kong and the Chinese mainland, but make themselves visible in China and Asia. Architects in Hong Kong are rarely burdened about "identity", but some architects have awareness on finding their own identity. This is the proposition in the beginning of this chapter "being Chinese in architecture", which is an ultimate discourse in Rocco Yim and some other people's eyes. Essy Baniassad commented on Yim, which may also be suitable for tradition and all works mentioned in this chapter. "We regard that (Chinese) tradition with admiration but it seems so narrow a scope for us individuals, for our self-expression, and for this time of increasing dimension and diversity. That tradition describes a world of governance, beliefs, and a daily life of artisan technology which, compared to the present, is a world of relatively simple institutional structure, a limited vocabulary of forms, and a culture closer to the ground. It seems so distant. Yet it endures in its simple composition in the depths of the emerging contemporary Chinese culture." "The (Yim's) works touch on the total scope of architecture, the house and the city, and each one is a complete work of architecture in itself. None of the designs set out to be Chinese. They are what they become" (Baniassad 2004, pp. 8–11).

If we view Hong Kong architects' evolution from the 1950s, there are several salient directions of pursuance. When facing a building task, architects will approach the solutions with various means. A total design concept is necessary. However, sharp characters were reflected in some people's designs. They can arguably be categorized as Table 8.1.

Architects in Hong Kong were educated and trained locally or from foreign countries. Except a couple of people bring in strong imprints from their education origin (for example Tao Ho), most people are challenged and adapted to perform in Hong Kong's special constraints and context. These architects' works are naturally formed by many forces in Hong Kong, and differentiate themselves with the western counterparts and are "what they become." They enriched Asian and world architecture in the late 20th century (Lim and Chang 2012). In Hong Kong, the project managers of many development companies are also architects. The developers and these project managers usually have clear and strong ideas of their building products. After many rounds of design improvement and amendment,

Table 8.1 Categories of architects' pursuance and tendency in Hong Kong

Trends	Representatives	Other people
Structural expression ("Brutalism")	Wai Szeto, Tao Ho, James Kinoshita (P & T)	Patrick Lau, Eric Cumine, Winston Shu
Chinese taste	Chung Wah-nan	Rocco Yim, CL3
Climate sensitive	Luke Him Sau, Patrick Lau	Anthony Ng, Ronald Lu, Oval Partnership, Winston Shu
Commercial	Eric Cumine, Wong and Ouyang	P & T, DLN, Andrew Lee, WCWP…
Geometry and simplicity	PWD (Alan Fitch, Ronald Phillips…), Rocco Yim	Simon Kwan, Oval Partnership
Traffic and pedestrian oriented	Rocco Yim, Aedas	AECOM
User-friendly	Bernard Lim (AD + RG)	Andrew Lee
Design and interior design driven	Gary Chang	Barrie Ho

design firms eventually fall to only act like a draftsman. The room for "creativity" is much more limited in Hong Kong than in the Chinese mainland.

The 1970s saw the taking off of Hong Kong's economy, with the change from handicrafts, light and home-based industries to a center of finance and services. Compared with those glamorous, world-renowned architects, Hong Kong architects fully understand the needs and budgets of government and private clients. Buildings in Hong Kong are silently solving the daily and technical problems of the city and the New Territories. The designs produced by Hong Kong architects reflect the pragmatic attitudes of the city. They humbly satisfy the functional requirements while following the aesthetic principles of geometry, abstract, mass, light and shadow, contrast, alignment, order and sequence.

In the Chinese mainland after the open-door policy was adopted, a number of international "celebrity architects" have occupied the market. Some buildings were built at the expense of the environment, rational structure and future budgets, regardless of people's complaints.[26] In this sense, the works of Hong Kong architects have particular significance. Inside China, a group of young architects have returned to the formal game and architectonics since 1996. Their works are labelled as "experimental architecture" and frequently appear in the international stages like exhibition and forum.[27] This trend is culminated by the appointment of a couple of Chinese architects as dean and chair of architectural schools of the top US universities and the awarding of Pritzker Architectural Prize to Wang Shu in 2012.

---

[26]For the importation of foreign designed architecture into the Chinese mainland, see two books of Charlie Q.L. Xue, *Global Impact: overseas architectural design in China*, 2006b; *World Architecture in China*, 2010.

[27]For the experimental architects in China, see Charlie Q.L. Xue, *Building a Revolution: Chinese architecture since 1980*, 2006a, particularly its Chap. 8; and Zhu (2009).

As ethnic Chinese, architects in the Hong Kong Special Administrative Region (HKSAR) are obviously marginalized in this trend. The spirit of "creation" trickles to Hong Kong through exchange activities like bienalle and seminars. However, the capitalist soil and cramped land in Hong Kong give little opportunity for "experiment." The serious academic journal of architecture does not exist (Xue, Tan and Xiao 2016). Any "experiment" beyond the commercial parameters will be lonely and helpless.

Rocco Yim's design of Bastille Opera House in Paris was selected as one of the three shortlisted works in 1983. The next year, Yim came to Shanghai and lectured at Tongji University. He spoke Cantonese, and Professor Luo translated his words into Putonghua. In 1989, I visited Yim in his office at Hopewell Center, Wanchai. An endless supply of fresh ideas sprung from this thin man. Tao Ho was also active in the 1980s and 1990s. He lectured at Science Hall of Shanghai on cosmopolitanism, Chinese culture and architecture. His office was made out of containers and located in the courtyard of a villa. The interior was lighthearted and bright. I visited Tao Ho in his office one autumn morning in 1989. The sudden rainfall splashed tiny water droplets on a window of sandy glass, beyond which could be seen the faint image of bamboo blowing in the breeze outside. It was as touching and unforgettable as a Chinese ink painting. Tao Ho was hit by stroke and now sits on armchair. It was as touching and unforgettable as a Chinese ink painting, this hero who survived so much, only to be brought down by the stroke that has so severely limited his existence over the past decade.

Professor Patrick Lau seemed akin to a movie star. With his strong energy, he was able to unite people and represent the design industry on the Legislative Council. He was the external examiner for our program for a long time. I had many opportunities to listen to him on how to teach. Of course, Mr. Chung Wah-nan's writing was full of energy and his Chinese ink calligraphy full of a patriot's enthusiasm. The people described in this chapter were high caliber and proactive people who were "successful" in their careers and lifestyles.

References

Baniassad, E. (2004). Architecture resolution. In Rocco Design (Ed.), *Being Chinese in architecture—Recent works in China by Rocco Design* (pp. 8–11). Hong Kong: MCCM Creations.

Chan, C., & Choi, H. (2005). *Journey of Space—Hundred year history of Hong Kong architecture.* Hong Kong: Joint Publication. 陈翠儿, 蔡宏兴主编. (2005). 空间之旅 – 香港建筑百年. 香港:三联书店.

Chung, W. N. (1982). *The art of Chinese garden.* Hong Kong: Hong Kong University Press.

Chung, W. N. (1989). *Inheriting the tradition of Chinese pavilion.* Hong Kong: Commercial Press. 钟华楠 (1989). 亭的继承. 香港: 商务印书馆.

Chung, W. N. (1991). Copy or surpass: On architectural design and urban planning. Beijing: China Architecture and Building Press. 钟华楠 (1991). "抄"与"超": 建筑设计城市规划散论. 北京: 中国建筑工业出版社.

Chung, W. N., & Zhang, Q. N. (2007). Globalization, sustainability and cross-culture design. Beijing: China Architecture and Building Press. 钟华楠、张钦楠 (2007). 全球化、可持续发展、跨文化设计. 北京: 中国建筑工业出版社.

DeHoff, J. N. (Ed.). (2013). *Reconnecting cultures—The architecture of Rocco Design.* London: Artifice Books on Architecture.

Department of Architecture, The Chinese University of Hong Kong. (2003). *Design parameters for elderly care architecture in Hong Kong.* Hong Kong: The Hong Kong Council of Social Service.

Goldhagen, S. W. (2001). *Louis Kahn's situated modernism.* New Haven, CT: Yale University Press.

Ho, T. (2000). *Tao Ho building a dream.* Hong Kong: Cosmos Books. 何弢 (2000). 何弢筑梦. 香港: 天地图书公司.

Khan, H. U. (1995). *Contemporary Asian architects.* Köln: Taschen.

Koolhaas, R. (1994). *Delirious New York: A retroactive manifesto of Manhattan,* New York: Monacelli Press.

Kvan, T., Lee, A., & Ho, L. (2000). *Anthony Ng Architects Limited: Building towards a paperless future.* Hong Kong: Centre for Asian Business Cases, School of Business, The University of Hong Kong.

Kwok, W. S. (2010). *Tao Ho–A modern architect in Hong Kong.* Hong Kong: City University of Hong Kong, Bachelor's degree dissertation.

Lim, B., Kan, K., & Wong, W. H. (2005). *Practitioners' guide to design and implementation of participatory projects.* Hong Kong: Department of Architecture, Chinese University of Hong Kong.

Lim, W. S. W., & Chang, J. H. (Eds.). (2012). *Non west modernist past—On architecture and modernities.* Singapore: World Scientific Publishing Co., Pte. Ltd.

Lim, W. S. W., Maki, F., Nagashima, K., & Jumsai, S. (1980). Contemporary Asian architecture: Works of APAC members. *Process Architecture, 20*

Lo, V. W. C. (2011). *A cultural and social architect: The works and career of Mr. Chung Wah-nan.* Bachelor's degree dissertation, City University of Hong Kong, Hong Kong.

Ng, K. C., & Chu, S. C. H. (2007). Story of the first generation of Chinese architects in Hong Kong. Hong Kong: Hong Kong Economic Journal Press. 吴启聪、朱卓雄 (2007). 建闻筑绩 - 香港第一代华人建筑师的故事. 香港: 经济日报出版社.

Rocco Design. (2004). *Being Chinese in architecture—Recent works in China by Rocco Design.* Hong Kong: MCCM Creations.

Rocco Design. (2012). *Presence—The architecture of Rocco Design.* Hong Kong: MCCM Creations.

RTHK. (2000). *Manifesto of architecture.* Hong Kong: Radio and Television Hong Kong. 香港电台(2000). 建筑宣言. 10集记录片.香港: 香港电台.

Wong, R. Y. C., & Cheng, J. Y. S. (1990). *The other Hong Kong report.* Hong Kong: Chinese University Press.

Xue, C. Q. L. (2006a). *Building a revolution: Chinese architecture since 1980.* Hong Kong: Hong Kong University Press.

Xue, C. Q. L. (2006b). *Global Impact: overseas architectural design in China,* Shanghai: Tongji University Press. 薛求理 (2006). 全球化冲击: 海外建筑设计在中国. 上海: 同济大学出版社.

Xue, C. Q. L. (2010). *World Architecture in China.* Hong Kong: Joint Publishing Ltd.

Xue, C. Q. L., & Xiao, J. (2014). Japanese modernity deviated: Its importation and legacy in the Southeast Asian architecture since the 1970s. *Habitat International, 44*(2), 227–236.

Xue, C. Q. L., Tan, Z., & Xiao, Y. (2016). Architecural magazine in Hong Kong for a century. *World Architecture, 36*(1), 40–44.

Zhang W. Z. (2005). I am myself—A story of Sze Wing Ching. Hong Kong: Cosmos Books. 张文中 (2005). 我就是我 - 施永青的故事. 香港: 天地图书公司.

Zhu, J. (2009). *Architecture of modern China—A historical critique.* New York: Routledge.

Part III
Backward and Forward Vision

Entering the twenty-first century, environment, sustainability, and conservation have set the trend and become strong voice. Society has high demand on protecting natural/artificial heritages and the environment we live. Through open design competition, new schemes continuously push the boundary of architecture and improve the progress in design and technology.

Chapter 9
Finding the Roots and Preserving Our Well-being

Hong Kong experienced many unexpected crises before 1970. The government was kept busy extinguishing fires and keeping the peace. Although people kept odd jobs that secured roofs over their heads, they lived from hand to mouth. In the wave of property upgrades in the 1970s, the colonial buildings of the 19th century were ruthlessly demolished as society looked on apathetically. The Antiquities Advisory Board and Antiquities and Monuments Office (AMO) were established in 1976, but were unable to prevent the demolition and were subservient to the dominance of commercial interests.[1] In the 1980s, people began to enjoy the relatively decent life afforded by economic development, and took pride in the luxurious mansions in Central and the magnificent landscape of Shatin.

The voice of democracy grew louder in the 1990s as Hong Kong was rolling near the sovereignty handover. Awareness of sustainable development, environmental protection and green architecture grew steadily during this era. This awareness is reflected in three aspects: to protect the harbor, conserve its heritage buildings and building green architecture. Although green building design and maintenance are mainly the businesses of architects, engineers and professionals, protecting the harbor and conserving the heritage buildings became the foci of social movements and debates between the politicians and government. Such a social atmosphere hastened sustainable development, no matter how substantial or shallow it is. This chapter discusses three related matters: protection of the harbor, conservation of the heritage buildings and green architecture, actions that have prevailed and converged in Hong Kong since 1990.

---

[1] In September 1976, the British government changed the position of Colonial Secretariat to Government Secretariat and that of Colonial Secretary to Chief Secretary; see (Cheng 1977). Moreover, Lui (2012) describes society and people's attitudes towards the colonial government. The Admiralty barracks were mostly demolished in the 1970s, see Chap. 7.

© Springer Science+Business Media Singapore 2016
C.Q.L. Xue, *Hong Kong Architecture 1945–2015*,
DOI 10.1007/978-981-10-1004-0_9

9.1   Defending "Our Harbor"

The City of Victoria started from the harbor and seashore. The nearby mountain rising up from the sea was mostly steep, and flat land was rare. In the mid-19th century, the government and private organizations reclaimed land from the sea and acquired large amounts of it for commercial use. In the early 20th century, reclamation pushed the sea wall to Gloucester Road and Connaught Road, located 200–500 m away from the original natural seashore. After the Second World War, land demand increased for Grade-A office towers, high-class hotels, art galleries, performing centers, piers, subways and express bypasses. More land was acquired from the harbor in the 50 years after the war than was acquired in the first 100 years of the city's history. The land slots divided in the 19th century are usually small, 20–30 feet wide in frontage. However, the commercial land slots reclaimed from the sea in the 20th century are much bigger. The peninsula for the Convention Center is located 1,000 m away from the original seashore. Record-breaking skyscrapers have continuously sprouted up and stand proudly on the waterfront. To strengthen the confidence of Hong Kong citizens, the government carried out "core projects" for the airport in 1989. Land in Central, West Kowloon, Tsing Yi, Tung Chung, Aldrich Bay and Hung Hom was acquired to develop new infrastructure and buildings.

The democratic voice grew louder in Hong Kong in the 1990s. People were astonished to find that the vast Victoria Harbor was quickly dwindling, ocean ecology deteriorated and would eventually dry out. The Society for Protection of the Harbour was founded in November 1995 and obtained 170,000 signatures from citizens to support relevant protection legislation. On June 27, 1996, a motion entitled *Protection of the Harbour Ordinance* proposed by civil activists and Legislative Council member Christine Loh was passed in the Legislative Council three days before the sovereignty handover and later became Chapter 531 of the Hong Kong Law. The motion stated that the harbor, as a special public asset and a natural heritage of the Hong Kong people, was subject to the "presumption against reclamation" principle. It primarily called upon the government to withdraw plans for reclamation of the harbor and to take urgent measures to ensure its protection and preservation.[2]

Traffic between Central and Wanchai expanded rapidly after 1997 and the roads could no longer bear the load. At the end of 2002, the Executive Council approved Phase III of the 23-ha Central Reclamation Plan. The Society for Protection of the Harbour asked for a judicial review, and the court adjudicated a loss for the Town Planning Board. The high court judgment of July 8, 2003 stated that the three tests of "compelling, overriding and present need," "no viable alternative" and

[2]Protection of the Harbour (Amendment) Bill 1997 (Minutes) 10 Feb 98, Legislative Council document (Legco.gov.hk 2015).

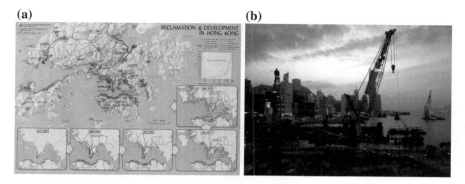

Fig. 9.1 Reclamation in the Victoria Harbor. **a** Reclamation from 1945 to 1996. **b** Filling the sea from Central to Wanchai, 2011

"minimum impairment to the harbour" had to be met before the presumption against reclamation could be rebutted (Fig. 9.1).

The project was immediately initiated after the court gave its decision. The government thought that stopping work would result in huge compensation claims from the contractors. The legal battle continued between the Society and government. The government actively reviewed its projects according to the three tests as stated by the court and explained the urgency of the Central-Wan Chai bypass to the citizens. At the end of 2003, the High Court decided that the Central reclamation basically conformed to the three tests, and the Society for Protection of the Harbour lost the case.[3]

Although the civil groups lost the case in court, street actions to protect the harbor often arose from 1997 to 2003. These actions aimed to educate both the government and citizens. Construction of the central waterfront green land began after the legal battle, and the waterfront promenade and Tamar Park were formed with the completion of the government headquarters building in 2011. This land accommodates citizens, invites tourists to play on the lawn and provides space for demonstrations outside the government building. The shortage of buildable land has perplexed Hong Kong for 60 years, and it becomes acute and more politicized when various groups of vested interest are wrestling in the public forum (Cheung 2015).[4] After the battle of Central reclamation, the government turned to be cautious in reclaiming the other parts of the sea.

---

[3]Protection of Victoria Harbour; see (Harbourprotection.org 2015), see also (Chu 2011).
[4]The debate on buildable land in Hong Kong will usually include voices from many different groups, for example, government planning department, local citizen and politicians. See report from Ta Kung Pao, Feb 2015 (Cheung 2015).

Fig. 9.2 Defending Queen's
Pier, June 2007

9.2   Two Piers

In the 21st century, the Central reclamation was pushed forward. According to the
newly approved reclamation plan and after public consultation with little adverse
opinions, the government demolished the Star Ferry Pier in December 2006. Built
in 1958 after the Central reclamation in the early 1950s, the Star Ferry Pier was a
functional structure with a thin floor/roof slabs, whitewashed external wall and a
clock tower. Although generally plain and modest, the pier faithfully reflected its
structure and material. The big clock on the pier was the last mechanical clock in
Hong Kong. Before its demolition, hundreds of citizens went on hunger strikes to
protect the pier. Their main demand was the "protection of collective memory."
Police arrested the protestors and formed a human shield to ensure the completion
of the demolition work.[5]

Just half a year later, the same scenario took place a few hundred yards east of
the old Star Ferry Pier at Queen's Pier. Built in 1953, Queen's Pier was aligned with
the front entrance of City Hall. If the Star Ferry Pier was considered "architecture,"
Queen's Pier was at most a "building" or a simple "sheltering" structure. During the
colonial era, when royal family members and new governors arrived in Hong Kong,
they usually took a boat to Queen's Pier, where they took part in a welcoming
ritual. The red carpet was extended from Queen's Pier to the front gate of City Hall.
Citizens were not permitted to attend these ceremonies. From the end of 2006 to
July 2007, a series of protests were held to maintain Queen's Pier, such as can-
dlelight vigils, overnight sit-ins and hunger strikes that often resulted in con-
frontations with the police.[6] The government finally demolished Queen's Pier and

---

[5]For more information about the Star Ferry Pier, see (Zh.wikipedia.org 2015).

[6]For more information about the Queen's Pier demolition, see information from *Ming Pao Daily
News* and *Singtao Daily*, July 30—August 1, 2007. E.g. (Lai 2007).

stored its components in a warehouse. Several schemes were suggested, such as rebuilding the pier in the same place or building the old components in a new location. The original location of Queen's Pier is now the center of an expressway, and the new location is positioned far away from City Hall. Neither scheme does much to protect the memory of the original pier (Fig. 9.2).

9.3   Conserving Heritage Buildings

Defending the Star Ferry and Queen's Piers involved defending the society's "collective memory." A collective memory is obtained from a society and recon-structed from the past. Such a collective memory belongs to different groups such as families, scholars, experts, politicians, ethnicities, social classes and countries. Each person is a member of different groups. In the field of architecture, the collective memory is built and interpreted through design and media (He and He 2014). Architecture represents a large portion of cultural heritage and best reflects human culture. Heritage buildings are structural witnesses to people's living attitudes, values and collective memory and provide a living record of the design and con-struction of a specific period. Architecture is a source of cultural identity and continuation. The Star Ferry and Queen's Piers, especially the former one, relate to Hong Kong citizen's daily life when ferry was the only way of crossing the harbor. In Queen's Pier, the welcoming ceremony was held when the new governors arrived in the colony. Such event has little relation with the ordinary citizens. However, in the high wave of finding root and especially after the fierce battles of protecting two piers, the preservation of heritage buildings has been common sense and a contemporary trend.

Although Hong Kong was developed as a port city in 1841, it contains traces of 6,000–year human activities. The village of the late Qing Dynasty (1644–1911) and 150-year-old colonial city left behind a group of valuable architectural heritage structures. The Antiquities Advisory Board has listed hundreds of heritage build-ings and categorized them into Grades I, II and III. Grade I buildings exhibit outstanding merit, and every effort should be made to preserve them if possible. Grade II buildings exhibit special merit, and efforts should be made to preserve them selectively. Grade III buildings exhibit some merit. Some form of preservation of these buildings would be desirable, and alternative means may be considered if preservation is not practicable. In accordance with the Antiquities and Monuments Ordinance, the Antiquities Authority may, after consultation with the Antiquities Advisory Board and with the approval of the Chief Executive (by notice in the *Gazette*) declare a place, building, site or structure as a monument. The Antiquities Authority is empowered to prevent alterations or impose conditions upon any proposed alterations as he/she thinks fit to protect the monument. Thus far, 105 structures have been declared monuments in the territory.[7] Examples include the main building of Hong Kong University (1910), the former Supreme Court in Statue Square (1905), Victoria Prison on Hollywood Road (1864), the governor's house (1855, 1944) and Sam Tung Uk Village (1786) of Tsuen Wan.

From 1996 to 2000, the Antiquities and Monuments Office carried out a territory-wide survey of historic buildings, during which around 8,800 buildings were recorded. This survey was followed up by a more in-depth study of about 1,000 items with higher heritage value. These buildings were subjected to six grading criteria to reflect their value: historical interest, architectural merit, group value, social value and local interest, authenticity, and rarity. As recommended by Members of the Antiquities Advisory Board, an expert panel comprising historians and members of the Hong Kong Institute of Architects, Hong Kong Institute of Planners and Hong Kong Institute of Engineers formed in March 2005 to undertake an in-depth assessment of the heritage value of these buildings.

Hong Kong hopes to keep its status as an international metropolis in Asia and to build more Grade-A office towers, classy residential buildings and various facilities. There is a sharp contradiction between development and conservation. Land is essential to the expansion of the population and economic development. Where does the land come from? During the economic boom of the 1970s, too many buildings with "collective memory" were demolished quickly and silently. When people came around in the 21st century, not many valuable heritage buildings remained. People treasure any structure related to history and memory, even simple shelters with little artistic and historic value (like Queen's Pier). Two piers in Central were demolished between the end of 2006 and summer 2007, further stimulating the sense of conservation in Hong Kong society. Old buildings are now being seen with new eyes, and both public and private sectors have contributed to the theme of preservation.

However, the owners of some historic buildings do not see in the above way. While they generally support the ideas of protecting the city's past, but if their properties were labelled as "heritage", they feel that their development rights are deprived by the government and "tyranny mass." Such conflicts often happen in old buildings of various districts. This section introduces some examples of conservation and discusses the problems caused by historic building preservation and possible solutions.

---

[7]For a classification and list of heritage buildings, see the webpage of the Antiquity and Monument Office, (Amo.gov.hk 2015) The Antiquities Advisory Board was established by government-appointed citizens. The Advisory Board voted on heritage building grades and monument confirmations. "Heritage buildings" were sometimes chosen over the course of debate. Civil organizations occupied Queen's Pier before its demolition. The Antiquities Advisory Board held an emergency meeting to designate Queen's Pier as a Grade I heritage structure, causing further debate. See *Mingpao Daily News* and *South China Morning Post*, March 25–27, July 28-August 2, 2007. E.g. (Parwani 2007).

9.3.1   Museum of Heritage Discovery (the Old Barracks)

When Britain occupied Kowloon in 1861, British rulers hoped to establish it as a barrier for Hong Kong Island. They assigned troops in Tsim Sha Tsui, Hung Hom and Stonecutters Island. Nathan Road, the thoroughfare of Kowloon, was used for military transportation.[8] The hills near Tsim Sha Tsui waterfront were developed into barracks for the British troops. According to the standard manual for South Asia colonies, the barrack buildings were constructed before 1910. A veranda was left on one side as a corridor to the rooms. Similar barrack buildings can be seen in several places on Hong Kong Island and in Kowloon. In 1967, the military land in Tsim Sha Tsui was returned to the government and redeveloped as Kowloon Park for the purposes of public leisure and entertainment. The historic museum used two barrack buildings from 1983 until 1998, after which it incorporated two purpose-built homes in East Tsim Sha Tsui. The Antiquity and Monument Office began using the two buildings as offices. In the 21st century, the two buildings were carefully renovated and turned over to the Heritage Discovery Museum in 2006. A glass box was inserted between the two buildings as a transition hall. The lecture theatre and main exhibition hall were organically integrated into the old building blocks. The old part remains fully displayed with the original architectural features, and the new part functions as a modest exhibition space (Fig. 9.3).

Preservation of military heritage was seen in overseas. But in Hong Kong, it is never considered seriously. A lot of barracks were demolished in the economic boom and gave way for shopping mall and skyscrapers. Before the Heritage Discovery Museum opened, government architects renovated the other barracks in Kowloon Park and turned them into a health education exhibition using a similar design method. In a series of renovation projects, the government architects accumulated experience and designed vocabularies, such as the connection of wood and steel and usage of large glass. The Heritage Discovery Museum showcases permanent displays and many topical exhibitions that enrich people's cultural lives.

9.3.2   Kom Tong Hall/Dr. Sun Yat-sen Museum

Chinese compradors and merchants have been raised in Hong Kong since the beginning of the 20th century. Sir Robert Hotung (1862–1956) and his family were outstanding representatives. Hotung's brother Ho Kom-tong was a comprador at Jadine Co. Ltd. He built his mansion at the junction of Castle Road and Seymour Street in Central. A British architect was hired to design the house, which had a 2,650-m^2 floor area consisting of a big living room, family rooms and bedrooms.

---

[8]For a description of Tsim Sha Tsui, see (Zheng and Tong 2000).

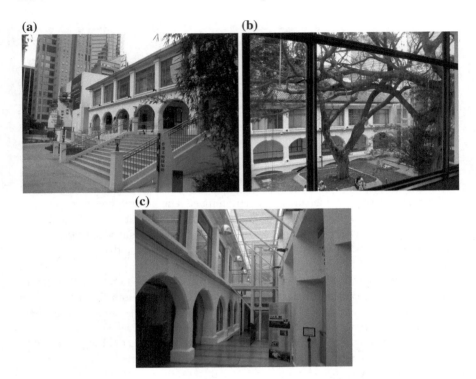

Fig. 9.3 Museum of heritage discovery **a** Entrance **b** Court **c** New part added into the old barracks

Made of stone and red brick, it served as home to several generations and dozens of servants. Completed in 1914, it was named Kom Tong Hall after the owner.

Making use of the topography, the entrance was set at the side of the building and the front was decorated with classical pillars. The mansion was magnificent. Its big stairs, arched terraces, flowery iron railings and multiple architraves are grand and delicate. Beginning in the 1960s, the building fell under management of The Church of Jesus Christ of Latter-day Saints, which installed a stone pool for Baptist rituals.

In 2004, after a long period of negotiation, the Hong Kong SAR government bought the premises for HK$53 million and converted it into the Dr. Sun Yat-sen Museum. The government architects and engineers attempted to find the original materials and paint the building to match its original appearance. At the back of the building, a lift was added to provide facilities for the disabled. The museum was opened to the public in December 2006. Beyond exhibits of the late Qing and early Republic, modern visitors can feel and experience the old built environment. The same year Kom Tom Hall was built in the 1910s, the Xinhai Revolution overthrew the Qing Dynasty (1644–1911). Sun was exiled to Japan and began planning the second revolution. Although Dr. Sun Yat-sen probably never entered this building, the Central, Mid-Level and high-low roads are all closely related to his trail in Hong

Fig. 9.4 Dr. Sun Yat-sen Museum **a** mansion in the mid-level; **b** living room

Kong.[9] Social activists in Hong Kong have appealed to collect and commemorate Dr. Sun's trail in past decades, and the Dr. Sun Yat-sen Historical Trail consisting of 15 locations was built. Dr. Sun's museum is appropriately located in this area (Fig. 9.4).

9.3.3 Lui Seng Chun

The preceding case is located in the commercial area of Kowloon, the second richest area of the Mid-Level on Hong Kong Island. The following two cases, including Tai Kok Tsui and Sham Shui Po, are located in more plebeian areas. Lui Seng Chun is owned by Mr. Lui Leung, who was born in Taishan, Guangdong and was one of the founders of the Kowloon Motor Bus Company (1933). In 1929, Lui purchased a piece of land at 119 Lai Chi Kok Road, Tai Kok Tsui from the government and appointed local architect W.H. Bourne, who specialized in designing shop-house, to begin construction. The construction work was completed in 1931. The ground floor was occupied by a bone-setting medicine shop known as Lui Seng Chun, and the upper floors served as living quarters for the members of the Lui family. The name "Lui Seng Chun" was derived from a pair of rhymed couplets that implied that Lui's medicine could bring a patient back to life. Lui passed away in 1944 and the shop closed a few years later. The building was subsequently used as living accommodations and let out as tailor shops. In 2000, the Lui family approached the Antiquities and Monuments Office to suggest donating the building to the government.[10]

Lui Seng Chun's restoration and research work began in late 2000. The consulting work consisted of two parts. The first part involved researching the

---

[9]For a description of Dr. Sun Yat-sen Museum, see (Xue 2007).

[10]For a description of Lui Seng Chun, see the webpage of the AMO, (Antiquities and Monuments Office 2015).

building's ownership, land deeds, construction, environmental effects, cultural value and historical context. The second part involved proposing a restoration plan that would facilitate plumbing, electricity, air conditioning and quantity surveying. The restoration work included strengthening the structure and piping and repainting the walls. In terms of heritage conservation, every effort was made to retain the original architectural features as much as possible, including the appearance of the *Kee-lau* (portico), railing decoration, veranda, windows and doors, tiles, and stone tablets engraved with the name of "Lui Seng Chun" on top of the building. The building's exterior decorative railings, veranda, floor tiles and concrete frame were kept. The front veranda railings, patio outfalls on each layer, stone plaque engraved with "Lui Seng Chun" and cornice and lintel decorations were preserved. The internal work included saving the Shanghai plaster, solid brick wall, plaster cornice and molding, granite doorway thresholds, wood and plaster wall lines, geometric patterns and colorful tiles, decorative plaster ceilings, wooden molding and ceiling lines, wooden doors and door frames with old-style hardware settings, windows and ornamental iron flowers on the window lintels and even the concrete slabs and column bases of the rear verandas (Fig. 9.5).

The revitalization work of the Lui Seng Chun building was completed in 2005. However, it took a long time to find appropriate operation partnership. Hong Kong Baptist University was ultimately selected through bidding to conserve the building and convert it into a Chinese medicine healthcare center known as Lui Seng Chun Hall. The hall consists of five clinic rooms, one herbal medicine and Chinese teashop, an exhibition gallery and a rooftop herb garden. It was completed in April 2012 and opened to the public (Baptist University 2015). Traditional Chinese clinical services including internal medicine, orthopedic, bone-setting, medical massage and TCM acupuncture services have been provided and free and concessionary medical consultations have frequently been offered since the revitalization.

(a)   **(b)**

Fig. 9.5 Lui Seng Chun **a** after renovation, 2005 **b** balcony

9.3.4 Jockey Club Creative Arts Center (JCCAC)

The 1950s witnessed the blossoming of small-scale cottage factories across Hong Kong. To show support for the local industry, the government set up factory areas in Sham Shui Po, San Po Kong, Kwun Tong, Tsuen Wan, Wong Chuk Hang and other places. These factories provided products of ironmongery, footwear, printing, watch manufactory and plastic works. These workshops made tremendous contributions to the Hong Kong industry and played an important role in the local economy. In the 1980s, the industry moved northward to the Pearl River Delta and left many factories abandoned. In the 21st century, the government has allowed these factory buildings to be converted into creative industry units. Creative buildings have begun to appear in the Fo Tan, Sham Shui Po and Kwun Tong districts. The Jockey Club Creative Arts Center (JCCAC) is one of many examples (Fig. 9.6).

Sponsored by the Hong Kong Jockey Club, the building housing the JCCAC was constructed on a nine-storey block in Shek Kip Mei. A glass roof atrium was built between two slab-shaped factory buildings. A platform was added in the

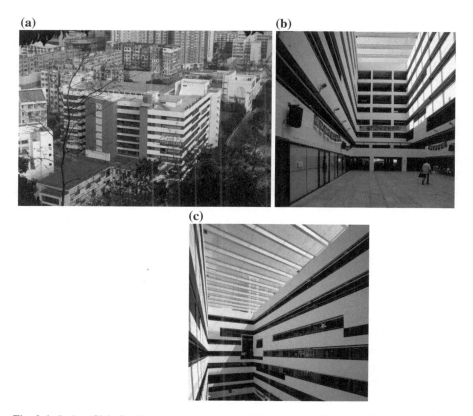

Fig. 9.6 Jockey Club Creative Arts Center **a** the building is located in the old Skep Kip Mei area **b** atrium **c** Skylight

atrium and appropriate treatments were made to the facade. The design respected the original structure of the factory buildings while adding a modern design language. The refurbished center now offers 124 affordable studios for rent to artists, arts groups and many volunteer-based community organizations related to the visual, performing and media arts and applied arts training and design. Most of the rooms have been rented out since the renovation of the building in 2006. Various community care and artistic activities are regularly organized at the building and have been greatly welcomed by arts groups and local residents.

9.3.5 Asia Society

In 1956, the Rockefeller Foundation founded the Asia Society, which has its headquarters in New York and a dozen branches located throughout the U.S. Along with the promotion of Sir Quo-wei Lee of Hang Seng Bank in 1990, a branch was established in Hong Kong. The Rockefeller Foundation also established the Asian Cultural Council, which remains active in Hong Kong. In 2002, the Asia Society applied to renovate the former magazine of the Admiralty barracks into its Hong Kong headquarters and activity center and received approval from the AMO. The magazine served mainly as storage for the Victoria barracks, and allowed for powder to be mixed, processed, packaged and distributed to the other defense bases in Hong Kong. The buildings were divided into upper and lower platforms. The upper platform of the magazine and former laboratory were completed in 1868. Between 1901 and 1925, Magazine B was built along with two anti-blasting safety embankments for separation. In the 1930s, the British army built Barracks GG on the lower platform as a supply outpost and magazine for military materials. Pacific Place was built in Admiralty after the British army moved out in 1979. The magazine was turned into workplaces and warehouses for various government departments. GG was used as a payroll office for the British Royal Army finance team and a workplace for maintenance contractors. When the military base was removed in the 1970s, this area was rezoned by the government (see Chap. 7). Because of its remote location, it escaped the fate of demolition and was abandoned after the 1980s.

Sponsored by the Hong Kong Jockey Club, the Asia Society acquired the site, and Tod William/Billie Tsien Architects of New York and AGC Design of Hong Kong designed the new plan. In early 2012, the conversion of the magazine was complete and a venue of office, social, exhibition and performance spaces was opened to the public. New lobbies, multi-function halls, restaurants and roof gardens rose up from the valley along the roadside. To avoid affecting the flying foxes living in the nearby woods, the overhead bridge was converted to a double-layer Z-shaped bridge and connected to the old building. The original three warehouses and laboratories were converted into offices, exhibition halls and small theaters. The new roof garden was positioned close to the back of the functional space. The double-layer Z-shaped bridge directs people to the wooded valley. Over 60 % of the Asia Society headquarter buildings were newly built, with the old magazines

Fig. 9.7 Asia Society **a** footbridge leading people to the old magazines **b** covered walkway to magazines **c** bird-eye view of the complex. Courtesy of Asia Society

organically inserted. The buildings lend a sense of elegance and appropriately treat space, enclosure and atmosphere. Asia Society dinners no longer have to be held at five-star hotels in Central. The concrete frame supports the reception and banquet hall from the valley. Galas are held in a natural setting surrounded by green trees (Asia Society 2015) (Fig. 9.7).

9.3.6   Bethanie in Pok Fu Lam

The Paris Foreign Mission Society moved from Macau to Hong Kong in 1847, and set up a nursing home in Pokfulam on west Hong Kong Island so that the Far East missionaries could have access to an infirmary. After Priest Osei purchased the land in June 1873, he designed the seminary and launched the project with the assistance of Fr. Charles Edmond Patriat, a priest who arrived from Singapore. The Hong Kong government donated granite materials. The Mission was completed and put into use in 1875 and Fr. Charles Edmond Patriat became its first president. In 1897, Bethanie conducted expansion and improvement projects. After 1949, all of the missionaries left the Chinese mainland. Coupled with advances in medicine, Bethanie's role gradually decreased. In 1974, the Mission moved out, and the property was sold to Hong Kong Land the following year. The original plan was to demolish the building and develop residential buildings, but the government proposed trading nearby land

Fig. 9.8 Bethanie in Pokfulam

and a dairy cowshed with Bethanie, which turned the land into government property. Between 1978 and 1997, Bethanie served as the office of Hong Kong University Press and the boy student hall of Hong Kong University.

In the 21st century, the government studied the possibility of restoring and revitalizing Bethanie. It was taken over in 2003 by the Academy for Performing Arts, which converted it into the Film and Television School at a cost of HK$83 million. The original building was refurbished and a new auditorium was added to the rooftop. During the more than two-year project, in addition to the renovation of buildings and the addition of teaching facilities, one daunting task involved recovering the precious relics lost when the building was sold in 1974, including 19 color-paint windows, icons, altars and altar screens inside the chapel (Fig. 9.8).

To reproduce the original appearance of Bethanie, the Hong Kong Academy for Performing Arts inquired widely about the whereabouts of these artifacts. It visited various religious and government warehouses in Hong Kong according to clues and appointed French historian to visit the Foreign Mission Biography Church in Paris. Project director Philip Soden visited many churches and finally found seven color-paint windows in Zetland Hall (Home for Freemasonry in Hong Kong), the shapes and sizes of which matched those of Bethanie Chapel. In 1985, an architect found a number of color-paint windows in Chi Fu Fa Yuen near Bethanie and deposited them in the government warehouses. The architect was then assigned to prepare Zetland Hall for its 50th anniversary. Because color-paint windows were required for the dining room, he applied to the government for use of the seven windows. Two windows remain stored in the government warehouses. Three photos of Bethanie in the 1950s confirmed that the glass windows from Zetland Hall and the government warehouses were from Bethanie, and the windows were eventually returned (Le Pichon 2006).

In the preceding cases, historic buildings were converted into artistic studios and cultural organization exhibitions. At home and abroad, the preservation of historic buildings is closely related to tourism and economic development. Tourists familiarize themselves with local history by visiting heritage sites and buildings, and the income incurred helps the preservation continue. The following are examples of commercial-led renovations.

9.3.7 The First-Generation Public House—Mei Ho Building

Chapter 1 introduces the first generation of resettlement house, which comprised the seven-storey H-plan blocks first built in Shek Kip Mei in 1954. The corridors, used for circulation and cooking, surrounded back-to-back rooms. The early public housing settled numerous families and nurtured generations of people under the Lion Rock. After 53 years, the Shek Kip Mei estate finished its mission in 2006 and had to give up the land for the new type of public housing that used taller blocks. All of the early settlement blocks were demolished except Mei Ho Building, which was listed as Grade I heritage.[11] At the same time, societal organizations organized the "Shek Kip Mei Humanity Display" in the old derelict public housing units to display the old furniture and home settings. Residents highly supported the event and donated their home utilities to the display.

In 2007, the HKIA, HKIE, HKIP and HKIS jointly ran a design competition for Mei Ho Building and received many innovative ideas from professionals and students. The government pushed forward the *Revitalising Historic Buildings Through Partnership Scheme* in 2008. Mei Ho Building was one of seven buildings involved in the scheme, and the project was awarded to Hong Kong Youth Hostel Association. AD + SG led by Bernard Lim designed the renovation project and converted Mei Ho Building into a 129-room youth hostel. Opened in 2013, the new youth hostel featured elevators, water treatment facilities and dining and meeting rooms for tourists. A portion of the building is used as the local history museum of Sham Shui Po. The old residents were invited to be docents to educate tourists about the history and life of the area (Youth Hostel Association Hong Kong 2015) (Fig. 9.9).

9.3.8 1881 Heritage

As mentioned in the case of the barracks, Tsim Sha Tsui shouldered the heavy function of defense in the early colonial period. In 1881, the marine police headquarters were built on the hill facing Victoria Harbor. The marine headquarters included a main building, a signal tower (round house), a stable block, the Kowloon fire-fighting bureau and the fire-fighter quarters. The building was declared a monument in 1994. In 1996, the marine police withdrew from Tsim Sha Tsui, and

---

[11]For a description of the public housing in Shek Kip Mei, see (Xue 2006).

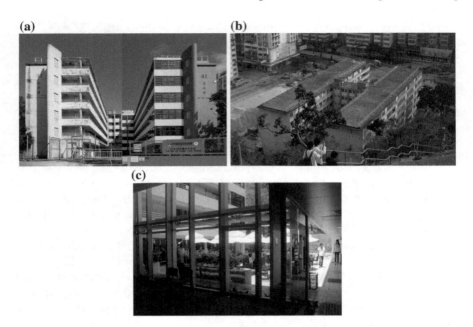

Fig. 9.9 Mei Ho Building. **a** Comparison of before and after renovation. Courtesy of Prof. Bernard Lim. **b** Before renovation, 2009. **c** Run as youth hostel

the property was left empty. In May 2003, the government issued a tender invitation. Cheung Kong Property bid HK$352 million for the land and a "best tender plan." Cheung Kong invested billions of dollars in renovating and rebuilding the land. After six years of construction the area became a tourist site populated by boutique shops, nostalgic restaurants and hotels and opened in November 2009. The current design makes use of the original hilly topography by incorporating terraces at different heights. Shops, platforms and fountains are scattered throughout the area at different levels. The former arched verandah of the marine police headquarters is now a restaurant lookout. The former stable block is now a high-class grill house. Although some of the old trees are gone, some of the banyan trees have been maintained. The 1881 Heritage building is located at the tourist hotspot of Tsim Sha Tsui and Canton Road, where brand shops are clustered. Conserving the old heritage buildings has brought lucrative business to the area (Fig. 9.10).

During high waves of conservation efforts, heritage buildings meet with different fates. The Wanchai Market was built in the 1930s according to the Bauhaus style. After many debates and workshops, only the facade was kept. Behind the facade stands a residential tower. The mediocre design of the Central Market was kept and renovated due to citizen outcry. The police headquarters and Victoria Prison on Hollywood Road were completely kept and functioned as the Hong Kong-Shenzhen biennale site in 2007 and 2008. Herzog & de Meuron from Switzerland established the renovation scheme. King Yin Lei, a private house built

Fig. 9.10 1881 Heritage. **a** Night view. **b** The slope is formed as terraced shopping arcade. **c** Courtyard

in 1937, was located at Mid-Level. The owner sought to demolish it and build multi-storey houses in 2007, triggering action from the public. The government mediated the matter and ultimately traded nearby land with the owner. After acquiring the property, the government solicited the partner to run the site.

For the buildings with historic value, government solicited "partners" from non-government organizations and institutions. If selected, the partner will repair the building and use it with new functions, for example heritage hotel in Tai O (old police station), cultural academy (old custom house and hospital) and cartoon and animation center (old tenement house). These projects are evaluated by the government and generally well accepted in the society. Some conservation projects have been criticized as neither fish nor fowl or as forms of gentrification. If a project wants to survive financially without taxpayers' subsidy, some commercial content is inevitable. In many cases, citizens are happy to enjoy the commercial services, for example, gift and coffee shops in the cultural facilities (Fig. 9.11).

However, functional usages are changing, and a building's structure and form are not normally altered after the building is erected. Buildings with historic value and unique designs are either kept idle, respected as antiquities or used by descendants. How can a historic building be used meaningfully and sustained for a longer time? Most of the conservation projects in Hong Kong are government

Fig. 9.11 Some preservation projects after 2010 **a** King Yin Lei, built in 1937 **b** and **c** The 19th century buildings were used as , immune station, prison and hospital, now Jao Tsung-I Academy, designed by Meta4 Design Forum. **d** and **e** Ten tenement houses of the 1920s. Some are demolished to form a courtyard, the others are used as Comix Home Base, designed by Aedas

supported. Individuals and NGOs have good intentions, but are not usually able to sustain sites.

This section introduces new examples of structures including private mansion, barracks, factories and public housing, and new functions including special museums, activity rooms, offices, hotels, arts centers and retail shops. With proper space, atmosphere and renovation, an old building can surely serve these new functions. Examples of museums that have been transformed from old buildings can be seen around the world. Old factory workshops have been extensively refurbished as art studios in foreign countries. In New York city, London, Sydney, Beijing and Shanghai, the renovation of old factory areas is mixed with real estate speculation labelled with "cultural district", SOHO or loft space. The Jockey Club arts center in Shek Kip Mei serves as completely local entertainment for grass-roots citizens and artists, and the 1881 Heritage building operates on the sheer basis of capital and brand shops. Both are suitable for their venues.

Sustainable development must be sustainable financially. No one doubts the value of heritage buildings to discovering a society's roots. However, the number of voices demanding how many of these buildings to keep and how to keep them operating varies, indicating an abuse of the democratic process. Some radical opinions hold that the type of conservation proposed by the government often leads to gentrification and expels local poor people. Heritage buildings should be conserved to please tourists and encourage them to spend money. Some projects have become the focus of debate between the government, developers, politicians and societal organizations.

Looking at the conservation work of world cities, the most direct support has come from the government, as exemplified by the Dr. Sun Yat-sen Museum and Heritage Discovery Museum described in this chapter. However, no matter how rich they are, governments are unlikely to shoulder all of the aspects of conservation, from property purchasing to maintenance and operation. Heritage conservation must rely on market forces and be organically integrated with commercial work. The New Horizon (*xintiandi*) in Shanghai is criticized as a form of gentrification. However, it maintains the physical form of Shanghai's lane house (*lilong*) and functions as a live "museum." The lifestyle of *lilong* belongs to the past. To people in the 21st century, *lilong* is both backward and uncomfortable. The marine police left Tsim Sha Tsui according to the same principle. The old building may still serve the current society, and contemporary people can use the property in a new way. Any heritage building should indicate its role in contemporary life.

9.4 Green Architecture

In the 1990s, the trends of sustainable development and green building spread throughout the world. A more direct meaning of "conservation" is to conserve the energy. The Building Research Establishment Environmental Assessment Method was founded in Britain in 1990. The U.S. developed the Leadership in Energy and Environmental Design (LEED) rating system. China launched the Green Building Label in 2003. At the turn of the 21st century, Hong Kong developed the Building Environmental Assessment Method (BEAM, later known as BEAM Plus). These systems share common characteristics and take local circumstances into account. For instance, the Hong Kong BEAM Plus incorporates many American LEED standards. The green building rating/assessment has become a business in its own right. Specialized associations organize such activities, charge fees and award certificates. Formed in 2008 by architects, engineers and surveyors among others, the Professional Green Building Council in Hong Kong is responsible for coordinating and organizing green building awards and establishing good practices. Since the inception of the council, over 300 projects in Hong Kong have been assessed, such as commercial, government/institutional, hotel, industrial and residential projects. From 2010 to 2014, 185 projects were assessed, half of which were residential buildings. Of these projects, 35 were granted platinum status, 44 were granted gold status, 29 were granted silver status, 30 were granted bronze status and 47 were unclassified (Hkgbc.org.hk 2015).

The Kadoorie Biological Sciences Building was erected in 2000 on the Hong Kong University campus at a location on a slope in the valley. If the building had been prostrate on the hillside according to the so-called organic growth approach, then ventilation in the laboratory would have been problematic. To avoid such problems, the 10-storey building was elevated 10 meters above the ground, supported by 8 groups of 4 inverted pyramid-shaped pillars. The layout of the building is about 30 × 60 m. Its core part comprises the high-tech laboratories under a symmetrical curved steel roof. The open steel staircases outside the main building are prominent elements of the facade and do not interfere with the use of the interior space (Fig. 9.12).

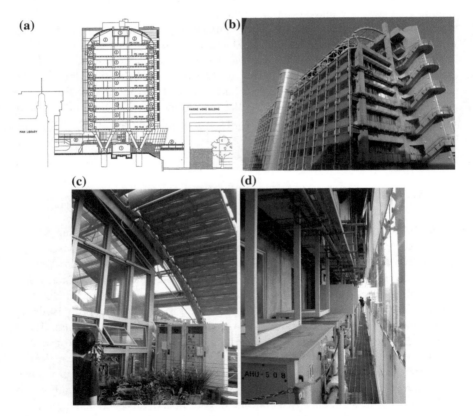

Fig. 9.12 Kadoorie Biological Sciences Building, HKU, 2000. **a** Section drawing. Courtesy of Leigh & Orange Architects. **b** Building rising from the valley. **c** Roof. **d** Between two skins

The east and west facades were designed with double skins with a 1-meter gap in between. The inside wall consists of quartz panels and windows. Part of the outside glass wall consists of frosted glass to prevent the sun from penetrating directly into the room. The space between the two skins is an effective buffer zone for the interior that enables hot air to rise naturally. Some of the building equipment is placed on the grid plates between the two layers in an attempt to enhance the interior flexibility. The solar panels on the top of the building provide an energy source. A greenhouse on the roof is used to cultivate plants and create a green indoor environment. Its flexibility and openness are in line with contemporary design trends. The building assumed a "green label" in 2000 due to its application of double walls, a roof greenhouse and solar panels. The Kadoorie Biological Sciences Building is an excellent example of the type of "green building" built in the early stages when sustainable architecture was popular. Designed by Leigh and Orange Ltd. along with structural consultant Arup, the project cost HK$400 million and set up a new prototype.[12]

During the same period, Leigh and Orange Ltd. and Integer, a British company dedicated to creating environmentally friendly buildings, co-designed "Integer Hong Kong Pavilion," a demonstration green building in Admiralty Tamar, Hong Kong. Constructed with tensile membranes and designed with natural ventilation, this temporary project serves as an ideal ventilation model of high-rise buildings and smart home devices. This exhibition promoted a local awareness of green buildings and their activities. After the 2001 show, the structure was dismounted and reconstructed in Beijing.

Green buildings in Hong Kong initially appeared in government-sponsored projects, such as the Electrical and Mechanical Services Department (EMSD) Building completed in 2004, a project converted from the original Kai Tak Airport Cargo Station Building No. 2 in Kowloon Bay. The building has eight storeys, and its seventh floor forms an additional part. Part of the facade in the old building was removed. While the workshops occupy the space from the underground to the fifth floor, the sixth and seventh floors function as offices. The roundabout of the old cargo station was retained and is used for circulation purposes in the multi-storey workshop. The newly constructed entrance hall on the lower ground floor contains a special exhibition hall, and the first floor is home to a well-equipped data center (Fig. 9.13).

The double-glazed facade of the sixth and seventh floors consists of an airflow device. The aluminum sunshade panels and perforated plates are installed on the workshop facade. These new devices beautify the facades and are characterized by fluid lines. The removal of part of the exterior walls has promoted air circulation and resulted in a cooling effect. Many environmental design solutions were adopted in the project, such as the installation of 2,300 pieces of solar panel on the periphery and roof of the building. The building is the largest in Hong Kong and can produce 350 kw of energy per year. The offices rely on heat insulation and soundproof double-glazing.

---

[12]For a description of the Kadoorie Life Science Building at Hong Kong University, see (Civcal.media.hku.hk 2015).

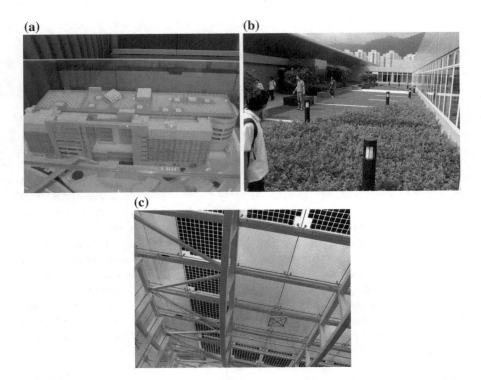

Fig. 9.13 Electrical and Mechanical Services Department (EMSD) headquarters, 2005. **a** Model. **b** Lower roof garden. **c** Solar panel installed on the skylight

Sun lighting tubes and a wastewater recycling system were also installed. The building won the Hong Kong Institute of Architects Merit Award in 2004.

The value-for-money report published by the Audit Commission on November 16, 2008 indicated that the EMSD Building had consumed 1,167 million kilowatt hours to 1,238 million kilowatt hours per year since its inception, an increase of 35–43 % over previous numbers. Furthermore, its electricity costs increased by 20–26 %, up to HK$10.26 million dollars. However, the floor area of the building is 1.5 % less than the previous area of the building before the move. Therefore, the Audit Commission thought that the EMSD needed to take measures to decrease its electricity consumption. In a response to this report, the EMSD observed that the newly provided facilities such as the data center for enterprise management, energy efficiency and security and the building's broad channels and high ceilings increased the building's electricity consumption (Director of Audit's Report: No. 51 2015). The EMSD Building demonstrated a "green building" problem, in that more energy was consumed due to the surplus of "green" gadgets and not due to the energy used to manufacture the solar panels.

The green building standards and practices implemented in Hong Kong and mainland China affect each other, and the two places make frequent exchanges.

In the 21st century, Tsinghua University in Beijing has designed demonstration green buildings on its campus. These buildings house offices, a learning center for building services engineering students and a variety of environmental protection facilities. Shanghai Institute of Building Science Research also set up green demonstration offices and residential buildings on its Minhang campus. Hong Kong has attempted to attract professionals to visit and discuss green buildings. The government has allocated land in Kowloon Bay, formerly owned by the Construction Industry Council (CIC), for the construction of green demonstration buildings. The CIC and Development Bureau co-developed "Zero-Carbon World," which was designed by Ronald Lu Architects and constructed by Gammon Construction Ltd. in 2012. This building, which has a 14,700-m^2 floor area and cost HK$240 million to build, serves as a place for groups and individuals to visit and gain green building knowledge (Zcb.hkcic.org 2015).

Zero Carbon World is a two-storey building, the roof of which slopes to the first floor and extends to the ground. The plants on the ground climb to the roof through the framing. Flat and cylindrical (absorbing sunlight in 360°) solar photovoltaic panels were installed on the tilted surface. The photovoltaic panels generate 30 % of the required energy, and biodiesel produces the remaining 70 % in the form of renewable energy. The interior spaces are open, with high-flow and low-speed ceiling fans installed and intelligent management systems automatically responding to the indoor and outdoor temperatures, humidity and light. An office is located downstairs, providing a variety of environmentally friendly equipment and solutions. Smart homes are exhibited upstairs. Architectural design tends to adopt a popular "green design" language, such as high headroom, semi-open public space, wind towers and external walls clad with wooden strips. Aside from the building, there is a wide range of local plants and doll sculptures of construction workers on the landscaped site. This low-rise building and its garden serve as a front courtyard for the surrounding high-rise buildings in East Kowloon, particularly the MegaBox shopping mall (Fig. 9.14).

The cost of "zero carbon" buildings is high. Calculating the full life-cycle of the materials involved, the initial energy consumption of zero carbon buildings is more than that of ordinary buildings. Since its opening, Zero Carbon World has not reached its true "zero carbon" condition. The majority of current "green buildings" are constructed in such a way that their iconic "sustainable" elements actually use more expensive materials and energy in terms of whole life cycle. Some of these elements are imported from other countries. The rating system tends to assess individual solutions separately and pay less attention to the whole life and overall energy efficiency of the building. In general, the development of "green buildings" in Hong Kong and mainland China remains in the initial superficial stage.[13]

---

[13]As stated in the text, despite the abundance of slogans and awarded "green projects," the development of green architecture has not yet matured. As such, we positioned the topic together with preservation in this chapter rather than relegating it to a new chapter.

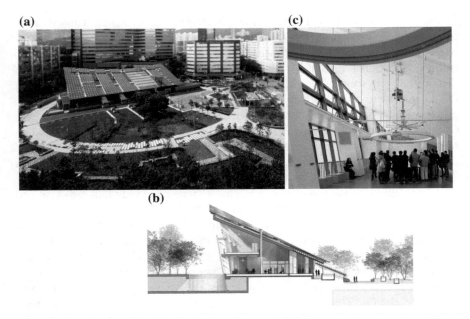

Fig. 9.14 Zero Carbon World, 2012. **a** Zero Carbon World is located in the old training field of CIC, now a park themed construction. **b** Section drawing. **c** Interior. Courtesy of Ronald Lu & Partners

9.5   Conclusion: Social and Environmental Sustainability

This chapter attempts to straddle a broad scope from defending the harbor to preserving heritage buildings, from the new usage of old building to newly-built "green" building. All the sessions and descriptions converge in a trend which has been obvious since the 1990s—that is sustainability. Defending the harbor from endless reclamation is to preserve Victoria Harbor, Hong Kong people's common wealth. Preserving heritage building in every means is to keep the society's history, tradition, root and identity. Both are socially sustainable and benefit to the continuation of a society. "Green building" relates to energy conservation, that is to retard the global warming and directly saves human being from looming disasters. It contributes to environmental sustainability.

In various social debates, sustainability, no matter social or environmental, always occupies the moral vantage point and it is un-challengeable. From defending the harbor, piers and some heritage buildings in Hong Kong, people's protest was gradually (and sadly) developed to confrontation, outlet of grievance towards government and show off of some politicians. However, green architecture falls to the realm and discussion of professional no-how. For most end-users and residents, green architecture is always admired and enjoyable.

In general, the pursuance of social and environmental sustainability is in tandem with the world trend in this global situation. As analyzed above, the exploitation of "sustainability" may be double-edged sword. In a buildable land of only 200 km^2, if more than one thousand old buildings could not be touched, where is the land for new development? If all building designs are attempted to satisfy every single index of green building criteria, the building cost and embodied energy will be immense. The territory is tumbled and evolved in this dilemma and learning process.

Hong Kong has fewer heritage buildings than Shanghai. During the high economic wave of the 1970s, the few heritage buildings in Hong Kong were demolished silently. Shanghai's economy started to take off in 1990, when the government and citizens were already aware of the importance of preserving historic buildings. Walking in the city center of Shanghai, one notices that many of the valuable old buildings of the 1930s have not yet been listed and remain in heavy daily use. I have witnessed the high demand for historic building preservation and "collective memory" in Hong Kong in the 21st century, for example, defending the two piers. If these buildings were in Shanghai, they would not be considered as heritage buildings based on their age and artistic quality. Indeed, we treasure our past along with pitiful and meager historic buildings.

References

Amo.gov.hk. (2015). *Declared monuments—antiquities and monuments office.* http://www.amo. gov.hk/en/monuments.php. Accessed December 11, 2015.

Antiquities and Monuments Office. (2015). *Adaptive reuse: Lui Seng Chun.* http://sc.lcsd.gov.hk/ gb/www.amo.gov.hk/textmode/b5/built_reuse1.php. Accessed July 22, 2014.

Asia Society. (2015). *Transformation of the former explosives magazine.* http://asiasociety.org/ hong-kong/visit/rebirth-former-explosives-magazine. Accessed December 5, 2015.

Baptist University. (2015). *Adaptive reuse: Lui Seng Chun.* http://scm.hkbu.edu.hk/lsc/tc/index. html. Accessed July 22, 2014.

Cheng, T. (1977). *The economy of Hong Kong.* Hong Kong: Far East Publications.

Cheung, A. (2015). *Getting every inch of land for building.* 张炳良:为建屋寸土必争. News.takungpao.com http://news.takungpao.com/hkol/topnews/2015-02/2921142_print.html. Accessed 8 August 2015.

Chu, W. (2011). Court of final appeal judgment meaning of "overriding public need" proposed proportionality principle on reclamation of victoria harbour (1st ed.). *Hong Kong: Society of protection of the harbour.* http://www.harbourprotection.org/media/490/proportionality.pdf. Accessed December 1, 2014.

Civcal.media.hku.hk. (2015). *Biological sciences building.* http://civcal.media.hku.hk/biosci/ introduction/default.htm. Accessed July 22, 2014.

Director of Audit's Report: No. 51. (2015) (1st ed., p. 5). Hong Kong. http://www.aud.gov.hk/ pdf_c/coer08_c.pdf. Accessed January 8, 2015.

Harbourprotection.org. (2015). Harbour Protection | Project & Press Release http://www. harbourprotection.org/en/projectandpress/. Accessed December 11, 2015.

Hkgbc.org.hk. (2015). Statistics—The Hong Kong Green Building Council (HKGBC) 香港綠色 建築議會 https://www.hkgbc.org.hk/eng/BEAMPlusStatistics.aspx. Accessed January 1, 2015.

Ho, P., & He, X. (2014). Construction of collective memory: memory in architecture, architecture in memory, in Cheng Peikai and Li Lin (Eds.), Wenhua yichan yu jiti jiyi (Cultural Heritage and Collective Memory) (pp. 55–70). Nanning: Guangxi Normal University Press. 何培斌,何心怡 (2014). 集体记忆的建构:建筑中的记忆,记忆中的建筑. 郑培凯、李璘主编. 文化遗产与集体记忆. 南宁:广西师范大学出版社.

Lai, C. (2007, May13). Heritage: Last resistance. *South China Morning Post*, p. A12.

Le Pichon, A. (2006). *Béthanie & Nazareth: French Secrets from a British Colony*. Hong Kong: The Hong Kong Academy for Performing Arts.

Lui, T. (2012). *The 1970s we might know*. Hong Kong: Chung Hwa Book Co. 吕大乐. (2012). 那似曾相识的七十年代. 香港:中华书局.

Parwani, A. (2007). Anger over plan to dismantle pier. *South China Morning Post*, p. B1.

Xue, C. Q. L. (2006, October 28). The last day of Utopia. *Wen Wai Pao*, p. A13. 薛求理 (2006年10月28日). 乌托邦的最后一天. 香港:文汇报, p. A13.

Xue, C. Q. L. (2007, February 13). The meaning of Dr. Sun Yat-sen Museum. *Wen Wai Pao*, p. A12. http://paper.wenweipo.com/2007/02/13/WW0702130006.htm. Accessed December 20, 2015. 薛求理 (2007年2月13日). 孙中山纪念馆的意义. 香港:文汇报. A12.

Youth hostel association Hong Kong. (2015). 美荷楼青年旅舍. Yha.org.hk. http://www.yha.org.hk/chi/meihohouse/index.php. Accessed July 22, 2014.

Zcb.hkcic.org. (2015). ZCB. http://zcb.hkcic.org/Chi/index.aspx?langType=1028. Accessed July 22, 2014.

Zheng, B., & Tong, B. (2000). *A century of Kowloon road and street*. Hong Kong: Joint Publishing Ltd. 郑宝鸿、佟宝铭 (2000). 九龙街道百年. 香港:三联书店.

Zh.wikipedia.org. (2015). 保留舊中環天星碼頭事件. https://zh.wikipedia.org/wiki/ 保留舊中環天星碼頭事件. Accessed December 5, 2015.

Chapter 10
Pursuing Excellence—Toward a Civic Architecture

1997 was a watershed year for Hong Kong. The anxiety and expectations surrounding the sovereignty handover drained away with the heavy rain on the evening of June 30. Following the "one country two systems" and "no-change for fifty years" policies, economic and building activities were carried out as usual. The Hong Kong Institute of Architects (HKIA) held a students' design competition to memorialize the return of sovereignty. The wave of globalization increased in the 1990s and had a direct effect on architecture. The globalization resulted in more foreign design firms in Hong Kong and the Chinese mainland, and the local acceptance of international trend such as green architecture and public engagement. After the sovereignty handover, the first obvious changes to buildings took place in the public sector.

10.1 Central Library and Design Competition

In a metropolis of seven million people, a central library was long overdue. Hong Kong Central Library was finally completed in 2001. With 12 floors and a gross floor area of 33,800 m^2, the library is the biggest in the city's public library system. Hong Kong Central Library is located in Causeway Bay, Hong Kong Island. According to its official website, the arch-shaped entrance at the front elevation represents the Gate to Knowledge. The circle stands for the sky, the square for the land and the triangle for the accumulation of knowledge. The Hong Kong Central Library is an intelligent building, built on a network flooring system to allow for a flexible power supply, telecommunications and further change and expansion.

© Springer Science+Business Media Singapore 2016
C.Q.L. Xue, *Hong Kong Architecture 1945–2015*,
DOI 10.1007/978-981-10-1004-0_10

Fig. 10.1 Central Library, 2001

It was designated as the depository library in Hong Kong for nine international organizations.

The Central Library has a neoclassical design and is intended to be monumental. However, it is often mocked by Hong Kong society for its use of historic architectural clichés. The building has enhanced and enriched public life through its provision of extensive book storage and reading areas. However, it challenges the notion of sustainability, as its over-decorated facade consumes a great deal of building materials and craftsmanship. The library is located at the perimeter of Causeway Bay opposite Victoria Park, a major public space in Hong Kong. It is easily accessible to visitors from the park and nearby stations. It serves to educate the public and promote reading culture (Fig. 10.1).

The library's ornamental extravagance has prompted fierce debate over the necessity of adapting neoclassical architectural design. When the design proposal was presented in the Legislative Council for fund allocation in 1997, members were generally not satisfied. Most of the public buildings were designed by government architects after the Second World War and by the ASD after 1986. Design competitions for important corporation headquarters such as those of Hong Kong Bank were held only in the private sector. The design of Honk Kong Central Library triggered a debate over the role of the ASD and the necessity of design competitions.

In 1998, Beijing held an international design competition for the national theatre. The three rounds of competition aroused extensive international interest and the results were fiercely debated. No matter which form of building was eventually selected, the process of the design competition demonstrated the opening up of China, which was long considered a country behind a curtain (Xue et al. 2010).

China's bold opening up to international design firms stimulated Hong Kong to a great extent.

In 2000, the Housing Authority and HKIA first held design competitions for public housing in Shui Chuen O of Shatin, which received a warm response.[1] Around the same time, Chief Executive Tung Chee-hwa mentioned youth services in a policy address. The government suggested building a youth development center in Chai Wan with public funding of HK$900 million. In June 2000, the Home Affairs Bureau and HKIA jointly held a design competition and in December received more than 60 entries. After two rounds of competition, a scheme designed by the young team of Humphrey Tak-ming Wong, Kenneth Tse, Steven Chu and Anson Tsang won first prize. Construction started in 2001 and stopped in 2003 due to a looming economic downturn. Construction resumed in 2005 and the building was completed and opened in 2010.

The lower floors of the Youth Center building are open or semi-open and inserted by the Chai Wan pedestrian bridge. They contain a long and wide ramp, a semi-open theater and a Y-shaped theater. The columns support over 20 floors. One wing contains a youth hostel and another contains activity rooms. The upper floors contain a hotel with a central patio. Many glass-clad staircases are exposed in the elevation. The glass facing the south and east is tinted with white strips to partially shade the direct sun. The activity rooms and library are flexible big spaces. The interactions between the staircase, escalators and lifts lend the building the atmosphere of a shopping mall. The interior design is bold and fashionable and fit for young people's taste. The youth center is owned by the government and managed by a private company. Due to its location in Chai Wan at the east end of Hong Kong Island, many of the shops are unavailable to rent out. The shining and bulky mass stands out from the residential areas of Chai Wan (Fig. 10.2).

As the population grew in the 1970s, the government built standard school buildings in needy areas. Classrooms and school halls were built according to standard designs. With the reform of education, such standard and monotonous school designs were challenged. In 2002, the Education Bureau held a design competition for Evangel College in Tseng Kwan O, where primary and secondary schools are joined together. Children in this college may spend 12 years from Y1 to graduation in a single secondary school that does not rank students and encourages equal learning opportunities. Three young architects made Z-shaped plans that included many outdoor spaces with open and semi-open decks. Primary and secondary schools have their own playgrounds, and some rooms can be flexibly connected or separated. Such bold designs stimulate children's freedom to grow and explore (Fig. 10.3).

---

[1]After several rounds of start and stop, Shui Chuen O Estate was completed in 2015 and accommodates 3,039 households.

Fig. 10.2 Youth Center, Chai Wan, 2010. **a** Model. **b** Open stair running along the external wall. **c** Facade. **d** Hostel in the upper floors. **e** Library. **f** From MTR to the youth center

Fig. 10.3 Evangel College, Tseung Kwan O, 2006. Courtesy of Prof. Paul Chu

10.2   West Kowloon Cultural District

Following this warm-up period, the West Kowloon Cultural District design competition was held. West Kowloon began as a plot of 42 ha reclaimed from Victoria Harbour when the Western Harbor Tunnel, international airport and airport expressway were built. In 1996, the land was designated as a cultural district. Although the land is only one twelfth the size of the 2010 World Expo site in Shanghai, it is valuable given its location in the city center of Hong Kong. In April 2001, an international open design competition was held and five schemes were selected from 140 entries. Foster & Partners from the U.K. won first prize. The winning scheme installed a "sky canopy" above the buildings and public space, which the authority appreciated.

With some concepts in mind, the government issued an invitation to develop the West Kowloon Cultural District in September 2003. The tenderer was asked to have experience developing, selling and managing large-scale comprehensive buildings and to inject HK$30 billion into the project. In April 2004, the government received five tenders. In November 2004, three entries were confirmed. An exhibition of three plans was displayed to the public for 15 weeks from December 2004 to March 2005. The tenderers comprised big property developers such as Cheung Kong, Sun Hung Kai, Henderson Land and Sino. The developers brought in international architects, engineers and various consultants. Each tenderer spent HK$10 million on models, display halls, lighting and brochures for its plan. The questionnaire sheet administered to the public was as long as a toilet tissue roll. The general public usually felt puzzled and did not know how to answer the questions. The tenderers and property developers transported their employees to "visit" and fill in the sheet (Fig. 10.4).

The people doubted the method of running the cultural district via a single consortium. The consortium invested huge amounts of money into "promoting" culture and expected the sum to be recouped through the development of commercial properties. The people questioned why this company was selected out of all of the other companies. Moreover, they questioned whether the property developers had enough experience to manage the cultural facilities. Under societal pressure, the government gave up the single-operator plan, sending 10 years of government, consortium and public effort went down drain. In 2008, the government established the authority of the West Kowloon Cultural District and applied for funding of HK$21.6 billion from the Legislative Council. In 2009, an invitation for a master plan competition was sent to international designers. Master plan works from three companies, including Foster & Partners, OMA and Rocco Design, were displayed to the public for three months starting in August 2010.

Lord Foster first came to Hong Kong in 1979. He participated in the design of Hong Kong Bank and the Hong Kong airport, train station and cruise pier. His designs paid attention to both the environment and technology. Foster & Partners demonstrated the theme of the "park in the city," according to which a park would be featured prominently in West Kowloon with all vehicular traffic diverted

Fig. 10.4 Schemes of West Kowloon Cultural District in 2004–2005. **a**, **b** Shortlisted master plan. **c** Swire Properties' scheme was not shortlisted. It exhibited "Vision of the Harbor" in its own shopping mall. The Design was led by Frank Gehry and Partners

underground. The dragon canopy was highlighted in the 2002 and 2004 designs. In this master plan, the canopy was replaced by large pieces of lawn and forest. The design made West Kowloon appear decent and elegant (Fig. 10.5).

Rocco Design focused on pedestrian and vehicular circulation. Its plan was relegated to a compact part of United Plaza that gradually gave way to a smooth path toward the sea. Local factors such as a market and stone slab streets were

Fig. 10.5 Scheme of Foster & Partners, 2010

Fig. 10.6 Scheme of rocco design, 2010

integrated into the site. Artistic raft pieces were floated on the sea as metaphors of Hong Kong fishing rafts (Fig. 10.6).

OMA is famous for many spectacular buildings including the CCTV headquarters in Beijing. Its designs have centered on circulation and people movement and have continuously broken through conventional concepts of "architecture." In the planning of West Kowloon, OMA designed three clusters of buildings, including the "East arts," "West performance" and "Central market" clusters. The grid layout of the "East arts" cluster was the Hong Kong version of CCTV headquarters from a visual standpoint. The "Central market" cluster was crowded. The design included a surprising stroke by adding a suspension bridge linking the Jordan and Austin Roads. There was no such requirement in the design brief and it extended the design beyond the site boundary. However, this ring bridge strengthened the celebratory atmosphere of the West Kowloon Cultural District and also connected the cultural district to the old city (Fig. 10.7).

All three of the plans considered internal and external traffic and prioritized pedestrian and bicycle routes. However, the quality of the works did not meet with people's expectations. The three companies were paid HK$ 50 million (US$ 6.45 million) each in compensation. Design competitions of a similar scale in mainland China typically pay HK$200,000–500,000 at most and attract similarly famous companies.[2] Foster & Partners ultimately won the bid for the master plan of West Kowloon Cultural District. The southwest portion of the district is a large park positioned on a gentle slope. Most of the district's performance and exhibition buildings are located close to Canton Road. Vehicular traffic is hidden underground. The roads and basement parking add to the problems of pollution and ventilation (Fig. 10.8).

---

[2]For more information about the West Kowloon Cultural District, see (Xue 2010); and the webpage of the Authority of West Kowloon Cultural District, http://www.westkowloon.hk/tc/home.

Fig. 10.7 Scheme of OMA, 2010

Fig. 10.8 Foster & Partners won the master plan of West Kowloon Cultural District, 2011

The cultural district will eventually be home to 14 buildings. In 2013, two buildings were confirmed. Bing Thom of Vancouver and Ronald Lu of Hong Kong jointly won their bid to design the Xiqu (Chinese opera) Center. Herzog & de Meuron from Switzerland, TFP Farrells and Arup & Partners HK won their bid to design the M+ Museum. Administration has been underway since 2008, with directors and many officers employed from overseas. With the "generosity" of the Hong Kong government, infrastructure construction began in 2013, and the estimated cost has already escalated to HK$47 billion, doubled the government's estimation in 2008[3] (Figs. 10.9 and 10.10).

---

[3]Chan Yuen-han, *Xijiu xin de guo?* (How can you trust the West Kowloon?) *AM730*, July 3, 2013. The escalation of construction fee is partly attributed to the shortage of construction workers. Young people are not willing to join the building industry, and the importation of labor is banned by worker's union and some politicians. In 2015, a rebar bending worker's wage is around HK $2,200 (US$ 270) a day. The high salary heavily burdens the development and city construction. See the report from Financial Time, (M.ftchinese.com 2015).

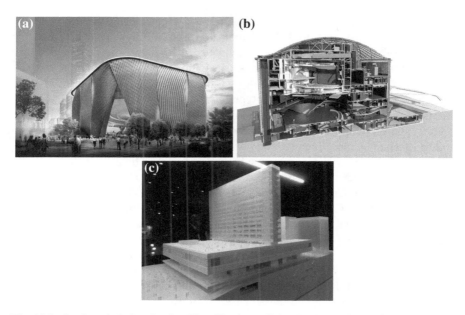

Fig. 10.9 Confirmed design in the West Kowloon Cultural District **a** and **b** Xiqu Center; Courtesy of Ronald Lu & Partners. **c** M+ Museum, Herzog & de Meuron won the design, 2013

Fig. 10.10 Construction site of West Kowloon Cultural District, Jan 2015

10.3 Campus Building

The 2001 West Kowloon design competition served as an example of soliciting excellent international design efforts. Overseas architects were already designing buildings on university campuses before construction began in West Kowloon. Daniel Libeskind Studio designed the **Creative Media Building at City University of Hong Kong** (CityU) and completed it in 2011. Coldéfy & Associes

Architectes Urbanistes of France designed the Hong Kong Design Institute Building and completed it in 2010. Zaha Hadid from the U.K. designed the Inno Tower of Polytechnic University and completed it in 2013. The private Chu Hai College initiated a new campus that was schematically designed by OMA and will be completed in 2016.[4] All of these designs were selected from competitions and created new academic building prototypes.

The School of Creative Media at CityU was founded in 1998. In the 21st century, the government allocated the nearby hilly land to the school, including 500 m of sloping road directed away from the main campus. In the summer of 2002, CityU invited design teams to submit schemes. The finalists included David Chipperfield, Michael Wilford and Associates of the U.K., OMA from the Netherlands, Studio Daniel Libeskind of the U.S. and Rocco Design of Hong Kong. On October 8, 2004, CityU announced that Studio Daniel Libeskind took first prize. The local architect was Leigh & Orange Ltd. The ground was broken in 2008, and the building was completed and began operations in autumn 2011. It currently provides classrooms, studio and offices for CityU's creative media, communication and architecture programs.

CityU hoped that the construction of a new building would allow the School of Creative Media to play an indispensable role in the Hong Kong media industry. The design and usage of the creative media center sought to attract the public, enhance the name of the school and strengthen the competitiveness of training students (Xue 2012).[5] After considering the university's opinions, Libeskind said, "I hope that the design can embody the ambition and liveliness of the fast growing university. This building should become an icon of the campus... The creative media center encourages various activities inside and the interaction between different studies (Libeskind and Goldberger 2008)."

The creative media building is located on the hill next to the ten 12-storey student hostel halls. Its drastic form pops out from the environment, inspiring feelings of tension and conflict. The building resembles a large split white rock whose massive volume and black strip windows create a contrasting and visually striking appearance. The two interlocking volumes produce many slanting walls (Fig. 10.11).

Several of the building's masses interweave and collide. Its internal spaces follow a seemingly random formation. Libeskind observed that a building should make material the designer's personal taste and style.[6] The buildings Libeskind designed in America and Europe are usually clad in metal. However, in this case, paint was only applied externally for budgetary reasons. The plans of each floor vary, and the large staircase acts as the center and spine of the internal space.

---

[4]The design of Chu Hai College was given to OMA in 2011. But it was found that the site was too small for the design. After the foundation was basically made, Rocco Design re-designed the project and fitted into the site.

[5]The information about the design of the CityU Creative Media Building is partly from "The Building in Brief," provided by Kevin Au, Project Manager of the CityU Campus Planning Office on 10 July 2008.

[6]From a speech made by Daniel Libeskind at City University of Hong Kong, 13 October 2006.

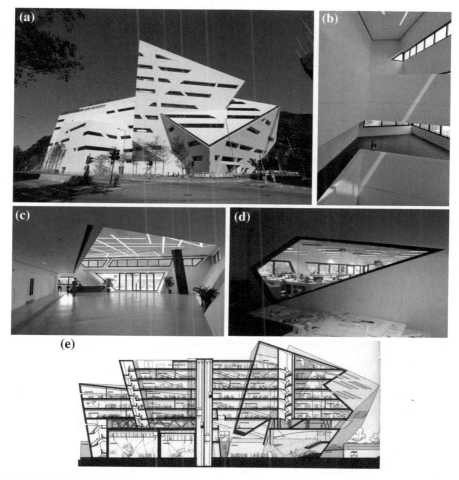

Fig. 10.11 CMC building, CityU, 2011. **a** Mass interlocking. **b** Stairway. **c** Lobby. **d** Architectural design studio. **e** Section. Courtesy of City University of Hong Kong

The shape and details of the windows and ceilings repeat the Libeskind motif, which can also be seen in the Jewish Museum of Berlin. The original design concepts have been respected over nine years of documentation, tendering, construction and many revisions (Fig. 10.12).

The site and users of these new campus buildings were investigated and the observations are recorded here.[7] The irregularity of the building interior causes many awkward interior spaces to appear. When these twisting boxes are

_____

[7]Studies of CityU, PolyU and HKDI buildings were conducted between 2012 and 2013. See Yang et al. (2015). The students' responses and comments in relation to the three campus buildings were taken from this investigation.

Fig. 10.12 Designer's image
of CMC building, CityU.
Courtesy of Studio Libeskind

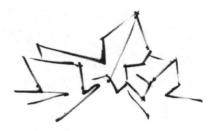

interpenetrated on a large scale, such as in the exhibition hall and function room, the resulting space functions well. However, when partitioned into small chambers such as the faculty office rooms, the space presents more intolerable conditions. Students sit in the open decks on every floor and on the balconies. 20 % of the students said it was not easy to determine where they wanted to go, perhaps due to the unclear directional signs and the variegated layouts of each floor.

The CMC building stands on a slope, where people can view Victoria Harbour across the Kowloon Peninsula to the south. The designer seemed to ignore this vantage point. The south-facing wall near the sea has narrow-strip windows, which are obviously not large enough to accommodate the sweeping view. Some of the strip windows are placed in the north-facing wall, which offers a view of the mountainside. The windows are drawn in the elevation in parallel lines regardless of the room partition. Therefore, some of the partition walls clash with the penetrations. Many teachers complained that they could not enjoy the sea view from such a privileged location.

The roof gardens are rarely used because they are located at the end of the plan. The unusual inner space, window shapes and leaning walls are the most disturbing factors and cause discomfort for the users inside. The slanting wall blatantly rising from the floor instills a feeling of awkwardness when one attempts to approach the windows. In addition, students have complained that although the new buildings are fashionable and spectacular in appearance, they are relatively poorly lit and enclosed compared with conventional academic buildings, which decreases the students' productivity. As a result, only 30 % of the students thought that the building helped to improve their work efficiency and productivity. The poor lighting conditions also result from the improper penetration mentioned previously. Even on sunny days, the classrooms and offices must use artificial lighting to meet the needs of academic activities. After several years' usage, the roof leaks in the raining days and the white slanting external wall is stained embarrassingly with trace of rain water. The other buildings at CityU rarely suffer from similar problems.

The School of Design at **Polytechnic University** (PolyU) was founded in the 1960s. The university hoped to build a home for the school to continuously contribute to the creative industry of Hong Kong.[8] In 2007, a jury of 11 members for

---

[8]For more information about the intention of PolyU to build the Inno Center, see (The Legislative Council 2009).

the new School of Design Building was formed and included two representatives from PolyU, Fumihiko Maki of Japan, and architects from Hong Kong and overseas. In April 2007, five teams were shortlisted for the project, including Sauerbruch Hutton from Germany, Zaha Hadid from the U.K., UN Studio from the Netherlands, SANAA from Japan and Rocco Design from Hong Kong. PolyU displayed the five schemes to the public from August 31 to September 13, 2007. According to the public sector procedure, the "two-envelop system" of technology and budget was adopted. Zaha Hadid received the highest mark in the process.[9]

The university expected the building to provide an ideal and innovative platform for study. The designer made the following observation in a note: "this building establishes a vision for the future and also salutes the long tradition of this university. A plural flexibility dominates the internal logic of the whole building (Hadid 2015)".

Established in 1980, the PolyU campus is unified by the dark brown tile of its external walls. The white, fluid and structurally sound **Inno Tower** is a loud shout on an otherwise conservative campus. Around 80 % of the students claimed to like the design of Inno Tower, and 46 % did not believe it to have a local identity.[10]

The outdoor podium provides an open public space and connection with the campus and interior lobby. Other designs by Hadid have also included podiums and ramps. In PolyU, they function mainly as traffic space. The ground and first floors are exhibition spaces. The third and fourth floors contain the library, lecture theatres and conference rooms. The sixth to eleventh floors include design studios and offices. The double traffic cores in the plan are interwoven with staircases and corridors. The double cores roughly divide the plan territories, shorten the traffic distance and enhance the public space and orientation (Fig. 10.13).

A signature method involving "lines" has often appeared in Hadid's designs. In the case of Inno Tower, several groups of lines flow in different directions and at different speeds. They can be found in the continuous illuminated strip in the ceiling, the lighting along the staircase and the railing along the balcony and staircase. The lines have different thicknesses and twist at different angles and gradients. They form the background of people's activities. Within the building, the boundaries between rooms are blurred and the different classrooms and studios are skillfully connected. The curtain wall is clad on an irregular plane and attracts seepage in raining. Water leakage problem is rarely seen in conventional buildings.

The **HKDI**, operated by the Vocational Training Council, was founded to offer design education in response to the growing demands from the emerging creative

---

[9]"Two envelop" system is used by the Hong Kong government to determine the tender in procurement. One envelop is technical, another is budgetary. The highest scored tenderer gets the job. For more about the process of selecting the scheme for the Inno Center, see (Ng 2008).

[10]The PolyU Inno Center study was conducted in autumn 2013. Of the 70 students who participated, 21 were from members of the Urban and Interior Design program and 49 were from other design programs.

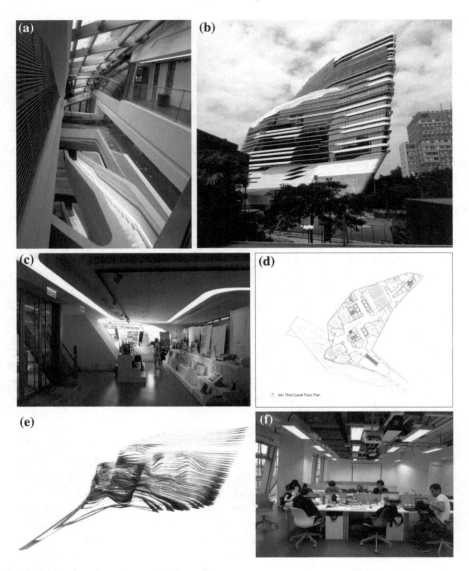

Fig. 10.13 PolyU Innovation Tower. **a** Atrium between two cores. **b** Inno Tower in campus. **c** Ground floor. **d** Plan. **e** Design idea. **f** Studio. Drawings courtesy of Zaha Hadid Architects

industries. It integrates design-related subjects, making it easier to concentrate resources and skills. The campus is located on the sea-reclaimed land of Tiu Keng Leng. From 2006 to 2007, the HKDI conducted an international design competition. The committee received 162 entries from 23 countries, including elite architects such as Kazuyo Sejima, Nobuaki Furuya and Zaha Hadid. Their works interpreted the designers' visions from various angles. A young French company known as Coldéfy & Associés won the competition with its submitted scheme and had its building constructed. The jury members included architect Richard Meier from the U.S., Leslie Lu from the University of Hong Kong and Shiling Zheng from Tongji University of Shanghai[11].

The theme of the winning design was the "white sheet," a metaphor for creativity and a common medium for designers. This "sheet" connects the lecture buildings in midair, suggesting the concept of interpenetration among the various disciplines. Simple and intense, it provides a large activity space and expresses an eternal theme: a square for the public, a tower for lectures and platforms for cooperation within departments. The jury committee commented, "This building provides opening and permeation to the largest degree to connect and interact with the city grid."[12] Compared with the other shortlisted entries, the Coldéfy scheme had clear ideas, a resolute method of arranging functions and a crisp treatment of both space and massing. The building mass consists of three main elements: the podium (first floor), platform (floors seven and eight) and derricks (interpenetrating the floor plates). The building's diagrammatic figuration seeks to both embrace the ambience and stand as a distinguished landmark. The landscape slope gently ascends 7 m from King Ling Road, providing a smooth transition from the street to the academic facilities and melding the school with its urban environment.[13]

Following the design competition and an efficient construction process, the late-initiated HKDI moved into its new building in 2010, a year earlier than the CMC of CityU. Students, neighborhood residents and passersby frequently use the exhibition halls, auditorium, canteen, coffee shop and semi-open space in the lower podium for various social activities. The swimming pool in the podium is open to the public on designated days of the week. The four supporting derricks contain departments and offices. In the upper podium, a library occupies the seventh floor and serves the entire institute, and the eighth floor contains studios. There is a roof garden located on the ninth floor, from which people can look out to the sea and the Tseng Kwan O area and enjoy the summer breeze. The building has a consistent structural logic and a crisp and clean design language (Fig. 10.14).

The spatial configuration of the HKDI inevitably sacrifices the efficiency of its space. Four towers take up only 60 % of the first floor area, and the terrace takes up

---

[11]This information about HKDI was taken in part from *Elevating Design/Hong Kong Design Institute International Architectural Design Competition*, Hong Kong Design Institute, 2007. Professor Leslie Lu later became Director of the HKDI.

[12]The comments of the jury were taken from Hong Kong Design Institute (2008).

[13]Some of the comments related to the HKDI design were taken from Hong Kong Design Institute (2008).

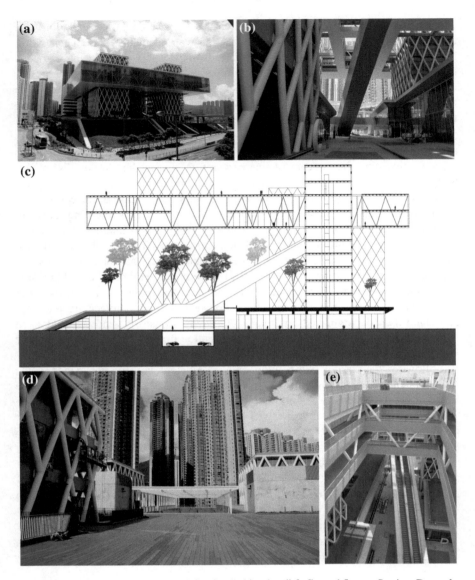

Fig. 10.14 HKDI building, 2010. **a** A floating "white sheet". **b** Ground floor. **c** Section. Drawn by Zang Peng. **d** Roof garden. **e** Atrium

the other 40 %. The platform void comprises more than 10 % of the total site area, a luxury in overpopulated Hong Kong. The ratio of open spaces to enclosed spaces on every floor of the building is almost 1:2.5. Due to the low space efficiency, many academic activities of the HKDI must be moved to the Kwun Tong campus several miles away.[14]

In regard of the above three new campus buildings, most of the students use and appreciate the buildings with confidence because they know they were designed by foreign or famous architects. Because some of the buildings' functions have been sacrificed, the university authorities have focused attention on their brand instead of utilities. The three buildings were constructed with the help of local project architects including Leigh & Orange for the CMC, AGC for Inno Tower and the P & T Group for the HKDI. Although local partners play an uncertain role in the final output, the feedback from the local architectural community can be sorted according to tone. Local architects and professionals frequented the buildings after they were opened. A few of the architects were interviewed and their responses were documented (HKIA 2012).[15]

In general, younger architects placed more value on the buildings and praised the refreshing quality they brought to the city. They believed that the three projects introduced international architects to Hong Kong, added diversity to the local practice and demonstrated alternative visions of Hong Kong architecture to the masses. Such eye-opening architectural events also altered the city's consideration of its local architects. The elder generation felt that such iconic buildings conflicted with the generic Hong Kong cityscapes in the street. To them, introducing more star architects and visionary buildings could only be disastrous for the city. People in the midst of their careers hoped that more opportunities could be given to the local architects. Local professionals noticed that their clients were willing to pay higher fees to bring in international architects and that this could add unnecessary project costs. Local architects expressed the concern that star architects usually adopted a universal approach and neglected the local context: "How much do we want them to be culturally sensitive like us, as they may bring something new to the city due to their foreignness?"[16] These buildings gave rise to discussions between local architects about the relationship of site-sensitive architectural practice.

---

[14]The author and his team investigated the three school buildings in 2012–2013. Major differences between the survey feedback received from the HKDI and CMC could also be identified. Most of the HKDI students would appreciate the space more if they were informed that the designer was a famous global architect. This indicates that design pedagogy might have enforced compulsory aesthetic norms on the interviewees. As a result, the students valued the design itself and believed that the convenience of the layout and circulation deserved to be compromised in favor of the free architectural expression. When asked such questions as "Do you like the color and the texture of the building?" "Do you find the appearance of the building creative?" "Do you think the building could inspire you?" and "How do you feel about the layout and the circulation of the building?" most students answered with the "moderate" option. Less than 30 % of the students highly commended the inspiration and improvement of work efficiency offered by the building. However, the students could not appraise the conflicts between the idiosyncratic spatial identity and its urban context. Publication of this investigation is listed in Yang et al. (2015).

[15]Some feedbacks were collected by the author and his team during the period of 2009–2014.

[16]The collection of Hong Kong architects' responses to the foreign-designed buildings has been conducted in several ways since 2011. We conducted formal interviews with three generations of

10.4   Usages of Urban Land: Formal and Informal

During urban transformation, old functions give way to new developments. In 1998, the airport moved to Chek Lap Kok and the Kowloon Walled City was left quiet. The government pushed forward a plan to rebuild Kai Tak that included filling in ditches and bays to produce 300 ha of land.[17] Kai Tak finally adopted a "zero filling" scheme in defense of the harbor. A new stadium, a MTR station and public housing were drawn into the outline zoning plan. The cruise pier was installed at the end of the runway. Designed by Foster & Partners, the cruise terminal was put in use in 2013. Airports around the world are being expanded, and very few have been discarded like Kai Tak. After 15 years of discussion and consultation, Kai Tak found its new usage. Compared with that in mainland China, construction in Hong Kong is extremely slow because of many stages of public hearing, engagement, consultation and budget approval (for public sector) in the Legislative Council. The public consultation meetings frequently happen in the government buildings or local districts, in weekdays or especially in weekends. Demonstration in Town Planning Board is seen almost in every meeting, as rezoning and change of use are closely linked with residents' interests. However, the opinions of various parties can be absorbed in a longer process and help to avoid the creation of "white elephant" and "ghost" cities.[18]

Admiralty once served as the naval base on the opposite bank of Kai Tak across the harbor. In 1990, the base moved to Stonecutter and the waterfront of Admiralty has been vacant since. Over time, various groups have used it for exhibition grounds, concerts, carnivals and even a tea party attended by 10,000 people. In 2002, the government allocated HK$5.2 billion to build its headquarters, legislative council and chief executive offices there, with a gross floor area of 136,000 m². The government adopted the BOT method to increase the speed of construction, a method led by the construction contractor. In May 2007, the works of four tenderers were displayed, including designs by Rocco Design, Aedas and Daniel Libeskind Studio (Fig. 10.15).

The joint venture between Gammon and Hip Hing took first place. Rocco Design designed the scheme, in which the government headquarters faced the new central waterfront park. All of the schemes responded to the requirements of the landscape and harbor. Rocco Yim's design followed an "open door" concept, featuring two

---

(Footnote 16 continued)

architects who were in their 30s, 40–50s and 70–80. All six of the architects were working actively in their age groups. Local architects and professionals were invited to attend seminars and students' work exhibitions in both of the buildings. Their opinions of the buildings were recorded.

[17] According to the *Basic Law of Special Administrative Region of Hong Kong*, the Hong Kong government can lease out land at most 50 ha a year. 300 ha is six times than one year's quota. See *Basic Law* of Hong Kong, 1990.

[18] "White elephant" and "ghost" cities have been widely covered by the media in China and overseas. In the government direction, some towns saw many housing estates emerge, but few people moved in. See Finance.southcn.com (2012).

Fig. 10.15 BOT tendering for the government headquarters in Admiralty, 2007. The three tenders were not selected

wings that embraced the green lawn of the waterfront park. One wing contained the circular legislative council building, and the other contained the chief executive and executive council offices. A bigger glass box contained boxes and platforms. The portal featured a 40-storey governmental office building. Yim's other works have made use of similar methods and gestures. The lawn penetrated through the building and linked with the sky bridge of the Admiralty MTR station. Compared with the other entries, this design resolutely embraced the environment. To avoid blocking the mountain, building heights were kept between 130 and 160 m (Fig. 10.16).

Construction in Hong Kong is slower than that on the Chinese mainland. However, after confirming the tender at the end of 2007, the government head-quarters was completed before the end of 2011, a level of efficiency that had never been attained. The "open-door" gesture allows the ocean breeze to reach the streets hundreds of meters away from the water. The building is made of double-pane black curtain walls and grey framing. Photovoltaic panels are installed on the rooftop. These are 21st-century technologies. Built in the 1950s, the "government hill" served three million people with machinelike efficiency. After more than 50 years, the government headquarters serve a more pluralistic and democratic society. The building itself should set up an example of sustainability and opening to society and nature. The lawn in front of the building provides a comfortable

Fig. 10.16 The winning tender from Gammon and Hip Hing was built according to Rocco Design's scheme. The government headquarters was completed in 2011

vantage point overlooking the harbor. Government officials and citizens are learning how to use the space, which has come to serve as a symbol of civic society.

Government headquarters is a most formal case of using the urban land. However, in this "international metropolis", there exists some "informal" or "illegal" space. The Kowloon Walled City was once an "independent kingdom" in the British Colony for hundred years (Girard and Lambot 1993). It was completely demolished and replaced by a park in 1995. However, the similar scene of Kowloon Walled City appears in many old districts packed with dilapidated tenement houses. Because of the cramped environment and escalated housing price, illegal structures exist on many rooftops and old buildings. Business takes place inside a lot of residential buildings, typified by Chungking Mansion in Tsim Sha Tsui, which was built in 1961. Backpackers from foreign countries especially Asia and Africa turn this residential building to low-price hostel, Indian curry restaurants, (fake brand) watch shops and numerous inconvenient businesses.[19] At weekend, tens of thousands foreign domestic helpers, mainly Filipino, Indonesian and Thai women, occupy plazas, pedestrian bridges, open ground floor of commercial buildings by chatting, eating, singing, dancing and praying. This has been a spectacular holiday

---

[19]Chungking Mansion in Tsim Sha Tsui contains more than 80 hostels and 400 shops and hawks. It was claimed by BBC and Time Magazine as "the most favorite ghetto" in Hong Kong, see Fitzpatrick (2015) and Mathews (2011).

Fig. 10.17 Informal space **a** citizen disobedient movement, 2014; **b** June 4th anniversary in Victoria Park; **c** domestic helpers at weekends

townscape of Hong Kong for the past 30 years.[20] In the Chinese New Year, June 4th anniversary, celebration or demonstration, the Victoria Park becomes cheerful or furious ocean. In the autumn of 2014, the streets of Admiralty, Causeway Bay and Mongkok were blocked and occupied for 79 days by the citizen disobedient movement. The vehicular traffic and bus transportation were paralyzed during that period. The occupiers met, sang, slept and read books in streets.[21] In daily life, one can see the exaggerated billboard for advertisement in streets, temporary buildings under the flyover or various clever "abusive" use of structure. Several books record the phenomenon (Chan 2009; Zhang 2009). The above informal, "abused", anarchic or illegal usages of urban spaces are experimenting various possibilities in a diversified and liberal city. They contrast sharply with most "formal" examples introduced in this book (Fig. 10.17).

---

[20]According to the statistics of government, there were 320,988 foreign domestic helpers in 2013, 46 % were from Indonesia and 51 % from The Philippines. They form around 3 % of Hong Kong population (Hong Kong Government 2014).

[21]The citizen disobedient movement in 2014 was triggered by the Chief Executive election method in 2017. The Chinese central government promised to allow "one person one vote", but the democratic alliance and students unions asked for more rights. See *South China Morning Post*, 30 September to 1 December 2014. Eg. (South China Morning Post 2014).

10.5   Conclusion: An Architecture of Civic Society

China has been experiencing from an enclosed to open state since the late 1970s. During its transition from British colony to a special administrative region in China, Hong Kong also experienced the similar path from enclosure to openness, especially in the field of public building design. The government architects once brought in the modernist method and created outstanding public buildings in the 1960s. However, in the following decades, some public buildings fell to mediocre level and were far away from society's expectation, because the government architects monopolized the design. Introducing the design competition and tendering system to the public building is a progress in the globalization era. After design was selected from competition for cultural and institutional building designs, the decision makers pay more attention on how the building can enhance their brand instead of practical utilities. Money was squandered on awkward buildings. People have every reason to demand for a better building environment and a context-sensitive design.

The government headquarters in Admiralty is the result of public competition. The comparison of old and new government headquarters buildings highlights the difference of governance in two historic periods. When the formal and spectacular monuments are rising up, many informal spaces spontaneously appear and disappear in front of our eyes. The "informal spaces" are sometimes embarrassing and inconvenient, but they reflect a diversified, democratic, vital and civic society. In the 21st century, Hong Kong sees Singapore and Shanghai as its rivals. However, none of the other two cities can tolerate such an informal and vital space.

Design competitions are always exciting, for the designers and for the public. Hong Kong eventually catches up with the international pace. Next to Hong Kong, Shenzhen claims to be a "capital of design." Of course, Shenzhen has much higher scales of exhibition and government support. Visiting the public exhibitions in parks, museums and commercial buildings in the twin cities is a pleasant pastime.

References

Chan, A. (2009). *Cooking Hong Kong. Hong Kong*: Joint Publishing Ltd. 陈雅妍. (2009). 香港の蛋 – 建筑与人对话. 香港:三联书店.

Finance.southcn.com. (2012). Construction stops and workers leave in Ordos. 鄂尔多斯康巴什众多楼盘停工 大批打工人员撤离. 南方网. http://finance.southcn.com/f/2012-04/26/content_44082718.htm. Accessed March 18, 2014.

Fitzpatrick, L. (2015). Hong Kong: 10 Things to do. *Time magazine*. http://content.time.com/time/travel/cityguide/article/0,31489,1850110_1850124_1852107,00.html. Accessed April 27, 2015.

Girard, G., & Lambot, I. (1993). *City of darkness: Life in the Kowloon Walled City*. Chiddingfold: Watermark.

Hadid, Z. (2015). Jockey club innovation tower—architecture—Zaha Hadid Architects. *Zaha-hadid.com*. http://www.zaha-hadid.com/architecture/jockey-club-innovation-tower/. Accessed December 24, 2015.

HKIA. (2012). Contemporary practice and global architecture. In H. K. I. A. Journal (Ed.), *Professional roundtable symposium* (pp. 26–29). Hong Kong: Hong Kong Institute of Architects.

Hong Kong Design Institute. (2008). *Special issue on information technology in design education* (8th ed., pp. 38–41). Hong Kong: BCI Asia Construction Information Pte. Ltd.

Hong Kong Government. (2014). 入境事務處二零一三年年報 (Annual Report 2013, Immigration Department). *Immd.gov.hk*. http://www.immd.gov.hk/publications/a_report_2013/tc/ch1/index.html#c6. Accessed April 27, 2015.

Legislative Council. (2009). The Hong Kong Polytechnic University's paper on proposed capital works project to develop the Innovation Tower (powerpoint presentation materials). http://www.legco.gov.hk/yr08-09/chinese/panels/ed/papers/ed0511cb2-1508-3-c.pdf. Accessed December 24, 2015.

Li, Z. (2015). Shortage of labor in Hong Kong's construction industry. 香港建筑业的"用工荒". M.ftchinese.com. http://m.ftchinese.com/story/001061481. Accessed August 7, 2015.

Libeskind, D., & Goldberger, P. (2008). *Counterpoint*. New York: Monacelli Press.

Mathews, G. (2011). *Ghetto at the center of the World—Chungking Mansions, Hong Kong*. Chicago: University of Chicago Press.

Ng, Y. (2008). *Impact of oversea star architects in Hong Kong*. Undergraduate final year thesis. City University of Hong Kong.

South China Morning Post. (2014). Occupy Central—the first night: Full report as events unfolded. *South China Morning Post*. http://www.scmp.com/article/1603331/live-tear-gas-fired-protesters-students-demand-cy-leungs-resignation. Accessed December 28, 2015.

Xue, C. (2010, Sep 22). Long Way of West Kowloon, Don't Waste Time. *Wen Wai Po*, p. A 12. 薛求理 (2010年9月22日). 漫漫西九路 切莫再蹉跎. 香港:文汇报, A12.

Xue, C. (2012). Free stroke—the creative media building of City University of Hong Kong. *Architectural Journal, 2*, 6–9.

Xue, C., Wang, Z., & Mitchenere, B. (2010). In search of identity: The development process of the national grand theater in Beijing. China. *The Journal of Architecture, 15*(4), 517–535.

Yang, K., Xue, C., Zang, P., & Tan, Z. (2015). From campus to brand, reading two campus buildings in Hong Kong. *New Architecture, 3*, 85–89.

Zhang, W. (2009). *The invisible logic*. Nanjing: Dong nan da xue chu ban she. 张为平. (2009). 隐性逻辑. 南京:东南大学出版社.

Chapter 11
Conclusion: "Made in Hong Kong" Design

In Preface, we raise the following questions

- As one of the major economic pillars, how did urban architecture help Hong Kong's transformation and economic miracles in its last 50 years before the sovereignty handover?
- How did the building projects represent and symbolize the various stages during this period of transformation?
- What are the driving forces for building development in different stages?
- What contributions has Hong Kong architecture made to China, Asia and the world?

This book tries to answer the above questions with many facets of architectural development in Hong Kong. In the post-war reconstruction, government led public housing gradually provided home for refugees. "Refugee" was an identity for all Hong Kong people in those years, no matter grass-roots or professionals. The society turned to peaceful and grassroots residents could work hard in factories to support Hong Kong's industrial revolution and economic taking off. The driving force came from government's determination of eliminating the shantytown and returning to normal societal order. In terms of limited land, resources and the percentage of beneficiaries in the population, the public housing plan was successful. From 1950 to 1970, the vital urban and infrastructural construction was accompanied by the serious learning of modernist architecture, which is evidenced by the English-language building construction magazine at the time.

From 1971 onward, emerging skyscrapers accommodated multi-national corporations for the rapidly growing economy, while private housing gave decent home, pride and identity for the burgeoning middle class. The driving force was from the property speculation and strong societal consuming demand. As demonstrated in chapters, Hong Kong architecture rarely pursues artistic expression, it is a result of functional pragmatism. In the capitalist market, buildings are chains in the profit making machine. For the commercial interests, buildings can be erected and demolished easily, regardless sustainability. Land lease and commercial building

© Springer Science+Business Media Singapore 2016
C.Q.L. Xue, *Hong Kong Architecture 1945–2015*,
DOI 10.1007/978-981-10-1004-0_11

design of Hong Kong once gave the Chinese mainland lesson of open-door reform. But some years later, the Hong Kong design (especially interior design) was seen as "too decorative" and old cliché. Hong Kong architecture and its central business district were once symbol of Asian can-do spirit and modernity. The commercial trend of Hong Kong architecture (and interior design) was reflected in the emerging Chinese-language magazines on building and construction.

In the 21st century, both private and public building projects have attempted to achieve excellence, establish brands and tell stories via "open-door," "white sheet" and "sailing forward" image designs. Only by opening itself to the world market can a client solicit a unique design that is able to spread the name of the owner and encourage profits in a commercial information-based society. Hong Kong and cities in mainland China continue to make efforts in this direction. The public buildings in Greater China have become new arenas for international architects. After China opened its door to the foreign design, Hong Kong firms act as both "insider" and "outsider". Compared to the foreign firms, they are based in Hong Kong, a part of China; compared to the Chinese mainland peers, they are designers from "outside". This gives convenience in obtaining the commitment and managing the project. In a relatively enclosed society, those who are able to move goods and services across the border could get the profits (Zweig and Chen 2007).

This book concludes the architectural trends of Hong Kong in the past 70 years since the end of WWII and lays a foundation for more specialized topical studies. These topical studies can be development of private housing, especially large scale housing estates for the middle class—planning and architectural design; the strategies of private developers—how these companies grow up in the Hong Kong and China conditions; the competitiveness of Hong Kong architects and building professionals—how the architects bid jobs in overseas; and new cases of 'rail village and mega-structure", for example, Ma An Shan Line, South Island Line, Shatin to Central Link. For the study of rail village, an integrated effort can be made in planning, architecture, land and property economics. Hong Kong architecture and the relevant topics have been and will further be a vital part of Hong Kong study.

Looking at the world history of the past 2,000 years, great architecture and arts were born usually in a thriving economic, cultural center and open society, for example, Athens in the Greek period, Florence in Renaissance, Paris in the 19th century and American cities after 1950. Since the 1980s, Hong Kong has been gradually approaching to such a situation. Hong Kong has placed second or third in the world competitiveness rankings since 1995.[1] In the economic freedom rankings run by the US Heritage Foundation and *Wall Street Journal*, Hong Kong has placed

---

[1]The World Economic Forum and Swiss Research Institute of International Management and Development have compiled the world's competitiveness rankings since 1989. The analysis relies on four aspects: economic performance, government efficiency, enterprise efficiency and infrastructure. See World Economic Forum (2015).

first for 20 consecutive years.[2] Furthermore, Hong Kong placed third after New York and London in the international financial center rankings,[3] pointing to the significance of New-Lon-Kong.[4] In addition to its financial and service industries, Hong Kong's film and popular music conquered China and Southeast Asia in the 1970s and 1980s. London and New York are doubtlessly the world's financial and cultural centers. They are home to many famous design firms, whose services extend to the entire world.

Compared with their peers in New York and London, design firms based in Hong Kong have long distances to cover. After China opened its door in 1978, the design forces in Hong Kong entered the mainland with a momentum and international experiences accumulated over 30 years. The Hong Kong design influence started from the Pearl River Delta and spread to Guangzhou, Shanghai, Nanjing, Beijing, Dalian and Northeast China. It was welcomed as "advanced and matured overseas design." Hong Kong developers and architects were in high demand for high-class hotels, retails and interior design. In the 1980s, their services were acquired for China Hotel in Guangzhou (1986), City Hotel (1984), New Jinjiang Hotel (1989), Hilton in Shanghai (1988), Jinling Hotel in Nanjing (1983) and Landmark complex in Beijing (1990). Hong Kong's land auction system and comprehensive design had a profound influence on the development of Chinese cities in the 1990s. The urban planning system, especially statutory drawing and outline zoning plan, of Hong Kong was directly learnt by Shenzhen (Xue 2006, 2012) (Fig. 11.1).

In the 21st century, some design firms in China have celebrated their initial performance in foreign countries, and "local" Hong Kong firms have already extended the overseas expedition they made in the late 1970s to places such as Taiwan, Vietnam, India and cities in the Middle East. In the world architectural 100 ranking released in 2015, six firms are in the list: Aedas, P & T, Leigh & Orange, Ronald Lu & Partners, Wong Tung & Partners and 10 Design. They all have works or set offices in the Chinese mainland, the busiest construction site in the world.[5] Overseas commitments currently account for 20–30 % of these companies' design workloads.[6] These include not only well-established companies such as P & T,

---

[2]The *Wall Street Journal* and American Heritage Foundation run economic freedom ranking based on 50 indexes of economic freedom to calculate the scores of countries. The average points are the mark of a country or area. See The Heritage Foundation (2015).

[3]International financial centers are global cities that provide financial services based on their tertiary industries. For a list of the international financial center rankings, see Wikipedia (2015).

[4]The term "New-Lon-Kong" is quoted from Michael Elliott, see Elliott (2008).

[5]The world architectural 100 ranking has been run by the *World Architecture* magazine in London for two decades. It announces the result in January every year. The result includes 100 largest design firms in terms of staff number and fee earning. It also includes statistics on the design of building types, like office, hotel, retail etc. See http://www.bdonline.co.uk/wa100-2015-the-big-list/5072847.article, accessed 30 Dec 2015.

[6]The design workload was estimated from the investigations conducted by the author in Hong Kong since 1999.

Fig. 11.1 Works of James Law Cybertecture. **a** Office building, Mumbai, 2013. **b** Technosphere, Dubai, including convention center, office, auditorium and hotel in a planet. **c** and **d** Bandra Ohm residential building, Mumbai. Courtesy of James Law Cybertecture

L & O, Wong Tung and Taoho, but also small firms such as James Law Cybertecture and IDA (see Chap. 8). James Law Cybertecture of a bit more than ten people has designed buildings in Dubai, Doha, Mumbai and won many awards for their design of high-rise apartments, offices and convention centers. The architectural education, local practice and government control in Hong Kong adheres to an English system, and drawings are annotated in English. Hong Kong design is a natural component of international building practice.

Despite these advantages, design from most Hong Kong firms reaches only as far as Taiwan in the east and stops in the Middle East in the west, rarely extending beyond Asia. As such, it cannot be compared with Japanese or even Singaporean design. How a city can provide design services to other places and how far these services can radiate are questions that reflect the competitiveness of the creative industry in Hong Kong. New York, London, Paris, Berlin, Hamburg, Rotterdam and Tokyo are obviously creative centers which send their designs to the world (*World Architecture 100*, 2010–2015). Aedas in Hong Kong is also, perhaps the only, global firm and sets example for the peers. For a long time, an inch of land in Hong Kong was more expensive than an inch of gold. The main developers have kept their eyes on profits rather than creative design. Design is only a single ring in the profitable chain of building production. On land such as this, creative design is both difficult to carry out and duly encouraged.

To the eyes of the outside world, Hong Kong is a typical high-density and compact city. As a case study, Hong Kong repeatedly appears in urban planning and design journals, conferences and forums. In the world statistics of gasoline consumption per capita, Hong Kong is at the low end and American cities such as Houston are found at the high end.[7] Owing to Hong Kong's small residential units and highly efficient public transportation, seven million residents and 50 million visitors pack themselves into a built area of 200 km^2 each year, a density ten to hundred times those of other world cities. Hong Kong's average family living space is 40 m^2, the smallest among those world cities and developed world and less than one quarter of that in the United States, however, Hong Kong people enjoy the longest life expectancy.[8] The old Kowloon Walled City and tenement houses represent a straightforward and bottomed-down life, and high-density locations such as Kowloon Station, Olympic Station and Tseng Kwan O cooperate with traffic hubs to represent a high quality and elegant life. High-rises and high density require delicate design and less disturbing construction. Although such design is difficult to measure according to traditional aesthetics, it heralds a sustainable future in which the planet's resources have depleted. Indeed, the high-density construction in Hong Kong sets an example for the world.

Hong Kong is located where East meets West. The city's identity is rarely discussed, especially in terms of its functional buildings. As stated in the preface, Hong Kong's architecture represents a high-density collectivity rather than an individuality. In the global wave of the 21st century, Hong Kong should actively find its position and identity and explore its own architectural technology and design language. Hong Kong design should work in parallel with its finances and once-popular film and music industries to add a unique color to the Oriental Pearl.

---

[7]For more information about the gasoline consumption and car ownership per capita, see Knaap (2006) and Paehlke (1989).

[8]For the life expectancy, living space and CO_2 emission of Hong Kong, Singapore, New York City, UK, Germany, Canada, USA and Australia, see Elsea (2014).

References

Elliott, M. (2008, January 17). A tale of three cities. *Time*. http://content.time.com/time/magazine/article/0,9171,1704398,00.html

Elsea, D. (2014). Learning from Hong Kong. *AECOM blog*. http://blogs.aecom.com/connectedcities/learning-from-hong-kong/

Knaap, G. (2006). Smart growth and urbanization in China: Can an American tonic treat the growing pains of Asia? In *The 2nd Megacities International Conference 2006* (pp.7–14). Guangzhou: South China University of Technology.

Paehlke, R. (1989). *Environmentalism and the future of progressive politics*. New Haven: Yale University Press.

The Heritage Foundation. (2015). *Index of economic freedom: Promoting economic opportunity and prosperity by country*. Heritage.org. http://www.heritage.org/index/. Accessed March 28, 2014

Wikipedia. (2015). *Financial centre*. Wikipedia.org. https://en.wikipedia.org/wiki/Financial_centre. Accessed March 28, 2014

World Economic Forum. (2015). *The global competitiveness report 2014–2015*. http://www.weforum.org/reports/global-competitiveness-report-2014-2015. Accessed December 26, 2015

Xue, Q. (2006). *The global impact: Overseas architectural design in China*. Shanghai: Tongji University Press. 薛求理 (2006). 全球化冲击: 海外建筑设计在中国. 上海: 同济大学出版社.

Xue, Q. (2012). Overseas design in China: 1978-2010. *New Architecture, 29*(3), 18–25. 薛求理 (2012). 海外设计在中国 1978-2010. 新建筑 29 (3), 18–25.

Zweig, D., & Chen, Z. (2007). *China's reform and political economy*. London, New York: Routledge.

Chronology of Hong Kong Architecture 1946–2015

1946 Japanese troop surrendered in August 1945. British military took over the power of Hong Kong. Population grew from 0.6 million after the war to one million in the beginning of 1946. The British government set up ten-year plan of development and welfare for its colonies. Bombed by the Allied Forces, demolished by Japanese troop and looted by local gang, buildings in Hong Kong were severely damaged. Expatriates returned to Hong Kong, and the only several hotels were fully occupied. The government approved plans to repair 143 European-type houses and 785 tenement buildings; and new buildings of 20 European-type houses and 70 tenement buildings.

1947 The population reached 1.8 million. The government invited Sir Patrick Abercrombie, the famous British planner, to visit Hong Kong and enact urban plan for the future 50 years. Committee of Tenement was established. Secretariat for Chinese Affairs set up a department of social welfare. T.T. Ng created a 'unit' housing selling mode.

1948 The government forcefully demolished residents' houses in the Kowloon Walled City. *The Hong Kong Preliminary Planning Report* was completed and sent to the Hong Kong government. Hong Kong Housing Society was established to provide housing for mid income families. There were 9,266 automobiles in Hong Kong and they caused traffic jam.

1949 Civil war in China was closing to the end, large amount of refugees fled to Hong Kong. Squatter areas were rampantly growing. People's Republic of China was born. People's Liberation Army pushed the frontline near Hong Kong. Kowloon Telegram Building of 13-story high was built, and was the tallest building.

1950 The population jumped to 2.1 million. Since the Korean War broke out, UK and USA implemented embargo policy towards China. The re-export trade of Hong Kong was blown, while the manufactory industry emerged. The new baby boom appeared in the 1950s. University of Hong Kong opened its Department of Architecture.

1951 Hong Kong Housing Society registered as a legal organization. Kowloon Methodist Church opened school, two buildings were linked together. Bank of China building was completed in Central.

© Springer Science+Business Media Singapore 2016
C.Q.L. Xue, *Hong Kong Architecture 1945–2015*,
DOI 10.1007/978-981-10-1004-0

1952 The population was 2.25 million. The government started the construction of new towns.

1953 Man Yee Building was completed. It was designed by Kwan, Chu and Yang. The squatter area of Shek Kip Mei was burned by big fire and made 53,000 people homeless. It stimulated large scale construction of public housing. Yau Yat Chuen, north of Boundary Street, was developed as low density housing, mainly for owners of factories.

1954 Two-story high temporary buildings were built in Shek Kip Mei, to settle the homeless refugees. "Hong Kong Housing Construction Committee" was formed. Government decided to carry out settlement plan. Eight multi-story settlement buildings, six-story high, were built in Shek Kip Mei.

1955 Building Ordinance 1935 was amended. Three subsidiary regulations, the Building (Administration) Regulations, the Building (Planning) Regulations, and the Building (Construction) Regulations, were issued. 35 articles were added or amended. The limit of building height was lifted. Empire Court, 17-story high and the tallest building in Hong Kong, was built in Causeway Bay. The developer Fok Ying Tung created "selling off plan" before construction completion.

1956 35 % private residential units had only 15 ft^2. floor area per capita. Hong Kong Society of Architects was founded. Chung Chi College started its construction in Shatin, five buildings were completed, designed by Robert Fan, Chau and Lee.

1957 North Point Estate, a low rental estate in Java Road, was ready for use. It was the first housing estate of Housing Authority. Kitchen and toilet were included in every unit. The monthly rental was $60–120. The applicant's monthly income should be between $300 and $900. Grantham Hospital in Wong Chuk Hang, designed by Chau and Lee, was competed. The Central government building was completed in the "Government Hill." Part of Causeway Bay Typhoon Shelter was reclaimed, and upon which Victoria Park of 19 hectares was built. It was the largest park in the Hong Kong Island.

1958 Building Contractors' School, designed by Wai Szeto, was completed. The building was now used by an international school. Takshing House, designed by Kwan, Chu and Yang, was completed. It was the first curtain wall building in Hong Kong. The runway in Kai Tak Airport was built and extended to the Kowloon Bay.

1959 21,000 people entered the resettlement house or public housing.

1960 Hot money flew in from Europe, America and South Asian Chinese and boosted the manufacturing. Land development companies were increasing. The government permitted structural engineers and surveyors to submit drawings for approval. So Uk public housing estate was completed, planned by Eric Cumine and buildings designed by Luke Him Sau, Chau & Lee and Leigh & Orange.

1961 Government promulgated plan of low rental housing. The bachelor degree of architecture at University of Hong Kong was accredited by the Royal Institute of British Architects (RIBA). Luk Hoi Tung Building, designed by Chu Ben, was completed. Union Building, 248 ft tall and 23 stories, was completed and recognized as the tallest building for three years. St. Peter's Church was completed in North Point.

1962 Typhoon Windy took toll of 130 lives, 600 injured, and 75,000 homeless. City Hall was completed in Central. It was a milestone of public building in Hong Kong. Hang Seng Building was the first building of steel column. Hilton Hotel, designed by Palmer and Turner, was completed.

1963 Chinese University of Hong Kong was founded. Repulse Bay Tower, designed by Luke Him Sau, was completed. ELCHK Truth Lutheran Church, designed by Eric Cumine, was completed in Yau Ma Tei. Elizabeth Hospital opened. The building of Elizabeth Hospital was granted Bronze Award by RIBA.

1964 Severe water shortage in Hong Kong. From January, water was supplied four hours a day. From June, water was supplied every four days, four hours each time. Shortage of water influenced the construction industry. Some contractors used salt water to mix concrete. This caused rebar rusted and concrete peeled off. Public housing estate Choi Hung was completed to house 43,000 people. Building regulation was amended. The volume calculation of development potential was replaced by site coverage and plot ration, which are used today.

1965 Bank crisis caused land and property price and rental slumping down. Supply over demand, there were 18,000 vacant units. The developers found difficult to finance. Government enacted planning outline to build high-density residential buildings. New types of settlement housing appeared, private kitchen and toilet in-situ in unit. There were one million population in public housing. The Hong Kong Society of Architects run its first annual award. Tung Ying Building, 17 story high, was completed, which was the tallest office building in Kowloon Peninsula.

1966 Mei Foo Sun Chuen—the first large scale private housing estate-started construction. Methodist church of North Point was completed. Harbor City in Tsim Sha Tsui opened to public. The wharf possessed double levels of shopping mall and double levels parking space.

1967 Street riot and confrontation, partly influenced by the "Cultural Revolution" in China. There were 346,000 units of public housing, sheltering one million people. Ngau Tau Kok Lower Estate was completed. It was the first resettlement building using prefabricated components (The buildings were demolished in 2000). AIA Building, designed by P & T, was completed and awarded by the Hong Kong Society of Architects. Residents moved in to Phase I of Wah Fu Estate.

1968 Report *Research of Hong Kong mass transportation* was published, which suggested to build subway rail system. Department of Transportation was founded. New pier in Wanchai, the Duchess of Kent Children's Hospital at Sandy Bay and public library in Sai Kung opened to public.

1969 On July 26, an earthquake measuring 5 on the Richter scale rattled Hong Kong and Macau. In November, Hang Seng Index was issued to reflect the fluctuation of stock market. The first cross harbor tunnel broke the earth. Trash incinerator of Lai Chi Kok, Tsing Yi Power Plant and Tang Shiu Kin Hospital were in use. Ching Chung Koon in Tun Men, a Taoist temple, was reconstructed. Technical college of Morrison Hill was founded.

1970 Property rental hiked up steeply. Government passed a temporary act to freeze rental. The old barracks at Tsim Sha Tsui was transformed to Kowloon Park.

Hong Kong participated the World Expo in Osaka, Japan to showcase the economic achievements. No. 500 public housing block and No. 50 public housing school were completed in Lam Tin. Public housing held 1.1 million residents.

1971 There were more than four million population. On Jan 25, Hang Seng Index went through 220. Wah Fu Estate, with a "new town" concept, was completed. Free primary school education was implemented. On Sep 6, Hong Kong Education TV Center opened. In November,Crawford Murray MacLehose arrived in Hong Kong and acted as 25th governor.

1972 Hung Hom Cross Harbor Tunnel opened for use. Kwai Chung Container Terminal and Plover Cove Reservoir were completed. "The Peak" was built on the Peak Tram Upper Terminus, 1,440 ft above sea level. The Hong Kong Society of Architects was renamed to Hong Kong Institute of Architects (HKIA).

1973 The government carried on "10-year public housing plan" to provide facilitated and reasonable living environment for 1.8 million residents. Housing Authority was restructured. Jardine House, 52-story, was built in the Central waterfront and became the tallest building in Asia.

1974 Sheraton Hotel was completed in Tsim Sha Tsui and awarded by HKIA. Six blocks of 1950s' resettlement buildings were remodeled to install kitchen and toilet for every unit. Bridge of Tsing Yi Island was completed to serve Tsing Yi's burgeoning industry.

1975 Oi Man Estate of Ho Man Tin was completed and double tower type of public housing blocks appeared. Her Majesty Elizabeth II and husband visited Oi Man Estate when they were in Hong Kong. Kowloon and Canton Railway terminal moved from Tsim Sha Tsui to Hung Hom Railway Station. World Trade Center, 42 stories, was completed in Causeway Bay. It provides exhibition and commercial functions partly for government.

1976 The population in Tsuen Wan new town reached 450,000. Major buildings in the main campus of Chinese University of Hong Kong were completed. Government promulgated policy of home ownership for lower middle class. International measuring system replaced English system in building ordinance and construction submission documents.

1977 Ocean Park opened, it was the largest theme park of its kind in Asia. Kwun Tong Industrial center became the largest industrial base in Hong Kong.

1978 High Island Reservoir was completed in Sai Kung. Phase I "home ownership" was on sale. Hong Kong Arts Center, designed by Dr. Tao Ho, was completed in Wan Chai. Heritage Association pleaded to the British government, hoping to protect the bell tower in Tsim Sha Tsui. New horse racecourse opened in Shatin. Structural engineers started to analyze structure and design with the aid of computer.

1979 Large amount of Vietnamese refugees poured to Hong Kong, and the number reached 100,000. Modified initial system of Hong Kong subway (now Kwun Tong Line of MTR) opened in October. Large scale construction appeared in Kowloon Bay and Mongkok to cooperate with the subway stations.

1980 The new campus of Hong Kong Polytechnic opened in Hung Hom. Hopewell Center, 66 stories and 216 m tall, was completed and it kept the tallest record in Hong Kong till 1989. Yau Oi Estate, a large scale public housing estate, was completed in Tun Men. MTR Central Station and Hong Kong Space Museum opened. In this fiscal year, 32,000 public housing, "home ownership" units and 28,600 private housing units were built.

1981 Two million people lived in the public housing administered by the Housing Authority. Lok Fu Estate and shopping plaza were completed. Sun Hung Kai Center and Union Center were completed in the Hong Kong Island.

1982 Tsuen Wan Line of MTR opened. Kowloon-Canton Rail Hong Kong part adopted double rails and electrificied. Shatin Train Station was put in use. New World Center in the waterfront of Tsim Sha Tsui was completed. Large scale row-house development Fairview Park saw its first group of residents. Fairview Park consists of 5,024 units of row-house, no higher than 3-story, 100 streets and large man-made lake. It was nicknamed as "poor people's luxurious house".

1983 Influenced by the looming future, Hong Kong dollar depreciated. Hong Kong dollar was pegged with US dollar, i.e. US$1 = 7.72–7.8 HK$. Phase II of Island Line MTR started construction. Aberdeen tunnel opened. Hong Kong Coliseum opened in Hung Hom. Phase I of Discovery Bay was completed, it set up precedence of large residential estate in an outlying island. Prince of Wales Hospital was completed in Shatin. From 1979 to 1983, averagely 26,000 residential units per year were delivered from private sector.

1984 Chinese and British governments jointly declared the return of Hong Kong sovereignty to China in 1997. City Polytechnic was founded. The Quarry Bay part of Island Eastern Corridor was completed. Taikoo Shing was partly completed. The supreme court in Admiralty, 22-story high, was completed. The original Flagstaff House (for the British army commander) was restored to Tea Ware Museum and opened to the public.

1985 Phase I of MTR Island Line opened. Light rail started construction in the northwest of New Territories. Tolo Highway opened for vehicles. Building of Academy of Performing Arts and Exchange Square were completed. Hong Kong Macau Ferry Terminal was completed. It was a typical traffic exchange and transition center with office tower and shopping mall.

1986 Edward Youde, governor of Hong Kong, passed away when he visited Beijing in December. The first generation new towns, Tsuen Wan, Shatin and Tun Men, accommodated 1.4 million people. Headquarters of Hong Kong and Shanghai Banking Corporation held opening ceremony. New Town Center, town hall and library opened in Shatin. Hong Kong participated World Expo in Vancouver. Dr Tao Ho designed the pavilion.

1987 Population in Hong Kong reached 5.6, 2 million in the New Territories. 80,000 residential units were built in this year, 35,000 in the public sector. Everyday, 2 million people took MTR, 3.5 million people travelled by rail between city and the new Territories. Architectural Services Department (ASD) was founded to administer, design and maintain government buildings. Government office tower, 49 stories tall and 54,000 floor m^2, stood up in Admiralty, into which ASD moved. Tun Men town hall, library and municipal services building in Ngau Chi Wan were completed. Bond Center, designed by Paul Rudolph, was completed. Hong Kong

University of Science and Technology held design competition for its campus design, Simon Kwan and Percy Thomas won the design. Parkview, classy residential area and hotel, was completed near Tai Tam Reservoir.

1988 City Polytechnic opened course of higher diploma in architectural studies. Chi Fu Fa Yuen and Whampoa Garden, both for middle class, were completed. Phase V of Kai Tak Airport expansion was completed to cope with 18 million passengers each year. Taikoo Plaza, together with hotels-office towers on the podium, was completed. New China Harbor in Tsim Sha Tsui was in use, and could handle 19 million passengers each year. Phase I of convention center opened in Wan Chai. Light rail from Yuen Long to Tun Men opened for use. Land Development Corporation was founded.

1989 In May and June, millions of people pulled to the streets to demonstrate the Tiananmen massacre and support students in Beijing. Hong Kong Open College was Founded. Kowloon Park was refurbished and reopened. Cultural Center opened in Tsim Sha Tsui. Bank of China headquarters was completed. The Waterloo Road campus of Baptist College was reconstructed and in use. Phase I of City Polytechnic was completed. Easter Harbor Crossing opened for vehicles. Tai Fu Tai, a 19th century house of Qing Dynasty, was restored for public visit. The Executive Council approved the plan of port and new airport.

1990 Housing Authority administered 144 estates, with 630,000 living units. The headquarters building of Housing Authority stood up in Ho Man Tin. The big Buddha of 60-m tall was installed in Lantau Island, it was the tallest Buddha in the Far East. Shing Mun Tunnel and Tseung Kwan O Tunnel opened for vehicle. New Chartered Bank building was completed. Aberdeen and Kwun Tong waterfront parks opened. Heritage buildings were restored, including Kun Tin Study Hall in Ping Shan, British primary school and royal observatory in Tsim Sha Tsui.

1991 Housing Authority administered commercial buildings including retail, bank and restaurants, total floor area 1.27 million m^2, 48,000 m^2 floor areas were completed in this year. Hong Kong University of Science and Technology campus was completed and received first cohort students. Chinese University of Hong Kong opened department of architecture. Science Museum and Art Museum opened in Tsim Sha Tsui. The old barracks in Admiralty was changed to Hong Kong Park, with big aviary.

1992 Kowloon Walled City was demolished after three years. Headquarters of Citibank was completed. Central Plaza, 78-story and 374 m hall, stood up in Wan Chai. It was the tallest concrete structure building in the world. Ma Heng public housing estate was completed. New Peak Tower was built in the Victoria Peak.

1993 Light Rail Tin Shui Wai Line and San Tin Highway were completed and open for use. The Land Development Corporation collected land in the old district of Causeway Bay and built Times Square, a comprehensive development project. Large development project Gold Coast was completed in the Castle Peak Bay, including hotel, yacht club, Mediterranean-type shopping arcade and high-rise residential buildings. Escalator and walking system from Central to Mid-level was open for public, with a horizontal length of 800 m and vertical height 135 m.

1994 Run Run Shaw Campus of Baptist University was completed. The Peninsula Hotel built new addition of tower. Ap Lei Chau Bridge opened. Large scale residential area South Horizon was on sale in Ap Lei Chau.

1995 Kowloon Walled City Park, designed by Tse Shun Kai of ASD, opened to public. Squatter area of Tiu Keng Leng was demolished. The permanent campus of Open College settled in Ho Man Tin.

1996 2.5 million people lived in the public housing. New campus of Lingnan College, designed by P & T, was completed in Tun Men. Massive fire in a commercial building of Yau Ma Tei took the toll of 40 lives and 80 injuries. The accident alerted the safety of old buildings with inadequate fire proof facilities. Hong Kong Institute of Architects (HKIA) started to print quarterly journal.

1997 Sovereignty of Hong Kong returned to China in July. Phase II of convention center was completed and hosted the sovereignty return ceremony. Tsing Ma Bridge and Western Harbor Crossing tunnel opened. Lantau Link, North Lantau Highway and Ting Kau Bridge opened for vehicles. Several large private residential estates were completed in Ma On Shan and Tseung Kwan O. Hong Kong Institute of Education moved into the new campus of Tai Po. Tai Po waterfront park opened. Government planned to build 85,000 residential units each year.

1998 Hong Kong International Airport moved to Chep Lap Kok, while Kai Tak Airport stopped operation. The limitation of building height for aviation in Kowloon was lifted. Hong Kong, Kowloon and Tung Chung Stations were completed for the opening of Tung Chung and Airport Lines. Chi Lian Nunnery built Tang-style wood temple by private donation, expertise from Hong Kong, China, Japan and Canada were used. Festival Walk shopping mall and office block opened in Kowloon Tong. History Museum opened in East Tsim Sha Tsui. 52 % residents lived in the self-own property. The government inspected aging buildings of 40–50 years old for their safety.

1999 Method of sustainable building assessment (HK BEAM) started in trial. The government carried on a study "Hong Kong 2030: planning, vision and strategies." Radio and Television Hong Kong (RTHK), HKIA and Hong Kong Economic Journal jointly run an election of "ten famous buildings in Hong Kong."

2000 Heritage Museum opened in Shatin. The government held design competition for Center for Youth Development in Chai Wan and Shui Chuen O public housing. The Costal Defense Museum, Yuen Long Theater and Kwai Tsing Theater opened. Stage II of Lai Chi Kok Park, with southern China flavor, opened to public.

2001 The government promulgated "joint practice note" to encourage measurements of green building design. Central Library was completed for public use. Open international design competition was held for the West Kowloon Cultural District. "Integer—green architecture exhibition" was held in Tama, Admiralty. Service apartments on sale, for example, Royal Peninsula in Hung Hom. To save the property market, the government decided to suspend the subsidized home-ownership plan.

2002 Science Park and Cyber Harbor finished their first stage. Phase I of Park Island was on sale. It was located in the outlying island of Ma Wan. In this fiscal year, there were 67,000 residential units ready for use, including 34,000 in private sector; 20,200 public housing rental units and 12,800 subsidized self-ownership units. 22 schools were completed, 26 were in construction. MTR Tseung Kwan O Line opened.

2003 Severe Acute Respiratory Syndrome (SARS) outburst. Ventilation and distance between buildings were paid attention. The property price plummeted, it was around 30 % of the price of 1997. West Line of Kowloon-Canton Rail opened. International Financial Center (IFC) stood up in Central, it was 415 m and 88-story, the tallest building in Hong Kong.

2004 Ma On Shan Line of Kowloon-Canton Rail opened. 129 Repulse Bay, schematically designed by Norman Foster, was completed. Ten buildings in Science Park started for rental. The waterfront of Tsim Sha Tsui, near the New World Hotel, was refurbished to Star Avenue. The movie stars palm prints were scripted on ground paving. Langham Place, shopping mall, office and hotel complex, was completed in Mongkok. It was a success of old district renovation. The government announced that the west Kowloon Cultural District will be developed and run by a single tender. Three corporations were shortlisted. Their schemes were exhibited for public voting.

2005 Phase I of Disneyland opened in Lantau Island. The old barracks were turned to Heritage Discovery Museum in Kowloon Park. The office building of government Mechanical and Electrical Department was renovated to showcase green architecture concepts. Four Season Hotel opened in Central. Asian International Exposition Pavilion opened in the airport. City University of Hong Kong run bachelor degree program of architectural studies.

2006 Wetland Park in Tin Shui Wai opened. Nan Lian Garden, constructed with private donation, opened, located next to the Chi Lian Nunnery. New high-rise public housing, 50-story high, was completed in Shek Kip Mei. Cable car from Tong Chung to Ngong Ping was constructed. Kam Tong House, of 1914, was bought by government and refurbished to Dr. Sun Yat-san Museum. Bethanie cloister, a French missionary sanitarium of mid-19th century, was restored to a campus of Academy of Performing Arts. Star Ferry Pier in Central, built in 1958, was demolished for new Central reclamation. It was strongly protested by the citizens.

2007 MTR Lok Ma Chau Line, Futian Checkpoint, Shenzhen Bay Bridge and west Checkpoint opened in the Hong Kong and Chinese mainland border. Terminal 2 of the airport was in use. The first Hong Kong –Shenzhen urban architecture biennale was held in November. The old Central police building was used as Hong Kong site. Jockey Club sponsored for the Inno Building of PolyU. In the international design competition, Zaha Hadid won the design. Visitor center of Ping Shan heritage trail was built on old police building. Government finished the report of "Hong Kong 2030: planning, vision and strategies". Queen's Pier in Central was demolished, and this triggered strong protest among society.

2008 West Kowloon Cultural District Authority was founded and got a government allocation of 21.6 billion dollars. Hong Kong pavilion appeared in the Venice Biennale of urban architecture. The marine police headquarters in Tsim Sha Tsui was renovated to "1881" complex shopping mall and hotel. The old terrace, building and clock were kept. The government started to demolish the public housing estates of the 1950s and 60s, to give way for the higher density development. These include North Point estate, So Uk estate and Ngau Tau Kok estate. New Central waterfront planning was exhibited to collect public opinions. Hong Kong started to run "Business of Design Week" every year to gather design professionals from all over the world.

2009 The second Hong Kong and Shenzhen biennale of urban architecture was held, and west Kowloon vacant land was the Hong Kong site. The Antiquity Advisory Board proposed 1,444 buildings for evaluation. Noel's Ark in Ma Wan opened. It was the same size as historic record. Tung Chung sport hall and library opened. Stonecutter's Bridge was in use, and Hong Kong-Macau-Zhuhai Bridge in construction.

2010 ICC and other high-rise buildings on the podium of Kowloon Station gradually completed, forming a complex of 1.7 million m^2 floor area on a podium. Three shortlisted planning schemes of West Kowloon Cultural District were displayed. Hong Kong Design Institute building was completed for use. New building of Open University was in use. The old North Kowloon Magistracy was turned to Hong Kong campus of Savannah College of Arts and Design, USA. Ma On Shan waterfront park opened for use. Guangzhou-Shenzhen-Hong Kong express rail applied for government allocation in the Legislative Council. People of different opinions confronted inside and outside the Legco meeting.

2011 Creative media building of CityU, designed by Daniel Libeskind, opened for use. Foster + Partners' scheme of West Kowloon Cultural District was confirmed as executive plan. Government headquarters and Legislative Council building was completed in Admiralty. Hung Hom waterfront park opened. Municipal services building of Tin Shui Wai was completed and awarded by HKIA. International design competition for Liantang and Heung Yuen Wai checkpoint was held.

2012 City Hall celebrated 50 years anniversary. Zero Carbon Building opened in Kowloon Bay. "Energizing Kowloon East" was launched, planned to turn the old industrial base of Kwun Tong and Kowloon Bay together with old airport Kai Tak to a new central business district.

2013 Maggie's Cancer Caring Centre opened in Tun Men Hospital, designed by Frank Gehry and local architect Ronald Lu & Partners. The construction company used BIM to find the spatial position of the non-linear form. Inno Center of Polytechnic University, designed by Zaha Hadid, opened for operation from the fall semester. In the West Kowloon Cultural District, the design of Xiqu Center was won by Bing Thom of Vancouver and Ronald Lu of Hong Kong; M+ Museum was won by Herzog & De Meuron from Switzerland.

2014 Hong Kong and Shenzhen urban architecture biennale was held. Kwun Tong Pier was the main venue for the Hong Kong side. The government wanted to open more land for public and private housing to alleviate shortage of housing. The development of Northeast New Territories was frustrated by local citizen groups. In autumn, "occupying Central" took place in Admiralty, Causeway Bay and Mongkok for over two months. Demonstrators asked for more democracy in selecting the candidates for the chief executive. The property price and building activities were not directly influenced. The Island Line of MTR extended to HKU and Kennedy City, and opened in December. Island Line of MTR extended to Sai Ying Pun, HKU and Kennedy City. In the HKU station, elevators transmit people from underground to the hill over 100 m height. Hong Kong Velodrome was completed in Tseung Kwan O.

2015 Hong Kong Architecture Center launched "My 10 Most 'Liked' Hong Kong Architecture of the Century". 15,111 valid votes were collected through online election. According to the number of votes, the following ten items were elected: Chi Lian Nunnery, international airport, Kowloon Walled City, Lui Seng Chun, Main building of HKU, Ocean Park, Tai O stilt house, old train station in Tsim Sha Tsui, Peak cable car and Central star ferry. During the construction of Shatin-Central Line, the MTRC found lots of antiquities of Song and Ming Dynasties. After consultation for six months, the company decided to preserve and exhibit the antiquities in the future hall of train station. 15 years after the design competition, Shuen Chuen O public housing estate was completed, and provided over 10,000 living units. Because of the housing shortage, part of the rental units was turned to be sold. To alleviate the housing shortage, Lee Shau Kee, founder and chairman of Henderson Land Development, donated several plots of land in the New Territories to build affordable housing for youth. He also offered to rebuild Tai Hang Sai Estate, a public housing property built in 1965, from housing 1,600 units into an estate of 5,000 units for low-income residents. Mr. Li Ka Shing, the richest person in Hong Kong and Asia, donated HK$ 1.5 billion to build a temple in Tai Po. The statue of Buddha is 76 m high.

Further Reading

British Colony and Hong Kong History

Abbas, M. (1997). *Hong Kong*. Minneapolis: University of Minnesota Press.

Akers-Jones, D. (2004). *Feeling the stones: Reminiscences by David Akers-Jones*. Hong Kong: Hong Kong University Press.

Blyth, S., & Wotherspoon, I. (1996). *Hong Kong remembers*. Hong Kong: Oxford University Press.

Cameron, N. (1979). *The Hongkong land company ltd: A brief history*. Hong Kong: The Hongkong Land Company.

Carroll, J. (2007). *A concise history of Hong Kong*. Hong Kong: Hong Kong University Press.

Castells, M., Goh, L., & Kwok, R. (1990). *The Skek Kip Mei syndrome: Economic development and public housing in Hong Kong and Singapore*. London: Pion.

Chen, A. (1990). *The other Hong Kong report*. Hong Kong: The Chinese University Press.

Ching, M., & Faure, D. (2003). *A history of Hong Kong 1842–1997* (2nd ed.). Hong Kong: Open University of Hong Kong.

Cumine, E. (1981). *Hong Kong: ways and byways—A miscellany of trivia*. Hong Kong: Belongers Publications.

Faure, D. (2003). *Colonialism and the Hong Kong mentality*. Hong Kong: Centre of Asian Studies, University of Hong Kong.

Girard, G., Lambot, I., & Goddard, C. (2011). *City of darkness*. Chiddingfold: Watermark.

Home, R. (1997). *Of planting and planning: the making of British colonial cities*. London: Spon.

Jameson, F. (1991). *Postmodernism, or, the cultural logic of late capitalism*. Durham: Duke University Press.

King, A. (2004). *Spaces of global cultures*. London: Routledge.

Ko, T. (2005). *Hong Kong: Past and present*. Hong Kong: Joint Publishing (Hong Kong) Ltd. 高添强 (2005). 香港今昔. 香港:三联书店.

Lee, H., & DiStefano, L. (2002). *A tale of two villages: The story of changing village life in the New Territories*. Oxford and Hong Kong: Oxford University Press.

Leung, M. (1999). *From shelter to home: 45 years of public housing development in Hong Kong*. Hong Kong: Hong Kong Housing Authority. 梁美仪 (1999). 家 – 香港公屋四十五年. 香港: 香港房屋委员会

Li, P. (2012). *Governing Hong Kong: Insights from the British declassified files*. Hong Kong: Oxford University Press. 李彭广 (2012). 管治香港- 英国解密档案的启示. 香港:牛津大学出版社

Liu, Z. P. (2010). *We all grow up in so Uk—A collective memory of public housing life in Hong Kong*. Hong Kong: Chung Hwa Book Co. 刘智鹏 (2010). 我们都在苏屋邨长大 – 香港人公屋生活的集体回忆. 香港:中华书局.

© Springer Science+Business Media Singapore 2016
C.Q.L. Xue, *Hong Kong Architecture 1945–2015*,
DOI 10.1007/978-981-10-1004-0

Lui, T. (2012). *The 1970s we might know*. Hong Kong: Chung Hwa Book Co. 吕大乐. (2012). 那似曾相识的七十年代. 香港:中华书局.

McDonogh, G., & Wong, C. (2005). *Global Hong Kong*. New York: Routledge.

Ngo, T. (1999). *Hong Kong's history: State and society under colonial rule*. London: Routledge.

Roy, A., & Ong, A. (Eds.). (2011). *Worlding cities: Asian experiments and the art of being global*. Chichester, West Sussex: Wiley-Blackwell.

Smart, A. (2006). *The Shek Kip Mei Myth: Squatters, fires and colonial rule in Hong Kong*. Hong Kong: Hong Kong University Press.

Stokes, E., & Morrison, H. (2009). *Hong Kong as it was-Hedda Morrison's photographs 1946–47*. Hong Kong: Hong Kong University Press.

Uduku, O. (2006). Modernist architecture and "the tropical" in West Africa: The tropical architecture movement in West Africa, 1948–1970. *Habitat International, 30*(3), 396–411. doi:10.1016/j.habitatint.2004.11.001

Wang, G. (1997). *Hong Kong History: New perspective*. Hong Kong: Joint Publication.

Wang, H. (2010). *A thankful life—Biography of H. K. Cheng*. Beijing: Zhongguo tie dao chu ban she. 王海文(2010). 感恩人生 – 郑汉钧传记. 北京:中国铁道出版社.

Welsh, F. (1997). *A history of Hong Kong*. London: HarperCollins.

Zheng, Y., & Lo, S. (1995). *From colony to SAR: Hong Kong's challenge ahead*. Hong Kong: Chinese University Press.

Urban Studies of Hong Kong and Statutory System

Bristow, M. (1984). *Land use planning in Hong Kong: History, policies and procedures*. Hong Kong: Oxford University Press.

Bristow, R. (1989). *Hong Kong's new towns: A selective review*. Hong Kong: Oxford University Press.

Cervero, R., & Murakami, J. (2009). Rail and property development in Hong Kong: Experiences and extensions. *Urban Studies, 46*(10), 2019–2043.

Cheng, P. (2000a). *Hundred years of Kowloon Street*. Hong Kong: Joint Publication Ltd. 郑宝鸿. (2000). 九龙街道百年. 香港:三联书店.

Cheng, P. (2000b). *Hundred Years of Hong Kong Street*. Hong Kong: Joint Publication Ltd. 郑宝鸿. (2000). 香港街道百年. 香港:三联书店.

Division of Building Science and Technology. (2003). *Building design and development in Hong Kong*. Hong Kong: City University of Hong Kong Press.

Division of Building Science and Technology. (2011). *Property development and project management in Hong Kong*. Shanghai: Tongji University Press.

Feng, B. (2001). *One hundred year history of Hong Kong real estate property*. Hong Kong: Joint Publishing Ltd.

Fong, P. (1986). *Housing policy and the public housing programme in Hong Kong*. Hong Kong: Centre of Urban Studies & Urban Planning, University of Hong Kong.

Freeman, Y. (1980). *Victoria barracks: Recreation and leisure area development study*. Hong Kong: Public Works Department, Hong Kong Government.

Ho, P. (2004). *Challenges for an evolving city: 160 years of port and land development in Hong Kong*. Hong Kong: The Commercial Press. 何佩然. (2004). 地挟山移:香港海港及土地发展一百六十年. 香港:商务印书馆.

Ho, P. (2008). *Ways to urbanization—Post-war road development in Hong Kong*. Hong Kong: Hong Kong University Press.

Ho, P. (2010). *History of construction industry in Hong Kong 1840–2010*. Hong Kong: The Commercial Press. 何佩然. (2011). 築景思城–香港建造業發展史1840-2010. 香港:商务印书馆.

Huang, T. (2004). *Walking between slums and skyscrapers: Illusions of open space in Hong Kong, Tokyo, and Shanghai*. Hong Kong: Hong Kong University Press.

Inglis, A. (1961). *City of Victoria, Hong Kong*. Hong Kong: Government Printer.

Jenks, M., & Dempsey, N. (2005). *Future forms and design for sustainable cities*. Amsterdam: Architectural Press.

King, A. (2004). *Spaces of global cultures—Architecture urbanism identity*. London: Routledge.

Lai, L. (1997). *Town planning in Hong Kong, a critical review*. Hong Kong: City University of Hong Kong Press.

Lai, L., & Fong, K. (2000). *Town planning practice: Context, procedures and statistics for Hong Kong*. Hong Kong: Hong Kong University Press.

Lai, L., Ho, D., & Leung, H. (2010). *Change in use of land: a practical guide to development in Hong Kong*. Hong Kong: Hong Kong University Press.

Leung, A., & Yiu, C. (2004). *Building dilapidation and rejuvenation in Hong Kong*. Hong Kong: Hong Kong Institute of Surveyors and City University Press.

Lim, W., & Chang, J. (2012). *Non West Modernist Past—On architecture and modernity*. Singapore: World Scientific Pub.

Lo, E., & Chan, L. (1998). *The introduction of urban planning in Hong Kong*. Hong Kong: Joint Publishing Ltd. 卢惠明、陈立天 (1998). 香港城市规划导论. 香港:三联书店.

Ng, E. (2010). *Designing high-density cities for social and environmental sustainability*. London: Earthscan.

Nissim, R. (2008). *Land administration and practice in Hong Kong*. Hong Kong: Hong Kong University Press.

Planning Department. (1990). *Hong Kong planning standards and guidelines*. Hong Kong: The Government of the Hong Kong Special Administrative Region.

Poon, A. (2011). *Land and the ruling class in Hong Kong*. Singapore: Enrich Professional Pub.

Preiser, W., & Vischer, J. (2005). *Assessing building performance*. Oxford: Elsevier.

Pryor, E. (1983). *Housing in Hong Kong*. Hong Kong: Oxford University Press.

Rowe, P. (2005). *East Asia modern*. London: Reaktion.

Sit, V. (2015). *Hong Kong: 150 years, development in maps*. Hong Kong: The Joint Publication Ltd. 薛凤旋. (2015). 香港发展地图集. 香港:三联书店.

Tang, B., Chiang, Y., Baldwin, A., & Yeung, C. (2004). *Study of the integrated rail-property development model in Hong Kong*. Hong Kong: Research Centre for Construction & Real Estate Economics, Dept. of Building & Real Estate, Faculty of Construction & Land Use, the Hong Kong Polytechnic University.

Waller, J., & Holmes, A. (2008). *Hong Kong, the growth of the city*. London, U.K.: Compendium.

Wong, L. (1978). *Housing in Hong Kong: A multidisciplinary study*. Hong Kong: Heinemann Educational Books (Asia).

Yeh, A. (1996). *Planning Hong Kong for the 21st century: A preview of the future role of Hong Kong*. Hong Kong: Centre of Urban Planning and Environmental Management, University of Hong Kong.

Yeh, A. G. O., Hills, P., & Ng, S. (2001). *Modern transport in Hong Kong for the 21st century*. Hong Kong: Centre of Urban Planning and Environmental Management University of Hong Kong.

Yuen, B., & Yeh, A. G. O. (Eds.). (2011). *High-rise living in Asian cities*. New York: Springer.

Hong Kong Architecture

Architectural Services Department. (2006). *Post 97 public architecture*. Hong Kong: MCCM CREATIONS.

Chan, C., & Choi, H. (2005). *Journey of space—Hundred year history of Hong Kong architecture*. Hong Kong: Joint Publication. 陈翠儿,蔡宏兴主编. (2005). 空间之旅 – 香港建筑百年. 香港:三联书店.

Christ, E., & Gantenbein, C. (2010). *An architectural research on Hong Kong building types*. Zurich: gta-Publ.

Chung, K. (2012). *My 36 years of model making in Hong Kong*. Hong Kong: MCCM Creations.

Chung, W. (1989). *Contemporary architecture in Hong Kong*. Hong Kong: Joint Pub. (H.K.).

Denison, E., & Guang, Y. (2014). *Luke Him Sau, architect*. Chichester: John Wiley & Sons Inc.

Fang, Y. (2005). *One building two system—The opportunity and challenge of Hong Kong architecture*. Hong Kong: Wan Li Book Co. 方元 (2005). 一樓兩制 - 香港建築的機遇和挑戰. 香港:萬里機構,萬里書店.

Farrell, J., Smith, S., & Farrell, T. (1998). *Kowloon transport super city*. Hong Kong: Pace Pub.

Frampton, A., Wong, C., & Solomon, J. (2012). *Cities without ground*. San Francisco: ORO Edition.

Ganesan, S., & Lau, S. (2000). Urban challenges in Hong Kong: Future directions for design. *URBAN DESIGN International, 5*(1), 3–12.

Gu, D. (2011). *Chung Chi original campus architecture*. Hong Kong: Chung Chi College, Chinese University of Hong Kong.

Hong Kong Institute of Architects. (2007). *Deeply loving architecture—Dialogue with 15 senior architects in Hong Kong*. Hong Kong: Hong Kong Institute of Architects. 香港建築師学会. (2006). 热恋建筑 -与拾伍香港资深建筑师的对话. 香港:香港建筑师学会出版.

Ho, P. (2009). *100 Traditional Chinese buildings in Hong Kong*. Hong Kong: Antiquities and Monuments Office, Leisure and Cultural Services Department.

Hong Kong Housing Authority. (2011). *Planning, design and delivery of quality public housing in the new millennium*. Hong Kong: Hong Kong Housing Authority.

Huang, H., & Chan, H. (2009). *Professional practice for architects in Hong Kong*. Hong Kong: Pace Publishing Ltd.

Jianzhuyouren (2013). *Zhu jue: Reading Hong Kong architecture*. Hong Kong: Joint Publishing Ltd. 建筑游人 (2013). 筑觉:阅读香港建筑. 香港:三联书店.

Krummeck, S. (2009). Railways as a catalyst for community building. *Hong Kong Institute of Architects Journal, 6*(54), 32–35.

Lam, T. (2006). From British colonization to Japanese invasion—The 100 years architects in Hong Kong 1841–1941. *Hong Kong Institute of Architects Journal,* 1(Issue 45), 44–55.

Lampugnani, V., Pryor, E., Pau, S., & Spengler, T. (1993). *Hong Kong architecture—The aesthetics of density*. New York: Prestel Verlag.

Lung, P. (1992). *The ancient and today's architecture in Hong Kong*. Hong Kong: Joint Publishing Ltd. 龙炳颐 (1992). 香港古今建筑. 香港:三联书店.

Ma, K. (2011). 11 stories of Hong Kong construction engineering. Hong Kong: Joint Publication Ltd. 马冠尧. (2011), 香港工程考:十一个建筑工程故事,1841–1953. 香港:三联书店.

Ng, K., & Chu, C. (2007). *Story of first generation Chinese architects in Hong Kong*. Hong Kong: Hong Kong Economic Journal Press. 吴启聪、朱卓雄 (2007). 建闻筑绩 - 香港第一代华人建筑师的故事. 香港:经济日报出版社.

Peng, H. (1990). *Hong Kong architecture*. Beijing: China Architecture and Building Press. 彭华亮主编. (1990). 香港建筑. 北京:中国建筑工业出版社.

Purvis, M., & Warner, J. (1985). *Tall storeys*. Hong Kong: Palmer and Turner.

Shelton, B., Karakiewicz, J., & Kvan, T. (2011). *The making of Hong Kong-from vertical to volumetric*. New York: Routledge.

Tan, Z., & Xue, C. Q. L. (2013). Trade magazines and the reflections on cities—About the contemporary urbanism of Hong Kong (1965–1984). *Architectural Journal,* (11), 14–19. 谭峥、薛求理(2013). 专业杂志与城市自觉—创建关于香港的当代都市主义(1965-1984). 建筑学报, (11), 14-19.

Tan, Z., & Xue, C. (2014). Walking as a planned activity: Elevated Pedestrian network and urban design regulation in Hong Kong. *Journal of Urban Design, 19*(5), 722–744.

Walker, A., & Rowlinson, S. (1990). *The building of Hong Kong*. Hong Kong: Hong Kong University Press.

Wang, H. (2008). *Chinese architects coming from Shanghai to Hong Kong after 1949*. Hong Kong: University of Hong Kong, Ph.D. dissertation.

Williams, S. (1989). *Hongkong Bank*. London: Jonathan Cape.

Woo, M. (2005). *Hong Kong style*. Hong Kong: TOM (Cup Magazine) Publishing Ltd. 胡恩威 (2005). 香港风格.

Xue, C. Q. L. (2006). *Building a revolution: Chinese architecture since 1980*. Hong Kong: Hong Kong University Press.

Xue, C. Q. L. (2014). *Contextualizing modernity: Hong Kong Architecture 1946–2011*. Hong Kong: Commercial Press. 薛求理. (2014). 城境:香港建筑1946-2011. 香港:商务印书馆.

Xue, C. Q. L., & Manuel, K. (2001). The quest for better public space: A critical review of urban Hong Kong, in Pu Miao. *Public Places of Asia Pacific Countries: Current issues and strategies*, 171–190.

Xue, C. Q. L., Manuel, K., & Chung, R. (2001). Public space in the old derelict city area—A case study of Mong Kok. *Hong Kong. Urban Design International, 6*(1), 15–31.

Xue, C. Q. L., Zhai, H., & Roberts, J. (2010). An urban island floating on the MTR station: A case study of the West Kowloon development in Hong Kong. *URBAN Design International, 15*(4), 191–207.

Yeung, A. (2002). Property development and railway: A marriage of convenience? *Hong Kong Institute of Architects Journal, 3*, 60–65.

Zhang, W. (2009). *The invisible logic*. Nanjing: Dong nan da xue chu ban she. 张为平. (2009). 隐性逻辑. 南京:东南大学出版社.

Zhang, Z., & Liu, S. (1998). *City image of central, Hong Kong*. Beijing: Pace Publication Ltd. 张在元,刘少瑜. (1997). 香港中环城市形象. 香港:贝思出版公司.

Index